BEYOND TRANSITION

Transition and Development

Series Editor: Professor Ken Morita
Faculty of Economics, Hiroshima University, Japan

The Transition and Development series aims to provide high quality research books that examine transition and development societies in a broad sense – including countries that have made a decisive break with central planning as well as those in which governments are introducing elements of a market approach to promote development. Books examining countries moving in the opposite direction will also be included. Titles in the series will encompass a range of social science disciplines. As a whole the series will add up to a truly global academic endeavour to grapple with the questions transition and development economies pose.

Also in the series:

Enhanced Transition Through Outward Internationalization
Outward FDI by Slovenian Firms
Andreja Jaklič and Marjan Svetličič
ISBN 0 7546 3134 6

Modeling Russia's Economy in Transition
Peter Wehrheim
ISBN 0 7546 3299 7

Foreign Direct Investment in Central and Eastern Europe
Edited by Svetla Trifonova Marinova and Marin Alexandrov Marinov
ISBN 0 7546 3026 9

Facilitating Transition by Internationalization
Outward Direct Investment from Central European Economies in Transition
Edited by Marjan Svetličič and Matija Rojec
ISBN 0 7546 3133 8

Emerging Market Economies
Globalization and Development
Edited by Grzegorz W. Kolodko
ISBN 0 7546 3706 9

Economic Reforms and Capital Markets in Central Europe
Ken Morita
ISBN 0 7546 0884 0

Beyond Transition

Development Perspectives and Dilemmas

Edited by

MAREK DABROWSKI
Center for Social and Economic Research, Poland

BEN SLAY
United Nations Development Programme Regional Center, Slovakia

JAROSLAW NENEMAN
Center for Social and Economic Research, Poland

ASHGATE

Published by
Ashgate Publishing Limited
Gower House
Croft Road
Aldershot
Hants GU11 3HR
England

Ashgate Publishing Company
Suite 420
101 Cherry Street
Burlington, VT 05401-4405
USA

Ashgate website: http://www.ashgate.com

British Library Cataloguing in Publication Data
Beyond transition : development perspectives and dilemmas.
- (Transition and development)
1. Monetary policy - Europe, Eastern - Congresses 2. Europe, Eastern - Economic conditions - 1989- - Congresses
3. Europe, Eastern - Economic policy - 1989- - Congresses
4. Europe - Economic integration - Congresses
I. Dabrowski, Marek II. Slay, Ben, 1958- III. Neneman, Jaroslaw
330.9'47086

Library of Congress Control Number: 2004049586

ISBN 0 7546 3970 3

Reprinted 2006

Printed in Great Britain by Antony Rowe Ltd, Chippenham, Wiltshire

Contents

List of Figures

List of Tables

List of Contributors

Anders Aslund – Senior Associate at the Carnegie Endowment for International Peace, Washington, formerly an economic adviser to the government of Russia and Ukraine, former Director of the Stockholm Institute of East European Economics and diplomat in Kuwait, Poland, Geneva, and Russia. Chairman of the CASE Advisory Council.

Leszek Balcerowicz – President of the National Bank of Poland, Professor of Economics at Warsaw School of Economics, former Deputy Prime Minister and Minister of Finance (1989-1991 and 1997-2000), a member of European Economic Association.

Andrew Berg – Deputy Chief of the Financial Studies Division of the Research Department of the International Monetary Fund, former Head of the US Treasury's Mexico Task Force and later Deputy Assistant Secretary of Treasury for East Asia and Latin America.

Olivier Blanchard – Chair of the Economics Department at MIT. A fellow and Council member of the Econometric Society, a member of the American Academy of Sciences, and the French Economic Advisory Council to the Prime Minister.

Eduardo Borensztein – Chief, Strategic Issues Division, Research Department, International Monetary Fund, formerly at the Banco Central de la Republica Argentina and FIEL, the Foundation for Latin American Economic Research.

Vittorio Corbo – President of the Central Bank of Chile, Professor of Economics at the Catholic University of Chile, Vice-President of the International Economic Association, a member of the Council of the Econometric Society and a member of the Governing Body of the Global Development Network. Formerly worked at the World Bank as Chief of the Macroeconomic Adjustment and Growth Division.

Marek Dabrowski – Co-founder and Chairman of the CASE Foundation Council, former deputy Minister of Finance of Poland (1989-1990), adviser to governments and central banks in many transition economies.

Daniel Daianu – Professor of Economics at Academy of Economic Studies in Bucharest, former Minister of Finance and Chief Economist at the National Bank of Romania.

Robert Ene – MA in Economics at the Central European University, Budapest, and MSc in Banking and Finance at the Lausanne University, Switzerland.

Irena Grosfeld – Professor of Economics at Centre National de la Recherche Scientifique, Departement et Laboratoire d'Economie Theorique et Appliquee (DELTA) in Paris. Former adviser to the Minister of Ownership Transformation in Poland, Member of the CASE Advisory Council.

Juan Francisco Jimeno – Professor of Economics at the Universidad de Alcala de Henares in Madrid, senior researcher at the FEDEA (Fundacion de Estudios de Economia Aplicada) in Spain.

Simon Johnson – Associate professor of Entrepreneurship at the Sloan School of Management, MIT. A member of the US Securities and Exchange Commission's Advisory Committee on Market Information and member of the NBER research group on corporate finance and international macroeconomics.

Vladimir Mau – Professor of Economics, a rector of the Academy of National Economy of the FR Government.

Paolo Mauro – Deputy Chief of the Strategic Issues Division in the Research Department of the International Monetary Fund.

Peter Mihalyi – Head of the Banking Programs in the Partners for Financial Stability (PFS) program of the USAID carried out by the East-West Management Institute (EWMI), former Chief Economist at the Privatisation Agency and the deputy Minister of Finance of Hungary.

Pradeep Mitra – Chief Economist, Europe and Central Asia Region of the World Bank. Formerly division chief, Russia Country Operations and director of the Poverty Reduction and Economic Management Department in Europe and the Central Asia Region.

Kalman Mizsei – Assistant Administrator and Regional Director, Regional Bureau for Europe and the Commonwealth of Independent States, UNDP; previously worked for the Institute of the World Economy, Hungarian Academy of Sciences, Institute of East West Studies in New York, Hungarian Export-Import Bank and AIG.

Jaroslaw Neneman – Lecturer at University of Lodz; Senior Researcher, Center for Social and Economic Research; Advisor to Polish Ministry of Finance.

Alari Purju – Professor and Dean of Faculty of Economics and Business Administration at Tallinn Technical University, former adviser to the Minister of Economic Affairs.

Jacek Rostowski – Professor of Economics at the Central European University, Budapest, member of the CASE Foundation Council, associate of the Royal Institute of International Affairs, London, adviser to the Governor of the National Bank of Poland.

Ben Slay – Director, UNDP Regional Center, Bratislava.

Nicholas Stern – Second Permanent Secretary and Managing Director, Budget and Public Finances, and Head of the Government Economic Service in the UK government. Formerly the World Bank Chief Economist and Senior Vice President, former Chief Economist and Special Counselor to the President at EBRD.

Jan Svejnar – Executive Director of The William Davidson Institute at the University of Michigan Business School, Department of Economics at the University of Michigan, and CERGE-EI, Prague.

Radu Vranceanu – Professor of Economics and Dean of Research at the ESSEC Graduate Business School in Paris.

Andrew Warner – Research Fellow at the Center for International Development at Harvard University.

Charles Wyplosz – Professor of International Economics at the Graduate Institute of International Studies in Geneva, Director of the International Centre for Money and Banking Studies, Director of the International Macroeconomics Program of CEPR.

Introduction

Marek Dabrowski, Jaroslaw Neneman and Ben Slay

The collapse of communist regimes in the former Soviet bloc and Soviet Union itself triggered a transition from centrally planned to market economies in the entire region. Most of countries of Central and Eastern Europe started their economic transition in 1989-1990, while the beginning of the similar process in the former Soviet Union happened at least two years later.

After more than decade of building a market system, it is legitimate to ask: 'Is the transition over?' There are two basic answers to this question:

The transition is not yet completed because many structural and institutional reforms are still needed in all former communist countries; or

The transition is completed in some countries (the new EU members) while others (Balkan and CIS countries) must continue this process.

The answer chosen depends very much on how the notion of transition is understood. If 'transition' is taken as referring to a movement from one institutional system or economic policy design to another, then the transition is not finished in any post-communist country. Such a general interpretation implies that almost every country experiences some kind of transition, since all countries must continuously adjust their economic institutions and policies in response to a dynamically changing environment. A broad interpretation of 'transition' therefore does not seem to be very practical because it blurs the historical context of moving from a centrally planned to a market economy.

A narrower interpretation of 'transition' leads us to accept the argument the transition is mostly over. Apart from few reform outsiders such as Turkmenistan, Uzbekistan, and Belarus, in all other post-communist countries, central planning and command management have been dismantled. All these economies are predominantly market-coordinated, although in several cases market mechanisms are still immature and heavily distorted. While all the former communist countries still have substantial reform agendas, the 'transition' character of these agendas is becoming less well defined. Reform challenges facing post-communist countries do not differ fundamentally from those experienced by other developed and developing economies.

The approaching end of the 'transition' era is also marked by the gradual disappearance of a single reform agenda. The results of the first decade of transition have been very uneven and geographically differentiated. While ten countries in the Central European and Baltic regions can be characterized alternatively as 'leading reformers' or as middle-income democratic-capitalist countries that are very close to the EU membership, the twelve CIS countries are much less advanced in reforms and can be characterized as lower- or lower-middle-income economies with distorted capitalisms and highly imperfect democracies. The Balkan countries can be placed into an intermediate category. They are less advanced reformers, and per capita income levels are on average lower than the new EU members. But improved prospects for EU integration (Bulgaria and Romania are already negotiating for accession, and Croatia and possibly some other West Balkan countries may join this list in not so distant future), political democratization, and acceleration of market reform processes during last few years make these countries closer to the 'reform leaders' than to the CIS group.

Differences in transition results necessarily mean at least some differentiation in post-transition reform agendas. The new EU members and the next tranche of candidates must focus on adapting national institutions and policies to EU standards (*acquis communautaire*). While their institutions work generally better than those in other post-communist countries, they still face challenges in upgrading their institutions to the standards prevailing in the incumbent EU and other developed countries. Growth prospects in the new EU members (similar to EU incumbents) are also constrained by their relatively large welfare states and high tax burdens. They also suffer from similar labor market rigidities. A significant part of the forthcoming reform agenda therefore resembles that of developed countries, pertaining among other things to social policy reform, restructuring costly and ineffective public services, and addressing the disincentives associated with progressive taxation and high marginal tax rates.

By contrast, the CIS countries have to date been left out of the European integration process. They cannot benefit from the institutional 'leverage' associated with the Copenhagen criteria and *acquis communautaire*, and must make their own institutional and policy choices. Geographic and geopolitical isolation, political/ethnic instability, and armed conflict create additional handicaps for many of these countries. In spite of some optimistic signs, such as rapid economic growth during 2000-2003, their income levels are low or very low, and the development gap—even compared to the new EU members—is substantial. Very poor countries like Mongolia, Tajikistan, Kyrgyzstan, Georgia, Armenia, Moldova, Albania or Macedonia require special attention from the international community, particularly international development and financial institutions. The CIS (and Balkan) economies also face problems similar to those of other developing economies. These include inadequate state capacity, fragile and unstable legal frameworks, underdeveloped financial sectors, underdeveloped (or deteriorating) infrastructure, aggressive corruption, large income inequalities, and rising social exclusion.

Many economic issues are common to all the post-communist countries, irrespective of their development level and past experience. Globalization is leading to increasing openness and economic interdependence. Heightened surveillance by international financial markets limits national sovereignty and room for discretionary economic policies. International competition is accelerating not only in product markets, but also in the service sector, capital and labor markets, legal and regulatory systems, taxation, corporate governance and currencies. These new phenomena constitute an important part of 'beyond transition' agenda, which not only the post-communist economies must deal with.

This book is drawn from papers first presented at an international conference entitled 'Beyond Transition', which was organized by CASE (Center for Social and Economic Research), a Warsaw-based international think tank working on the problems of post-communist economies, European integration and the world economy, celebrating in this way CASE's tenth anniversary of policy research and policy advisory activity.[1] The United Nations Development Programme's Regional Center in Bratislava[2] provided programmatic and financial support to the conference, as did a number of other sponsors.[3] The conference, which was held in April 2003 in Falenty (near Warsaw), featured 240 participants from Central and Eastern Europe, the Transcaucasus, Central Asia, Western Europe and the US.

This volume presents a selection of 18 chapters out of the more than 30 papers that were presented during the conference. These chapters are grouped into five thematic blocs.

The first section contains six chapters addressing various aspects of the exchange rate and monetary policy regimes in emerging markets. Global financial market integration increasingly limits national sovereignty in the sphere of monetary policy. Currency crises in Eastern Europe, Asia, and Latin America have demonstrated the fragility of such hybrid exchange rate regimes as adjustable pegs, crawling pegs, target bands, crawling bands, and managed floats. In a world of free capital movements, the only viable choice seems to be between maintaining an independent monetary policy with floating exchange rates versus surrendering monetary independence by adopting a hard peg variant (currency board or dollarization/euroization). For developing and transition countries that lack traditions of low inflation and independent monetary authorities, the key questions are: can and should independent monetary policies be maintained? Or should these countries join one of the major currencies in the near future?

This dilemma is extensively discussed in the first four chapters, where authors present different opinion and preferences. In light of the Latin American experience, Andrew Berg, Eduardo Borensztein, and Paulo Mauro (Chapter 1) and Vittorio Corbo (Chapter 4) are relatively optimistic about prospects for running independent monetary policies, via the application of direct inflation targeting regimes. On the basis of post-communist countries, Marek Dabrowski (Chapter 2) argues more for giving up monetary independence. Robert Ene and Jacek

---

1 This conference was the third in a cycle of CASE international conferences. The first one, 'Economic scenarios for Poland' was held on 18 January 1997; the second, 'Years After: Transition and Growth in Post-Communist Countries', was held on 15-16 October 1999.

2 The Bratislava Regional Center is part of UNDP's Regional Bureau for Europe and the CIS, which does research, programming, and policy advising in the post-communist economies.

3 These included: AIG Open Pension Fund, Freedom House, National Depository for Securities, Poland, Raiffeisen Bank Poland, and Westdeutsche Landesbank Poland. Other sponsors were: Bank of the Polish Cooperation Movement, CAIB Financial Advisers Ltd., Konrad Adenauer Foundation, USAID Partners for Financial Stability Program, PKO Polish Bank, Open Pension Fund 'Skarbiec-Emerytura', and Association for Development. The media patron was 'Gazeta Wyborcza' daily.

Rostowski in Chapter 3 try to delineate the economically justified expansion of the dollar and Euro zones, on the basis of a broad range of criteria related to optimal currency area theory, lender of last resort, and seigniorage issues. The two remaining chapters refer to the situation of the new EU members who are expected to join the Economic and Monetary Union after EU accession. Both Jacek Rostowski (Chapter 5) and Charles Wyplosz (Chapter 6) are in favor of rapid EMU entry, and skeptical about the 'classical' exchange rate mechanism (ERM-II) obligatory phase. Both look for a way to skip what they see as a very risky and crisis-prone arrangement, with Rostowski arguing strongly in favor of early unilateral euroization.

The second thematic bloc deals with the politically hot issues of labor market reform. The late twentieth century has seen a sharp change in labor market performance and policy preferences. In some cases, traditional labor concerns such as unionization, minimum wage, and health and safety codes have become less relevant, if not counterproductive. While providing some protection for some groups of workers, these institutions may also contribute to high unemployment rates by limiting labor market flexibility. In addition, demographic trends are making social security systems increasingly costly and are pushing some toward insolvency. The high payroll taxes needed to keep these systems afloat add to the tax wedge and further boost unemployment. Sustained reductions in unemployment require new, pragmatic approaches emphasizing flexible regulations that allow households adjust their behavior as workers in response to changes in their preferences as consumers.

Section Two contains three chapters analyzing various aspects of labor market regulation. Jan Svejnar in Chapter 7 presents a comparative analysis of labor market policies and institution in Central and Eastern Europe and sources of unemployment in transition economies. Svejnar concludes that '*The extent and effects of employment protection, labor market policies and unionization in the transition economies are similar to OECD and EU averages*'. From this point of view, the lessons of a quarter century struggle for more labor market flexibility in Spain presented in Chapter 8 by Juan Jimeno may be very helpful for countries of Central and Eastern Europe suffering similar rigidities. Olivier Blanchard in Chapter 9 discusses the extent of justified government intervention in labor markets and proposes concrete instruments for minimizing its negative side effects.

Free capital movement and labor market deregulation pose new challenges for national tax systems. The efficiency aspects of taxation often gain more attention than equity considerations in the unification of tax systems. The most important changes are occurring in direct taxation: the rationales behind highly progressive personal and corporate income taxes are increasingly being questioned. Both the number of taxes and magnitudes of tax rates have been reduced considerably in recent decades. Are flat income taxes only a dream of liberal economists, or are they an efficient and non-distorting source of income for the public sector? Do the economic benefits of such taxes outweigh their political and social costs?

These are the issues discussed in the third section of this volume, which is devoted to tax reform in transition economies. This bloc starts with a very complex and comprehensive overview of fiscal and tax policies in transition economies done by Pradeep Mitra and Nicholas Stern in Chapter 10. The authors concentrate on the impact of tax systems on business and investment climates, particularly in relation to small and medium-size enterprises and foreign direct investment. Further answers to these questions can be found in Chapter 11, where Alari Purju describes the Baltic countries' liberal tax systems, including the flat personal income taxes that are now spreading to other post-communist countries. Continuing this topic Daniel Daianu and Radu Vranceanu emphasize '*(...) the lack of well-functioning institutions as a source of major economic disruption and failure of conventional fiscal policy*'. This chapter calls attention to two very frequently noticed and partly interrelated phenomena: free rider behavior, and the fact that post-communist economies are too often on the right side of the Laffer curve.

Prudent corporate governance rules and practices also matter a lot in the international competition of economic systems and policies. Privatization of state-owned enterprises and the introduction of new forms of corporate governance are key pillars of enterprise reform around the world, not only in transition countries. These measures have produced very different results in enterprise restructuring and performance in different countries. The systemic causes of these differences, and the main factors behind successful linkages between privatization, better corporate governance, and better economic performance, need to be determined. Answers to these questions can be sought in examining the privatization and corporate governance patterns apparent in different new EU, Balkan, CIS, and Asian countries. The theoretical foundations and practical examples from countries with different privatization experiences both need to be explored. So do policy and institutional measures aimed at improving competition, hardening budget constraints, improving capital market and prudential regulation, protecting shareholder rights, and enforcing property rights.

These problems are comprehensively analyzed by Simon Johnson in Chapter 13, who stresses an importance of the legal framework. His main message is the following: '*Law definitely matters. Countries with better investor protection have better-developed financial markets and more growth. The determinants of law are complex, but the origin of the legal system is an important factor.*' By contrast, Peter Mihalyi in Chapter 14 (under the provocative title 'The Growing Irrelevance of Corporate Governance in Transition Economies') points out that, in the small Central European and Baltic economies, most of the largest firms belong to transnational corporations, and as such local management is effectively controlled by oversight from the parent company. Issues of domestic stock market regulation, the transparency of company activity, and minority shareholder protection therefore do not have key importance. In Chapter 15 Irena Grosfeld comes back to the role of privatization. She argues that '*institutions (law and regulations) appear as to some extent endogenous to the privatization process*', and that '*privatization is viewed as a precondition triggering the process of institutional change.*'

Finally, the fifth thematic bloc addresses the question of how the ongoing EU enlargement will influence other post-communist countries. The CIS and Balkan countries not currently negotiating for accession will have to deal with an enlarged EU in their direct neighborhood. Responses to the EU's external trade regime and barriers to the free movement of peoples will have to be developed. While most non-candidate transition countries do not have free trade and visa free travel agreements with the EU (many do not even belong to the WTO), they do have important economic, cultural, historical, geographical, and ethnic links with the new EU members (e.g. Ukraine, Belarus and Russia with Poland; Moldova with Romania; Serbia, Croatia, and Ukraine with Hungary; Croatia and other Yugoslav successor states with Slovenia). Additionally, the lack of clear prospects for accession to the EU and NATO could discourage political and economic reforms in these countries. What are the prospects for involving non-candidate countries in European integration? Can the EU's future eastern borders be kept free for the movement of goods, people, and capital?

Anders Aslund and Andrew Warner in Chapter 16 compare the EU's very open trade policies vis-à-vis the EU candidates with the protectionist trade policies it employs vis-à-vis CIS countries. EU trade barriers hamper growth prospects and slow market reforms in CIS countries. This topic is also discussed by Kalman Mizsei in Chapter 18, who contrasts the Balkan countries' European integration prospects with the lack of such in the CIS. Vladimir Mau in Chapter 17 presents possible developmental trajectories for the common European economic space between the Russian Federation and the enlarged EU, calling attention to the obstacles present on both sides.

Both authors and editors are very grateful to conference participants who gave valuable comments and remarks. The cases of substantial merit contribution are admitted in footnotes of individual chapters. The editors also want to thank Marcin Gasiuk, Jan Jarewicz-Jacinski, Jakub Kowalski, Kevin Price and Zuzana Vagnerova for their assistance in preparing the manuscript for this volume.

Foreword

Transition: A Guiding Model

Leszek Balcerowicz

This important book is about what has happened in the former Soviet block since the collapse of communism and about the remaining (or accumulated) problems, provocatively denoted as belonging to the 'post-transition' epoch. One cannot understand these problems very well without taking a look at past experience. What I find the most striking in post-communist developments is the enormous differentiation in economic and non-economic outcomes during the relatively short time of 11-13 years. The present differences in the living standards among the post-communist countries are much larger than those that existed a short while ago. These differences are apparent in growth of GDP, inflows of FDI, inflation, income inequalities, health, and ecological developments. Countries that have performed better on economic growth and inflation have also tended to have smaller increases and lower levels of inequalities, and better health and ecological developments.[1] Better performers overlap with the accession countries of Central and Eastern Europe while worse performers with those of the Commonwealth of Independent States.

The enormous differences in outcomes in post-communist countries obviously pose questions about its causes. There is a large empirical literature dealing with this issue (e.g., Aslund, 2002; Berg et al, 1999, Fisher et al., 2001). It focuses on explaining the relative growth performance of these economies; less attention has been paid to the determinants of the differences in other dimensions of welfare. It can be shown, however, that some crucial factors conducive to longer term economic growth are also conducive to ecological improvement and favorable health developments. For countries that inherited a wasteful communist economy, increased economic efficiency has been one of the fundamental causes of both economic growth and improved ecological performance. Diverse health developments can be linked to economic forces (for example, economic liberalization changed the availability and relative prices of more and less (un)healthy foodstuffs), which also affect growth. Differences in the ease of entry of new firms shape both economic growth and income inequality.

Empirical studies of the growth performance in the post-communist countries have found that differences in the initial economic conditions can explain only a part of the differences in growth, moreover only in the early phase following the collapse of communism. Poor economic performance may be also resulting

1 I have analysed these differences, drawing on EBRD reports, in Balcerowicz (2002), p. 35-39.

from unfavorable location (especially for Central Asian countries) as well as a lower level of market access with respect to exports to the European Union countries (see Chapter 16). However, the differences in long-term growth are mostly due to different degrees of market-oriented reforms, especially economic liberalization. The larger the scope of these reforms, the better on average, the growth record. I do not know of a single empirical study showing that less market-oriented reform, under comparable conditions, is better for economic growth than more reform.

The extent of market-oriented reforms is measured in statistical studies by the liberalization index developed by De Melo, Denzier and Gelb (1996), and by the EBRD transition indicators that focus on liberalization reforms (price, foreign trade and foreign exchange liberalization, liberalization of entry). The strong statistical link between these indicators and growth performance underlines how various state controls have blocked the development of former socialist economies and how important it is to abolish them, thus facilitating the growth of private entrepreneurship and market forces. These measures focus to a lesser extent on institution building (e.g., privatization as a fundamental enterprise reform, creation of an independent and efficient judiciary, restructuring of tax administration, setting up a stock exchange). However, a more casual analysis of post-socialist countries indicates that, on average, countries that achieved a larger extent of liberalization have also made larger advances in institution building (as well as in macroeconomic stabilization, which is linked both to liberalization and institution building).

Such a state of affairs should not be surprising. Given the inherited conditions of the communist institutional system, the extent of liberalization was directly linked to the scope of some crucial components of institutional restructuring: less liberalization meant more state controls, which required the preservation of the control apparatus.[2] This in itself reduced the scope of institutional restructuring and endangered further institution building. A large scope of initial liberalization was therefore a precondition for deeper institutional change. It was also necessary to eliminate shortages and to set in motion the spontaneous growth of the private sector. Both processes belonged to most important positive forces in the early phase of post-communist transition. Therefore, one may conclude that the larger the institutional reforms leading away from the communist institutional system towards a limited state and market economy, the better the performance.

This brief look at developments in the post-socialist countries (and the related debates) leads us to the problems of their future. The crucial question is the same as at the start of post-socialist transition: how to produce a sustained and rapid catch-up – real convergence for these economies. The basic question has remained the same because most of them failed to start catching up, and those that did are only at the beginning of this process.

---

2 I am omitting here the much-discussed issue of the order of financial liberalization, and especially the sequence of capital account liberalization. These problems deserve separate treatment.

Neoclassical growth theory does not give policy relevant responses to this basic question, and mainstream economics in general has only recently started to rediscover the fundamental role of institutional variables (frameworks, systems) in explaining differences in growth. I believe, however, that we know enough from older and newer non-orthodox research to be able to point, in general terms, to the desired institutional model, which should guide reforms aimed at generating sustained and rapid catch-up. This is a model of a limited state, which focuses on the protection of basic individual liberties, including economic ones. This definitional requirement implies that the state should not expand in ways that would restrict these freedoms, so it has to be limited. While such a limited state must protect individuals' basic liberties against intrusion from third parties, it cannot crowd out voluntary cooperation that includes both profit-oriented market transactions and various self-help or mutual help arrangements. There are nowadays few examples of a limited state. However, all the historical evidence we have suggests rather strongly that such a regime displayed a very good growth record, and I do not know of any evidence to the contrary (for more see Rabushka, 1985).

The expansion of the state's activity—the growth of state-imposed restrictions on economic freedom—is, broadly speaking, difficult to justify in terms of improved economic performance. Instead, the opposite seems to be true: the more radical the expansion of the state, the greater the economic damage. State expansion can be linked to corruption, tax evasion, the second economy, and the weakening of the state's fundamental role of protecting basic economic freedom. Many deviations from a limited state tend to increase the numbers of the most disadvantaged persons, i.e., the long-term unemployed.

It should not be assumed that a limited state (focused on the protection of basic liberties) would mean that certain services would not be provided and people would be worse off. The potential for voluntary cooperation should not be underestimated, and there are also various individual coping strategies. In fact, the expansion of the state may have driven out much non-state activity and blocked the development of the new, potentially beneficial, private arrangements.

There is therefore, a strong case for recognizing in principle that a limited state in normal circumstances is the optimal one. This implies that the burden of proof should fall on those who would argue for a larger state role.

The last twenty years have seen movement away from expanded states toward more limited ones. This shows that limiting the scope of the state's activity and thus releasing the potential of voluntary cooperation and individual initiatives is not impossible, even though the transition is far from completed and fraught with difficulties. The forces of statism will never cease to exist, as there will always be some people, who will see benefits (power, economic rents) in limiting other people's freedom. And there will always be some ideological statists who attach an emotional value to the state's power (or that of community) or distrust voluntary cooperation. This is why the struggle for a limited state will never end. But it is not a lost cause.

The classical vision of a state constrained by the framework of basic individual liberties could play an important role in this process. One should use every appropriate moment to anchor them in an effective constitution. There are other limits on the state's discretion, which are, in fact, surrogate defenses of individuals' freedom. Institutionalized fiscal constraints can help to limit growth in public spending and, therefore, in taxation. Central bank independence blocks the recourse to inflationary financing of budget deficits and thus protects individuals against the imposition of inflation taxes. Membership in the World Trade Organization limits the use of protectionist measures and helps to protect domestic taxpayers and consumers. These and other second line defenses of individuals' freedom matter, and they should be introduced or strengthened, using every appropriate moment.

References

Aslund, A. (2002), *Building Capitalism. The Transformation of the Former Soviet Bloc*, Cambridge: Cambridge University Press.

Balcerowicz, L. (2002), *Post-Communist Transition: Some Lessons*, London: The Institute of Economic Affairs.

Berg, A., E. Borensztein, R. Sahay and J. Zettelmayer (1999), 'The Evolution of Output in Transition Economies: Explaining the Differences', *IMF Working Paper*, No. 99/73.

De Melo, M., C. Denizer and A. Gelb (1996), 'From Plan to Market: Patterns of Transition', *World Bank Policy Research Working Paper*, No. 1564.

Fisher, S. and R. Sahay (2001), The transition economies after ten years, in: L. Orlowski (ed.), 'Transition and Growth in Post-Communist Countries: The Ten-years Experience', CASE.

Rabushka, A. (1985), *From Adam Smith to the Wealth of America*, New Brunswick: Rutgers - The State University.

Chapter 1

Is there Room for National Monetary Policy in the Global Economy?

Andrew Berg, Eduardo Borensztein and Paolo Mauro

Introduction

Over the past decade, many middle-income developing countries have moved away from intermediate exchange rate regimes and toward either extreme of floating rates or hard pegs such as currency boards or dollarization. Soft pegs, crawling pegs, and crawling bands were the norm; now, these options are increasing falling out of favor, particularly for those emerging market countries that are highly integrated in international financial markets.

This trend is perhaps clearest in Latin America. By 2001, a majority of Latin American countries had either adopted the US dollar as legal tender currency or instituted a floating exchange rate regime—the latter often combined with an inflation target.[1] Chile staged a gradual and orderly exit from an intermediate exchange rate system to a float. Other moves towards floating, such as those of Brazil and Mexico, took place under crisis or near-crisis circumstances. El Salvador and Ecuador dollarized fully, the former in an orderly way, the latter in the midst of a crisis. In 2002, Argentina moved to a float during an intense financial crisis, after having maintained a currency board for eleven years. Also in 2002 Venezuela moved to a float from an intermediate regime under milder external pressure conditions. And so on.

In the rest of the world, there has also been a move to the 'corners'. In Asia, Thailand moved from a de facto peg to an independent float, and Korea and Indonesia from a managed float to an independent float. The Philippines maintained a floating regime, while Malaysia, an outlier, has maintained a traditional fixed exchange rate since 1998. In contrast to Latin America, there have been no moves toward currency boards or currency unions.

The move to the corners has been primarily driven by heightened integration in international financial markets and sharp fluctuations in capital

1 Calvo and Reinhart (2002) and Reinhart and Rogoff (2002) have emphasized the difference between *de jure* regimes and *de facto* regimes, that is, between what the authorities do and what they say they do with respect to exchange rate policy. The move away from the middle can be observed, at least for Latin America, using either sort of classification (Otker-Robe and Bubula (2002), Berg et al. (2002)).

flows, which have led to the conclusion that intermediate regimes are more vulnerable to costly currency crises than are the 'corner' regimes. The increasing popularity of floating exchange rate regimes is also related to the generalized decline in inflation. Previously, a fixed exchange rate, often a band or a crawling peg, was a central instrument in many inflation stabilization plans. With lower inflation, floating exchange rate regimes are now more appealing.

Despite the increase in the number of floaters, important doubts remain about whether this is in fact a viable option for middle-income countries with broadly open capital accounts. Some influential observers have argued that emerging market economies rarely actually follow a practice of floating their exchange rates, whatever their announced policy. Calvo and Reinhart (2002) attribute this 'fear of floating' to a rational view on the part of central bankers that their need to establish inflation-fighting credentials trumps any gain that might accrue to a depreciated exchange rate. They also emphasize that financially fragile countries, particularly those that have substantial liabilities denominated in foreign currency, may find sharp exchange rate depreciations unbearably painful. Ricardo Hausmann and co-authors, in a similar vein, argue that interest and exchange rates in emerging market floaters do not in fact respond to shocks in ways that are helpful, because lack of credibility and financial fragility do not allow it.[2]

In this study,[3] we review some of the evidence about the performance of floating exchange rate regimes in practice in emerging markets, with particular attention to the financially vulnerable countries of Latin America. We do not dwell on definitional questions regarding whether countries are true floaters or not. For us, a floating exchange rate regime precludes neither substantial intervention in foreign exchange markets, nor close attention to the exchange rate in conducting monetary policy, as long as the nominal exchange rate moves frequently and substantially in response to market forces, and the authorities do not set a particular level or path for the exchange rate.

The key question on which we focus is whether flexibility in exchange rate and monetary policy achieves meaningful domestic objectives. To address this question, we briefly review the experience of a few emerging market economies over the latter half of the 1990s. We then look at the available systematic evidence. We review the literature on how a floating exchange rate should respond to various shocks, noting how various conditions specific to emerging markets, in particular lack of credibility and financial fragility, might modify this optimal response. We then examine available evidence on whether emerging market exchange rates and

---

2 See Hausmann, et al. (2001) and Hausmann, et al. (1999). Mishkin and Savastano (2002), Goldstein (2002) and Eichengreen (2002) provide useful discussions of general exchange rate issues for emerging markets; the latter concentrates on the same issues of concern to us here.

3 Authors are grateful to the discussants, participants of the Conference on 'Beyond Transition: Development Perspectives and Dilemmas', to Alex Werner and many IMF colleagues for useful discussions, as well as to Priyadarshani Joshi for helpful research assistance. The views expressed in this chapter are those of the authors and do not necessarily represent those of the IMF or IMF policy.

monetary policy appear to be useful tools of countercyclical and anti-inflationary policy.

Even if monetary policy flexibility is valuable, it may be too costly, in two respects. First, the lack of credibility associated with a floating exchange rate may imply higher real interest rates, perhaps due to a 'peso problem' of a looming if never realized collapse. Second, unstable expectations or unruly markets may generate excessive exchange rate volatility in emerging market floats. We briefly look at some evidence on these questions at the end.

Some Examples

We set the stage for a more systematic analysis by reviewing the experience of several emerging economies over the latter half of the 1990s. We compare Argentina (a hard peg) with Mexico, Chile, and Peru (all floating, to varying degrees), and Hong Kong (a hard peg) with Singapore (a managed float), during the turmoil period of the late 1990s. For each of these countries, we show the inflation rate, the real effective exchange rate, and real GDP growth (year over year) in the top panel of Figure 1.1 and the level of the nominal and real interest rate and the change (year over year) in the real effective exchange rate in the bottom panel, for 1996–2001.

In Argentina (Figure 1.1) the price level and the real exchange rate remained unsurprisingly stable, and the still strong credibility of the currency board kept interest rates flat through the turmoil of the Russia, LTCM and Brazil crises of 1998/1999. Only real GDP growth was adversely affected, with consequences that persist to this date.

Mexico's (Figure 1.3) response in 1998/1999 is strikingly different. While interest rates did spike up, the exchange rate was also allowed to weaken substantially. Real GDP growth dipped but resumed in 1999, and the exchange rate appreciated rapidly back up.[4] Two other points emerge from the figures. First, real interest rates have been quite low since the turmoil of 1998/1999, falling below 5 percent in 2001 when Mexico followed the recession in the United States. Second, inflation in Mexico has come down well below 10 percent. On the whole, Mexico's monetary policy has been flexible enough to allow interest rates to respond to cyclical downturns, taking advantage of the prevalence of lower inflation.

Peru (Figure 1.5) confirms some aspects of this story. Even this highly dollarized economy responded to the shocks of 1998/1999 through a combination of higher interest rates and a substantial, and in this case prolonged, depreciation in the real exchange rate. The outcome for growth was, however, not as cheerful as in Mexico, probably because of the weaker impulse from the strong U.S. economy. In

4 On Mexico's experience during this period, see Carstens and Werner (1999) and Edwards and Savastano (1998). It is striking to note the strong trend appreciation in the real exchange rate through the period under examination. It might be noted that this follows the sharp real depreciation of 1995. Of course Mexico benefited from the strong growth in the United States during this period, but the deviation in the real exchange rate from the trend appreciation is perhaps all the more remarkable.

contrast to Mexico, the authorities seem to have first attempted to raise interest rates without letting the exchange rate go, only subsequently allowing the weakening. In the event, inflation did not pick up much following the depreciation.

Chile's (Figure 1.2) story is also similar, but the response of interest rates seems to have been higher relative to that of the exchange rate, and the recession is sharper. Chile went through two episodes of exchange rate pressure, in 1999 and 2000. In the first episode, interest rates increased sharply, in the context of a monetary framework with objectives on both inflation and the exchange rate (an explicit band). In September 2000 the authorities abandoned the band for free float. Thus in the second episode, the sharp depreciation was not accompanied by any interest rate increase. As with the other countries, inflation did not raise much in response to this depreciation, and the economy recovered from the recession. One can perhaps infer from this experience either that Chile accrued credibility in 1999, using it in 2000, or that Chile learned not to fear floating.

The comparison between Hong Kong and Singapore suggests a parallel with that between Mexico and Argentina. In Hong Kong (Figure 1.4), the adjustment was, at least initially, in the form of higher interest rates and a large output drop. By contrast, Singapore (Figure 1.6) displays a sharp nominal and, eventually, real effective depreciation, with moderate monetary tightening and no recession. Three differences with Mexico/Argentina are worth noting. First, Singapore allowed only a brief and fairly modest interest rate response. Second, one cannot attribute its strong growth performance to its location. Third, Hong Kong's flexibility and small economic size resulted in a large, though lagged, disinflation that ultimately led to a substantial real exchange rate adjustment.

This anecdotal evidence suggests several tentative observations. (i) Floating countries do allow exchange rates to move in response to shocks, though sometimes interest rate responses are also sharp. (ii) Exchange rate flexibility seems to have been helpful in cushioning output despite adverse shocks. (iii) Peru's high degree of dollarization did not preclude some exchange rate response. (iv) At least for Mexico, real interest rates seem to have declined recently in response to the recession. (v) Pass-through seems to have been relatively low following exchange rate adjustments in floating countries. (vi) Hong Kong's price flexibility and small economic size clearly make it a more plausible candidate than Argentina is for a hard peg. (vii) Floating regimes seem to become gradually more effective over time, as evidenced by the case of Chile.

This perusal of cases can hardly be definitive, and others will no doubt look at these episodes differently (for example, Hausmann, et al., 1999). We now turn to more systematic evidence regarding the effectiveness of floating exchange rates in emerging markets.

The Taylor Rule as a Benchmark for Monetary Policy

Much of the discussion of design of optimal policy, especially for advanced economies, has focused on Taylor rules in recent years, following Taylor (1993). In this framework, monetary policy follows a rule of the form:

$$i_t^* = i^* + \beta(E\{\pi_{t,k}|\Omega_t\} - \pi^*) + \gamma E\{x_{t,k}|\Omega_t\} \quad \text{(See Table 1.1)}$$

where i_t^* is the target rate for the monetary policy instrument (for example, an overnight nominal interest rate), $\pi_{t,k}$ is inflation between periods t and $t + k$, π^* is the desired inflation rate, $x_{t,k}$ is the output gap (that is, the gap between desired and actual output) between t and $t+k$. E is the expectations operator, with Ω_t the information available to policy-makers as of time t. i^* is then the desired rate for the monetary policy instrument that would prevail when both inflation and output are at desired levels.[5]

This formulation is quite general: it says that the policy maker tries to move the monetary policy instrument so as to achieve some success at both keeping inflation on track and at reducing the output gap. The instrument usually is the interest rate, but it could be a monetary aggregate as well.[6] The values of the coefficients β and γ are useful summaries of policy. On the standard view that higher real interest rates contract both output and inflation, a coefficient of β above 1 suggests that policy will be stabilizing for inflation. Similarly, a coefficient of γ above 0 would be stabilizing for output.[7] Strict inflation targeting would be a restricted form of equation (1), in which the weight on the output gap is zero. (The output gap would still be in Ω, so it would still matter for policy, a point to which we return below).

A policy of the general Taylor-rule sort can be derived for a central banker in a closed economy who has a quadratic loss function in deviations in inflation and output from their targets, in an economy with nominal price rigidities. More generally, the Taylor rule benchmark is buttressed by the observation that the rule has provided a reasonably accurate way of describing how advanced economy central banks behave, notably those of the United States, Germany and Japan.

This theoretical literature was developed with reference to closed economies. It seems, however, that much of the closed economy story remains in

5 This discussion follows quite closely Clarida et al. (2000).

6 Taylor (2000) notes that a monetary instrument may make more sense when uncertainty about money velocity is lower than uncertainty about real interest rates, or when real shocks (such as export demand shocks) are large, as is likely to be the case for emerging markets.

7 It may help to note that the Taylor equation can be rewritten as:

$$r_t^* = r^* + (\beta - 1)(E\{\pi_{t,k}|\Omega_t\} - \pi^*) + \gamma E\{x_{t,k}|\Omega_t\},$$

where r_t^* is the ex ante real interest rate and r^* is the long run equilibrium real rate of interest.

open economies with floating exchange rates. The most obvious complication is the effect of the exchange rate, which provides additional channels for monetary policy to operate. The main effect is that interest rate contractions now affect inflation more rapidly through the exchange rate appreciation they induce, while their contractionary effect on output is also enhanced by the appreciation. Thus, smaller changes in the interest rate are appropriate for a given deviation from equilibrium values of output and inflation.[8] Nevertheless, a strict Taylor rule formulation would include the exchange rate only to the extent that, as part of Ω, it helps predict inflation or output gaps.

Can emerging markets float meaningfully and run an independent monetary policy along the lines of a Taylor rule? Three factors may make it impractical for emerging markets to do so: lack of credibility, high inflation pass-through, and powerful balance sheet effects of exchange rate movements.

Lack of credibility of the central bank may lead markets to interpret any loosening as a permanent shift towards higher inflation, implying that there is no benefit to discretion. This lack of credibility might derive from a lack of central bank independence and a vulnerability of the governing authorities to political pressures that will tend to lead to a time-inconsistent inflationary bias. Similarly, if fiscal policy dictates monetary policy in the long run, the monetary authorities may not be able to credibly claim not to resort to inflationary finance. If a lack of credibility were dominant, we would tend to observe higher real interest rates in floating exchange rate countries during periods in which they maintained price and exchange rate stability, since the expectation would remain that a large inflation was coming one day. We might also observe that central banks could not respond to shocks, as they would otherwise consider appropriate. For example, they could not loosen policy or at least allow the exchange rate to weaken in response to terms of trade shock, if observers would (even if wrongly) conclude that they might not just be responding optimally to the shock but also taking advantage of the opportunity to engage in an inflationary episode. Thus, whether in response to terms of trade and foreign interest rate shocks, or to weak domestic output or a domestic output gap, the central bank may not be able to allow the exchange rate to weaken.

High inflation pass-through may imply that exchange rate devaluations end up being predominantly inflationary, rather than expansionary. High pass-through may itself result from lack of credibility, as wage and price setters interpret exchange rate depreciations as signals of a monetary policy loosening, rather than a change in relative prices.

High incidence of foreign-currency-denominated liabilities in emerging markets may imply that exchange rate movements may have adverse real effects

8 Eichengreen (2002) shows this in a very simple model. Svensson (2000) reaches broadly similar conclusions based on simulations of a much more elaborate framework. He emphasizes not this result but the differences between the reaction function implied by inflation targeting and a Taylor rule defined, as in Taylor (1993), as one in which only current inflation and output gaps enter Ω. We follow Clarida, et al. (2000) in focusing on forward-looking Taylor rules in which Ω, can contain anything known at time t.

through the balance sheets of banks, firms, and the government. The implications of balance sheet effects for monetary policy are more complicated, though the basic closed economy results are likely to endure. The most obvious implication, that devaluations are less strongly expansionary, does not undermine the closed economy logic of the Taylor rule. Two further complications may have the stronger implications. First, the output effects of devaluations may be highly nonlinear (with large devaluations having dramatically different effects); the optimal response during crises might thus be different. Second, the authorities may care about the financial state of the banking sector beyond its implications for output and inflation (say for fiscal reasons). In either case, the central bank might pay attention to the exchange rate even beyond the extent to which it helps predict inflation and the output gap (see Eichengreen, 2002 and Cespedes, et al., 2000 for further discussion).

We have generalized about emerging market economies, but of course the credibility of the monetary authorities, the degree of pass-through, and the incidence of liability dollarization will vary importantly across countries. It is worth emphasizing that all three of these features of emerging markets are closely related to the phenomenon of de facto dollarization. Where a foreign currency is the unit of account, perhaps because of a history of high inflation, pass-through is also likely to be high. A lack of credibility of the monetary authorities is closely associated with dollarization. And of course the financial fragility associated with balance sheet effects of exchange rate changes is a direct function of dollarization of liabilities in the country. Thus, highly de facto dollarized economies are likely to be particularly vulnerable to these sorts of problems.

Do emerging market floaters follow a form of Taylor rule similar to that in the equation above? Table 1.1 reports the results obtained for Chile and Peru, from Corbo (2000) and Moron and Castro (2000), respectively. For comparison, (Table 1.1 lines 1 through 4) reports the baseline estimates for the G3 countries, drawn from Clarida, et al. (1997).[9]

The evidence is not conclusive but is consistent with the view that these emerging markets made effective use of monetary policy. The coefficient β for Chile is above 1 and is roughly comparable to that of the G3. Thus, Chile seems to have been able to manipulate its real interest rate in response to expected inflation. Similar results apply to Peru with respect to the money supply. The coefficient γ is closer to zero for both Chile and Peru, so that there is little evidence that the authorities respond to the output gap directly, beyond its implications for price pressures.[10] Nevertheless, even with a zero coefficient on the output gap, a regime in which the authorities respond only to inflation is still more countercyclical than

9 The results for the G3 confirm that central banks have since the 1980s raised (expected) real interest rates when inflation was high and lowered them when output was below equilibrium. The Fed seems to have given more emphasis to output after the initial disinflation period of 1979 through 1982 (line 4).

10 It might be interesting to examine the first-stage regressions that underlie these results, i.e., the extent to which shocks such as foreign interest rates, the terms of trade, or the exchange rate itself affect expected output and inflation.

a hard peg or dollarization, where uncovered interest parity suggests that the real interest rate increases when inflation is low. At the same time, neither Chile nor Peru seems to target exclusively inflation and the output gap: in Chile, there is evidence that the central bank also targets the current account deficit (indeed, this is an announced objective of the central bank); in Peru, deviations of the real exchange rate from trend seem to be resisted by the authorities.

These results are inevitably tentative. Compared to the developed country examples, the time series are short and the monetary policy regimes are changing during the sample, as we noted in the section above specifically for Chile. For Peru, Moron and Castro (2000) argue that during the turmoil of 1998/1999 the authorities were especially careful to avoid depreciation, and they show econometrically that the revealed aversion of the authorities to exchange rate weakness was especially strong during that period. Nonetheless, their results also show some countercyclical response. In addition, it is often more difficult to identify the instrument of monetary policy in emerging markets, most notably where the authorities attempt to control a monetary aggregate but do so only imperfectly at all horizons.[11]

Response to Important Shocks

A complementary approach to looking at Taylor rules is to ask whether emerging market floaters respond appropriately to important shocks to exogenous variables, such as the terms of trade and foreign interest rates.

Terms-of-Trade Shocks

Under floating rates, a negative shock to the terms of trade should depreciate the exchange rate.[12] An appropriate response for the monetary authorities would be to 'lean against the wind', in an attempt to keep inflation in check. The increase in interest rates should be limited however, as the negative terms-of-trade shock would also increase the output gap (see the second term in the equation above). To

---

11 Edwards and Savastano (1998) attempt to estimate a monetary policy reaction function for Mexico in 1996–97, using somewhat different techniques. Hausmann, et al. (1999) regress real interest rates on the output gap for a few emerging markets, and typically find a negative coefficient, implying higher real rates during recessions. At the same time, they find similar results for the United States. However, numerous other studies using more complete, Taylor-type regressions for the U.S. find that monetary policy seems to be countercyclical, thus casting doubt on the simpler Hausmann, et. al methodology.

12 Rogoff and Chen (2001) point out that in many plausible models the nominal exchange rate should depreciate with negative terms of trade shocks. With sticky domestic prices, for example, a permanent increase in the terms of trade will call for an almost corresponding appreciation to keep the relative price of domestic goods in line. In the Dornbusch (1976) model, similarly, a permanent change in the terms of trade requires full adjustment of the nominal exchange rate, in order to reproduce the flexible price equilibrium.

the extent that emerging markets central bank lack credibility, face high pass-through, or view devaluations as contractionary, a sharper interest rate response and a more limited depreciation might be appropriate.

There is evidence that emerging market floating exchange rate countries do, in fact, usefully depreciate in response to negative terms of trade shocks. Broda (2002) looks at a sample of 73 developing countries since 1973 and examines whether the response of real GDP, the real exchange rate and inflation to terms of trade shocks differs systematically across exchange rate regimes. He finds that, in response to negative terms of trade shocks, fixed exchange rate regimes suffer large and significant losses in terms of real GDP growth and display real exchange rate depreciations only after two years. By contrast, floating exchange rate countries display immediate large nominal and real depreciations, some inflation, and much smaller output losses.[13] Broda (2002) shows that emerging market floaters with a high degree of de facto dollarization do not look different in this regard.

A complementary approach considers how the nominal exchange rate responds to long-run trends that affect the equilibrium real exchange rate. One potential advantage of floats, compared with pegs, might be that they would permit the real exchange rate to trend without demanding changes in the price level. Rogoff and Chen (2001) examine the long-run relationship between the real exchange rate and real commodity prices for three small open developed countries, Canada, Australia and New Zealand. They find that world real commodity prices have a strong and fairly stable relationship with the real exchange rate of New Zealand and Australia, while the result is less clear for Canada. A long depreciating trend in the Australian real exchange rate is related to a similar downward trend in the real commodity prices of Australia's main exports. In the absence of a floating exchange rate, Australia would have had to experience deflation to achieve a similar adjustment.

This type of result seems to hold for many emerging markets as well. Cashin, et al. (2002) show that real exchange rate movements are highly correlated with commodity prices in most of the countries in their much larger sample of 58 commodity-export dependent emerging markets. Indeed, the real exchange rate is cointegrated with (trending) commodity prices in most of their sample. Thus, for these countries as well, nominal price levels would presumably have had to trend as well in the absence of exchange rate flexibility.

13 Negative terms of trade shocks above 3% of GDP lead to real output declines of 2% the first year and 7% cumulative over three years in countries with pegged regimes, compared to an average 1% decline the first year and 2% cumulative in countries with floats. The real effective exchange rate depreciates by only 2% in the fixed regime in the first year, and 4% overall, compared to a 7% depreciation on impact and 11% overall in countries with floats. Inflation is also somewhat higher in floats.

Foreign Interest Rate Shocks

An increase in foreign interest rates will, like negative terms of trade shock, tend to depreciate the exchange rate and hence cause inflation, prompting the monetary authorities again to raise interest rates. At the same time, since the domestic interest rate hike would tend to reduce output, the monetary authority should 'lean against the wind' but should permit some depreciation.[14] Permanent shocks to foreign interest rates should be more fully offset, as inflation will not tend to come down over time in the absence of a reduction in output. More generally, uncovered interest parity implies that a permanent increase in the foreign interest rate requires, in the long run, a corresponding increase in the domestic interest rate to maintain a stable inflation rate and output gap, independent of the exchange rate regime.

Hausmann, et al. (1999) find that the reaction of domestic rates to U.S. rates is not significantly different across exchange rate regimes, using monthly data from 1960 to 1998 for 11 emerging markets. Moreover, using daily data for 1998-99 for Mexico, Venezuela and Argentina, they find that the reaction of domestic interest rates to the international risk premium is highest in Mexico, the country with the most flexible exchange rate regime. In a more comprehensive study, Frankel, et al. (2002) regress quarterly and monthly domestic interest rates in several emerging market countries on the U.S. Federal Funds rate, along with several controls. They find mixed results: floats seem to have some insulating properties in their full sample, but not in a restricted sample consisting of the developing countries in the 1990s alone.

An alternative perspective is provided by Borensztein, et al. (2001), who examine the response of domestic interest rates and exchange rates to shocks to the U.S. Fed Fund rate and the risk premium on emerging market debt in a small sample of polar extreme regimes (Hong Kong, Singapore, Mexico and Argentina) as well as developed country floaters such as Australia, Canada and New Zealand for comparison. They attempt to identify the effects of surprises to the U.S. Fed Fund rate, rather than any movements in the rates that may reflect underlying factors affecting both emerging markets and the U.S. Moreover, they employ a dynamic specification to identify impact as well as long-run effects, a potentially important difference given that the optimal response to permanent and temporary shocks is likely to vary, as we have seen. They find that interest rates in Hong Kong seem to react one-for-one to U.S. monetary policy shocks. By contrast, interest rates in Singapore increase by about 0.3 basis points to a 1 basis point increase in U.S. interest rates, and Singapore's exchange rate depreciates somewhat. In these respects, Singapore thus looks very much like advanced country floaters such as Australia, Canada and New Zealand. The estimates for Mexico are less precise, making it difficult to discern a significant difference compared with Argentina. Thus this study does not confirm the result by Hausmann, et al. (1999) that shocks to U.S. interest rates cause interest rates in

---

14 These points are made by Eichengreen (2002) informally and by Parrado and Velasco (2002) in an optimizing model of a small open economy in the Obstfeld and Rogoff (1996) tradition.

Mexico to raise more than they do in Argentina. At the same time, it remains clear that the Mexican exchange rate does depreciate in response to U.S. interest rate shocks, consistent with the results in Frankel, Schmukler and Serven (2002).

Inflation Pass-through

In this section we address not a specific shock but rather the question of whether exchange rate pass-through is so high in some emerging markets that floating exchange rates are not a viable option. High pass-through from devaluation to domestic prices might be suggestive of low credibility of monetary policy, in that innovations to the exchange rate are in this case interpreted not as relative price shifts but as signs of an inflationary burst to come. Moreover, where recent history is highly inflationary, a foreign currency may serve as the unit of account, further enhancing inflation pass-through and impairing the role of the exchange rate.

Pass-through has been moderate in Mexico, Brazil, Russia, and other emerging markets that have recently undergone extremely large devaluations. This is confirmed by our country anecdotes reported above. More systematic analyses (Borensztein and De Gregorio, 1999; Goldfajn and Werlang, 2000) find that pass-through tends to be limited where output is below potential, the real exchange rate is initially misaligned, and the initial rate of inflation is low. This suggests that, in less extreme conditions, pass-through may be low where countries have established a track record of credibility with respect to their monetary policy in the context of a floating exchange rate.

We present some simple evidence on this conjecture for Mexico. We estimate inflation pass-through by regressing (the log of) prices on past prices and current and past exchange rate levels in a two-variable VAR. Figure 1.2 shows how an innovation of 1 percent in the exchange rate passes through into changes in the price level over time. The upper curve is based upon estimates for 1995–98, while the lower curve is based upon estimates for 1999–2001. While these results are tentative, they suggest that pass-through has become more moderate in Mexico as its float (introduced during the crisis of 1995) gained credibility over time.[15]

Do Emerging Markets Pay a Large Price in Terms of Credibility or Volatility?

Using a variety of approaches, we have presented evidence suggesting that emerging market floaters are often able to loosen monetary and exchange rate policy when this seems appropriate (e.g., in response to adverse external shocks). Does this flexibility impose a price in terms of higher inflation, higher real interest rates, or higher exchange rate volatility?

---

15 Carstens and Werner (1999) present further evidence to this effect.

First, floating regimes, which may become more popular in response to declines in inflation, do not seem to have led to a resurgence of inflation.[16] Second, there is tentative evidence that emerging market floaters suffered from chronically higher real interest rates as a result of lower credibility. Hausmann, et al. (1999) find that, even looking at lower inflation periods only, real interest rates were significantly higher in floating rate countries than in fixed rate countries in the 1990s (9 percent versus 5 percent). Ghosh, et al. (1997), in a much broader sample, also find somewhat higher real interest rates in floats that in pegs, although they find no systematic difference in economic growth across regimes. At the same time, it is difficult to disentangle the cases of countries that attempt to peg but are unable to sustain the peg because of inconsistent policies from those of countries that float as a deliberate choice. For the latter cases, it would be interesting to explore whether floaters gain credibility over time.

Third, is exchange rate volatility excessive in emerging market floaters? For advanced economies, there is evidence that volatility is largely unrelated to fundamentals. For example, Flood and Rose (1995) find that the only economic variable whose behavior depends systematically on the exchange rate regime is the real exchange rate, which is much more volatile in floats. There is no sign that the exchange rate volatility associated with floats achieves lower volatility in some other dimension (such as interest rates).[17] For emerging markets, 'fear of floating' considerations seem to lead most floaters to curb exchange rate volatility by increasing the volatility of interest rates and reserves. As a result, exchange rate volatility in Mexico has not been out of line with that observed in developed country floats, after the immediate post-crisis period of 1995 (Edwards and Savastano, 1998), despite presumably larger shocks in Mexico.

Conclusions

There is much debate about whether emerging markets can meaningfully and usefully float. In our view, they can. A useful and meaningful float is not necessarily an absolutely pure float. Indeed, emerging markets seldom conduct pure floats: they often intervene in the foreign exchange market and regularly conduct monetary policy keeping a close eye on foreign exchange rate

---

16 There is a debate on whether some monetary policy approaches (such as strict inflation targeting) in the context of floating are more effective than others. Corbo, et al. (2001) discuss this issue with a special focus on emerging markets.

17 Jeanne and Rose (2002) suggest in a model how 'noise traders' could explain this result. Flood and Rose (1999) instead focus on how volatility in the exchange rate can be self-fulfilling in that it can generate high and volatile risk premia that, in turn, justify the exchange rate volatility. In this context, a *credible* peg could fix expectations around the stable equilibrium and reduce volatility in the exchange rate without increasing volatility elsewhere in the economy. Importantly, Reinhart and Rogoff (2002) have called some of these sorts of general empirical results into question, noting that they are sensitive to differences between *de facto* and *de jure* exchange rate regimes, particularly the prevalence of multiple exchange rates.

developments. But so do advanced country floaters, including strict inflation targeters — to the extent that the exchange rate determines inflationary expectations. What is important is whether exchange rates and interest rates seem to move in useful ways.

From a look directly at evidence on policy reaction functions, and at the response of interest rates and exchange rates to shocks of various sorts, a picture has emerged. First, exchange rate fluctuations seem to play a stabilizing role in many cases. The contrast between Singapore and Hong Kong during the Asia crisis is perhaps the clearest case. There is also strong systematic evidence, though, both in the short run and over the long term, that terms of trade shocks lead to appropriate adjustments in the exchange rate and relative prices, adjustments that would be painful if they had to take place directly through changes in nominal prices instead. Second, there is more tentative evidence that interest rates in floating exchange rate countries do fall in response to depressed domestic activity and especially relatively low inflation.

One issue that deserves further study is the question of how emerging market floating exchange rate regimes evolve over time. If performance under floating regimes can remain acceptable in terms of overall price stability, one can hope for a number of developments that will further enhance this effectiveness. Wage indexation and backward looking inflation expectations in general may disappear as the central bank gains in credibility.[18] Firms may change their financial structure to reduce their vulnerability to exchange rate fluctuations, reducing the magnitude of balance sheet effects.[19] We saw some anecdotal evidence for improved performance in our examination of the Chilean experience of 1998/2000. It may be, as noted above, that the move to a more pure float and enhanced willingness to let the exchange rate absorb the shocks is a function of the gradual increase in credibility of the regime. Before we become too optimistic about floating exchange rates, we should note that this dynamic also can run in the other direction. For countries that start with little credibility, the costs of establishing that credibility may be extremely high, and further poor performance can increase liability dollarization and financial fragility.[20]

The answer to the question posed by our title is thus 'yes, there is room for a national monetary policy, even in financial fragile emerging markets.' This

18 We saw some evidence consistent with this for Mexico. Corbo, et al. (2001) argue that this has been observed more generally in Latin American inflation targeters in the 1990s.

19 Eichengreen (2002) makes the point that, even if the economy on the whole cannot reduce its exposure to foreign-currency-denominated debt, firms can rearrange it so as to minimize risks. Martinez and Werner (2001) find some evidence that the floating exchange rate in Mexico has reduced foreign currency mismatches in the borrowing of Mexican firms over the 1992 to 2000 period.

20 Caballero and Krishnamurthy (2001) illustrate how insufficient exchange rate volatility in the aftermath of a crisis (due to rational 'fear of floating') may lead private agents to accumulate inefficiently small amounts of international liquidity *ex ante*. In their framework, it would be optimal for central banks to commit to allow more flexibility than they would like to *ex poste*. Their paper is nominally about post-crisis periods, but the idea may apply better to financially fragile countries in more normal times.

does not mean that floating is right for every country. In a companion paper (Berg, et al. (2002) we review the relative merits of the other hard corner, the adoption of a common or foreign currency ('dollarization'). We conclude that dollarization may be appealing to those countries lacking credibility and where *de facto* dollarization has already reached high levels. We also have not discussed the case of those mostly poorer countries that are substantially closed to capital flows. For them, intermediate options remain viable. Thus, we can expect to continue to observe a spectrum of exchange rate choices for some time to come.

References

Berg, A., E. Borensztein and P. Mauro (2002), 'An Evaluation of Monetary Regime Options for Latin America' *North American Journal of Economics and Finance,* Vol. 85, pp. 1-23.

Borensztein, E. and J. De Gregorio (1999), 'Devaluation and Inflation' unpublished working paper (Washington: International Monetary Fund).

Borensztein, E., J. Zettelmeyer and T. Philippon (2001), 'Monetary Independence in Emerging Markets: Does the Exchange Rate Regime Make a Difference?' IMF Working Paper No. 01/1 (Washington, DC: International Monetary Fund).

Broda, C. (2002), 'Terms of Trade and Exchange Rate Regimes in Developing Countries' Staff Reports Number 148 (New York, NY: Federal Reserve Bank of New York).

Calvo, G.A. and C.M. Reinhart (2002), 'Fear of Floating' *Quarterly Journal of Economics,* Vol. 117, Issue 2 (May), pp. 379-408.

Carstens, A. and A. Werner (1999), 'Mexico's Monetary Policy Framework under a Floating Exchange Rate Regime' Working Paper (Mexico City, Mexico: Banco de Mexico).

Cashin, P., L.F. Cespedes and R. Sahay (2002), 'Do Developing Countries Have Commodity Currencies?' working paper, forthcoming (Washington, DC: International Monetary Fund).

Cespedes, L.F., R. Chang and A. Velasco (2000), 'Balance Sheets and Exchange Rate Policy', NBER Working Paper No. 7840 (Cambridge, MA: National Bureau of Economic Research).

Clarida, R., J. Gali and M. Gertler (1997), 'Monetary Policy Rules in Practice: Some International Evidence' National Bureau of Economic Research Working Paper, Working Paper Entry: 200012 6254.

Clarida, R., J. Gali and M. Gertler (2000), 'Monetary Policy Rules and Macroeconomic Stability: Evidence and Some Theory' *Quarterly Journal of Economics,* Vol. 115, Issue 1 (February), pp. 147-80.

Corbo, V. (2000), 'Monetary Policy in Latin America in the 90s' Working Paper No. 78 (Santiago, Chile: Central Bank of Chile).

Corbo, V., O. Landerretche and K. Schmidt-Hebbel (2001), 'Assessing Inflation Targeting after a Decade of World Experience' *International Journal of Finance and Economics,* Vol. 6, Issue 4 (October), pp. 343-68.

Dornbusch, R. (1976), 'Expectations and Exchange Rate Dynamics' *Journal of Political Economy,* Vol. 84, Issue 6 (December), pp. 1161-76.

Edwards, S. and M.A. Savastano (1998), 'The Morning After: The Mexican Peso in the Aftermath of the 1994 Currency Crisis', NBER Working Paper No. 6516 (Cambridge, MA: National Bureau of Economic Research).

Eichengreen, B. (2002), 'Can Emerging Markets Float? Should They Inflation Target?' Working Paper Series 36 (Sao Paolo: Banco Central Do Brasil).

Flood, R.P. and A.K. Rose (1995), 'Fixing Exchange Rates: A Virtual Quest for Fundamentals' *Journal of Monetary Economics,* Vol. 36, Issue 1 (December), pp. 3-37.

Flood, R.P. and A.K. Rose (1999), 'Understanding Exchange Rate Volatility without the Contrivance of Macroeconomics' *Economic Journal,* Vol. 109, Issue 459 (November), pp. F660-72.

Frankel, J.A., S.L. Schmukler and L. Serven (2002), 'Global Transmission of Interest Rates: Monetary Independence and Currency Regime' NBER Working Paper No. 8828 (Cambridge, MA: National Bureau of Economic Research).

Goldfajn, I. and S.R. da Costa Werlang (2000), 'The Pass-Through from Depreciation to Inflation: A Panel Study' Working Paper Series No. 5, (Brasilia: Banco Central Do Brasil).

Ghosh, A.R., A.M. Gulde, J.D. Ostry and H.C. Wolf (1997), 'Does the Nominal Exchange Rate Regime Matter?' NBER Working Paper No. 5874 (Cambridge, MA: National Bureau of Economic Research).

Hausmann, R., M. Gavin, C. Pages-Serra, and E. Stein (1999), 'Financial Turmoil and the Choice of Exchange Rate Regime' Working Paper Series No. 400 (Washington, DC: Inter-American Development Bank).

Hausmann, R., U. Panizza and E. Stein (2001), 'Why Do Countries Float the Way They Float?' *Journal of Development Economics,* Vol. 66, Issue 2 (December), pp. 387-414.

Jeanne, O. and A.K. Rose (2002), 'Noise Trading and Exchange Rate Regimes' *Quarterly Journal of Economics,* Vol. 117, Issue 2 (May), pp. 537-69.

Martinez, L. and A. Werner (2001), 'The Exchange Rate Regime and the Currency Composition of Corporate Debt: The Mexican Experience.' Paper presented at the NBER Interamerican Seminar on Economics, Cambridge, MA, July 20-21.

Mishkin, F.S. and M.A. Savastano (2002), 'Monetary Policy Strategies for Emerging Market Countries: Lessons from Latin America' *Comparative Economic Studies,* Vol. 44, Issue 2-3 (Summer-Fall), pp. 45-82.

Moron, E. and J.F. Castro (2000), 'Uncovering the Central Bank's Monetary Policy Objectives: Going Beyond Fear of Floating' Working Paper (Lima, Peru: Universidad del Pacifico).

Obstfeld, M. and K. Rogoff (1996), *Foundations of International Macroeconomics* (Cambridge, Mass. and London: MIT Press).

Otker-Robe, I. and A. Bubula (2002), 'The Evolution of Exchange Rate Regimes since 1990: Evidence from De Facto Policies' Working Paper No. 02/155 (Washington, DC: International Monetary Fund).

Parrado, E. and A. Velasco (2002), 'Optimal Interest Rate Policy in a Small Open Economy' NBER Working Paper No. 8721 (Cambridge, MA: National Bureau of Economic Research).

Reinhart, C.M. and K.S. Rogoff, (2002), 'The Modern History of Exchange Rate Arrangements: A Reinterpretation' unpublished manuscript (Washington, DC: International Monetary Fund).

Rogoff, K. and Y.C. Chen, (2001), 'Commodity Currencies and Empirical Exchange Rate Equations.' Paper presented at the Conference on Empirical Exchange Rate Models, Madison, Wisconsin, September 28-29.

Taylor, J.B (2000), 'Using Monetary Policy Rules in Emerging Market Economies.' Paper presented at the 75th Anniversary Conference of the Bank of Mexico, Mexico City, Mexico, November 14-15.

Taylor, J.B. (1993), *Macroeconomic Policy in a World Economy: From Econometric Design to Practical Operation* (New York and London: Norton).

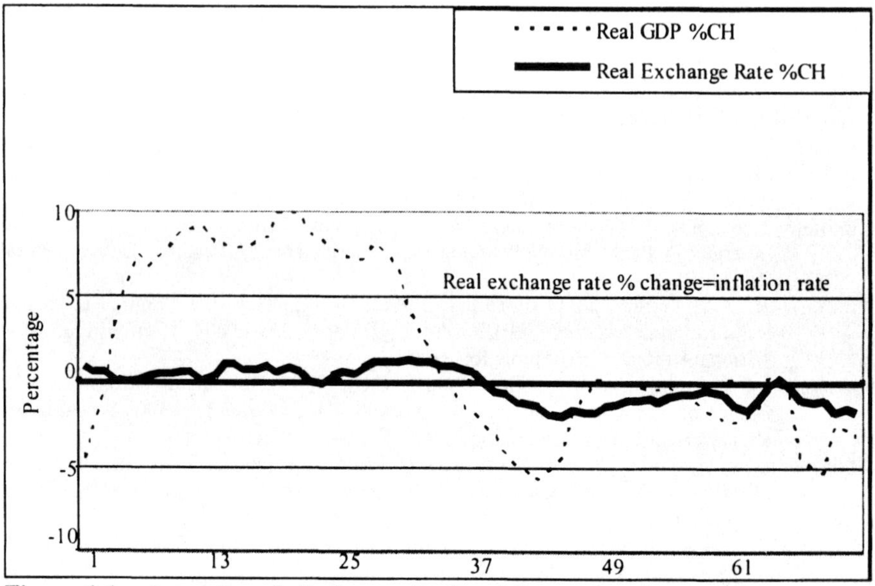

Figure 1.1a Argentina: Inflation, output and the real exchange rate

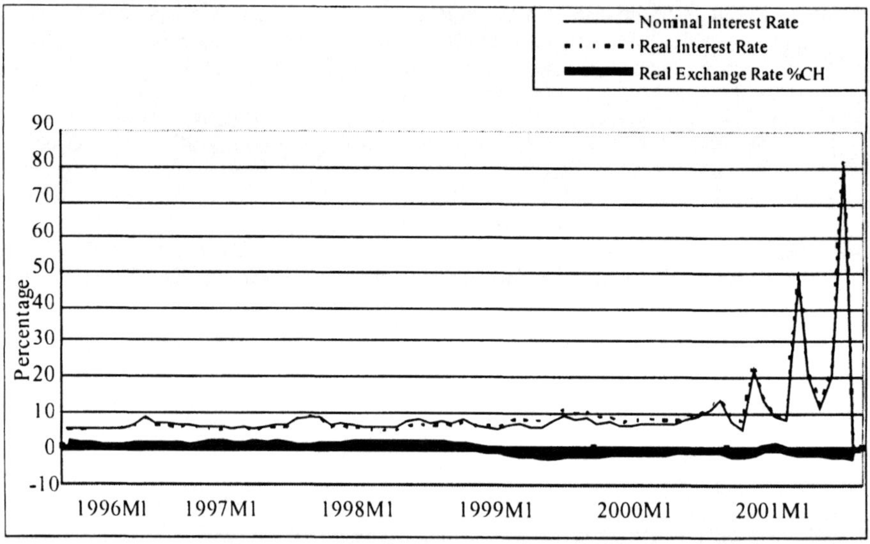

Figure 1.1b Argentina: Changes in exchange rate and interest rates

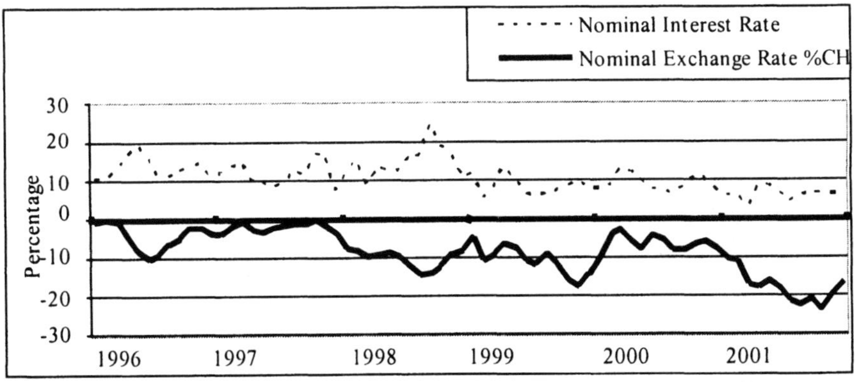

Figure 1.2a Chile: Nominal exchange rate changes and interest rate

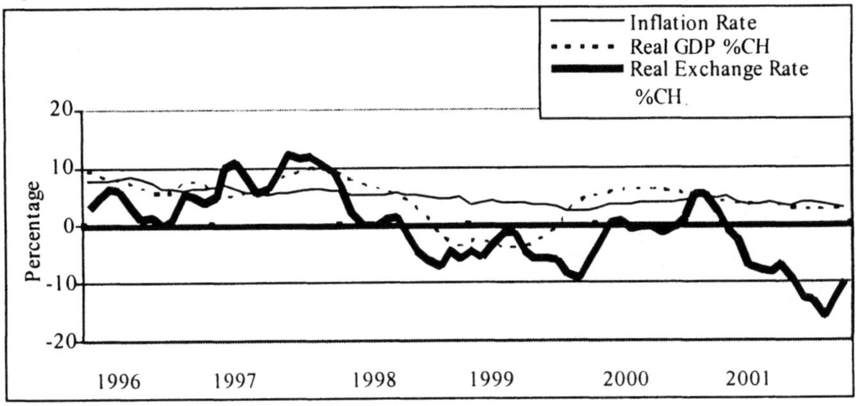

Figure 1.2b Chile: Inflation, output and changes in real exchange rate

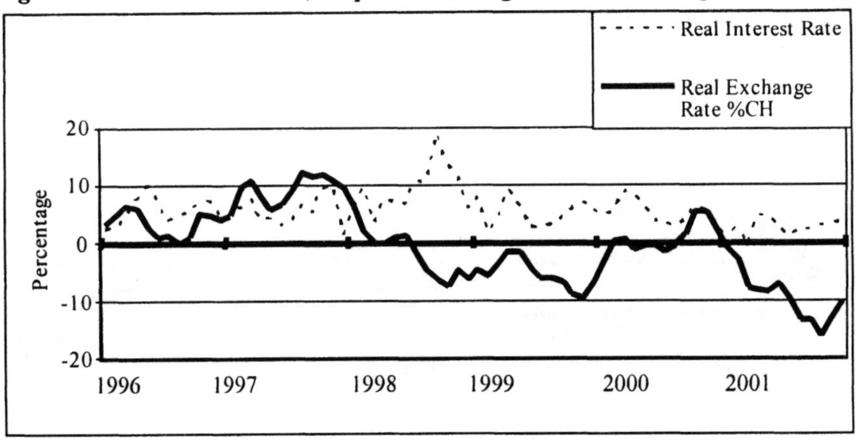

Figure 1.2c Chile: Real exchange rate changes and interest rate

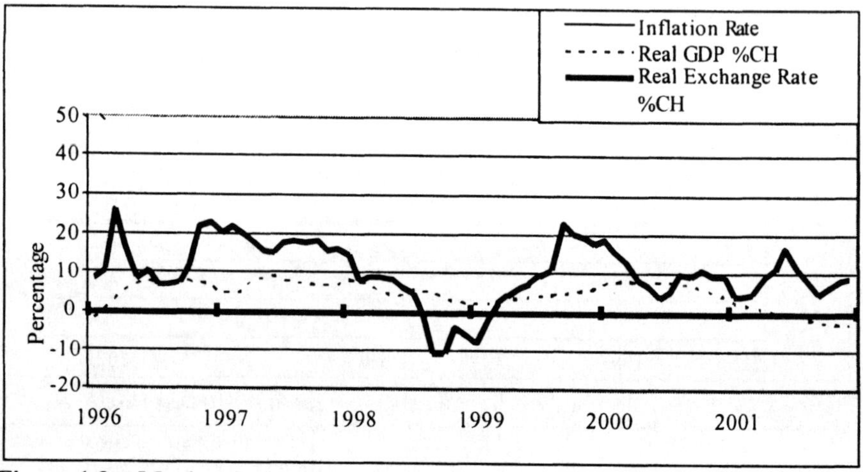

Figure 1.3a Mexico: Inflation and the real exchange

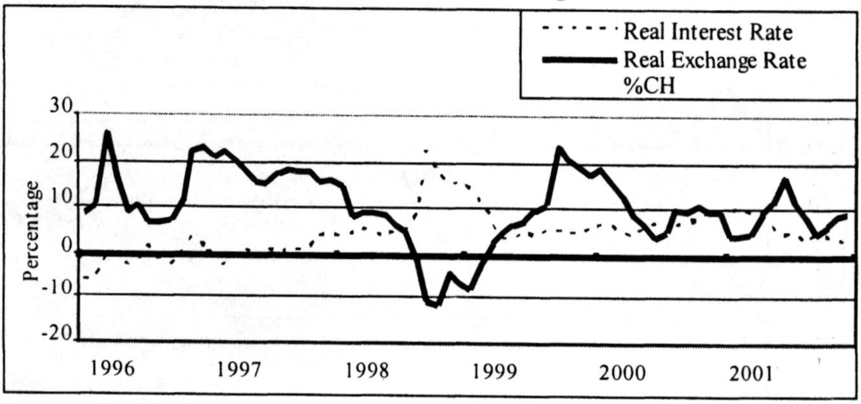

Figure 1.3b Mexico: Real rate changes and interest

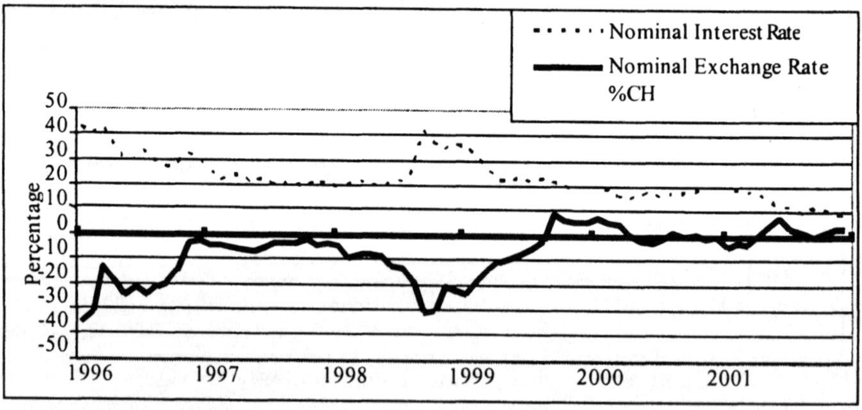

Figure 1.3c Mexico: Nominal exchange rate changes and interest rate

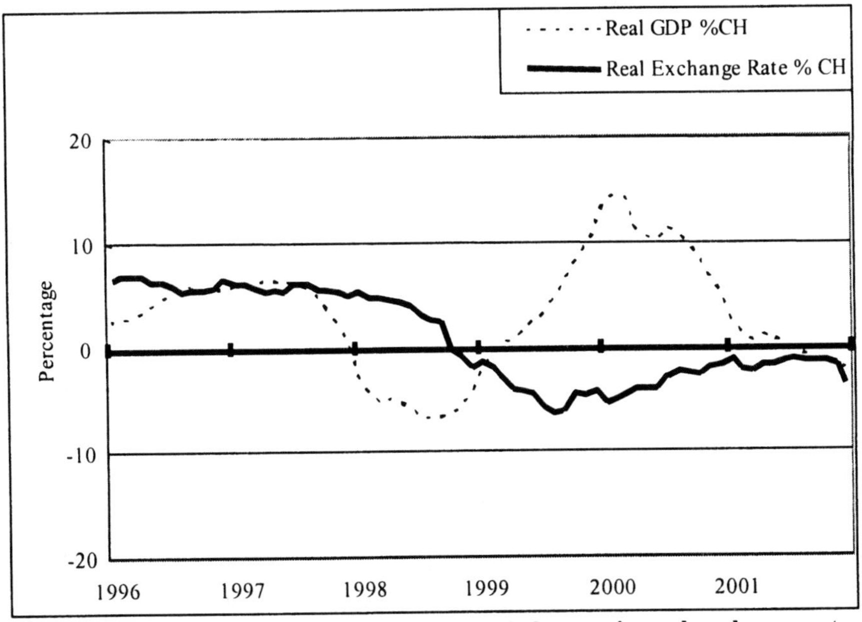

Figure 1.4a Hong Kong: Inflation, output and changes in real exchange rate

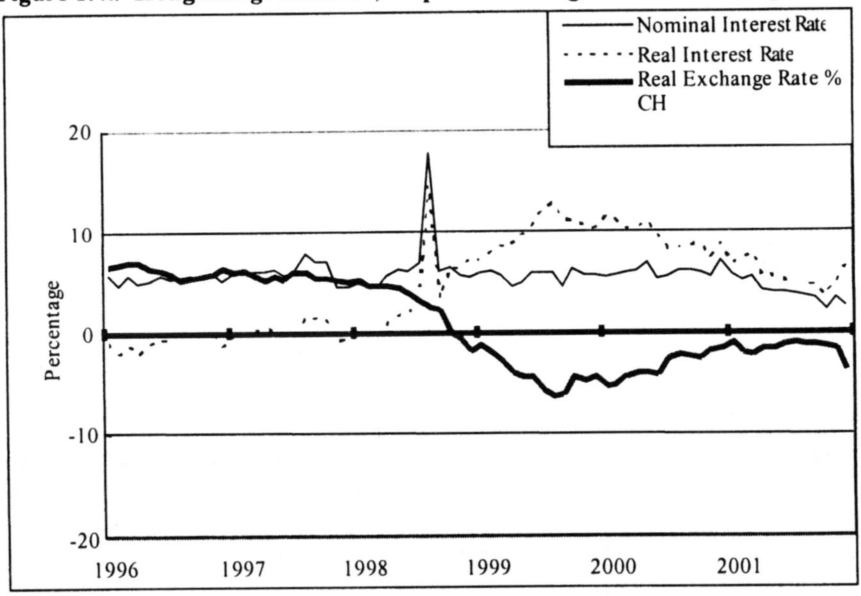

Figure 1.4b Hong Kong: Changes in exchange rate and interest rates

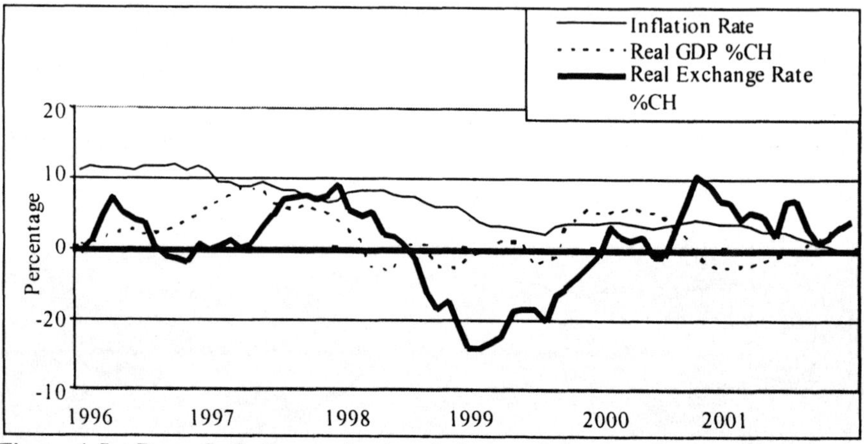

Figure 1.5a Peru: Inflation, output and changes in real exchange rate

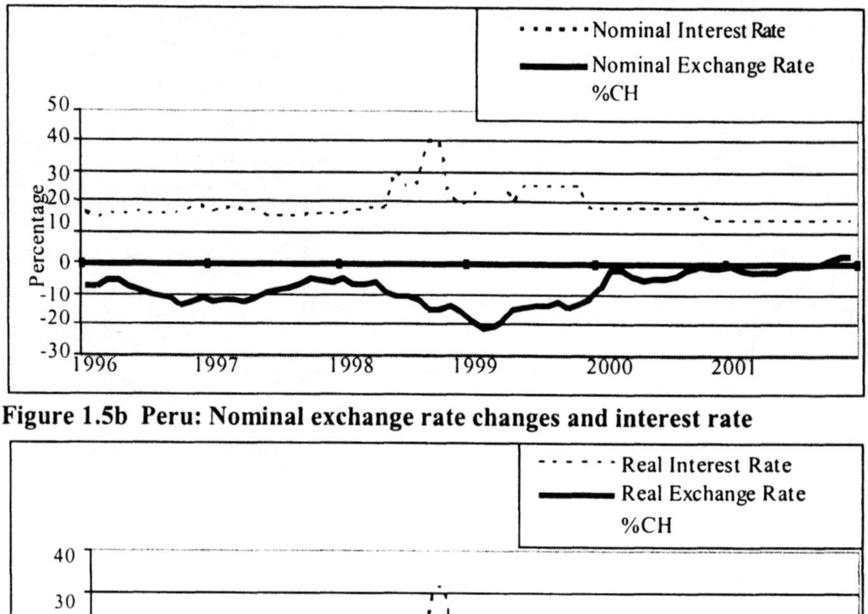

Figure 1.5b Peru: Nominal exchange rate changes and interest rate

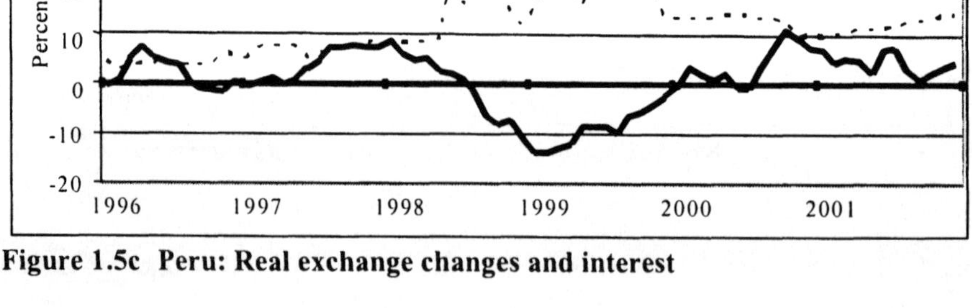

Figure 1.5c Peru: Real exchange changes and interest

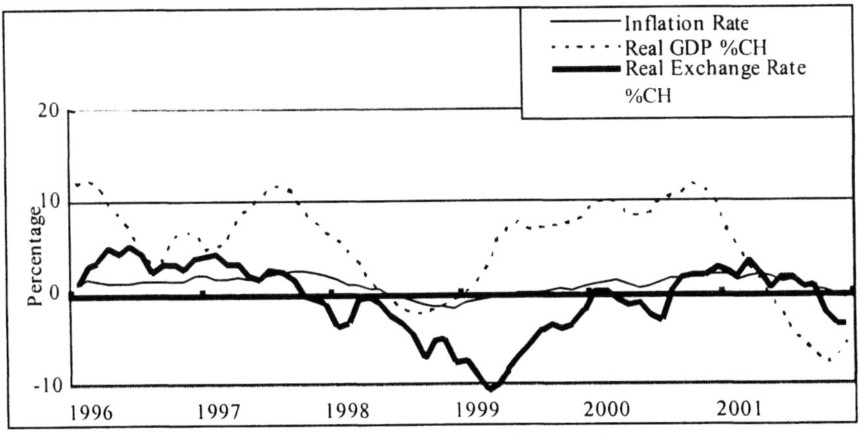

Figure 1.6a Singapore: Inflation, output and changes in real exchange rate

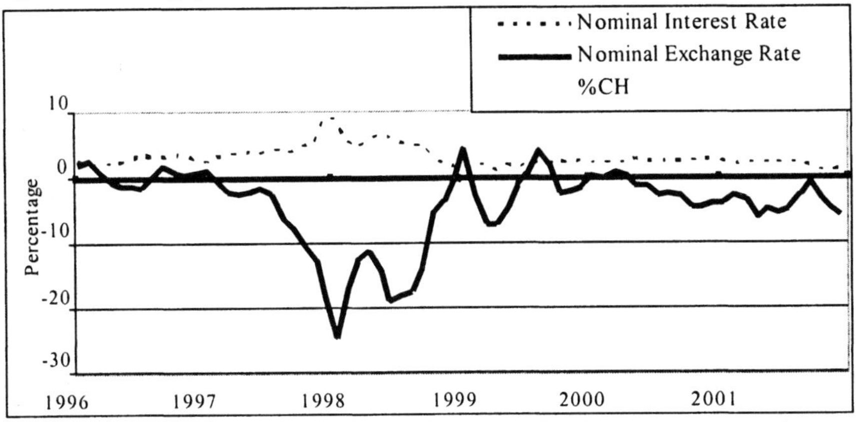

Figure 1.6b Singapore: Nominal rate changes and interest

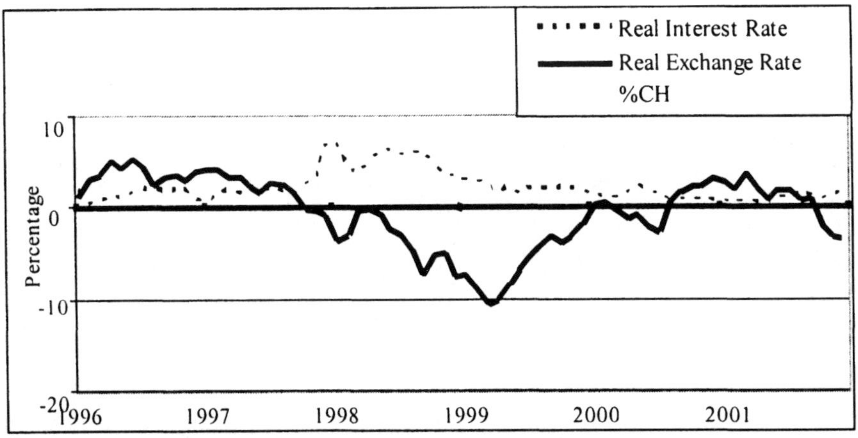

Figure 1.6c Singapore: Real rate changes and interest

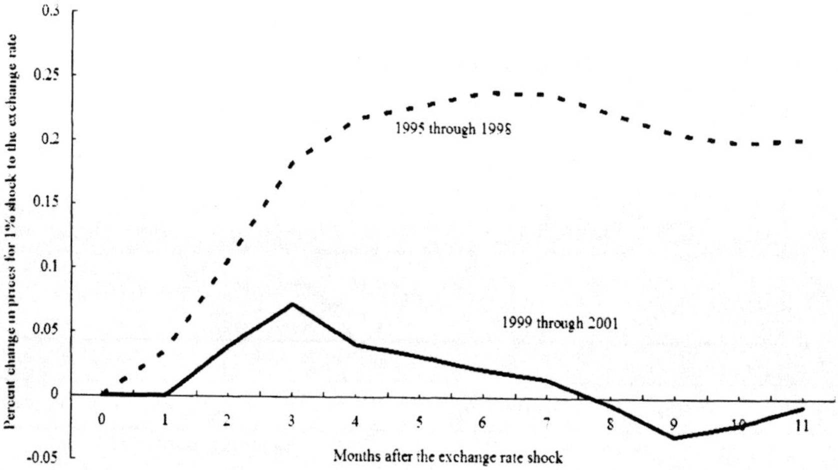

Figure 1.7 Percent change in prices for 1 percent shock to the exchange rate

Table 1.1 Taylor equations for various countries[1]

	β	γ	Coefficient on additional variables in eq. (1) (as noted)
Germany[2]	1.31 (0.09)	0.25 (0.04)	
Japan[2]	2.04 (0.19)	0.08 (0.03)	
United States[2]	1.79 (0.18)	0.07 (0.06)	
post 82:10	1.83 (0.45)	0.56 (0.16)	
Chile[3]	1.24 (0.18)	0.36 (0.32)	
including CA deficit deviation from 4% target[4]	1.68 (0.29)		0.61 (0.24)
Peru[6] (Includes the deviation of the real exchange rate from trend.)	-0.0022 (0.0008)	-0.0007 (0.0001)	-0.1106 (- 0.048)

Notes

1. All these results derive from GMM (that is instrumented) regressions of the sort described by equation (1) in the text. Standard errors are in parentheses. The developed country results are from Clarida, et al. (1997), Chile is Corbo (2000), while Peru is from Moron and Castro (2000).
2. Monthly data, from 1979 through 1994.
3. Quarterly data, from 1990:1 through 1999:4. The dependent variable in this regression is the real interest rate; for purposes of comparison we have added 1 to the reported coefficient of 0.236, to correspond to the dependent variable, which is the nominal interest rate in the other regressions. The standard error is not adjusted. Corbo (2000) emphasizes that 0.236 is not significantly different from 0.
4. Chile has a declared objective of maintaining a current account deficit below 4 percent of GDP. The observed sign implies that an increase in the deficit led to a counter-cyclical increase in the real interest rate.
5. For Colombia, Corbo (2000) used the deviation of the unemployment rate from trend rather than the output gap; here we present the opposite sign from that in Corbo (2000), for comparability. It may be that a difference in units explains the difference in magnitudes.
6. From Moron and Castro (2000), estimated with the change in base money as the dependent variable from Jan. 1992 to Dec. 1999. The coefficients are not comparable because of the different dependent variable. The signs are as expected, in that low inflation, low output, and a depreciated exchange rate imply higher subsequent base money growth.

Chapter 2

Costs and Benefits of Monetary Sovereignty in the Era of Globalization

Marek Dabrowski

Introduction

This study[1] discusses the new challenges facing monetary policy regimes in developing and transition countries in the era of globalization. Most of these countries run sovereign monetary policies based on fiat money and central banks discretion, and this seems to be the standard solution of the last half of the century. However, frequent speculative attacks against individual currencies and resulting severe currency crises demonstrate that this contemporary standard solution is not free from serious flaws.

Challenging the status quo is never an easy task, particularly when it is considered the standard solution by mainstream economic theory and political practice. This seems to be the case with activist national monetary policies. However, rapid progress in financial-market integration and the increasing influence of international financial markets on national macroeconomic and financial stability force us to rethink even the most obvious paradigms and assumptions.

This study does not pretend to cover all aspects of contemporary monetary regimes or all the challenges facing the monetary policies of developing and transition economies. It instead contrasts some of the theoretical arguments in favor of each of the so-called 'corner' solutions (i.e., either continuing sovereign monetary policy, or giving up monetary sovereignty), with a focus mainly on the former communist countries. While generally this group does not differ dramatically in its basic characteristics and problems from other regions (particularly Latin America), the balance of some particular arguments may not be the same.

The chapter is organized as follows. Section 2.2 summarizes the critique of the so-called intermediate (hybrid) regimes which leads to the recommendation that countries should choose between the two extreme 'corner' solutions: either sovereign monetary policy with a freely floating exchange rate, or the surrender of monetary sovereignty by adopting a 'hard' peg. The remainder of the chapter is

---

1 This is the revised version of my comments to Berg, Borensztein and Mauro (2002), which was prepared for the CASE International Conference on 'Beyond Transition: Development Perspectives and Dilemmas' held in Falenty, Poland on 12-13 April 2002.

devoted to discussing various theoretical aspects of this choice. Section 2.3 revisits optimum currency area theory. Section 2.4 discusses the advantages of flexible exchange rates. Section 2.5 addresses the credibility issue and analyzes the phenomenon of currency substitution. Section 2.6 introduces the political economy dimension to the choice analyzed, and Section 2.7 introduces the issue of 'network externalities.' Section 2.8 analyzes the case of the transition economies of Central and Eastern Europe and the former Soviet Union. Finally, Section 2.9 offers short summary.

Critique of Intermediate Regimes

The first serious critique of national monetary policies, particularly after the currency crises of the 1990s, focused on the so-called 'intermediate' monetary regimes in which central banks tried to control both the exchange rate and monetary aggregates (or interest rates). Such regimes were the standard solutions under the Bretton Woods system of fixed but adjustable pegs. However, it is worth remembering that as a result of the Great Depression and World War II, the world economy at that time was much less integrated than either at the beginning of the 20th century or now, and international financial flows were heavily restricted. So the simultaneous management of exchange rates and national liquidity did not necessarily violate the principle of the so-called 'impossible trinity' formulated by Frankel (1999).[2] Nevertheless, even under the Bretton Woods system individual currencies did face speculative pressures quite often (Eichengreen, 1996).

As increasing numbers of countries abandoned capital controls, the Bretton Woods system came under growing strain and finally collapsed at the beginning of the 1970s. Many developing countries nonetheless continued using intermediate regimes. An increasing number of severe currency crises in the 1990s, even among countries without bad macroeconomic fundamentals, lent additional weight to the argument that intermediate regimes were not a viable option (Obstfeld and Rogoff, 1995; McCallum, 1999; Eichengreen and Hausmann, 1999; IIE, 1999).[3]

Why have intermediate regimes, including adjustable pegs, crawling pegs, crawling bands, targeted bands, and managed floats turned out to be so flawed? The first and the most fundamental reason is that hybrid regimes are unlikely to provide the advantages of either extreme: they are unable to provide either the exchange rate stability associated with 'hard' pegs or the discretion in managing domestic liquidity that come with free floats. On the contrary, intermediate regimes may create substantial exchange rate variability (actual or expected when the peg is

2 According to this principle a country must give up one of the following three goals: exchange rate stability, monetary independence, and financial market integration. It cannot have all three simultaneously.

3 The opposite view is expressed, among others, by Williamson (2000), who tries to defend the intermediate regimes (however, he recommends also resorting to some forms of capital controls).

not viewed as credible) while making the money supply largely exogenous (beyond the control of the monetary authorities). Second, regimes with low credibility are technically very difficult to operate because of a fluctuating demand for money and changing market expectations. Moreover, short-term economic and political pressures may tempt policy makers to ignore trade offs between the two goals and attempt the impossible feat of stabilizing the exchange rate and pursuing discretionary monetary policies simultaneously. Third, the transparency—and therefore credibility—of intermediary regimes is lower than that of the corner solutions.

Assuming that the increased capital mobility we have at present is irreversible, it follows that an increasing number of countries will face the choice between monetary independence and exchange rate stability. In practice this means either retaining monetary independence under a freely floating exchange rate or giving up monetary independence by adopting such options as a currency board, monetary union, or the unilateral adoption of a foreign currency.

This choice is not easy and requires consideration of the various, sometimes contradictory, arguments coming both from theoretical models and empirical experience. Below we try to discuss some of these.

Limited Usefulness of OCA Theory

Discussions of the advantages and disadvantages of potential monetary unions (complete surrender of monetary independence) usually start from optimum currency area (OCA) theory and try to find some empirical evidence verifying the arguments of this theory in relation to a particular country of group of countries. This is, for example, the case of Berg, Borensztein and Mauro (2002), who discuss monetary-regime options for Latin America.

However, not all authors are sufficiently aware of limitations of the OCA theory and do not articulate sufficiently its numerous shortcomings. The original OCA theory in the version proposed by Mundell (1961) and McKinnon (1963) reflected the post-WWII economic landscape with its extensive trade, current account and capital account restrictions, its increasing microeconomic rigidities and an almost universally activist approach to monetary and exchange rate policies (aimed at stabilizing output and employment rather than fighting inflation). Although the Bretton Woods system was designed to provide some degree of exchange rate stability, this was definitely not meant to be stability forever. As we mentioned before, exchange rates could be and were subject to corrections in the case of major imbalances, thus serving as the ultimate shock absorber and adjustment tool. In fact, OCA theory at this point seemed to discourage abandoning exchange rate flexibility, rather than promote the idea of monetary unification.

Today's world economy is different from that of the 1950s. Most currencies are convertible and trade liberalization is much more extensive. Global product and financial markets are increasingly integrated: we live in a world of free capital and product mobility. Thus, international factor mobility, which was the key concern of Mundell's (1961) model, does not need to be a serious obstacle any longer. Even if labor mobility is still seriously restricted (internationally but also internally), the associated problems can in principle be attenuated by far-reaching capital mobility.

However, the biggest problem with OCA theory in its original version relates to its static character. Asymmetric shocks and limitations in factor mobility are viewed as being exogenous. This may be true in the short to medium-term, but in the longer run they can become endogenous. Obviously, monetary unification will promote trade and capital flows within the common-currency area, and create pressures to synchronize fiscal policies. It may also encourage the further deregulation of labor, capital and product markets (see below). All these factors will reduce the incidence of the asymmetric shocks and increase factor mobility.

Summing up, the adoption of a more dynamic approach to OCA theory in the contemporary world means that the criteria for monetary unification are not so difficult to meet.

What are the Advantages of Exchange-Rate Flexibility?

Let us look now at the opposite extreme ('corner solution'). Asking why flexible exchange rates are needed for policymakers, the standard OCA theory answer is: as the ultimate shock absorber. What does this mean, however, in a world of a free capital movement? Obviously, in countries with low credibility monetary policymakers have almost no direct influence on the real exchange rate. Thus, competitive devaluations without large collateral damage become almost impossible.[4] However, nominal (and real) exchange rates may automatically adjust to changing terms of trade and changes in capital flows unless other factors work in an opposite direction.

Flexible exchange rates also leave certain room for discretionary monetary policies focusing on achieving goals other than price stability. However, hard pegs do not fully eliminate the counter-cyclical role of monetary policy. If the central bank of a country with an anchor currency does pursue such a policy and the business cycle conditions in a hard-pegged country do not differ significantly from those in the anchor county, monetary conditions will help to close an output gap. The problem occurs when a country with a hard-pegged currency must deal with asymmetric shocks or business cycle conditions, notwithstanding the influence of monetary unification on harmonizing business cycles and promoting trade inside the common currency area (as described in the preceding section).

There is, however, another question: to what extent is the central bank of a developing/transition country able to 'lean against the wind?' Berg, Borensztein and Mauro's (2002) answer in relation to Latin America is that such a stance is possible, but I think that this issue needs further investigation on both theoretical

4 Policymakers can still provoke a currency crisis and resulting real depreciation of a national currency. However, the side effects of such experiments, including the political costs for its sponsors, are likely to exceed the potential benefits.

and empirical grounds, taking into account both the credibility issue and political and technical constraints.

Another question relates to the choice of the intermediate monetary target. If a developing/transition economy does not want to rely on a credible exchange rate anchor (in order to retain exchange rate and monetary policy flexibility) it needs to find another nominal anchor. Berg, Borensztein and Mauro (2002), Corbo (2002), Corbo and Schmidt-Hebbel (2001) suggest direct inflation targeting (DIT), an increasingly popular strategy in the contemporary world. This is really the most transparent variant of an independent monetary policy, helping to discipline both the monetary authorities and inflationary expectations. However, this strategy is not so easy in practice to operate, and many developing and transition economies may have serious problems with its effective adoption.

Let us list some of the necessary conditions for effective DIT. First, because DIT involves, by definition, significant room for policy discretion, it needs to be backed by a strong conceptual and political anti-inflationary consensus. Second, this consensus should take the form of central bank independence, with strong legal guarantees that are respected in practice. Third, DIT is technically quite complex and sophisticated, and needs well-developed analytical and forecasting skills, both inside and outside the central bank, as well as quality monetary, fiscal, price, balance of payments and output statistics. Fourth, effective transmission of the policy to the economy requires well-developed and transparent financial markets, which are not always the case in emerging-market economies. For example, banking sector fragility and extensive currency substitution can be serious obstacles to establishing effective transmission channels.

Overcoming these technical problems does not eliminate the other serious policy dilemmas that face monetary authorities operating DIT, particularly those of economies with chronically high or moderate inflation—which is quite frequently the case in developing/transition countries. If a central bank wants to build its credibility in order to achieve rapid disinflation at relatively low output/employment costs, it must stick quite resolutely to the low inflation target, and without compromising it in favor of other goals. This means giving up most of the potential advantages that an independent monetary policy is supposed to have compared to the hard peg variant—at least for the period of disinflation and subsequent consolidation of the low inflation environment.

Other variants of intermediate targets, such as, for example, monetary aggregates, are not necessarily technically easier to operate for monetary authorities, but may be less understandable and transparent for the wider public.

Credibility and Currency Substitution

Insufficient credibility of monetary/macroeconomic policy in many developing/transition countries seems to be the main argument for surrendering monetary independence and choosing a hard peg.[5] Insufficient credibility can result

5 This argument was also raised in Mundell's later works—see Mundell (1973).

from experience with or expectations of moderate/high inflation (or even hyperinflation), past currency crises, political instability, or the lack of a sustainable domestic political and intellectual consensus in favor of price stability. Building credibility is a long lasting and costly process (in terms of high real interest rates and increased macroeconomic vulnerability), and there is no guarantee of success. Joining one of the major currency areas can eliminate this kind of problem as well as the danger of currency crises.

However, the credibility problem need not be automatically solved by introducing a hard peg regime. While the adoption of another currency may be an irreversible step, a currency board definitely need not to last forever. Economic history knows of many hard pegs that were abandoned, for example, during the gold standard period (see Eichengreen, 1996) even though these pegs were declared to be immutable and were based on very solid legal foundations. Argentina's abandonment of its currency board in 2002 may have increased uncertainty for those countries running currency boards that do not have credible macroeconomic policies and solid rule-of-law traditions.

A chronic lack of credibility is reflected, among other things, in low levels of monetization (particularly when measured in domestic currency), high ratios of currency substitution (spontaneous dollarization or euroization using Berg, Borensztein and Mauro's (2002) terminology), and the inability to borrow long term in the domestic currency, called *original sin* by Hausmann (2001).

The phenomenon of competition between currencies (currency substitution) is particularly important (see Dabrowski, 2001). The integration of international trade and financial transactions and the expansion of new financial techniques and instruments have substantially increased opportunities for arbitraging between currencies. Contrary to past experience, when currency substitution was the exceptional practice (during episodes of major political or financial instability), in the contemporary economy traders can freely choose the currency of use, at least for savings and credit purposes,[6] and they do so.

Currency substitution is caused not only by credibility problems, interest rate differentials or anticipated exchange rate instability, but also by the fact that most international trade and financial transactions are conducted in a few major currencies. Thus, even in economies having a good track record in macroeconomic management, but being small and open to international trade, a certain degree of currency substitution caused by transaction needs may be unavoidable.

Currency substitution (arbitrage), regardless of whether it is conducted between countries or between currencies in one country, undermines the monopoly power of the monetary authority to issue the national currency and to collect *seigniorage*. In practice, monetary authorities must compete with central banks of other countries (particularly those of major currencies), which may remind us, to

6 In most countries, there are still restrictions on using foreign currency in some types of domestic transactions such as paying wages and salaries, tax obligations or selling goods and services on the domestic market.

certain extent, of *free banking*[7] or may refer to Hayek's (1978) idea of the *denationalization of money*.

Currency substitution and *de facto* competition among central banks can therefore further reduce the effectiveness of activist monetary policies (and, therefore, also reduce the potential advantages of flexible exchange rates), at least in countries where the monetary authorities do not enjoy sufficient credibility. This observation should lead to the rethinking of many textbook macroeconomic models and macroeconomic policy proposals,[8] which assume (either explicitly or implicitly) that economic agents must exclusively use the national currency, and that currency substitution is not an effective option.

Seen in this context, proposals to follow the EMU experience and introduce new regional currency for Latin America (see Berg, Borensztein and Mauro, 2002) or Southeast Asia (see Sakakibara, 2002) can raise serious credibility concerns. The experience of building the Euro zone in Western Europe (based on the credibility of the D-Mark and other European currencies) is unlikely to be repeated in other regions, particularly in Latin America, in the foreseeable future. Exactly for the same reasons, attempts to build the ruble zone in the CIS in early 1990s after the collapse of the USRR must be assessed *ex post* as completely unrealistic (see Dabrowski, 1997; Odling-Smee and Pastor, 2001).[9]

The real choice for countries willing to surrender their monetary independence seems to be between the US dollar and the Euro zone. All other currencies, including the Japanese yen, would be less practical because of their limited role in international trade and financial transactions. In addition, apart from a dozen EU candidates with the prospect of eventually becoming full EMU members, all others can consider only unilateral participation in a monetary union, without the possibility of directly influencing the decisions of the Fed or ECB.

Political Economy and Politics

Credibility is closely related to politics and incentives that encourage politicians to conduct responsible macroeconomic policy and needed policy reforms. Giving up monetary independence means domestic de-politicization of money following Rudi Dornbusch (2000, p. 15) suggestion that '*money is too serious to be left to politicians: in these matters, there is no such thing as a responsible politician; democratic money is bad money.*' Depriving politicians of the monetary/exchange adjustment tool may force them to think seriously about fiscal, structural and institutional reforms making an economy more balanced, flexible and competitive.

---

7 For episodes of free banking in Scotland (18th and the first half of 19th century) and US (before the Civil War) – see Friedman and Schwartz (1986).

8 At least in relation to countries that do not possess major international currencies.

9 In addition, establishing a supranational currency needs also in adequate political and institutional infrastructure, as in the case of the European Union. Such an infrastructure and international political commitment does not exist in any region other than Europe. Neither did it exist in the former Soviet Union when the idea of a ruble area was a serious subject of economic and political debate.

These microeconomic reforms are the 'first-best' solutions that should be employed to fix existing inefficiencies; monetary/exchange rate accommodation is a second best solution (see Gillman, 2001).

While the hard peg creates strong incentives for politicians to put fiscal accounts in order, liberalize the economy and make it more flexible, there is no guarantee that they will do so. Adopting a hard peg without introducing first-best structural reforms can generate macroeconómic and credibility crises that undermine the hard peg regime (the case of the currency board in Argentina in 2001-2002). Moreover, introducing a hard peg creates can create more room to maneuver in the fiscal sphere (through a substantial decrease in interest rates), which may be used either to balance a budget (the positive scenario) or to expand non-interest payment expenditure (the negative scenario). The same concerns private investment: if banking and corporate sectors suffer major inefficiencies, the capital inflow stimulated by the lack of exchange rate risk will be misallocated, causing dangerous imbalances (the case of Asia in the first half of the 1990s).

Network Externalities

Another argument in the discussion about which of the two 'corner solutions' might be better concerns the prevailing monetary regimes outside the country, particularly in its close neighborhood. This is the problem of 'network externalities' emphasized strongly by Eichengreen (1996). For example, when all major economies followed the gold standard before World War I, it was very difficult for any individual country to live outside this regime. But after the collapse of the Bretton Woods system of fixed but adjustable parities in 1973 when exchange rates between major currencies (the US dollar, D-Mark and Japanese yen) started to float, the situation changed dramatically. A stable peg in relation to any major currency became difficult, unless it was a particular country's dominant currency for trade and financial transactions.

As a consequence, even small open economies that do not wish to use discretionary monetary policies may encounter difficulties in entering a monetary union because of the diversified currency structure of its trade and financial transactions. Although entering the monetary union can be expected to affect this structure in favor of the anchor currency, this will not happen overnight. In the meantime, the country can suffer asymmetric shocks coming from the changing cross exchange rates among the major currencies. The currency basket reflecting a country's foreign transactions structure, being the standard solution under the intermediate regimes, is technically difficult to operate under a currency board regime. It is obviously impossible to use in the case of adopting another country's currency.

On the other hand, some new approaches to this issue under the currency board arrangement seem to be possible. First, an interesting empirical example is provided by Latvia, which fixes its currency to the SDR (which de facto plays the currency basket role). While Latvia has not formally declared the introduction of a currency board, its monetary regime is very close to that of a currency board.

Another idea has been raised by Oppers (2000), who proposed a 'dual' currency board with a second anchor currency that would be automatically activated when the initial anchor currency appreciates beyond a specified level. Still, if all of a country's major trade and financial partners belong to a single currency area, staying outside this bloc could put important trade and investment opportunities at risk.

Thus, according to the 'network externalities' argument, if more countries irrevocably join a particular currency bloc, this can push others to do the same. Such a snowball effect can be already observed in Europe, where one may expect the progressive expansion of the Euro zone to the rest of the continent, as well as to the Mediterranean and North Africa during the next two decades. Whether this will happen in Latin America in relation to the US dollar remains an open question.

Attempts to investigate the prospects for dollarization or euroization based mainly on analyses of trade links (see Chapter 3) show considerable room for further expansion of the euro zone (mainly in relation to current EU candidates) and rather limited room for expansion of the dollar zone in Latin America (with only Mexico, Honduras and Guatemala being able to benefit from dollarization).

Increases in the number of countries using international currencies (the US dollar and the Euro) may also push the monetary authorities of the currencies concerned toward taking into consideration the economic situation outside the home country (area), in order to avoid negative feedback resulting from their decisions that are then transmitted by international capital markets. These considerations have been taken into account by the Fed on more than one occasion.[10] In the fall of 1998, for example, when facing the danger of international financial turmoil, the Fed acted as if it were the global central bank.

One could expect the IMF to play an important role in encouraging suitable countries to adopt a hard peg (and there are plenty of such candidates among developing and transition economies). This would be consistent with the historical mandate of this organization to facilitate exchange rate stability and discourage competitive devaluations that damage international trade.

Unfortunately, this has not been the case so far. After limited involvement in some currency boards experiments in the 1990s (Bulgaria in 1997 was the last such episode) the IMF became increasingly hesitant to support this 'corner solution.' Instead, many small developing and transition economies with low credibility have been pushed by the IMF to experiment with independent monetary policy and more flexible exchange rate arrangements (this is true, for example, of the CIS countries after 1998-1999 financial crises). As many of those countries suffer serious credibility problems and have operational difficulties with introducing free floats,[11] the actual effect of IMF policies has been a continuation

10 Although this did not occur in the context of dollarization of other countries, an idea does not evoke, delicately speaking, the enthusiasm and support of the Fed. The ECB is even more hostile to this idea, openly discouraging the EU candidate countries from earlier unilateral euroization (see Bratkowski and Rostowski, 2002).

11 Calvo and Reinhart (2000) call this phenomenon 'fear of floating'.

of the intermediate (hybrid) regimes, which as we have seen usually offer the worst solutions.

What is the Choice for Transition Economies?

Most transition economies must deal with a legacy of high inflation, low macroeconomic policy credibility (reflected, among others, in high real interest rates, extensive currency substitution, and low monetization levels), and repeated temptations to use monetary policy for other purposes than achieving price stability. They therefore seem to be good candidates for surrendering their monetary sovereignty. Some of these countries have already done so. Estonia, Lithuania, Bosnia and Herzegovina, and Bulgaria run currency boards. Latvia, Croatia and Macedonia, although they have more conventional pegs, have a monetary policy stance that is not so distant from a currency board. In addition, Montenegro and Kosovo are cases of unilateral euroization.

Three countries—the Czech Republic, Poland, and Hungary—have chosen the opposite 'corner', i.e. a DIT strategy. Slovakia and Slovenia allow for substantial exchange rate flexibility but without a clear nominal anchor. The remaining countries run intermediate regimes, most frequently declared formally as a managed float, but de facto closer to a peg formula.

Looking at the detail of trade and monetary characteristics, one can obtain a differentiated picture of pros and cons related to potential monetary unification. While Central European countries (particularly the Czech Republic and Slovakia) enjoy relatively high macroeconomic policy credibility (compared to other post-communist countries), their economies are already highly integrated (in terms of trade and investments) with the Euro area. From the credibility point of view, they probably could continue sovereign monetary policies, but the EU accession timetable is pushing them to think about how to join the Euro zone in the coming years. Moreover, the overall balance of arguments (including 'network externalities') seems to favor accelerating this process (see Chapter 3; Rostowski, 2002).

At the other extreme, CIS countries with extremely low credibility of their currencies represent a much more diversified trade structure (in terms of transaction currency) and do not have the chance of joining the EU in the foreseeable future. This reminds one, to certain extent, of the Central versus South American picture (see Berg, Borensztein and Mauro, 2002). However, in the light of all the above arguments, the CIS countries to not have the chance to sustain their own independent monetary policies at reasonable cost. Moreover, they can face problems with running currency boards because of a general lack of credibility of their state institutions. This means that they should think seriously about unilateral dollarization/euroization (see the arguments of Dabrowski, Paczynski, and Rawdanowicz, 2002 in relation to Russia).

Conclusions

While a national monetary policy with a freely floating exchange rate seems to be a reasonable choice for large developed economies with a good credibility record such as the US, the Euro zone, Japan, the UK, Canada, Australia, and New Zealand, the balance of costs and benefits of this option for developing and transition countries seems to be more ambiguous. Moreover, continued progress in trade and financial-market integration is likely to further reduce the attractiveness of the true float 'corner solution', even for economies not suffering credibility problems but heavily involved in international trade and financial flows. Indeed, trade and financial integration will increasingly push for more monetary integration and hard-peg regimes.

As traditional theoretical approaches to monetary union, such as OCA theory, seem to be outdated and do not fit contemporary realities well, they appear to require serious reconsideration. The same holds true for some other traditional paradigms, such as the importance of the exchange rate as a shock absorber and of monetary policy as an instrument for fine-tuning demand and stabilizing output and employment. All these issues need further theoretical discussion and empirical investigation. Some other issues, such as insufficient policy credibility, currency substitution, network externalities, and the political economy of fiscal discipline and structural reforms, also need to be taken into consideration.

References

Berg, A., E. Borensztein and P. Mauro (2002), 'An Evaluation of Monetary Regime Options for Latin America', *North American Journal of Economics and Finance*, Vol. 85, pp. 1-23.

Bratkowski, A. and J. Rostowski (2002), 'The EU attitude to Unilateral Euroization: misunderstandings, real concerns and ill-designed admission criteria', in A. Brzeski and J. Winiecki (eds.), *A Liberating Economic Journey: Post-communist Transition, Essays in Honour of Ljubo Sirc*, CRCE London, pp. 379.

Calvo, G.A. and C.M. Reinhart (2000), 'Fear of Floating', *NBER Working Paper*, No. 7993, November.

Corbo, V. (2002), 'An Evaluation of Monetary Regime Options for Latin America. Andrew Berg, Eduardo Borensztein and Paolo Mauro. A Comment', paper prepared for the CASE Conference on 'Beyond Transition. Development Perspectives and Dilemmas', Falenty, Poland, April 12-13.

Corbo, V. and K. Schmidt-Hebbel (2001), 'Inflation Targeting in Latin America', paper prepared for presentation at the Workshop in Open Economy Macroeconomics and International Finance, Catholic University of Chile, January 15-18.

Dabrowski, M. (1997), 'The Reasons for the Collapse of the Ruble Zone', in L. T. Orlowski and D. Salvatore (eds.), *Trade and Payments in Central and Eastern Europe's Transforming Economies*, Greenwood Press, Westport CT.

Dabrowski, M. (2001), 'Global Integration of Financial Markets and Its Consequences for Transition Economies', in L. T. Orlowski (eds.), *Transition and Growth in Post-communist countries. The Ten-year Experience*, Edgar Elgar, Cheltenham.

Dabrowski, M., W. Paczynski and L. Rawdanowicz (2002), 'Inflation and Monetary Policy in Russia: Transition Experience and Future Recommendations', CASE - Center for Social and Economic Research, Warsaw, *Studies and Analyses*, No. 241.

Dornbusch, R. (2000), *Keys to Prosperity*, The MIT Press, Cambridge.

Eichengreen, B. (1996), *Globalizing Capital: A History of the International Monetary System*, Princeton University Press, Princeton.

Eichengreen, B. and R. Hausmann (1999), 'Exchange Rates and Financial Fragility', *NBER Working Paper*, No. 7418, November.

Frankel, J.A. (1999), 'No Single Currency Regime is Right for All Countries or at All Times', *NBER Working Paper*, No. 7338, September.

Friedman, M. and A.J. Schwartz (1986), 'Has Government Any Role in Money?', *Journal of Monetary Economics*, vol. 17, pp. 37-62.

Gillman, M. (2001), 'Evaluating Government Policy in Transition Countries', in M. Dabrowski and J. Rostowski (eds.), *The Eastern Enlargement of the EU*, Kluwer Academic Publishers, Boston/ Dordrecht/ London.

Hausmann, R. (2001), 'The Polish road to the Euro: An envious Latin American view', paper prepared for the Conference on 'The Polish Way to the Euro' organized by the National Bank of Poland, October 22-23.

Hayek, F.A. (1978), *Denationalization of Money*, Institute of Economic Affairs, London, 2nd extended edition.

IIE (1999), 'Safeguarding Prosperity in a Global Financial System. The Future International Financial Architecture', a Council of Foreign Relations-Sponsored Report, Institute for International Economics, Washington, DC.

McCallum, B.T. (1999), 'Theoretical Issues Pertaining to Monetary Unions', *NBER Working Paper*, No. 7393, October.

McKinnon, R.I. (1963), 'Optimum Currency Areas', *American Economic Review*, Vol. 53, pp. 715-725.

Mundell, R. (1961), 'A Theory of Optimum Currency Areas', *American Economic Review*, Vol. 51, pp. 657-665.

Mundell, R. (1973), 'Uncommon Arguments for Common Currencies', in H. Johnson and A. Swoboda (eds.), *The Economics of Common Currencies*, London: George Allen & Unwin Ltd., pp. 114-132.

Obstfeld, M. and K. Rogoff (1995), 'The Mirage of Fixed Exchange Rates', *NBER Working Paper*, No. 5191.

Odling-Smee, J. and G. Pastor (2001), 'The IMF and the Ruble Area, 1991-93', *IMF Working Paper*, WP/01/101.

Oppers, S.E. (2000), 'Dual Currency Boards: A proposal for Currency Stability', *IMF Working Paper*, WP/00/199.

Rostowski, J. (2002), 'The Eastern Enlargement of the EU and the Case for Unilateral Euroization', in M. Blejer and M. Skreb (eds.), *Financial Problems and Policies for Emerging Markets*, MIT Press, Cambridge, MA.

Sakakibara, E. (2002), 'Regional Cooperation in Asia', paper prepared for the FONDAD Conference on 'Financial Stability in Emerging Economies: Steps Forward for Bankers and Financial Authorities', De Nederlandsche Bank, Amsterdam, June 3-4.

Williamson, J. (2000), 'Exchange Rate Regime for Emerging Markets: Reviving the Intermediate Option', Institute for International Economics, *Policy Analyses in International Economics*, No. 60, September.

Chapter 3

Assessing Dollarization

Robert Ene and Jacek Rostowski

Introduction

The decision about which exchange rate system to adopt has become more difficult as world trade and capital markets have become more integrated. New problems have emerged, and with them, new answers to the question of the best exchange regime to promote each country's economic objectives. The future of the international monetary architecture may depend on the newest of these solutions: full dollarization.[1]

The emergence of the European Monetary Union spurred the debate on dollarization in Latin America. The launch of the euro in 1999 stimulated U.S. Senator Connie Mack to promote the adoption of the dollar by countries within the U.S. economic sphere. The other impulse toward common currencies and dollarization came from the financial crises of 1997-99. Amid the increasing global financial instability of the 1990s, some Latin American countries concluded that neither soft pegs nor floating currencies are viable options, and that the only choice left is a 'hard peg', as in the case of Ecuador's and El Salvador's complete dollarization.

According to Fischer (2001), at the end of 1999, 45 of the IMF's then-182 members had hard peg exchange rate systems, either with no independent legal tender, or in a currency board. Except for the 11 countries in European Union's Economic and Monetary Union (EMU), all of the 37 economies without independent legal tender were small. Since the exit of Argentina, Hong Kong is the biggest economy with a currency board. Since the end of 1999, however, Ecuador and El Salvador have dollarized, so that over a quarter of the IMF's now 183 members have very hard pegs, and their proportion in terms of GDP has remained similar (mainly because of the EMU).

The rest of this chapter is organized as follows. In the next 3 sections we assess the impact of dollarization by examining the realization of some of the optimal currency area (OCA) conditions and by addressing the lender of last resort and seigniorage issues. In Sections 3.5 and 3.6 we analyze the benefits from dollarization resulting from reduced transaction costs, increased trade and

---

1 We use the term dollarization to mean the adoption of a foreign currency as legal tender and the abandonment of the use of a national currency. This may refer also to the use of the euro, i.e., euroization.

improved credibility. The last section develops a framework for measuring the net benefits of dollarization and attempts to foresee the spread of dollarization in the countries of Latin America and Central and Eastern Europe, so as to provide a tentative appraisal of how the international monetary system is likely to look in the future.

The argument for dollarization turns on assessments of the gains stemming from lower transaction costs for trade and investments and from mfaintaining price and exchange rate stability. Dollarization is seen as a way of establishing fiscal and monetary credibility because inflating the currency to cover fiscal deficits is no longer an option. It also eliminates the devaluation premium built into many countries' interest rates (since the domestic currency cannot be depreciated), and it leads to the strengthening of the financial system. On the other hand, dollarization limits the central bank's ability to serve as lender of last resort to troubled commercial banks during a banking crisis, and a dollarizing country gives up the revenue it enjoys from seigniorage.[2] Above all, dollarization's opponents point out that the dollarized country would lose control of its monetary policy.

How useful a stabilization instrument is monetary policy, working through domestic short-term nominal interest rates and a floating nominal exchange rate? What does a nation give up, in terms of the ability to pursue macroeconomic stabilization policies by surrendering monetary sovereignty, and how can it offset the loss of the monetary instrument? It is clear that if a country never intends, or it is not able, to use the exchange rate as an adjustment mechanism, then retaining it is at best superfluous and is in fact likely to be counter-productive (Calvo 2000). These are the central questions that produced the theory of optimal currency areas (Mundell, 1961; McKinnon, 1963; Kenen, 1969). The theory asks which of a set of national economies would benefit from having irrevocably fixed exchange rates with one or more of the other countries. The following characteristics of the individual national economies have been argued to determine the desirability of abolishing the national currency: foreign trade orientation, correlation in business cycles, and commodity composition of exports. The common thread is that countries that are highly integrated in terms of international trade are more likely to constitute an optimal currency area.

2 The balance of the argument would be tilted if a politically acceptable means could be found of transferring seigniorage to dollarizing countries. The Mack bill would have done that, suggesting that at least in the case of the dollar, some means of transferring seigniorage could eventually become politically feasible. Such arrangements are in place in the Rand area in South Africa, Lesotho and Namibia.

Optimal Currency Area Criteria for Dollarization

When analyzing the advantages for Latin American and Central and East European countries in adopting the dollar or the euro, the aim is to determine the degree to which these economies are integrated through trade with the US or the EMU, respectively. Openness, measured by total trade as a percentages of gross domestic product (GDP), is one criterion for membership in an OCA, since greater trade leads to greater savings on transactions costs and greater costs resulting from exchange rate risk. Further, the high marginal propensity to import associated with an open economy reduces output variability and the need for domestic monetary policy, since openness acts as an automatic stabilizer. The importance of bilateral trade in 1999 with the 'metropolitan' country as a share of GDP and as a share of total trade is presented in Table 3.1.

The data show that the trade links between the EMU and the Central and East European countries (CEECs) are more important than those between the US and the Latin American countries (LACs).[3] For CEECs, trade with the EMU varies from 37 percent for Lithuania to 80 percent for Albania. Almost all CEECs, except Bosnia, Latvia and Lithuania,[4] pass the first test of the optimal currency area theory. They are open economies trading mainly with the EMU. The situation for Latin America is highly differentiated between Central America (which trades a great deal with the US) and South America (which does not).

According to OCA theory, if the actual proportion of intra- versus inter-industry trade in bilateral trade is high, then business cycles are expected to become more similar across countries. The share of intra-industry trade (IIT), as measured by the Grubbel-Lloyd (GL) index,[5] increased between 1993 and 1998 for all CEECs except Bulgaria, Lithuania and Latvia (Kaminski 2000).[6]

---

3 Indeed, for some Latin American countries, the EU is a bigger trading partner than US. For example, for Argentina and Brazil, EMU trade in total trade is around 25-30% compared with 15-20% for US.

4 Among the CEECs, the Baltic states trade the least with EMU members because an important share of their trade goes to Sweden, Denmark and the U.K. Although these countries are not EMU members, these countries' strong integration with the euro area can be seen as something akin to "quasi-EMU" status, effectively increasing the EMU share of trade for the Baltic states.

5 The index is computed as the share of absolute value of intra-industry trade in total trade: $GL = 1 - \frac{\sum|X_i - M_i|}{\sum(X - M)}$, where X and M are total exports and imports, and X_i and M_i are exports and imports by commodity groups i.

6 The largest increase in the value of GL index registered Estonia followed by Slovakia, Czech Republic, Romania and Poland.

Table 3.1 Trade integration in 1999: CEECs-EMU, Latin America-US

Country	Trade with EMU/GDP (%)	Trade with EMU/Total Trade (%)	Total Trade/GDP
Albania	25.6	80.0	31.9
Bosnia & Herzegovina	30.7	42.2	72.9
Bulgaria	39.3	54.2	72.5
Croatia	29.7	49.8	59.6
Czech Republic	65.1	61.7	105.6
Estonia	62.0	45.1	137.3
Hungary	73.2	68.7	106.6
Latvia	30.9	46.8	66.1
Lithuania	26.5	36.0	73.7
Macedonia	49.6	56.9	87.1
Poland	27.6	58.5	47.2
Romania	34.7	66.4	52.3
Slovakia	58.9	56.8	103.8
Slovenia	61.8	67.1	92.0
	Trade with US/GDP (%)	**Trade with US/Total Trade (%)**	**Total Trade/GDP (%)**
Argentina	2.7	15.7	17.1
Bolivia	10.8	27.8	38.9
Brazil	4.3	23.2	18.5
Chile	9.0	20.5	44.1
Colombia	11.3	44.1	25.7
Costa Rica	41.6	45.9	90.7
Ecuador	21.2	33.9	62.5
El Salvador	25.4	48.6	52.3
Guatemala	24.4	44.8	54.4
Honduras	99.0	62.5	158.6
Mexico	55.5	81.1	68.5
Nicaragua	40.6	36.5	111.2
Panama	16.9	32.0	52.7
Paraguay	8.4	15.7	53.1
Peru	7.7	30.5	25.2
Uruguay	2.7	9.2	29.5
Venezuela	17.7	49.9	35.5

Source: IMF Direction of Trade Statistics 2001 and authors' calculations.

While the GL index summarizes two-way trade in the same categories of products, it does not fully take into account the most dynamic ingredient of world trade occurring in international production networks organized around multinational corporations (MNCs) (see Kaminski and Ng, 2000). Kaminski (2000) provides evidence that suggests that some CEECs have become part of a new division of labor resulting from participation in global networks of production and distribution. Estonian and Hungarian producers in particular seem to have already become complements to EU-based production and marketing networks. The share of network-related trade in trade of other CEECs has been also rapidly growing as incorporation of CEEC producers offers significant benefits to both CEECs and MNCs.[7]

Another way to assess structural similarity and hence the likelihood of asymmetric shocks is to directly examine the fluctuations of business cycles between OCA economies. Research on the convergence of cyclical unemployment fluctuations revealed a high degree of convergence of cyclical unemployment fluctuations between Germany and Hungary, the Czech Republic, Slovenia and Poland (see Boone and Maurel, 1998; 1999).[8] We follow Bayoumi and Eichengreen (1996) in using the standard deviation of changes in the log of relative GDP between the economies. This indicator is defined formally as follows:

$$ASSYMETRY = \sigma\left(\log\left(\frac{GDP_i^t}{GDP_{US/EU}^t}\right) - \log\left(\frac{GDP_i^{t-1}}{GDP_{US/EU}^{t-1}}\right)\right) \qquad (3.1)$$

If the cyclical component of output is exactly equal in the two countries, this indicator will be equal to 0, even if growth trends are different across countries. The indicator increases in direct proportion with the asymmetry between the cycles. To compute the level of asymmetry, we use yearly GDP series[9] and as a benchmark,[10] and we include in the second part of the table the calculation of economic cycle asymmetry of France and Italy with respect to Germany. The results are presented in Table 3.2.

The highest levels of asymmetry, among CEECs, are recorded by Bulgaria, Latvia and Lithuania while Slovenia, Poland and Czech Republic are the most suitable for a currency union. Actually, four CEECs have a lower asymmetry

7 In their study on IIT between EU and the CEECs, Djankov, et al. (1997) distinguish between horizontal and vertical IIT. The latter consists of exchange of similar goods of different quality and the former comprises exchange of similar goods that are differentiated by characteristics other than quality. In the OCA context the distinction may be relevant because the level and growth in horizontal IIT may be an indicator of the extent to which the CEECs are 'similar' to the EU. Findings in Djankov, et al. (1999) suggest that vertical IIT accounts for 80 to 90 percent of total IIT with the EU, and is positively associated with product differentiation, economies of scale, labor intensity of production, and FDI. If it is important to have horizontal IIT instead of vertical IIT, then the CEECs and EU may not satisfy the OCA criterion.

8 See Chapter 5 for more extended description of this work. Similar research was done for non-candidates countries and for example for Croatia the percentage is 79 percent.

9 The period is 1991-1999 for Latin America and 1993-1999 for Central and Eastern Europe.

10 For Latin America the benchmark country is Panama.

index than Italy. It is worth pointing out that all Central American countries, except Mexico, list a low asymmetry index *vis-à-vis* the United States, and are therefore strong candidates for full dollarization.

If we consider GDP growth correlations for Latin American countries, only Argentina, Brazil, Ecuador and Mexico register positive correlations (Table 3.3). Therefore, dollarization in LACs does not seem optimal from this point of view. However, correlated cyclical movements do not necessarily make coordination easier. For example, suppose an exogenous shock affects two partners of a bloc in the same way and one of them decides to increase trade barriers[11] and impose capital controls. In a crisis situation, the other country will not be inclined to tolerate such deviations. But the reaction could have been more tolerant if the second country had not received the impact of the shock.

Hausmann, Panizza, et al. (1999) offered a compelling argument for dollarization by questioning the benefits of floating in economies that are susceptible to shocks. For example, in the oil-based Venezuelan economy, if the price of oil goes up, the exchange rate will appreciate. The question is whether a country's residents would willingly save in their domestic currency if they were allowed to save in another. People need to have savings with a maximum buying power when their incomes are low, because when their incomes are high, their marginal utility is lower. Therefore, households are likely to diversify away from a domestic currency that is positively correlated with income.

11 This was indeed the case between Argentina and Brazil in 1999.

Table 3.2 Economic cycle asymmetry index for LACs and CEECs

US	Argentina	Bolivia	Brazil	Chile	Colombia	Costa Rica	Ecuador	El Salvador	Guatemala
	0.070	0.045	0.204	0.109	0.175	0.047	0.052	0.047	0.060
	Honduras	Mexico	Nicaragua	Paraguay	Peru	Uruguay	Venezuela		*Panama*
	0.064	0.181	0.047	0.097	0.115	0.075	0.128		*0.037*
Germany	Bulgaria	Czech Republic	Estonia	Hungary	Latvia	Lithuania	Poland	Romania	Slovakia
	0.184	0.058	0.110	0.079	0.151	0.147	0.054	0.115	0.071
	Slovenia							*Italy*	*France*
	0.025							*0.083*	*0.020*

Source: IMF - IFS CD-ROM and authors' calculations.

Table 3.3 GDP growth correlations: LACs (1990-1998), CEECs (1993-1999)

Country	Argentina	Brazil	Chile	Colombia	Ecuador	Mexico	Peru	Venezuela	US	Average
Argentina	1.0	-0.112	0.160	-0.285	0.492	0.611	0.157	0.074	0.063	0.145
Brazil		1.0	-0.065	0.582	0.003	-0.268	0.813	-0.520	0.244	0.085
Chile			1.0	0.337	0.323	-0.493	0.050	0.326	-0.106	0.066
Colombia				1.0	0.266	-0.521	0.468	-0.081	-0.084	0.085
Ecuador					1.0	0.211	0.220	0.470	-0.451	0.192
Mexico						1.0	-0.235	0.009	0.192	-0.002
Peru							1.0	-0.488	0.299	0.161
Venezuela								1.0	-0.784	-0.120

	Bulgaria	Czech Republic	Estonia	Hungary	Latvia	Lithuania	Poland	Romania	Slovakia	Slovenia
Germany	0.38	0.03	0.53	0.75	0.76	0.50	0.37	-0.11	0.74	0.81

Germany-EU (average) = 0.71

Germany-EMU (average) = 0.69

Source: Ortiz (1999) and IMF - World Economic Outlook 2000.

All in all, there is no firm consensus on the way in which integration affects trade specialization patterns and business cycles. There are two contrasting hypotheses. On the one hand, Krugman (1993) argues that monetary integration accentuates specialization, as each country has increased incentives to exploit its comparative advantage. This should increase the asymmetry of cycles insofar as the shocks that affect specific industries are idiosyncratic. On the other hand, Frankel and Rose (1998) suggest that increasing monetary integration means more synchronicity in the cycles, because intra-industry trade grows faster than inter-industry trade. Therefore, optimal currency area conditions may well be endogenous to the type of monetary regime in a given area. Moreover, they have tested whether income correlation depends positively on trade integration or negatively and the result was a positive dependence, suggesting that the Krugman specialization effect may not dominate.

Seigniorage Loss

Dollarization involves two kinds of seigniorage losses. The first is the immediate 'stock' cost: as the dollar is introduced and the domestic currency is withdrawn from circulation, the monetary authorities must buy back the stock of domestic currency held by the public and banks, effectively returning to them the seigniorage that had accrued over time. This cost can be measured as the stock of notes and coins (C0) relative to GDP:

$$S_{stock} = \frac{C0}{GDP} \tag{3.2}$$

Second, the monetary authorities would give up future seigniorage earnings stemming from the flow of new cash printed and minted every year to satisfy the increase in demand for cash. This flow cost can be measured as the present value of the annual change in cash (C0) to GDP or as the present value of (the cash stock multiplied by the annual interest rate (i)) as proportion to GDP:

$$S^1_{flow} = \frac{\sum_{t=0}^{\infty} \frac{C0_{t+1} - C0_t}{(1+i)^t}}{GDP} \quad \text{or} \quad S^2_{flow} = \frac{\sum_{t=0}^{\infty} \frac{iC0_t}{(1+i)^t}}{GDP} \tag{3.3}$$

Table 3.4 displays the significance of seigniorage losses[12] for LACs and CEECs as a percentage of each country's gross domestic product (GDP).[13] The stock seigniorage loss varies from 6 percent of GDP for Argentina, Slovenia and

12 The flow cost of seigniorage was calculated for a nominal interest rate of 5 percent.

13 We have used figures for the somewhat larger money base (MO) rather than the cash stock because of their greater availability. The difference between the two series is commercial bank reserves held at the central bank, which need not be held in foreign cash by the 'central bank' of the dollarizing country. Instead they can be held in the form of US or EU government bonds. In that case the seigniorage on these amounts is not lost.

Mexico to 25 percent for Czech Republic and 38 percent for Chile. These figures may explain why the dollarization idea has been clearly more popular in Argentina than in Chile.

The different magnitudes of seigniorage flows reflect the different degrees to which governments have relied on money creation to finance their budgets. Table 3.4 also shows that seigniorage flow is only 2 percent of total government revenue in Argentina. Therefore losing seigniorage flow would not require a major fiscal adjustment in that country. But in Chile domestic money creation is responsible for almost 8.5 percent of government revenue. As a consequence, dollarization would require Chile to find new and significant sources of tax revenues or to significantly reduce government expenditures.

For countries that do not already have enough foreign reserves to buy up their domestic currency so as to dollarize, the acquisition of the initial stock could add indirect costs. However, almost all countries in CEE and more than half in Latin America have enough reserves to cover the cash stock. The conclusion is that dollarization would imply a fairly large seigniorage transfer from a dollarizing country to the United States. This is not the case for the transition countries that are EU candidates. As emphasized by Rostowski (2000), at the moment of EMU accession the Central Bank income generated by the assets backing the monetary base are transferred to European Central Bank, which is exactly the same outcome as in the case of unilateral euroization. The only loss that remains is the present value of seigniorage flow during the period between euroization and EMU accession (see also Chapter 5).

The Lender of Last Resort

Even though the lack of a lender of last resort (LOLR) function may result in a healthier system (due to less moral hazard), banking systems are often thought to be naturally vulnerable to exogenous liquidity shocks that require intervention from the Even though the lack of a lender of last resort (LOLR) function may result in a healthier system (due to less moral hazard), banking systems are often thought to be naturally vulnerable to exogenous liquidity shocks that require intervention from the central bank or some other agency. A major concern about dollarization is that the central bank would be unable to play this role. How could the liquidity insurance implicit in the LOLR function be preserved under full dollarization, and at what cost? Several important aspects should be emphasized.

First, there are two misconceptions about LOLR. The first lies in the belief that a central bank is always able to guarantee the liquidity of domestic currency deposits in the banking system, because it can always print enough money to convert deposits into cash through LOLR operations. However, central banks do not necessarily have an unlimited ability to guarantee the liquidity of the domestic currency deposits. As the central bank issues more currency through last resort lending, the central bank either loses international reserves or the exchange rate depreciates. In fact, in several recent banking crises, such as those in Venezuela and Ecuador, central bank commitments to provide liquidity led to a full-blown currency crisis. The perception that the domestic money supply was increasing in an unsustainable manner lead to a collapse in money demand, the depletion of international reserves, and a major depreciation of the currency. In Ecuador, in order to avoid hyperinflation the government was compelled to freeze deposits.

The second misconception assumes that since central banks in dollarized economies cannot print money, they lose completely the ability to provide liquidity. Although dollarization may imply the reduction in central bank reserves (in order to purchase the outstanding notes in circulation), it certainly does not imply that central bank reserves will necessarily fall to zero. This permits the central bank to continue to provide liquidity (see Chapter 5).[14] Another alternative is the outsourcing of the LOLR function to the private sector. There are at least three ways in which a private lender of last resort can be conceived: as a contract between a consortium of international banks and the central bank; individual contracts between banks; or as a reflection of the self-interest of foreign owners in their local subsidiaries.[15]

A dominant role for large and solid foreign banks[16] in the banking system (which presumably would be encouraged by dollarization) would also reduce the danger of a weakened LOLR. This is because such banks can be expected to know the true condition of their subsidiaries better than any central bank, and could directly provide liquidity out of their own 'deep pockets'. They could also indirectly bring support from foreign central banks through their headquarters, and because depositors' confidence on the financial backing of these institutions would be likely higher.

---

14 In addition, this will depend on the existence of a treaty for seigniorage sharing and on the way the arrangement is set up. For example, if the monetary treaty creates a mechanism based on a currency swap (i.e., a swap of the dollarizing country's notes for US dollars), then the dollarizing country maintains its initial stock of reserves. If instead seigniorage is paid in annual amounts, this may be used to set up a liquidity fund or as collateral.

15 An innovative version of the first type of arrangements was in place in Argentina. This was a repo contract that involved a swap between the central bank and a foreign consortium. In the event of a crisis, authorities were allowed to get instant credit in exchange for government dollar-denominated bonds. The annual fee Argentina had to pay for the option to have access to this swap is 32 basis points. The cost of funds implicit in the repo agreement was roughly LIBOR plus 205 basis points. The size of the agreement was USD 6.7 billion, or 9 percent of the deposit base. Assuming that the Argentine government has the bonds to be used in the swap operation, in non-crisis periods the contract represents an annual cost of approximately USD 21.5 million. In crisis periods, the cost of drawing down the funds from the repo were considerably smaller than the rate at which the Treasury would have had to borrow. Thus, private insurance seems to be a convenient substitute for a LOLR under dollarization.

16 This argument is also pointed out by Bratkowski and Rostowski (2000). In CEECs, according to IMF World Economic and Financial Surveys 2001, the proportion of total bank assets controlled by foreign-owned banks rose from 8 percent in 1994 to 56 percent in 1999.

Benefits of a Common Currency and Reduced Transaction Costs

The uncertainty associated with exchange rate changes acts as a tax on trade and, more importantly, a tax on investment in traded-goods industries. Although it is possible to hedge against exchange rate risk by using derivative instruments, risk cannot be hedged perfectly if the size of foreign currency exposure is not known.

An exchange rate change, however, affects not only the domestic currency values of the future foreign currency receipts and payments, but also the foreign currency values by affecting the volume and value of future trade flows. Moreover, a common currency reduces the administrative transaction costs associated with the need to deal with multiple currencies, even in cases where exchange rates are perfectly stable.

How important are these transaction costs? For the case of EMU, the report of the European Commission (1990) estimates transaction costs savings to be at 0.25-0.5 percent of GDP per year for the average union member. In the absence of a detailed calculation, we estimate the benchmark EMU transaction savings of 0.4 percent of GDP as an appropriate upper bound of this benefit for LAC and CEECs, although we might expect significantly higher transaction costs since the spreads between buying and selling prices should be greater when less liquid exchange rate markets are involved.

Table 3.5 Foreign bank ownership by assets

CEECs	Percentage	LACs	Percentage
Albania	20.0	Argentina	48.6
Bulgaria	12.4	Brazil	16.8
Croatia	83.2	Chile	53.6
Czech Rep	70.0	Colombia	17.8
Estonia	97.0	Mexico	18.8
Hungary	56.6	Peru	33.4
Lithuania	59.8	Venezuela	41.9
Poland	70.0		
Romania	52.6		
Slovakia	50.0		

Source: IMF, World Economic and Financial Surveys (2001), and EBRD, Investment Profiles (2001)

Rose (2000) points out that being a member of a currency union reduces the standard deviation of annual real exchange rates by 6 percentage points. He concludes that real exchange rates have much lower short-term volatility among currency-union countries, even holding constant the volatility of the nominal exchange rate. That is, the reduction in real exchange rate variance is not solely attributable to fixed exchange rates; currency-union membership appears to stabilize real exchange rates through other channels as well.

A second, related argument for fixed rates asserts that exchange rate changes give rise to protectionist pressures and can thus prevent the realization of the gains from trade. This argument has appeared periodically in different contexts. In Europe, for example, protectionist pressures produced by the exchange rate changes of the early 1990s were cited frequently by advocates of monetary union, who said that an irrevocable fixing of exchange rates was the only way to insulate the Single European Market from such pressures in the future. Finally, the depreciation of the Brazilian currency in 1999 caused Argentina to erect trade barriers that stalled and threatened to reverse trade liberalization in Mercosur.

Recent studies on the intensity of bilateral trade between the Canadian provinces and the U.S. based on the gravity model (McCallum, 1995) suggest that the combined effect of exchange rate volatility and transaction cost can be much greater than discussed above. These authors found that, after controlling for distance and size of the economies, bilateral trade between two Canadian provinces was on average 20 times larger than trade between a Canadian province and a US state. This result is surprising, since these countries have a very long common border, share the same language and cultural values, and have a free trade agreement that minimizes trade barriers. While there are other transaction costs associated with international trade, the need to exchange currencies might at least partially explain these surprisingly large effects. Recent research by Rose (2000) provides ample support to the hypothesis that currency transaction costs are in fact important for trade. If one takes the results at face value, the impact is enormous. His estimate of the currency union effect implies that trade between countries that share the same currency will be more than three times as large as that between countries with different currencies, other things equal.

The Risk Premium

An immediate benefit from full dollarization is a reduction in borrowing costs. Using the US dollar or the euro eliminates the risk of devaluation to foreign lenders and should therefore reduce interest rates for credit that was previously denominated in domestic currency.

Lower interest rates and more stability in international capital movements should cut the cost of servicing the public debt,[17] and encourage higher investment[18] and economic growth. The magnitude of this potential gain is hard to

---

17 A simulation on Argentina's public debt suggests that for every 100 basis points fall in the interest rate, there would be a saving of some USD 3.6 billion (today's present value) for debts rolled over up to year 2009. Then there would be a continuing effect of at least some USD 0.9 billion each year from 2009 onwards, reaching a steady state reduction of about USD 1 billion (Guidoti, et al., 2000). Rostowski (2000) points out that in Poland, in the case of euroization, the annual savings from reduced interest rates on government paper could be 1.5 percent of GDP.

18 Hausmann, Gavin et al. (1999) argue that dollarization is likely to increase the set of assets that can serve as collateral. In a dollarized system, real estate could be considered

measure. However, sovereign or default risk is still present after dollarization, and investors still respond to financial crises, whether prompted by economic shocks or political and social conditions (see Berg and Borensztein, 2000).[19] The key question, then, is: Would full dollarization, by eliminating currency risk, substantially reduce the default risk premium on dollar-denominated debt? The answer will be yes if dollarization is perceived as an irreversible institutional change toward low inflation, fiscal responsibility, and transparency. Even without this, dollarization holds the promise of a steadier market sentiment, as the elimination of exchange rate risk will tend to limit the incidence and magnitude of crisis and contagion episodes.

Hausmann and Powell (1999) stress that a step-by-step process in which the adoption of a strong common currency is preceded by the introduction of healthy pre-announced reforms makes financial markets reward good reform performance with lower interest rates and lower exchange rate pressures during the transition process. This reward in itself makes it easier for the governments to strengthen fiscal and financial systems, in preparation for the monetary switch. The decision to dollarize in an orderly and pre-announced manner can create incentives to put in place a set of reforms that would not be feasible in the absence of that commitment.

A Simple Framework for Assessing Dollarization

Are the benefits of dollarizing greater than the costs? Clearly, one problem is that while many of the costs are easily quantifiable, some of the benefits, possibly much more important in the long term, may be difficult to assess in terms of present value. We try to determine these long-term benefits by evaluating the impact of a common currency on trade and output.

Rose (2000) estimated the effect of currency union membership on international trade. He found that bilateral trade was higher for a pair of countries that used the same currency than for a pair of countries with their own sovereign monies. More precisely, the coefficient on a currency union dummy in an empirical model of bilateral trade was found to be positive and significant. Its value around 1.2 implies an effect of currency union on trade of around 300 percent. This was true even after controlling for a number of other factors that might affect trade through the 'gravity' model. However, the results did not answer questions about the size of the trade effect for a country joining a currency union. To conduct this

---

collateral while it usually is not used for international transactions because of the inherent exchange rate and convertibility risk.

19 Argentina, when it used a currency board under which the peso rate was fixed to the U.S. dollar, provided a good example of the difficulties. There, a higher interest rate for borrowing in pesos than in U.S. dollars persisted as evidence that lenders—correctly—continued to perceive a devaluation risk. Interest rates on dollar-denominated Argentine government and private securities also exceeded those on industrial countries' debt, reflecting an (again correctly) anticipated risk of default by the country on those securities.

exercise, we use the Rose and Wincoop (2001) estimates to assess the benefits derived from increase in trade for a dollarizing country.

In the Rose and Wincoop (2001) model, trade between countries depends on their bilateral trade barrier relative to average trade barriers with all trade partners. Thus, more goods will be sold to a region with which exporters face relatively low trade barriers. Consequently, the larger the pre-union trade among the members of a currency union, the smaller the percentage increases in trade among currency union members. For example, there would be a smaller percentage increase in trade when Mexico dollarizes than when Argentina dollarizes, as Argentina trades less with the US than Mexico does.

Using complete bilateral data for a set of 143 countries, Rose and Wincoop (2001) find that the currency union is estimated to raise bilateral trade by 250 percent.[20] However, the result ignores the effect of multilateral trade resistance, which is an index that depends positively on trade barriers between a specific country and all of its trading partners. The effect of currency unions on trade, more realistically incorporating multilateral resistance effects, is presented in Table 3.6. The trade-creating effects of currency union are still large. Nevertheless, instead of EMU causing trade to rise inside euroland by 250 percent, the increase is estimated to be only 58 percent.

Table 3.6 Impact of currency unions on trade

Geographical area	Trade Increase (%)	Standard Error
EMU	58	12
EMU+UK	44	9
EU	40	5
Argentina dollarizes	132	37
Ecuador dollarizes	106	26
Mexico dollarizes	53	13
Canada dollarizes	39	9
Mexico + Canada dollarize	27	8
World monetary union	10	2

Source: Rose and Wincoop (2001).

The 58 percent value seems to be a good fit in assessing the benefits for CEECs, as the level of their trade with EMU is very similar to that among EMU members. For LACs this value probably underestimates the potential increase in trade, because they trade far less on average with the US and other dollarized countries. Therefore, we will use 58 percent as the estimate for the trade creating

20 The currency union coefficient is 0.91 with a standard error of 0.18. This implies an effect on trade of $e^{0.91}$=2.48

effects for all CEECs in the simulation. In the case of LACs, the estimates[21] vary between 53 and 132 percent, depending on the ratio of trade with dollarized countries[22] to total trade.

In order to calculate the benefits of dollarization we need to determine the effect that currency union has via trade[23] on output. Frankel and Rose (2000), using a gravity model and an output regression, estimate that every 1 percentage point increase in the openness ratio (e.g. trade/GDP ratio) leads to 1.18 percent increase in the GDP over a twenty year period.[24] Thus, for Mexico, total trade to dollarized countries was 81.3 percent and non-dollarized countries trade was 19.7 percent of total trade in 1999. According to the Rose and Wincoop (2001) results, dollarization will increase trade with dollarized countries by 53 percent and, therefore, the increase in total trade will be around 44 percent. As a consequence, the openness ratio (total trade/GDP) will increase by about 29 points (0.44 × 68.5). Finally, in the case of Mexico, dollarization will lead to a 35 percent increase in GDP over twenty years.

In order to determine the *net* benefit (cost) of dollarization, we calculated present values (PV) for the increase in GDP and for the loss of seigniorage. In order to account for the fact that the benefits of a GDP increase are likely to be concentrated in the first part of the 20 year time span, we considered that 66 percent of the increase occurs in the first 10 years and the remaining 34 percent in the last 10 years. Then, we divided the GDP increase by a factor of 10 to obtain the yearly GDP increase for the two 10-year periods. Finally, the benefit was calculated as the present value of the yearly increase in GDP for the 20-year period. As for the costs, we determined the present value of seigniorage flow,[25]

---

21 The 53, 58, 74, and 132 percent values correspond to the following four groups of countries: 1st group: Mexico; 2nd group: Argentina, Bolivia, Brazil, Chile, Paraguay and Uruguay; 3rd group: Costa Rica and Guatemala; 4th group: Colombia, Honduras, Nicaragua, and Peru.

22 Trade with dollarized countries includes trade with US, Ecuador, Panama, and El Salvador.

23 We assume that there is a causal link between trade and output and that trade drives growth.

24 Frankel and Rose (1998) use samples ranging from 95 to 150 countries and find that coefficient of openness in an output equation goes from 0.8 in an OLS regression to 2.0 with instrumental variable estimates, and remains statistically significant.

25 Let π denote the inflation rate, g the domestic real growth rate, r the real interest rate, and i the nominal interest rate. We assume that the income elasticity of the demand for real balances in the economy is unity, so that real money balances are growing at the rate $(1+g)(1+\pi)$. Then the present value of the seigniorage flow is given by:

$$S^2_{flow} = \frac{\sum_{t=0}^{\infty} \frac{[(1+g)(1+\pi)]^t iM0}{(1+i)^t}}{GDP} = \frac{iM0}{i-(g+\pi+g\pi)} \times \frac{1}{GDP} \approx \frac{iM0}{r-g} \times \frac{1}{GDP}$$

, where M0 is the money base in dollars. We assume for the simulation that i = 5%, r = 4%, and g = 3%.

which was then added to the seigniorage stock for the LACs, while for CEECs only the present value of seigniorage flow was retained. For CEECs, the present value of the flow seigniorage cost was calculated under two scenarios: (i) a delayed EMU accession[26] scenario with a delay of ten years for the first entrants; and (ii) a fast accession[27] to EMU with the first countries becoming members in eight years. The results are presented in Table 3.7.

According to the results for the delayed accession to EMU scenario for Central and Eastern Europe, all countries will gain from unilateral euroization except Albania, Bulgaria, and Latvia. Also, the largest benefits in terms of percentage of GDP are registered by Hungary, followed by the Czech Republic, Slovenia and Slovakia. In the case of a fast accession to EMU scenario, all the CEECs benefit, except Albania. Not surprisingly, the closer the expected date of EMU accessions the greater are the benefits of unilateral euroization.

In the case of LACs, there are only two *net* beneficiaries from dollarization: Honduras and Mexico. In terms of *gross* benefits, the most suitable candidates are the countries from Central America, while the Mercosur countries seem to have the least advantages. This reinforces the evidence that South America's economies are not natural candidates for a currency union with the US. Apart from Mexico and other Central American countries, few economies are closely integrated in terms of trade with the US or converge with U.S. macroeconomic performance. Nevertheless, Central American countries also have the biggest seigniorage losses if they opt for dollarization. Therefore, the proposal for a seigniorage sharing agreement with US is even more important for these countries than for South America, and would bring the most benefits.

If one or more countries decide to dollarize/euroize, what will be then the benefits (costs) for non-dollarized countries?[28] There will probably be three effects: a substitution effect, an income effect and a competition effect. The *substitution effect* is related mainly to the trade diversion effect, which means that the dollarizing countries will face lower transaction costs and will therefore have a competitive advantage over non-dollarized countries in trading with others in the dollar zone. As a consequence, the non-dollarized countries will trade less with the dollar zone. Nevertheless, the *income effect* may prevail because, as a dollarized country registers an increase in income, this will lead to a growth in its trade with its all of its trading partners, dollar zone and non-dollar zone.[29] This would then represent an additional incentive for unilateral dollarization by non-dollarized

26 Scenario 1 assumed the year of the EMU accession for CEECs, except Albania, Bulgaria, Croatia, Macedonia and Romania, 2010. For Bulgaria, Croatia and Romania the accession year was considered 2015, and for Albania and Macedonia—2020.

27 Scenario 2 assumed the year of the EMU accession for CEECs, except Albania, Bulgaria, Croatia, Macedonia and Romania, to be to be 2008. For Bulgaria, Croatia and Romania the accession year was considered 2011 and for Albania and Macedonia 2020.

28 Clearly the failure of Brazil's link to the dollar has threatened Argentina financially, and the change in the real exchange rate has disrupted trade relations among the Mercosur partners. The benefits to one country of a firmer dollar link are enhanced if others are moving in the same direction.

29 We assume that the two or more countries have significant trade relations.

countries. Finally, the *competition effect* means that the non-dollarized countries face a lower probability of competitive devaluation by countries that had previously had their own currencies, but which had in the meantime dollarized. They may therefore be tempted to adopt competitive devaluations themselves, knowing that their dollarized competitors cannot respond. However, Hausmann, Panizza, et al. (1999) argue that flexible regimes face heavy costs when they attempt to improve competitiveness through devaluation. Improvements come at the cost of an increase in inflation and tend to be rather short-lived since *de facto* wage indexation and the pass-through effect of higher import prices offsets the changes in competitiveness. Thus, for the non-dollarized countries a feasible alternative would also be to dollarize themselves, especially as they are no longer threatened by competitive devaluation by their already dollarized neighbors. In other words, dollarization should benefit from network externalities.

When we calculate again the benefits for the remaining non-dollarized countries once an earlier group has dollarized, then some of them now report a net benefit from dollarization (see Appendix 3.1). Among the CEECs, under the first scenario, the new candidates are Bulgaria and Latvia, while for LACs only Guatemala now has a net benefit.

However, the more countries dollarize, the smaller the likely increase in trade with the dollarized area. In the case of CEECs, we conducted a simulation that considered a *simultaneous* move toward euroization. In this case we assumed only a 29 percent increase in trade with EMU (half of the 58 percent increase in the original simulation). Even on such a restrictive assumption, the results suggest that half[30] of CEECs should euroize (see Appendix 3.1).

To sum up, according to our cost-benefit simulation, the majority of CEECs should unilaterally euroize, while for Latin America, only a few countries enjoy clear advantages from dollarization. The reason for this difference is firstly the much higher level of trade integration of CEECs with EMU than of LACs with the US, and secondly the absence of the stock seigniorage cost in Europe.

30 These countries are Croatia, Estonia, Hungary, Macedonia, Slovakia and Slovenia.

Table 3.7 Costs and benefits of dollarization: CEECs and LACs

	Total EMU /Total Trade (%)	Trade /GDP (%)	GDP increase (%)	PV benefit (% GDP)	Flow /GDP	Scenario 1 PV Flow (% GDP)	Scenario 1 Euroize?	Scenario 2 PV Flow (% GDP)	Scenario 2 Euroize?
Albania	80.0	31.9	17.5	17.1	1.1	60.8	No	60.8	No
Bulgaria	54.3	72.4	26.9	26.3	0.6	27.8	No	22.4	**Yes**
Croatia	55.7	59.6	22.7	22.2	0.4	16.8	**Yes**	13.5	**Yes**
Czech Republic	61.8	104.9	44.3	43.4	1.3	43.4	**Yes**	37.1	**Yes**
Estonia	45.1	138.4	42.7	41.9	0.8	26.6	**Yes**	22.7	**Yes**
Hungary	69.0	106.6	50.3	49.3	0.6	19.1	**Yes**	16.3	**Yes**
Latvia	46.8	66.1	21.2	20.7	0.7	23.4	No	20.0	**Yes**
Lithuania	36.0	73.7	18.2	17.8	0.5	16.6	**Yes**	14.2	**Yes**
Macedoni a	57.9	87.1	34.5	33.8	0.3	19.3	**Yes**	19.3	**Yes**
Poland	58.5	47.3	18.9	18.5	0.4	14.9	**Yes**	12.7	**Yes**
Romania	66.5	52.3	23.8	23.3	0.5	22.1	**Yes**	17.8	**Yes**
Slovakia	56.8	103.9	40.4	39.6	0.8	26.4	**Yes**	22.5	**Yes**
Slovenia	69.6	91.6	43.6	42.7	0.3	9.9	**Yes**	8.4	**Yes**

	Total USD area /Total Trade (%)	Trade /GDP (%)	GDP increase (%)	PV benefit (% GDP)	Flow/ GDP (%)	M0/GDP (%)	PV Flow (% GDP)	PV Cost (% GDP)	Dollarize?
Argentina	16.1	17.1	4.3	4.2	0.3	5.8	16.3	22.2	No
Bolivia	30.4	38.9	18.4	18.1	0.5	9.1	25.6	34.7	No
Brazil	23.4	18.5	6.8	6.6	0.3	6.6	18.6	25.2	No
Chile	21.8	44.1	15.0	14.7	1.9	37.7	105.4	143.1	No
Colombia	47.7	25.7	8.4	8.2	0.3	6.6	18.4	25.0	No
Costa Rica	49.3	90.7	39.0	38.2	0.6	12.3	34.4	46.6	No
Guatemala	53.1	51.2	23.7	23.2	0.4	7.8	21.9	29.8	No
Honduras	62.7	150.8	64.7	63.3	0.8	15.2	42.5	57.7	**Yes**
Mexico	81.3	58.1	29.5	28.9	0.3	6.0	16.9	22.9	**Yes**
Nicaragua	47.2	103.6	33.5	32.8	0.8	15.9	44.6	60.5	No
Paraguay	15.8	47.5	11.7	11.5	0.7	13.1	36.7	49.8	No
Peru	32.5	24.4	12.3	12.1	0.7	13.1	36.5	49.6	No
Uruguay	9.7	27.6	4.2	4.1	0.7	14.0	39.2	53.2	No
Venezuela	51.4	31.6	14.2	13.9	0.4	8.1	22.7	30.8	No

Note: Trade and GDP data are for 1999.

Source: Authors' estimation.

Conclusions

What are the prospects for dollarization/euroization in the twenty-first century? The purpose of this chapter was to take an objective look at this question, with particular emphasis on the factors most likely to influence the spread of the dollar and the euro. After the string of financial crises in the 1990s, many economists questioned the merits of intermediate exchange rate regimes, both in the short run (during a stabilization program), as well as in the longer run. Preferences shifted towards the extreme positions: super-fixed (through a currency board or dollarization) and floating rates. Then the debate focused on the choice between the two extremes: truly fixed vs. clean floating.

In the chapter, we have analyzed some of the costs and the benefits of dollarization. The OCA criteria were applied in order to investigate some of the consequences of dollarization. These suggest that most of the CEECs constitute an optimal currency area with EMU, while most LACs do not do so with US. We also contend that the loss of the lender of last resort function can be mitigated through the dominant presence of international banks in the domestic banking sector.

The last part of the chapter attempted to measure the net benefits of unilateral dollarization, and to anticipate the spread of dollarization in Latin America and CEECs. The results were encouraging mainly for the CEECs, as most of them record significant benefits from euroization, but only partially for the LACs, as only Guatemala, Honduras and Mexico registered net benefits. However, the analysis points to significant benefits and significant losses for Central American countries in the case of a unilateral dollarization, and as a result the importance for Central America of a seigniorage-sharing agreement with US.

How is the international monetary system likely to look in 2020? The outcome is that two out the three main regions[31] of the world economy, the Americas and Europe, are likely to move towards full dollarization/euroization. In Europe, where integration is a political as well as an economic phenomenon, monetary integration is likely to deepen and widen. This may happen even sooner than expected as the advantages of a unilateral euroization for EU candidates and poorer members make themselves felt. In the Americas, the US will not pursue a EU-style monetary union in the near future. This leaves unilateral dollarization as the only option, which is likely to be most attractive for small countries in Central America with particularly strong economic and financial links to the US. Some countries may even try to link their currency to both euro and dollar.[32]

All in all, it is reasonable to believe that, as dollarization/euroization expands and as other economies reconsider the costs and benefits of maintaining a national currency, more countries will adopt very hard pegs, and there will in the future be fewer national currencies.

31 The third region, Asia, is likely to continue floating. As trade and financial flows are diversified, neither dollar nor yen or euro represents an attractive currency anchor.

32 The Argentine authorities considered such a solution during 2001.

References

Bayoumi, T. and B. Eichengreen (1997), 'Ever closer to heaven? An optimum currency area index for European countries', European Economic Review 3-5 (April).

Berg, A. and E. Borensztein (2000), 'The Pros and Cons of Full Dollarization', IMF Working Paper No. 50, International Monetary Fund, Washington DC (March).

Boone, L. and M. Maurel (1998), 'Economic Convergence of the CEECs with the EU', CEPR Discussion Paper No. 2018, Centre for Economic Policy Research, London (November).

Boone, L. and M. Maurel (1999), 'An Optimal Currency Area Perspective of the EU Enlargement to the CEECs', CEPR Discussion Paper No. 2119, Centre for Economic Policy Research, London (March).

Calvo, G.A. (2000), 'Capital Markets and the Exchange Rate: With Special Reference to the Dollarization Debate in Latin America', Mimeo, University of Maryland (April).

Djankov, S., A. Chonira and B. Hoekman (1997), 'Determinants of Intra-Industry Trade between East and West Europe', World Bank Working Paper.

EBRD Investment Profiles (2001), European Bank for Reconstruction and Development, London.

Fischer, S. (2001), 'Exchange Rate Regimes: Is the Bipolar View Correct?', paper prepared for the meetings of the American Economic Association, New Orleans, January 6.

Frankel, J.A. and A.K. Rose (2000), 'An Estimate of the Effect of Currency Unions on Trade and Growth', NBER Working Paper, No. 7857, National Bureau of Economic Research, Cambridge MA.

Frankel, J.A. and A.K. Rose (1998), 'The Endogeneity of the Optimum Currency Area Criteria', The Economic Journal 108 (July), pp. 1009-1025.

Guidotti, P.E., A. Powell and G. Escude (2000), 'Dollarization in Argentina and Latin America', Working Paper, Central Bank of Argentina.

Hausmann, R. and A. Powell (1999), 'Dollarization: Issues of Implementation', mimeo, InterAmerican Development Bank.

Hausmann, R., U. Panizza and E. Stein (1999), 'Why Do Countries Float the Way They Float?', Paper prepared for the Inter-American Seminar in Economics, CEMA, Buenos Aires, (December 3).

Hausmann, R., M. Gavin, C. Pages-Serra, and E. Stein (1999), 'Financial Turmoil and the Choice of Exchange Rate Regime' InterAmerican Development Bank, Working Paper #418.

IMF World Economic Outlook (2001, 2000), International Monetary Fund, Washington DC.

Kaminski, B. (2000), 'How Accession to the European Union Has Affected External Trade and Foreign Direct Investment in Central European Economies', paper prepared for the 'Prague 2000 Accession' session at the IMF/World Bank annual meeting, Prague, September 2000.

Kaminski, B. and F. Ng (2000), 'Trade and Production Fragmentation: Central European Economies in EU Networks of Production and Marketing', The World Bank, Washington DC.

Kenen, P.B. (1969), 'The Theory of Optimum Currency Areas: an Eclectic View', in R.A. Mundell and A.K. Swoboda (eds.), Monetary Problems of the International Economy, Chicago, University of Chicago Press.

Krugman, P. (1993), 'Lessons of Massachusetts for EMU', in F. Giavazzi and F. Torres (eds.), Adjustment and Growth in the European Monetary Union, Cambridge, Cambridge University Press, pp. 241-261.

Mundell, R.A. (1961), 'A Theory of Optimum Currency Areas', American Economic Review 51 (September), pp. 657-665.

McCallum, J. (1995), 'National Borders Matter: Canada-U.S. Regional Trade Patterns', American Economic Review 85-3, pp. 615-623.

McKinnon, R.I. (1963), 'Optimum Currency Areas', American Economic Review 53, (September), pp. 717-725.

Ortiz, G. (1999), 'Dollarization: Fad or Future for Latin America?', IMF Economic Forum, International Monetary Fund, Washington DC, June.

Rose, A.K. and E. van Wincoop (2001), 'National Money as a Barrier to Trade: The Real Case for Monetary Union', paper presented at the American Economic Association Meeting session on 'Currency Unions', January 6.

Rose, A.K. (2000), 'One Money, One Market: Estimating the Effect of Common Currencies on Trade', Economic Policy 15, April30, pp. 7-46.

Rostowski, J. (2002), 'The Eastern Enlargement of the EU and the Case for Unilateral Euroization', in Financial Vulnerability and Exchange Rate Regimes: Emerging Markets Experience, M. Blejer and M. Skreb (eds.), MIT Press, Cambridge, MA.

Appendix

Table 3.A1 Costs and benefits of dollarization in stage two of the simulation: LACs and CEECs

Country	Trade Euro Area/ Total Trade (%)	GDP increase (%)	PV Benefit (% GDP)	PV Cost (% GDP)	Dollarize?
Albania	85.7	18.7	18.3	59.1	No
Bulgaria	61.8	30.6	30.0	27.8	Yes
Latvia	67.4	30.5	29.9	23.4	Yes
	Trade USD Area/ Total Trade (%)	GDP increase (%)	PV Benefit (% GDP)	PV Cost (% GDP)	Dollarize?
Argentina	17.8	4.7	4.6	22.2	No
Bolivia	32.0	19.4	19.0	34.7	No
Brazil	25.2	7.3	7.1	25.2	No
Chile	25.8	17.8	17.4	143.1	No
Colombia	50.9	8.9	8.7	25.0	No
Costa Rica	53.6	42.4	41.5	46.6	No
Guatemala	61.2	48.8	47.8	29.8	Yes
Nicaragua	62.8	44.5	43.6	60.5	No
Paraguay	16.1	12.0	11.7	49.8	No
Peru	35.4	13.4	13.2	49.6	No
Uruguay	11.5	4.9	4.8	53.2	No
Venezuela	53.7	14.8	14.5	30.8	No

Table 3.A2 Costs and benefits of a simultaneous euroization: CEECs

Country	Trade Euro Area/ Total Trade (%)	GDP increase (%)	PV_Benefit (% GDP)	PV_Cost (% GDP)	Dollarize?
Albania	87.92	40.09	9.41	60.85	No
Bulgaria	62.18	85.41	15.08	22.41	No
Croatia	70.45	71.73	14.06	13.55	Yes
Czech Republic	76.90	128.27	27.03	37.10	No
Estonia	55.92	160.79	25.93	22.75	Yes
Hungary	77.23	130.42	27.58	16.34	Yes
Latvia	67.62	79.05	14.98	19.97	No
Lithuania	50.56	84.52	12.49	14.21	No
Macedonia	76.49	106.37	22.32	19.35	Yes
Poland	66.68	56.39	10.56	12.72	No
Romania	74.81	63.62	13.11	17.80	No
Slovakia	86.30	129.84	30.04	22.51	Yes
Slovenia	84.35	114.06	25.91	8.44	Yes

* The benefits are calculated under the assumption of 29 percent increase in trade.

Chapter 4

Exchange Rate and Monetary Regimes

Vittorio Corbo

Introduction

This chapter evaluates the relative merits of the two exchange rate and monetary-policy regimes to which most Latin American countries are converging today: hard pegs (dollarization and currency board) and floating exchange rate regimes.

It is well-known by now that for countries that can make a choice, today's consensus view holds that the potential benefits from monetary union or dollarization (or a 100 percent credible currency board) stem from low(er) inflation, elimination of currency risk and its associated premium, elimination of currency transaction costs, and elimination of currency mismatch in foreign assets and liabilities. These benefits could be particularly important in countries without much room to run an independent monetary policy. At the other extreme, maintaining a domestic currency under a free float offers potential benefits derived from allowing for nominal (and hence more real) exchange-rate flexibility, an independent monetary policy employed for stabilization purposes, direct access to seigniorage revenue, and direct central bank exercise in providing lender-of-last-resort services on a temporary basis.

A host of structural and policy conditions determines the extent of the previous gains and losses associated with each regime choice. Traditional optimal currency area (OCA) factors to be considered comprise: the degree of international factor mobility and correlations of factor prices, the extent of domestic price and wage flexibility, the degree of foreign trade openness and integration, the degree of symmetry of domestic and external shocks and business cycles, and the extent of domestic output, export, and portfolio diversification. Other important factors, mostly in the realm of policies and financial markets, have been added recently: completeness and depth of domestic financial markets and their integration into world markets (particularly in their ability to hedge exchange risk and to accept domestic-currency denominated issues of foreign debt) and coordination of monetary union or dollarization with overall economic and political union, transfer payments, and adoption of similar regulatory and tax codes.

It is far easier to list the latter costs, benefits, and determining factors in choosing exchange regimes than putting numbers to such choices. In fact, an overall evaluation of the relation between regime choice and welfare is hampered by three serious limitations. There is no well-established encompassing framework that takes account of the various dimensions and variables that determine regime choice; there is not much agreement on the empirical weight of different costs and benefits associated with such a decision; and the costs and benefits may change over time in response to regime changes. Hence, regional or country specific evaluations of exchange regimes tend to be partial, emphasizing each factor separately.

The rest of this chapter covers the following topics: the cost and benefits of alternative regimes (Section 4.2),[1] elements to consider when choosing a rigid exchange rate regime, i.e., dollarization, currency union or currency board (Section 4.3), and the choice of monetary framework for the countries that decide to float, including an inflation-targeting (IT) (Section 4.4).[2] Finally, I end up with some concluding remarks (Section 4.5).

Alternative Exchange Rate Regimes: Costs and Benefits

In general, exchange rate regimes can be grouped into three broad categories: hard peg regimes (dollarization, currency unions and currency boards), intermediate regimes (fixed-but-adjustable pegs, flexible pegs, crawling pegs, target zones) and floating regimes (managed floats with occasional interventions and free floats).[3] Hard peg regimes have many benefits. First, they eliminate (and intermediate regimes reduce) volatility in the nominal and real exchange rate and, when accompanied by supporting macro policies, are less prone to generate misalignments that are unrelated to change in fundamentals.[4] Second, hard pegs, as well as fixed-but-adjustable regimes with infrequent adjustments (FBAR) also provide a nominal anchor for the evolution of the price level and allow for more efficient adjustments when shocks are of a nominal nature. The anchor is stronger for hard pegs than for FBARs. Also, a commitment to an exchange rate anchor is easier to understand and monitor than a commitment to a monetary anchor. Third, an additional advantage for countries with a poor track record on the use of monetary policy is that it also reduces the scope for an independent monetary policy.

However, hard-peg regimes (and to a lesser extend, FBARs) also have some important costs. First, in the presence of nominal downward price and wage rigidities, they make a real depreciation difficult to achieve when a change in fundamentals requires one, generating important costs in terms of output and

1 This section and the next draw on Corbo (2002b).
2 This section draws, in part, on Corbo and Schmidt-Hebbel (2001).
3 Corden (2002) distinguishes nine regimes that go all the way from absolutely fixed regime (dollarization and monetary unions) to the pure floating regime.
4 Empirical work on Latin America shows that the variability of the real exchange rate has a detrimental effect on export growth and on investment and output growth (Caballero and Corbo, 1989, Corbo and Rojas, 1993, and Reinhart and Reinhart, 2001). Furthermore, Baxter and Stockman (1989) compare the variability of a set of real variables across different exchange rate regimes, finding that, controlling for fundamentals, there were no mayor differences except for the real exchange rate, which was more volatile for flexible regimes. Furthermore, there was a tendency for long-lasting misalignments.

unemployment. Thus, it has also been found that adjustment to real shocks under fixed exchange rate regimes (hard pegs and FBARs) are more costly than under more flexible regimes (Broda, 2000). Second, when agents underestimate the risk of an exchange rate change, they facilitate over-expansion of foreign indebtedness, exposing agents to high costs when an exchange rate adjustment does take place. These costs could be high in economies with weak financial systems. Furthermore, an additional difficulty for hard pegs and especially for FBARs, which has been much stressed in the recent literature (Fischer, 2001; Mussa, et. al., 2000), is that they are prone to costly speculative attacks in countries that are increasingly integrated into world markets through trade, direct foreign investment, and other types of capital flows.[5] The costs here are multidimensional: the central bank losses associated with the exchange rate intervention, the macroeconomic and financial effects of the high interest rates needed to defend the peg, the balance-sheet and relative price effects of an abrupt change in the exchange rate, and the political and economic costs usually associated with the abandonment of a peg. Balance-sheet effects can emerge when there is a severe currency mismatch between assets and liabilities, that is, when the liabilities of private agents are dollarized while their assets or income-generating abilities are in local currency. In this type of situation, a drastic exchange rate adjustment could unleash generalized bankruptcy. Third, a fixed exchange rate regime—both of the hard peg and FBAR varieties—also requires forgoing the use of monetary policy to help control demand to stabilize output. This is not a minor cost, since with a flexible exchange rate monetary policy is the most effective stabilization tool in the presence of nominal price rigidities. Some of these benefits of having a less rigid system should not be underestimated. Indeed, there is an emerging consensus that the countries, which suffered least from the Great Depression were the ones that abandoned the rigid gold standard earlier rather than later.[6]

Floating regimes reduce most of these costs of the fixed regimes. However, floating regimes also have their costs. First, they usually deliver higher inflation than fixed-rate regimes. Thus, an explicit nominal anchor, most likely in the form of an inflation target regime, must complement any flexible exchange rate regime. Second, flexible exchange rate regimes show more volatility in nominal and real exchange rates and sometimes lasting misalignments in the real exchange rate. This could be an important cost of flexible regimes, as volatility and misalignments have real costs in terms of reduced trade and capital flows and, ultimately, growth and welfare. How high volatility may rise is well illustrated by the exchange rate between the yen and the dollar, which went from 147 yen per dollar in August 1998 to 115 in October of that same year. If these sharp movements occur for the currencies of the two largest countries in the world, with

---

5 The experience of Hong Kong currency board illustrates this point. Thus, at the height of the Asian crises doubts about the survival of the system resulted in high interest rates and a substantial growth slowdown.

6 See Eichengreen and Sachs (1995), Eichengreen (1992), and Bernanke (1995) for industrial countries and Diaz-Alejandro (1982), Corbo (1988), and Campa (1990) for Latin America.

deep markets to cover exchange rate risks, anything could happen for the currencies of smaller countries. The exchange rate volatility costs of a flexible exchange rate system in the form of balance-sheet effects could be important. Calvo (2000) has made this point forcefully while advocating a hard peg (currency board or dollarization). However, balance-sheet effects could be ameliorated through appropriate regulation and supervision of the financial system and the aggressive development of instruments and markets to cover exchange rate risks as well as the development of deeper capital markets in domestic currency (Caballero, 2002; Goldstein, 2002). Thus, a flexible exchange rate system must be accompanied by appropriate supervision and regulation of banks and by the promotion of instruments to hedge exchange rate risks, including encouraging issuance of local currency denominated debt.

It is sometimes claimed that countries have a fear of floating and therefore, although they claim to have a flexible exchange rate system, they do not use the flexibility that it entails. Fear of floating (see Calvo and Reinhart, 2002) could be due to a high pass-through effect of devaluation on inflation or to the commercial risks associated with an abrupt exchange rate adjustment in an economy where the currency composition of assets and liabilities is mismatched. However, recent analytical and empirical work shows convincingly that pass-through effects—from depreciation to CPI inflation—are much weaker than initially thought (Obstfeld and Rogoff, 2001 and Goldfajn and Werlang, 2000). This is especially so for those countries with a well-established and credible monetary framework of the IT (inflation targeting) type. Under these circumstances, agents trust that the central bank will prevent the acceleration of inflation above the set target, in the process reducing the pass-through from depreciation to inflation.[7]

As Taylor (2000) emphasizes, more than the exchange rate today, producers are particularly concerned about expected future exchange rate trajectories. The case of Brazil following the sharp depreciation of early 1999 is very important. Although there was no previous record of responsible policy management, and the inflation rate surged following the depreciation, it returned slowly to low levels without having any important long run effects. The experience of Chile also points in the same direction. After abandoning the exchange rate band, there have been some important ups and downs in the exchange rate, but the effects on inflation have been quite modest.

In a formal model where monetary policy follows a Taylor rule, fear of floating could be merely the normal reaction of monetary authorities that are concerned about inflation, especially if they also have a separate target for the real exchange rate (or for the current account deficit) as an independent monetary policy objective. However, a hidden cost of having a separate exchange rate objective—due to fear of bankruptcies or its potential effects on trade flows—is that the IT framework becomes less transparent and less credible.

7 However, the pass-through from depreciation to a rise in import prices still could be high, as shown by Campa and Goldberg (2002).

It should be kept in mind that, in the ideal case of the absence of any market friction, there is no gain from exchange rate flexibility or from having an independent monetary policy. There is likewise not much to be gained by giving up the domestic currency, as currency transaction costs are nil and perfect financial markets hedge the currency risk premiums and currency mismatch. The only residual issue would be a minor one, related to the international distribution of seigniorage revenue.

Is it possible to combine a fixed exchange rate regime and a flexible one? In their heyday a decade ago, the intermediate regimes of adjustable pegs and exchange rate bands seemed to provide a perfect combination of credibility (with the nominal anchor provided by the exchange rate peg or band) and flexibility (through the limited and gradual adjustment of the nominal and real exchange rate in response to shocks). However, in a world with large capital movements and high levels of workers' remittances, these exchange rate regimes have become very vulnerable to highly costly speculative attacks (Mexico in 1994, Asia in 1997, Russia in 1998, Brazil in 1999, and Turkey in 2001). As a result, after a decade of growing disappointment with intermediate regimes (including FBARs), the current consensus has shifted in favor of the two pure cases: credible fixed or fully flexible (Eichengreen, 1994; Obstfeld, 1995; Summers, 2000; Mussa, et al., 2000; Fischer, 2001). A minority view in favor the intermediate option is presented in Frankel (1999) and Williamson (2000).

For countries that are well integrated into world capital markets, intermediate regimes are prone to crises; a strong policy interest in finding less costly options has emerged. The main options are to establish a credible hard-peg exchange rate system (dollarization, currency unions, or a currency board) or to employ a more flexible exchange rate system where there is no explicit commitment to a given exchange rate value, developing, at the same time, instruments to cover exchange rate risk and building in parallel a monetary framework capable of delivering low inflation. An increasingly popular framework of this sort is the inflation targeting one.[8]

8 A third option, proposed in certain cases to avoid exchange rate crises, is to introduce capital controls. However, it must be kept in mind that, given the increasing integration of world trade and direct foreign investment and the lower communication and information costs and advances in information technology, the world is an ever more integrated market, so that capital controls are very difficult to implement and, at best, are only temporarily effective (until the private sector finds ways to avoid them). For a recent review of the effectiveness of capital controls, see Edwards (1999).

Hard Pegs: Dollarization, Currency Unions, and Currency Boards

Hard pegs are extreme cases of fixed pegs and, as such, they share the costs and benefits of such systems discussed above. A successful hard peg has some prerequisites. First, it must be credible, so the central bank must have sufficient foreign reserves to buy back the monetary base or back it up. The fiscal and financial situation must also be strong enough to facilitate the normal development of the private economy. Otherwise, unacceptable economic outcomes (high interest rates, low growth, high unemployment) reduce the credibility of the system, making it vulnerable to attack. Second, as they rule out the use of the nominal exchange rate to adjust to negative real shocks that require changes in the real exchange rate, hard pegs must be accompanied by sufficient downward flexibility in nominal prices and wages to reduce adjustment costs to these types of shocks. In the specific case where the hard peg is part of a currency union, adjustment is also facilitated by the possibility of labor and capital mobility within the union. Third, the financial system must be solid enough to survive without a lender of last resort. However, in the event of a financial crisis, provision must be made for emergency loans from foreign commercial banks or from a monetary authority of industrial country, presumably the Federal Reserve Board or the European Central Bank, and/or the fiscal situation must be robust enough to obtain financing in case of a financial emergency. Fourth, any successful hard peg requires a solvent government, in which country-risk-augmented interest rates do not crowd out private demand. Furthermore, the government must have the capacity to carry out counter-cyclical fiscal policy in situations when the country faces shocks that result in a reduction in aggregate demand. This is the functional fiscal policy of Corden (2002).

Nevertheless, the discipline inherent in a hard peg means that a government must be ready to endure, and have the political support to weather, the temporary high real interest rates (and high unemployment) that are an integral part of an adjustment to a drop in foreign reserves. Changing reserve requirements, impeding market-determined increases in the interest rate, or reducing the backing of the monetary base in a currency board scheme may backfire, resulting in reserve losses and/or higher interest rates, as the credibility of the system comes into question.

Hard pegs of the weaker currency board type are not fully protected from the effect of financial contagion. Indeed, financial turmoil and contagion in open economies that have adopted currency boards (e.g., Argentina and Hong Kong), and protracted high exchange rate risk premiums after nine years of Argentina's currency board (reflected both directly and indirectly through large country-risk premiums, as described by Powell and Sturzenegger, 2000) mark some recent disillusion with currency boards. Thus, some believe that, to reduce the cost associated with distrust of the authorities' ability to maintain a currency board, it is necessary to renounce one's domestic currency and adopt that of a larger country with a history of monetary discipline, such as the dollar. Indeed, this option was openly discussed in Argentina at the end of the Menem administration as a way of reducing the growing currency risk despite having a currency board system.

However, if fiscal solvency and a sound financial system are not established in advance, the market default risks will still be in place, with high economic costs in terms of unemployment and output losses.

There is a related question of the most appropriate exchange rate regime to provide a nominal anchor to reduce inflation in a country that starts from high inflation and is prepared to carry out a fiscal adjustment compatible with low inflation. Here, a hard peg has the advantage of providing a clear and transparent signal of the course of policy as well as a direct anchor for the price of imports and exports. However, early on and once inflation has been reduced to low levels, it could become advantageous to move toward a flexible regime—accompanied by IT with strong institutional backing—to facilitate adjustment to external shocks. The longer it takes to exit the fixed peg, the higher the cost of the transition, as agents will gradually adjust to the fixed peg. Here there is a clear trade-off between credibility and flexibility. Again, this could be a major advantage for countries with extensive downward price rigidities. Otherwise, the high unemployment costs that usually accompany the adjustment to a negative shock could be large to endure.

A Monetary Policy Framework for the Floaters: The Case for Inflation Targeting

Free floaters by definition have dispensed with the use of the exchange rate as a nominal anchor and thus must select a monetary regime capable of delivering low inflation. Two fundamental options can be considered: a money anchor and an IT anchor.[9] A monetary anchor relies on a pre-committed path for the money supply to anchor inflation. In the case of IT, the anchor for inflation is the publicly announced inflation target itself. The credibility of this policy relies on the power given to the central bank to orient monetary policy chiefly toward achieving the target and its willingness to use the power and policy instruments at its disposal for this purpose.

The effectiveness of the use of a monetary aggregate as a nominal anchor for inflation depends, first of all—as with an inflation target—on the authority and capacity of the central bank to carry out an independent monetary policy aimed at achieving and maintaining low inflation (including that induced by exchange rate depreciations). But in this case, the effectiveness of the policy depends also on the stability of the demand for the monetary aggregate that is used as the anchor. That stability provides a link between the monetary anchor and the inflation rate. The stability of the demand for money presents a problem in cases where there is considerable financial innovation or a sudden change in the level of inflation.

In particular, in an economy that has experienced periods of high and variable inflation, the demand for money becomes very unstable, as economic agents develop ways to economize in the use of domestic money balances.

9 On monetary anchors, see Calvo and Vegh (1999); Bernanke and Mishkin (1997), and Bernanke et al. (1999).

Therefore, when the rate of inflation is reduced, hysteresis effects emerge, generating a breakdown in the former relationship governing the demand for money. That is, when the inflation rate returns to previously observed lower values, the quantity of money demanded is lower than what was expected before the outburst of inflation. In cases like these, one would overestimate the quantity of money demanded, and the use of a money target could be very ineffective in achieving a given inflation objective. Thus, it is not surprising that as countries have moved toward more flexible exchange rate arrangements, they have searched for a new monetary anchor regime.[10] In recent years, inflation targeting as an anchor has become increasingly popular. An additional advantage of the IT over monetary aggregate targeting is that, as the credibility of the policy increases, the central bank can engage in short-term stabilization policy.

In the case of the Americas, five of the seven floaters (Brazil, Canada, Chile, Colombia, and Mexico) have gradually established an IT framework. Meanwhile another floater, the United States, uses the high credibility of its central bank, the Federal Reserve Board, as a monetary anchor, but recently there have been suggestions to move toward an explicit ITF framework.

An IT framework was initially introduced in Canada (February 1991), and Chile (1991), and was later extended to Colombia (1999), Brazil (June 1999), and Mexico (1999). Under the IT, the target rate of inflation provides a monetary anchor and monetary and fiscal policies are geared toward achieving the inflation target. The advantages of this framework are that it does not rely on a stable relationship between a monetary aggregate and inflation for its effectiveness, and at the same time, it avoids the problems associated with pegging the exchange rate. An additional advantage for emerging countries is that the trajectory of the market exchange rate provides important information on the market evaluation of present and future monetary policy, such as the information provided by nominal and real yields on long-term government bonds in industrial countries (Bernanke, et al., 1999).

A well defined IT has to satisfy a set of conditions (Svensson, 2000; King, 2000). First, it must include a public announcement of the strategy of medium-term price stability, and an intermediate target level for inflation for the relevant period in the future in which monetary policy affects inflation. Second, an institutional commitment to price stability must be in place, in the form of rules of operation for the monetary authority. Third, operational procedures must be transparent and there must be a clear strategy concerning how monetary policy will bring inflation close to the announced target. The strategy, in practice, usually starts from a conditional inflation forecast for the relevant period. It also establishes specific operational procedures for the central bank to adopt when the inflation forecast differs from the target. The procedures should be transparent and the monetary authority should be accountable for attaining the objective that has been

10 One should be careful not to oversell this argument. Inflation targeting also benefits from a stable demand for money although all that it is required is a stable relation between inflation and its determinants, including the interest rate. However, for this relation to be stable, the money demand must also exhibit some stability.

established. Central bank autonomy is an important institutional development that reinforces the credibility of an IT.

Given lags in the operation of monetary policy, the inflation target must be set for a period far enough into the future to ensure that monetary policy can have a role in determining future inflation. In practice, central banks announce a target for the next eighteen to twenty-four months. They then develop a conditional inflation forecast for this timeframe—based on the existing monetary policy stance and a forecast of the relevant exogenous variables—and provide a strategy and communicate to the public the policy actions they will adopt should inflation deviate from target levels. When the conditional inflation forecast is above the inflation target, the level of the intervention interest rate is raised to bring inflation closer to the target. One advantage of IT is that inflation itself is made the target, committing monetary policy to achieve an explicit inflation objective and thus helping to shape inflation expectations. However, herein also resides its main disadvantage. As inflation is not directly under the control of the central bank, it becomes difficult to evaluate the monetary stance on the basis of the observed path of inflation. Furthermore, as monetary policy operates with substantial lags, pre-committing to an unconditional inflation target—irrespective of changes in external factors that affect inflation—and to using monetary policy to bring inflation back to the target can be costly. Aiming at the inflation target when a shock causes a temporary rise in inflation can be very costly in terms of a severe growth slowdown and increased output volatility (Cecchetti, 1998).

To address some of these problems, several options have been proposed. First, the inflation target can be set in terms of a range rather than a point. Second, a target can be set for core inflation rather than observed inflation. Third, changes in indirect taxes, interest payments, and energy prices can be excluded from the targeted inflation measure. Fourth, the target can be set for sufficiently long periods so that short-term inflationary shocks do not require a monetary response.[11]

Emerging market countries that adopted an IT framework when inflation levels were well above their long-run objectives have had to deal with the problem of inflation convergence. Usually, these countries have started reducing inflation without a full-fledged IT in place. Once they had made sufficient progress in reducing inflation, they announced annual targets and gradually put in place the components of a full-fledged IT framework, as they moved toward low and stationary inflation (Australia, Chile, Canada, Israel, New Zealand, and the United Kingdom are good examples here).

A floater that chooses an IT should adjust the interest rate or a monetary aggregate to keep inflation close to the target. Corbo (2002a) studies Taylor-type reaction functions for a set of countries in Latin America (Chile, Colombia, Costa Rica, El Salvador and Peru) drawing on the work of Clarida, Gali, and Gertler (1998). Corbo finds that in two of the five cases studied (Chile and Colombia) since their central banks became independent, monetary policy has been clearly geared to getting inflation closer to its target value. From the other three cases

11 For a review of the costs and benefits of these alternative options, see Bernanke et al. (1999), chapter 3.

(Costa Rica, El Salvador and Peru), in El Salvador there is some evidence that monetary policy is at least neutral. That is, shocks to the inflation rate do not result in a change in the real interest rate, while in the other two countries, higher real interest rates are not utilized to bring inflation close to its target.

In general, it is found that when setting monetary policy central banks look beyond just inflation, taking into account other variables that many times are spelled out in their charter. These other variables are not considered because of their predictive power for future expected inflation but as separate monetary policy objectives. Thus, in the case of Chile it was found that the size of the current account deficit, as a share of GDP, was also a variable taken into account when deciding the stance of monetary policy. In contrast, the output gap was significant only in the second half of the 1980s, but not in the 1990s when the central bank became independent. A similar type of result was found for Colombia, where the unemployment rate was significant only in the 1980s but not in the 1990s.

In the case of Costa Rica, both the output gap and the real exchange rate are statistically significant, while in El Salvador, the output gap is statistically significant and in Peru both the output gap and the real exchange rate are statistically significant.

Conclusions

For countries with poor records of macroeconomic stability, dollarization could be beneficial. However, they have to be able to provide the fiscal underpinning for the stabilization. The benefits of dollarization are derived from: lower interest rates resulting from the elimination of currency risk and its associated premium, elimination of currency transaction costs, lower variability in relative prices of tradable goods, and the elimination of currency mismatches in foreign assets and liabilities. The reduction of these microeconomic costs and market friction should result in an improved integration to the world economy, a higher income level and higher growth rates. The benefits of dollarization would be higher yet if labor markets are flexible and they have developed the appropriate institutions to support the financial system in case of a sudden crisis. Of course if all these conditions are fulfilled one could then ask, why to dollarize?

In contrast, for open economies with a good record of financial stability and large tradable sectors, in which exports are highly diversified by commodity and geography and where downward nominal rigidities are widespread, dollarization could be a major hindrance to the adjustment to a negative real shock that requires a real depreciation. For this type of country, a more flexible exchange rate regime would be preferable. Indeed, the combination of prudent monetary policy and exchange rate flexibility has facilitated adjustment in most countries in the region. With capital mobility, exchange rate flexibility also leaves the door open for the use of discretionary monetary policy in response to unexpected domestic and external shocks.

In the Americas we have today a very wide range of different exchange rate arrangements. While few countries are willing to go the route of dollarization

(Ecuador, El Salvador and other Central American countries), a larger number is moving towards the use of more flexible systems. However, more flexible systems must be accompanied by the development of forward and future exchange rate markets, to enable market participants to hedge against exchange rate volatility. Otherwise, the real costs of real exchange rate variability could be high. As countries move towards the use of more flexible exchange rate arrangements, they will need to make the selection of the monetary anchor more explicit. Here, much progress has been made in the region in implementing quite successful full-fledge IT regimes. Thus, for countries that have built strong macro fundamentals, and that have a safe and sound financial system, the alternative of keeping its own currency, combining a floating exchange rate system with IT may be a better choice.

References

Baxter, M. and A.C. Stockman (1989), 'Business Cycles and The Exchange Rate System', *Journal of Monetary Economics* 23, pp. 377-400.

Bernanke, B. (1995), 'The Macroeconomics of the Great Depression: A Comparative Approach', *Journal of Money, Credit and Banking*, 27 (1), pp. 1-28.

Bernanke, B. and F. Mishkin (1997), 'Inflation Targeting: A New Framework for Monetary Policy?', *Journal of Economic Perspectives*, 11 (2), pp. 97-116.

Bernanke, B., T. Laubach, F. Mishkin and A. Posen (1999), *Inflation Targeting*. Princeton, New York: Princeton University Press.

Broda, C. (2000), 'Terms of Trade and Exchange Rate Regimes in Developing Countries', Mimeo, MIT, December.

Caballero, R. (2002), 'Coping with Chile's External Vulnerability: A Financial Problem', *Central Bank of Chile Working Paper 154*, May.

Caballero, R. and V. Corbo (1989), 'Real Exchange Rate Uncertainty and Exports: Multi-Country Empirical Evidence', *World Bank Economic Review*, 3 (2), May, pp. 263-278.

Calvo, G. (2000), 'Testimony on Dollarization', presented before the Subcommittee on Domestic and Monetary Policy, Committee on Banking and Financial Services, Washington, DC.

Calvo, G. and C. Vegh (1999), 'Inflation Stabilization and BOP Crises in Developing Countries', Chapter 24 in J. Taylor and M. Woodford (eds.), *Handbook of Macroeconomics*, Vol. 1C. Amsterdam: Elsevier Science.

Calvo, G. and C. Reinhart (2002), 'Fear of Floating', *Quarterly Journal of Economics*, 117 (2), May.

Campa, J. M. (1990), 'Exchange Rates and Economic Recovery in the 1930s: An Extension to Latin America', *Journal of Economic History*, 50 (September), pp. 677-82.

Campa, J. M. and L. Goldberg (2002), 'Exchange Rate Pass-Through into Import Prices' A Macro or Micro Phenomenon?' *NBER Working Paper*, No. 8934.

Cechetti, S. (1998), 'Policy Rules and Targets: Framing the Central Banker's Problem', *Federal Reserve Bank of New York Economic Policy Review*, 4 (2), June.

Clarida, R., J. Gali and M. Gertler (1998), 'Monetary Policy Rules in Practice: Some International Evidence', *European Economic Review*, 42, pp. 1033-68.

Corbo, V. (1988), 'Problems, Development Theory and Strategies of Latin America' in *The State of Development Economics: Progress and Perspectives*, G. Ranis and T. P. Schultz. London: Basil Blackwell.

Corbo, V. (2002a), 'Monetary Policy in Latin America in the 90s', in N. Loayza and K. Schmidt-Hebbel (eds.), *Monetary Policy and Transmissions Mechanisms*. Santiago: Central Bank of Chile.

Corbo, V. (2002b), 'Exchange Rate Regimes In The Americas: Is Dollarization The Solution?' Paper prepared for presentation at the Conference organized by the Institute for Monetary and Economic Studies of the Bank of Japan on Exchange Rate Regimes in the 21st Century, Tokyo, Japan, July 1-2, 2002.

Corbo, V. and P. Rojas (1993), 'Investment, macroeconomic stability and growth: The Latin American experience', *Revista de Analisis Economico* 8 (1), pp. 19-35.

Corbo, V. and K. Schmidt-Hebbel (2001), 'Inflation Targeting in Latin America', *Central Bank of Chile Working Paper 105*, September. In José A. Gonzales, Vittorio Corbo, Anne O. Krueger and Aaron Tornell (eds.) forthcoming. *Financial and Fiscal Policy in Latin America*. Chicago: University of Chicago Press.

Corden, M. (2002), *Too Sensational: On the Choice of Exchange Rate Regimes*. Cambridge, MA: MIT Press.

Diaz-Alejandro, C. (1982), 'Latin America in Depression, 1929-39', in *The Theory and Experience of Economic Development*, M. Gersovitz, C. Diaz-Alejandro, G. Ranis and M. Rosenzweig (eds.) London: George Allen and Unwin.

Edwards, S. (1999), 'How Effective are Capital Controls?', *Journal of Economic Perspectives*, 13 (4), pp. 65-84.

Eichengreen, B. (1992), *Golden Fetters: The Gold Standard and the Great Depression, 1919-1939*. New York: Oxford University Press, 1992.

Eichengreen, B. (1994), *International Monetary Arrangements for the 21st Century*. Washington, DC: Brookings Institution.

Eichengreen, B. and J. Sachs (1985), 'Exchange Rates and Economic Recovery in the 1930s', *Journal of Economic History* 45, pp. 925-46.

Fischer, S. (2001), 'Exchange Rate Regimes: Is the Bipolar View Correct?' *Journal of Economic Perspectives*, 15 (2), Spring, pp. 3-24.

Frankel, J. (1999), 'No Single Currency Regime is Right for all Countries or at all Times', *NBER Working Paper*, No. 7338, September.

Goldfajn, I. and S. Werlang (2000), 'The Pass-through from Depreciation to Inflation: A Panel Study', *Banco Central do Brasil Working Paper No. 5*, July.

Goldstein, M. (2002), 'Managed Floating Plus', *Policy Analyses in International Economics 66*, March, Institute for International Economics.

King, M. (2000), 'Monetary Policy: Theory in Practice', address to the joint luncheon of the American Economic Association and the American Finance Association. Available at http://www.bankofengland.co.uk/speeches/speech67.htm.

Mussa, M., P. Masson, A. Swoboda, E. Jadresic, P. Mauro and A. Berg (2000), 'Exchange Rate Regimes in an Increasingly Integrated World Economy', *IMF Occasional Paper 193*.

Obstfeld, M. (1995), 'International Currency Experience: New Lessons and Lessons Relearned', *Brookings Papers on Economic Activity*, 1, pp. 119-96.

Obstfeld, M. and K. Rogoff (2001), 'Perspectives on OECD Economic Integration: Implications for US Current Account Adjustment', paper presented at the symposium *Global economic Integration: Opportunities and Challenges* sponsored by the Federal Reserve Bank of Kansas City, August.

Powell, A. and F. Sturzenegger (2000), 'Dollarization: The link between Devaluation and Risk Default', mimeo, Universidad Torcuato di Tella.

Reinhart, C. and V. Reinhart (2001), 'What hurts most? G-3 Exchange Rate or Interest Rate Volatility', *NBER Working Paper*, No. 8535, October.

Summers, L. (2000), 'International Financial Crises, Causes, Prevention and Cures', *American Economic Review*, 90 (2), pp. 1-16.

Svensson, L. E. O. (2000), 'Open-Economy Inflation Targeting', *Journal of International Economics*, 50, February, pp. 155-183.

Taylor, J. (2000), 'Low Inflation, Pass-through, and the Pricing Power of Firms', *European Economic Review*, 44, pp. 1389-1408.

Williamson, J. (2000), 'Exchange Rate Regimes for Emerging Markets: Reviving the Intermediate Option', *Policy Analyses in International Economics 60*, September, Institute for International Economics.

Chapter 5

Why Unilateral Euroization Makes Sense for (some) Applicant Countries

Jacek Rostowski

Key Elements of the Unilateral Euroization Proposal

Andrzej Bratkowski and I first presented our proposal for unilateral euroization in 1999 (Bratkowski and Rostowski, 1999). Comments by some economists indicate that the details of our proposal have not always been understood clearly. This is why we wish to begin by restating the main elements of the proposal.

We propose that in transition countries applying for EU membership, the domestic currency should be replaced as quickly as is practicable by the euro.[1] This means that domestic cash in circulation and in bank vaults would be replaced by euro notes and coins, which would be bought using a country's international reserves. At the same time all domestic currency denominated bank deposits, private contracts, wages and tax obligations would be re-denominated into euro at the 'conversion rate' chosen by the government of the country concerned.[2] We wish to make it absolutely clear that we are *not* proposing, and never have proposed, the introduction of a 'Polish euro' or of a 'Czech euro'—i.e., a new currency that would be different from that created by the European Central Bank (ECB).

We believe that it would be most beneficial for some transition applicant countries (TACs) if unilateral euroization were implement with the acceptance of the European Union (what we call 'consensual unilateral euroization'). Thus, by 'unilateral euroization' we mean that euroization would be implemented by buying the necessary euros using a country's international reserves and before the country becomes a member of the Economic and Monetary Union (indeed, possibly before it becomes a member of the European Union). We do not mean that unilateral euroization should be implemented without prior discussions with the EU, and without attempting to obtain EU acceptance of it. At present the EU is opposed to unilateral euroization. We believe that this EU opposition is not well grounded in EU law or in the interests of current EMU member states (on the former see

1 The technical preparations would probably take about one to two years.

2 Whether the euro would become a country's 'national currency' or whether there would cease to be a national currency in the accession countries after the abolition of the zloty or crown is a legal question which we leave to lawyers. From an economic point of view it is a secondary matter.

Appendix 1, on the latter Bratkowski and Rostowski, 2001). It should therefore be possible to convince the EU as to the merits of unilateral euroization for both sides, and to agree on terms that would obviate any well-founded concerns that the EU or the ECB might have. TACs should therefore start talks aimed at convincing the EU to change its stance, while at the same time preparing the legal and institutional basis for the change.[3]

Failure in these negotiations need not mean that TACs would have to give up the idea of unilateral euroization (it could still proceed with 'non-consensual unilateral euroization'. However, it might be better under such circumstances to adopt a currency board arrangement instead. Such a system is very similar to unilateral euroization, but would be slightly less beneficial (Rostowski, 2001a).

Finally, our proposal for unilateral euroization is a response to the acute 'problems of success' that face advanced transition economies as they approach EU membership. Successful market reforms in the TACs and anticipated EU accession lead to expectations of rapid growth. This in turn means that domestic residents wish to save less, so as to smooth consumption, while foreign investors are willing to provide the financing needed to bridge the gap between savings and investment. The result is high capital account surpluses and their corollary high current account deficits, which makes the TACs very susceptible to capital inflow 'stops' (reversals are not necessary) leading to currency crises. In the case of Poland the current account deficit has been around 5-8 percent of GDP since the end of 1990s, which is usually considered well within the 'danger zone' in which a currency 'stop' may threaten due to fears of unsustainability by investors.

Neither monetary nor fiscal policies can be *counted on* to keep these developments in check. Under a floating exchange rate regime, contractionary monetary policy will cause the domestic currency to appreciate, which in the traditional Mundell-Fleming view is likely to increase the current account deficit even further. Expansionary monetary policy will lead to faster inflation and make the achievement of the Maastricht inflation criterion impossible. Under a fixed exchange rate, monetary policy is not available as an instrument. Fiscal policy (which can be used with either floating or fixed exchange rate regimes) may also prove ineffective in improving the current account balance, as a tightening of the fiscal stance may simply make foreign lenders more willing to lend to domestic private borrowers (we know that foreign investors nowadays look at the overall indebtedness of a country's residents, both public and private). Expansionary fiscal policy would, in the traditional way, increase aggregate demand and thus tend to increase the CA deficit.

Given the difficulty of reducing high CA deficits, many TACs are very exposed to the risk of a sharp depreciation of their currency, commonly called a currency crisis. In countries with high levels of 'liability dollarization/euroization' (Calvo, 1998) such crises can lead to increases in the real debt burden and to depression (Indonesia in 1997-1998 is an example).

In the rest of this chapter we shall not repeat the above arguments in favor of unilateral euroization *in extenso*. Those who are interested are referred to our

3 For instance, setting up the Banking Sector Liquidity Fund which we discuss below.

previous papers (Bratkowski and Rostowski, 2001 and Rostowski, 2002). Sections 5.2 to 5.5 deal with some new monetary, fiscal and exchange rate *policy* considerations (including consideration of which of the TACs already constitute an optimum currency area with the EMU countries). Sections 5.6 to 5.8 deal with the fiscal and financial costs and benefits of unilateral euroization. Appendix 5.1 deals with some of the legal and political aspects of EU opposition to unilateral euroization.

The Effectiveness of Monetary and Fiscal Policy in the Absence of Unilateral Euroization in the Run-up to EU and EMU Membership

It cannot be denied that fiscal policy *may* be effective in limiting current account deficits. The existence of the countervailing effect we describe means that a given fiscal tightening will have that much smaller an impact on the current account. Thus the shift of the US to a fiscal surplus during the 1990s did not prevent its current account deficit from growing. We suspect that, given normally low interest rates, a very large fiscal tightening would be needed in many countries to reduce the current account deficit to a supposedly safe level of about 5 percent of GDP. Such a tightening (of say 4 percentage points of GDP) might often not be politically feasible. This does not mean that we are not in favor of fiscal tightening, we are. But we wish to see it for its own sake, in order to free resources for private sector development, and not to achieve a doubtful improvement in the current account balance. In the meantime, current account improvement cannot wait.

Developments in Poland suggest that monetary policy *can* be used effectively to reduce the current account deficit. Very high real interest rates during 1999-2000 limited aggregate demand sufficiently to reduce the current account deficit to about 5 percent of GDP in 2001, in spite of a large nominal—and massive real—appreciation of the zloty against the euro during the period. However, the cost has been considerable, with annual real GDP growth slowing from over 6 percent in 1997 to about 1 percent in 2001.[4]

Thus, the traditional path to EU and EMU accession either exposes fast growing applicant countries to a high risk of currency crisis, or forces them to grow far more slowly than they could with unilateral euroization. Since real convergence is one of the purposes of EU accession for the TACs, the orthodox path is at variance with the ultimate goal, something which cannot be desirable. This is the crux of our argument.

4 Given the size of the real appreciation of the zloty, even this lower CA deficit may turn out not to be adequate protection against a currency crisis.

Optimum Currency Area Considerations

Asymmetric risks are a danger if a country and the monetary union it proposes joining do not constitute an optimum currency area (OCA). Our view is that many TACs satisfy the OCA conditions *to the same degree as present members of EMU*, or are very close to doing so. Since the TACs are committed by their acceptance of the *acquis communautaire* to joining the EMU at some stage, what is good enough for the EMU's current members should be good enough for the TACs. Even if some of the TACs satisfy OCA conditions a little less than current EMU members, this merely makes them slightly more vulnerable to idiosyncratic shocks than current EMU members. In making a choice on unilateral euroization, these slightly higher risks must be set against the very high above-mentioned costs of keeping one's national currency in the pre-accession period.

The main reason we think that many TACs are close to satisfying OCA requirements to a similar degree as current EMU members is their very high level of trade integration with EMU countries (see also Chapter 3). Trade with other members of a currency area as a share of GDP is a good indication of the extent to which idiosyncratic shocks to a country's economy are likely to be amortized by its trade with the rest of the currency area. Trade with other members of a currency area as a share of total trade is a good indication of the extent to which a country is exposed to movements in the exchange rate of the common currency against the currencies of 'third countries'. Thus Table 5.1 shows that in 1999:

1. *All of the TACs* traded a higher share of their GDP with EMU countries than did the weighted average of EMU members in the year preceding the launching of the euro.

2. *All of the TACs* traded a higher share of their GDP with EMU countries than six of the current 12 EMU members (including the four largest: Germany, France, Italy and Spain).

3. *All of the TACs* traded a higher share of their total trade with EMU countries than two EMU members, and *six* of the TACs traded a *higher* share of total trade with EMU than *all but two* current EMU members.

Thus, if these ratios were the only criteria for satisfying OCA requirements, we could conclude that many TACs satisfy them.

It is argued (e.g. Fidrmuc and Schardax, 2000) that a higher share of intra-industry trade within a currency area will lead to more synchronous business cycles, because industry specific supply or demand shocks are then more likely to be symmetric across countries. We therefore measure intra-industry trade with EMU/GDP for EMU members and applicant countries, and find that seven TACs have a share of intra-industry trade with EMU/GDP that is higher than that of three EMU members.

Table 5.1 Degree of TACs' trade integration with EMU compared to that of EMU countries

Country	EMU trade/GDP	Intra-industry EMU trade/GDP*	EMU trade/total trade
Belgium-Lux.	81.4	59	56.8
Hungary	*73.2*	*43*	*68.7*
Czech Republic	*65.1*	*43*	*61.7*
Estonia	*62.0*	*24*	*45.1*
Slovenia	*61.8*	*37*	*67.1*
Slovakia	*58.9*	*29*	*56.8*
Netherlands	48.8	38	47.9
Ireland	44.2	22	33.2
Bulgaria	*39.3*	*13*	*54.2*
Portugal	38.5	19	67.1
Austria	37.6	26	63.2
Romania	*34.7*	*10*	*66.4*
Latvia	*30.9*	*7*	*46.8*
Poland	*27.6*	*12*	*58.5*
Lithuania	*26.5*	*6*	*36.0*
Spain	25.5	17	58.3
France	21.7	18	51.9
Germany	20.8	17	43.8
Finland	20.7	10	34.0
Italy	19.5	12	49.3
Greece	17.4	5	53.4

* The shares of intra-industry (II) trade with EMU countries in GDP were estimated by taking the 1997 shares of II trade with the EU in Fidrmuc and Schardax (2000) and applying them to columns 2 and 4.

Source: Eurostat. Data is 1999 for accession countries and 1998 for EMU countries.

However, it needs to be remembered that inter-industry trade also contributes to the convergence of business cycles in a currency area. Although it need not protect a country from an asymmetry of industry-specific shocks with the rest of the area, inter-industry trade does reduce the asymmetry of aggregate shocks. Thus, an increase in aggregate demand in EMU (but not in a particular TAC) will increase the demand for the TAC's exports, whatever the nature of these, and an asymmetric increase in aggregate costs (for instance as a result of increased energy prices which affects the TACs more than EMU) will be partly cushioned by the smaller fall in EMU output and therefore demand.

Thus, it is hardly surprising that studies show that business cycles are more correlated between the advanced TACs and Germany than between important EMU members. Boone and Maurel (1999), using de-trended unemployment, show that between 55 percent (Poland) and 86 percent (Hungary) of the advanced TACs' cycles are explained by German cycles, whereas only 43 percent of Spanish and 18 percent of Italian cycles can be explained in this way. Fidrmuc and Schardax (2000) find that Poland's industrial production is as closely correlated with Germany's as is Austria's, and more so than those of Switzerland or Italy. Hungary's and Slovenia's industrial outputs are more closely correlated with Germany's than is that of Italy, although those of the Czech Republic and Slovakia are far less correlated (see also Chapter 3).

It should be repeated, however, that business cycle synchronicity is not in itself a requirement for a small country to join a much larger currency area. Thus, *ex ante,* if shocks are mainly demand-generated, a small country whose autonomous aggregate demand is negatively correlated with that of a large currency area may benefit from acceding to it. Downturns in domestic demand will be offset by increases in demand in the rest of the area, reducing overall output variability. Joining the currency area will increase trade within it, and may therefore increase the smoothing effect by more than the elimination of the exchange rate effect reduces it.[5] *Ex post* this would result in fluctuations becoming more correlated.

Inflation and Exchange Rate Misalignment after Currency Conversion

Wojcik (2000) worries about exchange rate misalignment as a result of inflationary inertia after the domestic currency is converted into euro. Our solution is a simple up front devaluation at the moment of euroization (Rostowski, 2001b). Wojcik claims this will make inflation 'harder to control'. This is clearly only the case if the 'pass-through' effects of a devaluation are large.[6] But if they are then devaluation will not affect the real exchange rate much, freedom to devalue is worth little, and one may as well euroize.

Furthermore, our recommendation is based on the existence of high rates of labor productivity growth in the TACs.[7] On the one hand this productivity growth generates the problem in the first place, because rapid expected GDP growth is what causes residents to wish to be net borrowers, and foreigners to be willing to be net lenders to (or investors in) the country. On the other hand, rapid labor productivity growth means that a mistake in initially setting the conversion rate for the domestic economy, such that a margin of output does become uncompetitive, is likely to be made up quickly.[8] Of course, this suggests that TACs with a long record of relatively slow labor productivity growth, such as the Czech Republic, may have less to gain and more to lose from unilateral euroization.

The argument made by some opponents of unilateral euroization, that the rate of labor productivity growth is irrelevant because trade unions will force real

5 The 'exchange rate smoothing effect' is due to the fall in the value of the currency of the country in which demand falls relative to that of the country in which demand rises.

6 There will, clearly, be some inflationary effect of the up-front devaluation, our point is that we do not expect it to be large.

7 In the absence of the very tight macroeconomic policies required to contain the current account deficit within safe limits.

8 We are grateful to Eduardo Borensztein for this point.

wages to rise by more than productivity gains so that unit labor costs increase whatever the rate of productivity growth, is not a convincing argument for exchange rate flexibility. Unions that are strong and clever enough to appropriate more than the full amount of labor productivity growth are likely to be strong and clever enough to enforce wage increases that will compensate their members for any real depreciation!

Finally, we see no reason why the credibility of the regime should be dramatically undermined, as suggested by Wojcik (2000), just because the euroization is *unilateral*. While we fully expect unilateral euroization to be somewhat less credible than full EMU membership, we expect it to be somewhat *more* credible than a currency board arrangement, such as exists in Estonia, Lithuania or Bulgaria. And currency boards have proved very credible, far more so than soft-pegs of the ERM variety. We expect unilateral euroization to be more credible than a traditional currency board in a *non-applicant* country for two reasons:

1. Although a domestic currency could in principle be re-created to enable depreciation, the technical preparations would be long and complicated and impossible to keep secret, giving speculators a large amount of warning. This would in itself reduce the benefits to a government contemplating such a move, and therefore speculators' expectations of such an event. In currency boards the domestic currency already exists, so all that needs to be changed are the constitutional provisions which set up the CB arrangement. Thus, with euroization the 'poison pill' defense against speculation is even stronger than in the (strong) case of a currency board.

2. unilateral euroization would be expected to last only a relatively short time (say five years) before the TAC concerned would join EMU as a fully-fledged member.[9] Also, it would be absurd for a country whose strategic goal is EU and EMU membership (within about 4 and 6 years respectively) to reintroduce a national currency.

Generally, the credibility of unilateral euroization would be reflected in the interest rates that would subsequently obtain. We return to this absolutely central matter in Section 5.6.

9 *This* factor does not make unilateral euroization more credible than a currency board in an advanced TAC expected to shortly join the EU and EMU.

Satisfying the Maastricht Inflation Criterion

There is considerable confusion regarding the implications of unilateral euroization for a TAC's ability to fulfill the Maastricht inflation criterion. Fast growing countries such as the TACs usually exhibit the Harrod-Balassa-Samuelson (H-B-S) effect, with the prices of non-tradables rising faster than the prices of tradables, and the rate of increase in the relative prices of non-tradables being faster than in slower growing countries.[10] If tradables' price inflation in a TAC were the same as in the EMU (as would be the case under unilateral euroization), then overall inflation would be higher—possibly sufficiently higher to make it impossible for TAC to fulfill the Maastricht inflation criterion. With a flexible exchange rate, inflation can be lowered to the required level by allowing the domestic currency to appreciate; at present, the so-called 'reference value' that defines this level is 1.5 percentage points above the average inflation rate in the three best performing EMU countries. This would put downward pressure on domestic tradable goods prices, as well as reducing domestic non-tradable goods inflation. Since this option would not be available under unilateral euroization or a currency board, their opponents claim that either of these systems would make satisfying the Maastricht inflation criterion and therefore joining the EMU impossible for many years (maybe for as long as two decades) (Gomulka, 2001).

We disagree strongly with this view. In the first place, all that will have to be done under unilateral euroization is to reduce domestic demand sufficiently for non-tradables' price inflation to fall sufficiently for average inflation to satisfy the present 'reference value' of the MIC. In the case of Poland, non-tradables for which prices are market determined account for about 30-40 percent of the CPI basket. Thus, if inflation in the three best performers in EMU were to be 1.5 percent (see fn.11), then the reference value would be 3 percent, and if tradables' and non-tradables' inflation were the same within the EMU, then the maximum level of non-tradables goods' inflation which would still allow Poland to satisfy the present reference value of the Maastricht inflation criterion would be 5.25-6.5 percent. This does not seem to be an unimaginably low level to achieve through a tightening of fiscal policy. Should traded goods' inflation in the EMU (and Poland) be lower than the 1.5 percent assumed above, then the allowable level of non-traded goods' inflation in Poland would be even higher.

As discussed, with a floating exchange rate a temporary tightening of monetary policy will result in nominal appreciation of the currency and downward pressure on both traded and non-traded goods' inflation. In the traded goods sector nominal price *reductions* may even be required.[11] Under unilateral euroization the

---

10 This is a result of faster growth of labor productivity in their tradables sector than in: (1) their non-tradables sector; and (2) the tradables sector of slow growing countries such as the EU.

11 Domestic prices would certainly need to rise less than in the three best performing EMU member states. Since the ECB average inflation target in the EMU is 2 percent, inflation in the 3 best performers is likely to average 1.5 percent. Even in the EMU, tradable goods inflation will, if anything, be lower than average inflation, leaving practically no room for

non-traded (services and construction) sector would bear more of the costs of the temporary reduction in inflation below trend required by the Maastricht inflation criterion. This could be achieved by a temporary 'social pact' restraining wages in the non-traded sector and limiting the growth of administratively set prices, or by a temporary tightening of fiscal policy, or by a combination of all three. A reduction of domestic aggregate demand would suspend the functioning of the H-B-S effect, which operates through employers in the traded goods sector, which has rapid labor productivity growth and which competes for employees in the non-traded sector. This pushes up wages, costs, and prices in the non-traded sector. It is important to stress that in both cases (a floating exchange rate and unilateral euroization) the contraction would be quite short-term (one to two years), since the reference value of the Maastricht inflation criterion only needs to be satisfied for one year. It therefore seems to us that this problem has been blown out of proportion.

Furthermore, we recommend that after accession to the EU, new members should argue for an adjustment of the Maastricht inflation criterion. The criterion itself merely requires 'lasting and sustainable convergence of inflation rates' as defined by the reference value. However, the reference value itself can be changed by the European Council;[12] the Maastricht treaty need not be amended. Since most new members will experience the H-B-S effect, and some will have currency boards, a strong lobby will exist for adjusting the Maastricht inflation criteria so that it applies only to tradable goods inflation. Such calls will be all the more persuasive since the Maastricht inflation criterion calls for 'sustainable convergence'. Yet because of the H-B-S effect, rapidly growing countries such as Ireland were only able to satisfy the Maastricht inflation criterion reference value for a short time before entry into EMU, after which they exceeded it by considerable margins.

Like fast-growing EMU members, countries that have unilaterally euroized can have inflation in excess of the present Maastricht inflation criterion reference value only as a result of the H-B-S effect, since the prices of their tradable goods will be the same as in the EMU.[13] Therefore, a country that has euroized, has its fiscal accounts in order, and is growing rapidly (showing that it remains competitive in its traded goods sector) can be said to have satisfied the spirit of the Maastricht inflation criterion, even if it cannot satisfy the present reference value. Thus, not only is there likely to be a significant lobby in favor of changing the Maastricht inflation criterion after 2004, but there are also strong

---

stable tradable goods prices. The key question is: how large a tradable goods recession would a country need in order to bring about a modest fall in domestic tradable goods prices under a flexible exchange rate? The answer might be: not a very large one. With rapid labor productivity growth, prices of tradables could fall while wages in the tradable goods sector continued to rise (but not quite as rapidly as might otherwise be the case).

12 Although only current EMU members would be able to vote on this change.

13 These countries could also have high demand driven inflation in the non-tradables sector if they had large increases in their budget deficits. But this would likely breach the Maastricht fiscal deficit criterion, which would prevent EMU entry.

objective reasons for doing so in the case of countries that will have unilaterally euroized or will have well-established currency boards.

Of course, unilateral euroization only makes sense for those TACs that are capable of maintaining basic fiscal discipline. This is (correctly!) a requirement for EMU membership. Unilateral euroization would reduce the costs of servicing public debt. It is our assumption that this relief would be used to reduce the fiscal deficit rather than to increase public expenditures if doing so would maintain fiscal deficits at unacceptably high levels. We see unilateral euroization as a better (less painful) route to EMU than the traditional one. We do not see it as way of avoiding the need for EMU membership with all its constraints. The current fiscal problems of the Czech Republic, Hungary and Poland cast doubt both on their ability to achieve EMU membership and to benefit from unilateral euroization. Unilateral euroization can help put a country's fiscal house in order, but it cannot, and should not, be a substitute for fiscal discipline or rapid EMU membership. We are constantly reminded by the opponents of euroization that it is not a panacea, and all we can do is humbly agree.

Will Interest Rates Fall under Unilateral Euroization?

One of the most striking points in Wojcik (2000) is the claim that unilateral euroization need reduce medium and long term interest rates, because the abolition of the domestic currency, although abolishing currency risk in lending by foreigners to domestic residents, may increase their default risk. This could happen because devaluation is no longer available as a tool to increase the competitiveness of domestic producers. Interest rates on loans to domestic businesses might therefore rise, as might rates on loans to the government (whose tax revenue depends on the profitability of domestic business). This argument is illustrated using the case of Argentina, where in the late 1990s real interest rates were similar to those of Poland, implying that Polish rates need not fall after euroization, since Argentina had a currency board (linked to the US dollar) with many similarities to unilateral euroization. But Wojcik does not explain just how exceptional the Argentine situation is. The country conducts only 16 percent of its trade (worth only 2.7 percent of its GDP) with the United States. In fact, Argentina is one of the countries in the world that *least* satisfies conventional OCA criteria for establishing a currency union with the United States.[14] It is this, together with fiscal irresponsibility, that exposed Argentina to the problems described.

However, we have seen (Section 5.3) that Poland and many other TACs satisfy the OCA requirements at least as well as half of the existing EMU members. Thus, the Argentine example, while polemically useful, is in practice irrelevant, unless one wishes to argue (as many US economists have done) that the present EU is itself far from being an optimum currency area. If one believes this, then TACs should perhaps *never* join the EMU, since they are unlikely to become

14 There are other, non-conventional, non-trade criteria, which Argentina may satisfy better, see Mundell (1973).

even more integrated in terms of trade than they are at present (except in the share of intra-industry trade to GDP). However, in that case, neither should they join the EU, since ultimate EMU membership is a *requirement* of EU membership.

Absence of a Lender of Last Resort under Unilateral Euroization

We have addressed this argument at length in Bratkowski and Rostowski (2000), where we made some of the following points. First, monetary expansion is of course inconsistent with any fixed exchange rate system (unless the expansion is very modest). Nevertheless, as Goodhart et al. (1998) point out, the lender of last resort (LOLR) function need not involve any monetary expansion. The central bank can lend to an affected bank, and at the same time undertake liquidity reducing open market operations, so that the money stock remains unchanged. Under euroization, although the central bank is unable to increase the money supply, the LOLR function can be performed by the government in guaranteeing loans to the stressed bank (as long as the government itself is solvent). The money supply would remain constant, but the distribution of liquidity would be changed in the direction desired by the authorities.

Second, in countries with currency board arrangements, the LOLR function is in any case very limited, and this will not change as a result of euroization.

Third, pure LOLR activity is aimed at preventing the illiquidity of *solvent* banks. In many TACs, foreign owned banks held over half of all bank assets in 1999 (EBRD 2000). The foreign owners should know the financial condition of these banks sufficiently well to provide them with liquidity when they are illiquid but solvent (see Chapter 3). For the remaining, domestically owned, banks we have suggested the creation of a 'banking sector liquidity fund' (BSLF), into which the international reserves of the national bank remaining after euroization would be placed. In the case of Poland, after allowing for a modest 10 percent up front devaluation of the zloty at the time of conversion, we have 'coverage' by the BSLF of 100 percent of sight deposits and 25 percent of total deposits (including the foreign currency deposits for which there is no LOLR or BSLF at present).[15] In countries with very high shares of foreign currency deposits (such as Croatia, where the share is about 90 percent), the LOLR function is already limited by the level of the central bank's international reserves and its ability to increase them by borrowing.

Finally, solvency (rather than liquidity) crises require recapitalization rather than LOLR support. They therefore depend on the *solvency* of the government of a country (as the 'borrower of last resort') rather than on the *liquidity* of the central bank. Most, though not all, TACs are borrowers in good standing.

15 The existence of a funded deposit insurance scheme further reduces the danger of illiquidity at solvent banks (whoever may own them), and reduced the likelihood of the need to recapitalize insolvent ones.

The Seigniorage Costs of Euroization

It is usual to calculate both the 'flow' and 'stock' seigniorage costs of adopting a foreign currency. The flow cost is the loss of revenue resulting from the fact that during the period of euroization (between the abolition of the domestic currency and entry into EMU as a fully-fledged member) the central bank of a euroized country will no longer receive interest on that part of its international reserves that have been exchanged for the domestic cash that has been withdrawn. This loss of seigniorage revenue definitely exists, and in most TACs it varies between 0.5 percent and 1 percent of GDP. These revenues are reduced when the central bank engages in sterilized interventions, however, as sterilization costs offset seigniorage revenues.

The stock seigniorage cost of adopting a foreign currency results from the need to exchange the existing stock of domestic currency notes and coins for foreign notes and coins. In the case of Poland, this would be about 6.5 percent of one year's GDP, a very large amount. However, this stock cost is not in fact borne in the case of euroization, where only the flow seigniorage cost is relevant. This is because upon joining EMU, a country's national central bank (NCB) will be obliged to transfer to the ECB all of the income from the assets that correspond to (or 'back') its monetary liabilities. This revenue from all the NCBs that are members of the European System of Central Banks (ESCB) will then be redistributed to NCBs (after deduction of ECB expenditures) on the basis of their share in ECB capital.[16] Each NCB's share of the ECB's capital depends in equal proportions on the population and GDP of its country, and is thus *completely independent of NCB monetary liabilities*. A TAC that had previously euroized unilaterally, and has bought in all of its monetary liabilities in exchange for euro notes and coins, will thus enter EMU *without any monetary liabilities*. As a result, it will not need to transfer *any* income to the ECB, but it will receive the same income from its share in ECB capital as it would have had it not euroized first.

This system for redistributing seigniorage revenue is equivalent to NCBs having to transfer to the ECB assets corresponding to their monetary base. Put even more simply, it is equivalent to the NCBs having to *buy* the euros used to replace their monetary base from the ECB.[17] A unilaterally euroizing country merely completes this transaction before joining EMU, rather than at the moment of joining. No stock seigniorage costs of euroization therefore exist for such countries.

---

16 After the expiry of a transitional period. This period is due to end before any TAC joins EMU, be it by the traditional route or after a period of unilateral euroization.

17 Since a monetary union occurs after this transaction, the base can be bought by the NCB from the ECB for any good quality assets including domestic ones. International reserves need not be used.

Conclusions

There will be no stock seigniorage costs for unilaterally euroizing applicant countries. The suggestion that short-term interest rates may not fall as a result of euroization is weakly grounded. The example of Argentina is not apposite, as on traditional criteria that country clearly does not form an optimal currency area with the US, to which its currency was 'hard-pegged'. According to traditional OCA criteria, most TACs do belong to an OCA with EMU countries to the same extent as a number of current EMU members. On some criteria they do so to a greater extent than the majority of current EMU members. The absence of an unlimited LOLR capability after euroization should not increase the risk to the banking system significantly in the majority of countries in which there is a large share of foreign ownership of banks, or in those in which there is a large share of foreign currency denominated deposits, or in countries that have currency board arrangements. For domestically owned banks with previously domestic currency denominated deposits, a banking sector liquidity fund may be established.

Any initial exchange rate misalignment at the time of conversion can and should be avoided by an 'up-front' devaluation and will in any case to be eroded over time if there is faster productivity growth in TACs than in the present euro zone. Monetary and fiscal policies *may* be effective as a means of limiting dangerously large current account deficits. But the question is rather whether it *will* be *reliably* effective. We believe that we have shown that one cannot count on that. As a result, without euroization TACs are at severe risk from 'capital inflow stops' and currency crises.

References

Boone, L. and M. Maurel (1999), '*An Optimal Currency Area Perspective of the EU Enlargement to the CEECs*', Discussion Paper 2118, Centre for Economic Policy Research, London.

Bratkowski, A. and J. Rostowski (1999), 'Zlikwidowac zlotego (Eliminate zloty)' *Rzeczpospolita* March 6-7.

Bratkowski, A. and J. Rostowski (2000), 'Unilateral Adoption of the Euro by EU Applicant Countries: The Macroeconomic Aspects', paper presented at the Sixth Dubrovnik Economic Conference on 'Exchange Rate and Financial Vulnerability in Emerging Markets', June 29-30.

Bratkowski, A. and J. Rostowski (2001), 'The EU Attitude to Unilateral Euroization: Misunderstandings, Real Concerns and ill-designed Admission Criteria' in *A Liberating Economic Journey: Post-communist Transition, Essays in Honour of Ljubo Sirc,* A. Brzeski and J. Winiecki (eds.), CRCE London, pp. 379.

Calvo, G. (1999), *On Dollarization* available online at: http://www.bsos.umd.edu/econ/ciecpn5.pdf

Ecofin (2000), European Council (2000), November 7, 'Conclusions of the Council on the Exchange Rate Strategy of Candidate Countries' available on http://ue.eu.int/newsroom.

EBRD (2000), *Transition Report* European Bank for Reconstruction and Development, London.

EBRD (2001), *Investment Profiles* European Bank for Reconstruction and Development, London.

European Commission (2000), 'Exchange Rate Strategies for EU Candidate Countries', *Note for the Economic and Financial Committee*, Directorate General, Economic and Financial Affairs, ECFIN/521/2000 – EN, 22 August, Brussels.

Fidrmuc, J. and F. Schardax (2000), 'More 'Pre-Ins' Ante Portas? Euro Area Enlargement, Optimum Currency Area, and Nominal Convergence', *Transition,* 2000:2, pp. 28-47, Austrian National Bank, Vienna.

Goodhart, C., P. Hartmann, D. Llewellyn, L. Rojas-Suarez and S. Weisbrod (1998), '*Financial Regulation: why, how and where now?*' Routledge and Bank of England, London.

Gomulka, S. (2001), 'Poland's Road to Euro: a review of options', paper presented to the Conference on Poland's Road to the Euro, National Bank of Poland, Warsaw, October 2001.

Mundell, R. (1973), 'Uncommon Arguments for Common Currencies' in *The Economics of Common Currencies,* H.G. Johnson and A.K. Swoboda (eds.), Allen and Unwin, pp.114-32.

Rostowski, J. (2001a), 'Do euro na skroty, przez *currency board* i dwu walutowosc (The Short Way to Euro: Through Currency Board and Bi-currency Arrangement)', *Polityka*, September.

Rostowski, J. (2002), 'The Eastern Enlargement of the EU and the Case for Unilateral Euroization' in *Financial Vulnerability and Exchange Rate Regimes. Emerging Markets Experience,* M. Blejer and M. Skreb (eds.), MIT Press, Cambridge, Mass.

Solbes, P. (2001), *Unia i Polska (The EU and Poland)*, No.18 (70), October 2001, Warsaw.

Wojcik, C. (2000), 'A Critical Review of Unilateral Euroization Proposals: the Case of Poland', *Transition,* 2000:2, pp. 48-76, Oesterrichisches Nazionalbank, Vienna.

Appendix: The Legal Aspects of Unilateral Euroization

In the European Commission's note (August 2000), it is claimed that the sequencing of steps in adopting the euro is set out in the Treaty of Amsterdam. This sequencing is therefore seen as part of the *acquis communautaire,* and must therefore be accepted by EU applicant countries as it stands. What is more, since unilateral euroization does not conform to this sequencing, unilateral euroization cannot be adopted by applicant countries. If this were indeed the case, then we would favor the adoption of currency boards by those countries for which we have recommended unilateral euroization. Currency boards are now accepted by the EU as a suitable path to EMU. The same arguments advanced for unilateral euroization hold for a currency board, only the benefits are slightly smaller. Interest rates are likely to be slightly higher under a currency board than under unilateral euroization, and speculation is more likely against a currency board since it is easier to abandon. However, less seigniorage is foregone with a currency board than with unilateral euroization.

Nevertheless, it is our view that on a close reading the Amsterdam Treaty does *not* set out a sequence of steps that have to be undertaken before a country adopts the euro, and that therefore such a sequence is not part of the *acquis.* Applicants could be admitted to the EU as Member States with a derogation regarding the EMU. This derogation is defined (art. 122(3) of the Treaty) as the country not being subject to articles 104(9) and (11), 105(1), (2), (3) and (5), 106, 110, and 112(2) b of the Treaty, as well as Chapter IX of the Statute of the European System of Central Banks (ESCB). These articles concern a country's membership of the ECB, the ESCB, its liability to sanctions should it break the fiscal deficit requirements of the Treaty, its right to vote in the European Council on exchange regime agreements between EMU and non-Community countries and on the EMU's exchange rate policy, as well as being subject to the *requirement* that *only* euro notes be legal tender on its territory.

None of these things will happen as a result of unilateral euroization. The candidate country will evidently not accede to EMU institutions, nor will it have the right to vote on EMU exchange rate policy. It will not be subject to sanctions for failure to abide by the fiscal deficit limits of the Treaty, nor will it be *required* to make euro notes the only legal tender on its territory. If it *decides* to make euro notes the only legal tender on its territory, this will be a free choice, not because of the requirement of the Treaty. An applicant that unilaterally euroizes therefore fully meets the Treaty's definition of a Member State with derogation from EMU. Thus, unilateral euroization does *not* fail to conform to the *acquis*.

From our point of view, the biggest problem is presented by art.123(5). This states that if it is decided to abrogate a member State's derogation from EMU (i.e., to admit it to EMU institutions on the basis of it having fulfilled the Maastricht convergence criteria set out in art. 121 (1)), then the Council shall in agreement with the Member State[18] concerned 'adopt the rate at which the euro shall be substituted for the currency of the Member State (…)'. Clearly if a national currency does not exist then 'the rate at which the euro shall be substituted' for it cannot be adopted, either by the Council or anyone else. However, the EU should accept that this paragraph applies only to those countries that actually have a national currency upon entering the EU, but that it does not apply to those that do not have such a currency. Indeed, if a country's *national* currency was already the euro, as would be the case after unilateral euroization, it would be strange (to say the least) to suggest that some rate other than 1:1 should be adopted. We believe that if the EU becomes convinced that unilateral euroization is in the interests of applicants and not against the interests of Member States, then such an interpretation of art. 123(5) will be adopted.

Art. 123(5) states that, at the abrogation of the derogation, apart from adopting the rate at which the euro shall be substituted for the national currency of the Member State concerned, the Council will also 'take the other measures necessary for the introduction of the euro as the single currency in the member State concerned.' We believe that this does not rule out unilateral euroization, because unilateral euroization means adopting the euro as a country's national currency. We only have the 'introduction of the euro as the *single currency* (our italics) in the Member State concerned' when that State comes to participate in the common institutions that determine the EMU's monetary and exchange rate

18 The Council acts with the unanimity of the member States, on a proposal of the Commission and after consulting the ECB.

policies. This of course will not happen upon unilateral euroization, but only once the derogation is abrogated.

Our interpretation of the Treaties is supported by the noticeably softer line on euroization that was taken by the Ecofin Council of Finance Ministers meeting on 7 November 2000, and which was subsequently confirmed by the Nice Summit of 16 December 2000. Unlike the Commission's note discussed above, Ecofin's Conclusions (Ecofin 2000) do not state that unilateral euroization is illegal for applicants, merely that it 'would run counter to the underlying economic reasoning of EMU in the Treaty.' After stating that 'participation in ERM2 before adoption of the euro[19] is a legal requirement', the Opinion continues: 'The only clear incompatibilities *vis-à-vis* the ERM2 that can be identified already at this stage are fully floating exchange rates, crawling pegs and pegs against anchors other than the euro.' *Finis*, with no mention of euroization.[20] The red herring of the supposed illegality of unilateral euroization seems to have finally been laid to rest by Pedro Solbes (the Commissioner responsible) himself, who in an interview on 13 September 2001 in Budapest stated: 'We never said that unilateral euroization is illegal' (Solbes, 2001).

19 i.e., before 'abrogation of the derogation' as defined above.

20 European Commission (2000) on the other hand went on at this point to say: 'Euroization is of course excluded by the Treaties.'

Chapter 6

Exchange Rate Regimes after Enlargement

Charles Wyplosz

Introduction

The process of acceding to the European Union (EU) is currently being masterminded by the European Commission.[1] This is a massive task that deals with a huge range of issues, from the essential to the mundane. It is also largely a mechanical task, since there is not much to be discussed: the accessing countries must take on board all the *acquis communautaires*, as was decided a decade ago in Copenhagen.

However, the case of exchange rate regime requires special treatment. The road map envisions a transition period that leads to membership in the EU's Economic and Monetary Union (EMU). This map was drawn up more than a decade ago, and was specifically designed to deal with the 'old' members of the EU. The Central and East European countries (CEECs) are very different in a number of respects, and the world has changed since the EMU was first devised. Logically, therefore, the road map ought to be adjusted. So far, however, the Commission has not shown much flexibility, and the incumbent countries display no interest in reopening a chapter that they themselves closed years ago.

In so doing, considerable risks are being imposed upon the accessing countries. Two logics clash: the legal logic, which calls for equal treatment, and the economic logic, which calls for taking important specific factors into account. This chapter reviews both logics and concludes that it would be a serious mistake to ignore, as is currently the case, the economic logic.[2]

---

1 In addition to Cyprus and Malta, negotiations are held with ten applicants from Eastern and Central Europe: Bulgaria, the Czech Republic, Estonia, Hungary, Latvia, Lithuania, Poland, Romania, Slovakia, and Slovenia.

2 This is a revised version of my remarks at the CASE conference 'Beyond Transition: Development Perspectives and Dilemmas', held on 12-13 April, 2002 in Falenty, Poland. This paper is partly based on the report Begg et al. (2002) prepared for the European Commission. I thank Jean-Joseph Boillot for help with data.

The Legal Logic

Upon joining the EU, the CEECs are expected to adopt the European Monetary System (EMS) II exchange rate mechanism, while they prepare themselves for joining the eurozone. Their admission, in turn, is subject to their fulfilling the convergence criteria laid down in the Maastricht treaty that created the EMU. If they pass this test, the CEECs can adopt the common currency as early as two years after entry.

Joining the exchange rate mechanism of the EMS has a number of preconditions. These include: declaring a fixed central parity vis-à-vis the euro, to be decided jointly with the current members of the EMS (the eurozone and Denmark); keeping exchange rates within a margin of ±15 percent around the declared parity; and intervening in the foreign exchange market should this fluctuation band come under threat.

Next, in order to gain EMU membership, the CEECs must satisfy the Maastricht treaty's five nominal convergence criteria: (1) the inflation rate should not exceed by more than 1.5 percentage point the average rate in the three lowest-inflation countries;[3] (2) long term interest rates should not exceed by more than 2 percentage points the average rate in the three lowest-inflation countries; (3) the exchange rate should not be devalued during the two years preceding EMU entry; (4) the budget deficit should not exceed 3 percent of GDP; and (5) the public debt should not exceed 60 percent of GDP.

Table 6.1 shows the extent to which the CEECs are in compliance with these various criteria. Since 2005 would be the earliest year in which these figures would have policy significance, these numbers should not be taken as indicating the actual judgment that will be made. It is clear that, with the exception of Bulgaria, the CEECs do not have a problem vis-à-vis the debt criterion and that, when they need to, they will probably be able to satisfy the budget deficit criterion as well. Inflation is likely to vary significantly, and the interest rate will follow, but most of the CEECs have achieved impressive victories over inflation. It would be surprising that this success will deteriorate when it matters, but there are reasons, detailed below, to be concerned about compliance with this criterion.

The Economic Logic

The design of the Maastricht convergence criteria reflected the fact that most European Union countries had achieved a high degree of real convergence, but exhibited, for a sustained period, serious nominal divergence. While the view that nominal convergence is a necessary condition for EMU membership was, and remains, controversial, the goal was both understandable and doable.

3 It is not clear that reference to the three lowest inflation rates makes sense once most countries belong to the eurozone. It would be helpful that this small technical point be clarified, for example, making only reference to the euro-wide HICP index.

Table 6.1 Compliance with the Maastricht criteria

Country	Inflation (2002)	Interest rate (2001)	Public deficit as % of GDP (2001)	Public debt as % of GDP (2001)
Bulgaria	4.0	4.7	0.7	76.9
Czech Republic	3.9	3.8	5.5	23.7
Estonia	3.8		-0.2	4.8
Hungary	5.7	9.8	-4.3	55.9
Latvia	2.5		1.6	16.0
Lithuania	3.0		3.3*	23.6*
Poland	5.0	14	3.5*	40.9*
Romania	28.0	35	3.8	22.8
Slovakia	5.0	5	4.7	32.4
Slovenia	6.0	6	2.3*	25.8*
Eurozone	*1.6*	*4.3*	*0.5*	*69.1*

* 2000. The interest rate is indicated as short term.

Source: Inflation: DREE, Ministry of Finance, Paris; Interest rates: UN ECE; Budget and debt: Enlargement paper No. 8, European Commission.

The CEECs have made some progress towards real convergence, but they remain far from that goal as Table 6.2 indicates. For most of them, it will take at least 20 years—and possibly much more—to approach the range of the current EMU members. Thus, unless the untold intention is that EMU membership will have to await both nominal and real convergence—which is impossible for reasons spelled out below—the CEECs are being asked to achieve nominal convergence without real convergence. This raises a number of difficulties, which challenge the legal logic.

In addition, the situation has changed within Europe. In particular, EMS II differs from its predecessor EMS I in a crucial respect. Under EMS I, all member currencies were bilaterally tied to each other, and the burden of intervention in support of each pair of currencies was fully shared. Under EMS II, each currency is tied to the euro, and the ECB makes no commitment to support the parities. The EMS has evolved from a jointly managed system into a hub-and-spoke system that relies on unilateral commitments from countries on the periphery. Each member country alone bears the burden of defending its parity. Since EMS membership with a stable parity is a necessary condition for EMU membership, the stakes are high.

Table 6.2 GDP per capita (PPP) as a percentage of European Union average

Country	1992	2000
Bulgaria	27.0	24.0
Czech Republic	58.1	58.7
Estonia	34.6	37.3
Hungary	46.1	52.0
Latvia	28.8	29.3
Lithuania	36.2	29.3
Poland	31.6	38.7
Romania	29.2	26.7
Slovakia	41.1	48.0
Slovenia	60.3	71.6
Average		38.7

Source: World Bank.

Nominal Convergence without Real Convergence

The fact that the CEECs are undergoing a process of catching-up with the EU carries two main implications: trend real appreciation and sizeable capital flows.

Trend Real Appreciation: the Balassa-Samuelson Effect

Price levels are lower in poorer than in richer countries. When a country catches up, its price level, expressed in foreign currency terms, rises. This process of real appreciation can be achieved through stable prices and nominal exchange rate appreciation, through a stable exchange rate and higher inflation, or through a combination of both. This effect, the Balassa-Samuelson effect, is well documented. Estimates for the CEECs (Halpern and Wyplosz, 2001) put this effect at some 2 percent per year.

This effect is part and parcel of productivity gains that result from real convergence and, as such, should be interpreted as a positive development. Yet, it creates difficulties for nominal convergence. If the exchange rate vis-à-vis the euro is kept roughly constant, inflation will be higher in the CEECs than in the euro zone. If the differential is indeed in the vicinity of 2 percent annually, the Maastricht treaty's inflation criterion will be violated. To achieve equal inflation, the CEECs would have to allow the nominal exchange rate to appreciate by about 2 percent annually. Since the fluctuation band is large, this seems the easy way out, especially if the transition period does not last more than a few, possibly two years. Two risks remain, though. First, the longer the transition period, the smaller the room for maneuver. Second, a continuous exchange rate appreciation is bound to be seen—incorrectly—as a loss of competitiveness and could generate political opposition. Again, the longer this process lasts, the less manageable it will be.

Capital Flows

Accession will be accompanied by two important macroeconomic changes. The *acquis* require that the accessing countries fully liberalize their current and capital accounts. This implies full capital mobility, which is known to be largely incompatible with fixed exchange rates. In addition, as a low-cost part of the common market, the CEECs are likely to attract strong capital inflows: direct investments as firms relocate and investors seek higher profits; and shorter-term flows attracted by potentially rapid gains, especially if the exchange rate is on a nominal appreciation trend. This is not only good news, but also a threat. Liberalizing countries, from Latin America to South East Asia, have observed this phenomenon before, and the lessons from their experience are not too encouraging.[4]

A first lesson is that powerful capital inflows are hard to manage. They exert strong upward pressure on the exchange rate that, if unchecked, soon knocks down competitiveness, which can undermine the very growth prospects that attracted the capital in the first place. If the central bank intervenes to prevent the exchange rate from appreciating, since only unsterilized interventions work, monetary policy soon becomes far too lax, and rising inflation wipes out competitiveness. Furthermore, as part of the intervention process, the central bank acquires low-yielding foreign assets while issuing high-yielding liabilities, which brings it close to insolvency—the so-called quasi-fiscal costs of intervention. Not only do public revenues significantly decline, but also the central bank becomes vulnerable to government pressure since the government effectively underwrites the bank's solvency.

A second lesson concerns the emergence of significant currency misalignments. Capital inflows are typically in foreign currencies (this would be euros flowing into the CEECs), largely intermediated through local financial institutions that grant loans in local currency. Entire banking and financial systems have been wiped out in so-called 'economic miracle countries' because of currency misalignments between assets and liabilities.

A third lesson is that capital can flow in fast, and out even faster. Capital flow reversals, as the phenomenon is called, have been the rule. It is easy to see why they occur and why their effects are destructive. The inflows produce overvaluation, rising inflation, and an increasingly weak central bank. International investors grow increasingly nervous and scramble for the exit as soon as a spark (which can be bad economic numbers, political difficulties or an external shock) is ignited. The currency misalignment then takes over and transforms a currency crisis into a banking and financial crisis, which can lead to an all-out economic crisis.

---

4 The classic references are Calvo, Leiderman and Reinhart (1996) and Hausmann and Rojas-Suarez (1996).

The CEECs are next in line for the highly disruptive capital inflows that EU accession may trigger. The wide EMS II band will soon appear to be dramatically narrow.

Possible Solutions

If we ignore, for the time being, the legal logic, what is the most desirable solution to these problems from an economic viewpoint? Five possibilities are explored.

Floating

Floating, with some management, is the best way to cope with the capital inflow problem. It allows the central bank to tread a fine line between overvaluation and inflation. It sends a powerful signal that currency misalignment is dangerous. It allows countries to deal with capital inflows and subsequent reversals. Floating also allows countries to deal with the Balassa-Samuelson effect. Over the medium term, the national authorities can aim at some nominal appreciation in order to try and achieve the required rate of inflation.

Managed floating, however, requires a skilled central bank and political authorities able to cope with possibly large exchange rate gyrations. It also requires exchange and financial markets deep and efficient enough to deal with a succession of shocks, and to price and allocate the attendant uncertainty.

EMU Membership

Joining EMU eliminates most of the consequences of the capital inflow problem. There can be no currency mismatch and there is no need for delicate and expensive foreign exchange market interventions. Local inflation can be high without affecting significantly the overall inflation rate. Because the CEECs are economically small, capital flows within the eurozone are unlikely to disturb the smooth functioning of the whole system.

Early EMU membership also lifts the constraint of satisfying the entry criteria. This eliminates the difficulties created by the Balassa-Samuelson effect and, of course, the risk of repeated postponements that may result from capital reversals and devaluations hurriedly arranged in the midst of a crisis. Early EMU membership will obviously not eliminate the effects of capital inflows; it will merely transfer the pressure elsewhere. This may mean unsustainable booms followed by rising inflation. Risk taking by banks and financial institutions may become excessive and result in failures. In the absence of currency misalignment, such failures are likely to be manageable. This has been the case, so far at least, in Ireland.

Euroization

Unilateral euroization (see Chapter 5) is nearly identical to eurozone membership, with a few differences. The benefits are the same, except for the fact that the governor of the national central bank does not sit on the governing council of the European Central Bank.

There are a few additional costs, however. To start with, countries that euroize unilaterally may be tempted to seek support from the eurozone in the event of serious tensions, e.g., in the banking system. Not only would this create serious difficulties but it could also set a precedent. Next, there is a serious financial cost. Upon joining EMU, a country swaps its currency for euros, which it therefore receives for free. In the case of euroization, the monetary authorities would first need to acquire the euros before distributing them to the population against its now-worthless currency. Table 6.3 shows the size of the monetary base that would have to be purchased at full cost. This amounts to about 10 percent of GDP, a considerable amount for each country, with a negligible gain for the incumbent eurozone members.

Table 6.3 Monetary base in 2000 (percent of GDP)

Bulgaria	Czech Republic	Estonia	Hungary	Latvia
5.6	25.1	15.7	11.9	13.1
Lithuania	Poland	Romania	Slovak Republic	Slovenia
8.7	7.1	9.6	12.8	5.3

Source: International Monetary Fund.

Finally, there is the question whether those countries interested in euroization should first reach an agreement with current EMU members. Since the incumbents have made it abundantly clear that they are strongly against early euroization, Rostowski (see Chapter 5) argues that interested countries should act unilaterally. This is an appealing idea, but one that faces a number of serious political hurdles. The first one is grounded in the legal logic: the incumbents see unilateral euroization as entering EMU through the back door while they themselves used the front door. The incumbents worry that, with unilateral euroization, the exchange rate would be decided unilaterally as well, which runs against the letter and the spirit of EMU. They also fear that new EU members that euroize unilaterally may be able to seek support in the event of serious tensions, e.g. in the banking sphere.

Currency Boards

Currency boards are often seen as nearly equivalent to euroization. The Argentine crisis of 2002 has shown that this is definitely not the case. A currency board is just an extreme form of a fixed exchange rate regime. It shares with standard regimes the risks of speculative attacks. Even though its defenses are sturdier, they are not infinitely sturdy. On the other hand, like any fixed exchange rate system, a currency board can be a good temporary arrangement. It requires an adequate exit strategy, and EMU membership provides just that. A currency board that ties the currency to the euro can be used to satisfy the convergence criteria and, once they are fulfilled, the exit strategy is simply to adopt the euro.

The main problem is that capital inflows will require the central bank to carry out unsterilized interventions with a potentially strong impact on inflation. Similarly, the Balassa-Samuelson effect will deliver higher inflation than in the eurozone. It would seem natural to reach an understanding that the inflation and interest rate criteria would be lifted for countries that adopt a currency board. Indeed, in such a system, the authorities have no control over inflation and the interest rate, and cannot be held responsible for the outcome.

EMS II (or currency boards) and Capital Controls

Fixed exchange rate regimes are known to be vulnerable to speculative attacks. These regimes also encourage financial intermediaries and firms to tolerate currency misalignments on their balance sheets. As a result such regimes are often subject to forced devaluations, however the consequences for balance sheets can be lethal. As the incumbent EMS countries discovered in 1992-1993, speculative attacks are considerably harder to manage when capital is fully mobile.

If the incumbent countries insist on EMS II, it would seem natural that they grant an exemption from the *acquis* requirement of full capital mobility until the CEECs join EMU. Well-designed capital controls do not offer firm protection against speculative attacks, but they may provide some precious breathing space. This can make all the difference between a managed EMS-style depreciation and an Asian-style currency collapse.

Waiting for Real Convergence?

Given the difficulties associated with nominal convergence in the absence of real convergence, postponing EMU membership might be reasonable. Since real convergence lies decades away, this would be a radical move. But postponing EMU entry could be highly unwise for two main economic reasons, not to mention the political backlash that it could easily trigger in the CEECs.

First, at the logical level, nominal convergence is a requirement with a limited rationale. It was devised in the specific circumstances of the late 1980s, chiefly to address German fears of rogue EMU membership. If anything, EMU membership will speed up real convergence: after all, EMU was invented to reap the full benefits of the common market.

Second, at the practical level, EMS II with capital mobility is not sustainable in the long run. It will collapse long before real convergence is achieved. In fact, should that path be adopted, the euro would soon start circulate in the CEECs as a parallel currency. Spontaneous euroization would also be encouraged by the monetary authorities rightfully fearful of an indefinite EMS II arrangement. In other words, postponement of EMU entry and indefinite EMS II membership is not an option.

Conclusions

So far, the issue of monetary and exchange rate policies to be adopted by the CEECs following their accession to the EU has been dealt with on the basis of legal agreements reached earlier, the *acquis* principle. While this principle is backed by strong legal logic, it clashes head on with economic logic. One lesson, often learned and soon forgotten, is that attempts to violate economic principles usually result in severe stress. The decision that, upon accession to the EU, the CEECs must both join EMS II and fully liberalize their capital accounts is likely to be a case in point.

It is true that, for the incumbent countries, the stakes seem low today. The arrangement they are imposing on the CEECs implies that all the costs and risks—defending the currency and facing the consequences of destabilizing capital flows—are borne by the accession countries. Since this is presented as leave-it-or-take-it issue, the CEECs are too eager to join the EU to take the risk of derailing the process for what seems today a remote threat. This is not just bad economics, it is myopic: serious economic and financial stress in the CEECs will reverberate throughout the EU, and no one will escape unhurt.

Many solutions are technically possible. Over the last years, the CEECs have adopted different exchange rate regimes and ought therefore to be treated differently. Some countries—Bulgaria, Estonia, and Lithuania—currently operate currency boards. For them, it makes no sense to give up the tight euro-peg to temporarily face the vagaries of a soft peg before finally adopting the euro. Immediate EMU membership, or even costly euroization, is the natural next step.[5] Other countries, like the Czech Republic, Hungary, Slovakia, and Poland, have finally exited their narrow-peg exchange rate regimes and currently operate managed floating exchange rate regimes. It would be dangerous for them to return, for a temporary period, to the fixed exchange rate regime from which they have successfully exited. They should be allowed to retain their current strategies, including inflation targeting. Yet other countries (Slovenia for example) operate a de facto narrow peg regime, often backed by capital controls. EMS II membership is feasible provided they are able to retain some restrictions on capital movements. They could as well wish to either soften the peg, in order to deal with the Balassa-Samuelson effect, or to harden it and join early, or euroize, in order to reduce financial instability.

References

Begg, D., B. Eichengreen, L. Halpern, J. von Hagen and Ch. Wyplosz (2002), 'Sustainable Regimes of Capital Movements in Accession Countries', CEPR.

Calvo, G., L. and C. Reinhart (1996), 'Inflows of Capital to Developing Countries in the 1990s', *Journal of Economic Perspectives* 10(2), Spring, pp. 123-39.

5 It would only be fair to find ways to alleviate the massive costs of unilateral euroization, even though most of these costs are now sunk due to the operation of the currency boards.

Halpern, L. and Ch. Wyplosz, (2001) 'Economic Transformation and Real Exchange Rates in the 2000s: The Balassa-Samuelson Connection', *Economic Survey of Europe* 1, pp. 227-39.

Hausmann, R. and L. Rojas-Suarez (eds.) (1996), *Volatile Capital Flows: Taming Their Impact on Latin America*, Inter-American Development Bank, Johns Hopkins University Press, Baltimore.

Chapter 7

Labor Market Flexibility in Central and East Europe

Jan Svejnar

Introduction

The fall of communism created expectations that the centrally planned economies would experience rapid economic growth and gradually catch up with middle-income developed countries as they moved to a market system. Yet, the relative performance of the transition economies since 1989 has fallen short of expectations for three principal reasons: advanced western economies did unusually well in the 1990s; the economic problems associated with the transition were underestimated; and policymakers made a number of errors. The question therefore arises as to what has worked and what could have been and still could be done better.

In this chapter[1] I provide an assessment of the extent to which labor market institutions and regulations in Central and East European (CEE) economies have contributed positively or negatively to economic performance since 1989. An understanding of the role played by the labor markets in the CEE countries, apart from being of interest *per se*, is important for at least four reasons. First, at a fundamental level an analysis of the functioning of nascent labor markets provides clues about the functioning of one of the basic pillars of a market system. The transition provides an interesting laboratory, with tremendous variation in key variables, as exemplified for instance by the rise of unemployment rates from zero to double digits in most CEE economies and the sizable declines in wages and employment in firms during the first years of the transition. Analyses of the labor market are hence able to capture the 'big bang' effect of introducing a market system. From the policy standpoint a particularly important issue is why the unemployment rate rose fast in the early 1990s in some but not all countries, and why it recently stabilized in the single digit range in some CEE countries (e.g., the Czech Republic, Estonia, Hungary, and Slovenia), but rose to the 15-20 percent range in others (e.g., Bulgaria, Poland and Slovakia). It is notable that the

1 The final version of this chapter greatly benefited from comments provided by participants of the CASE Conference 'Beyond Transition' in Falenty, Poland, 12-13 April 2002. I would also like to thank Cristina Negrut for her valuable assistance with preparing the tables and figures for this chapter. While writing this chapter, I was supported by the National Science Foundation Grant No. SES 0111783, ACE grant P98-1129-R and ACE grant P98-1008-R.

significant rise in unemployment in the CEE countries in the early 1990s occurred despite major declines in labor force participation, competitive devaluation of the currencies, reductions in formerly generous unemployment benefits, and the introduction of active labor market policies.

Second, there is an important political consideration since voters' response to high unemployment has been quite negative in all the CEE countries. The discontent reflects anxiety that reforms require economic sacrifices without ensuring adequate social security. A major policy question therefore arises as to how the transition economies can strike a balance between reducing further government intervention and completing the establishment of market incentives, while still providing an adequate social safety net that ensures public support for these policies.

Third, in the context of accession to the European Union, the policy debate has by and large moved from macro stabilization (which continues to be essential but requires standard policies) to microeconomic issues such as the rate of creation of new firms, corporate governance in existing firms, enforcement of market-friendly legal frameworks, enhancing the functioning of a flexible labor market, and attracting foreign direct investment. A significant emphasis has been placed on the link between unemployment and the wage and employment setting in the newly created firms, privatized versus state owned firms, and foreign owned firms. Labor market analyses may be particularly useful in providing policy guidance in this area.

Fourth, the economies of Central and East Europe were the first to launch the transition process and they differed from one another in their initial conditions, policies, and outcomes. The results of studies dealing with these economies therefore provide useful information for policy makers in economies that started transition later.[2]

The initial labor market conditions varied across the CEE countries. While it was functioning, the Soviet-type economic system was characterized by full employment of labor (zero open unemployment) and centrally set wages, prices and output targets for state-owned enterprises. Income distribution was maintained at relatively egalitarian levels, most people were required to work and enterprises were allocated funds to provide the needed jobs. Starting in the 1960s, however, many CEE countries experienced slowdowns in economic growth and, as a result of popular pressure, the system started undergoing reforms. Full employment at centrally set (and low) wages was maintained but in many countries the

2 Poland and Hungary for instance entered the transition with a significant private sector in agriculture and services and limited government control over enterprises. In contrast, the Czech and Slovak economies were highly centralized and almost completely state-owned. Yet, the Czech Republic and to a lesser extent Slovakia have carried out massive privatization of state property, while others, such as Bulgaria, Poland, and Romania, have been slower in privatizing their state sector. Some, such as the Czech Republic, have pushed through massive privatization, leaving the restructuring of firms for later. Others have stressed more the commercialization of existing state enterprises (e.g., Poland), reorientation of exports from east to west, attracting western capital (Hungary), and creating new firms.

requirement to work (e.g., for housewives) was not fully enforced. Rather than merely soliciting information and imposing targets, central planners increasingly engaged in bargaining with enterprise managers about plan targets, employment levels and financial allocations. Firms increasingly operated under soft budget constraints, being able to receive bailouts from the central authorities when producing losses. Moreover, firms could increasingly trade with one another outside of the scope of the central plan and in some countries, e.g., Poland and Hungary, workers and managers seized a significant degree of control over enterprises from the planners. By the time of the fall of the Berlin wall in 1989, the system was rapidly disintegrating in countries such as Poland and Hungary, but it still remained fairly intact in East Germany and Czechoslovakia.

The economic strategy during the transition consisted of what I have called Type I and Type II reforms (Svejnar, 2002). Type I reforms were launched rapidly in all the transition economies and they focused on the removal of the authoritarian state and introduction of basic policies aimed at softening up the impact of the transition. At the micro level, the goal of Type I reforms was to move towards the liberalization of prices, reduction of direct subsidies to trusts and state-owned enterprises, allowing trusts and firms to restructure or even break up, removing barriers to the creation of new firms and banks, carrying out small scale privatizations, and introducing a new social safety net. These reforms caused a sizable reallocation of labor away from the state-run firms, some of which went to the new private firms and some of which ended up in nonemployment.

Type II reforms have emphasized the creation of a reliable state apparatus that would provide a level playing field for the market economy and enhance its functioning. They have been more fundamental than Type I reforms and the extent of their implementation has varied across the transition economies. These reforms have involved the development of new laws, regulations and institutions that would ensure a successful market-oriented economy. They have included the in-depth development of labor market regulations and institutions related to industrial and labor relations, unemployment compensation and retirement systems, privatization of large and medium-sized enterprises; establishment and enforcement of a market-oriented legal system and accompanying institutions; further in-depth development of a viable commercial banking sector and the appropriate regulatory infrastructure, and assistance for the creation and growth of new firms.

The nature and extent of Type II reforms that have been carried out in different economies should, along with differences in initial conditions and exogenous shocks, provide the possibility to explain differences in economic performance across the transition countries. Note that four leading transition economies shown in Figure 7.1—Poland, Slovenia, Hungary, and Slovakia—have pursued a relatively complete set of reforms, including maintaining relatively clear property rights and corporate governance. The Czech Republic belongs to the leading group but it underestimated the importance of the latter two sets of reforms and was the only economy in Central Europe to suffer a recession in the second half of the 1990s. Reforms in other countries have been more limited.[3]

In the next section, I discuss the principal differences in the institutional and regulatory framework in the transitional labor markets and examine the extent to which they explain relative economic performance of the CEE countries.

Institutions and Regulation in the Transition Labor Markets

The transition countries have differed considerably in the nature and speed of the development of labor and social regulations and institutions and the differences have been substantial even within clusters such the CEE countries.

Employment Protection

Building on their existing legislation and using the assistance provided by the International Labor Office (ILO) and the European Union (EU), the transition economies established various forms of employment protection legislation in the 1990s. By the end of the 1990s, the CEE candidates for admission to the EU had developed a set of labor market institutions and regulations that broadly resemble those found in EU countries (Riboud, Sanchez-Paramo and Silva-Jauregui, 2001). The CEE countries in fact fall in the middle of the EU-based flexibility index used by Riboud, et al. (2001)—the index takes on values of 1 to 6, with higher values corresponding to stricter employment protection legislation. They have therefore adopted employment protection legislation that is less flexible than those found for instance in the United Kingdom and Ireland, but more flexible than those found in the southern EU countries.

As in the EU, however, there are important differences across the CEE countries in terms of the exact nature and extent of employment protection. Riboud, et al. (2001) show that in the late 1990s rules for hiring and firing of permanent workers (including notification requirements and severance payments) as well as rules related to collective dismissals were more flexible in Hungary and Poland than in the Czech Republic, Estonia, Slovakia and Slovenia. Legislation related to temporary employment was in turn much more flexible in the Czech Republic and Hungary than in Estonia, Poland, Slovakia and Slovenia. Overall, among 26 OECD and CEE countries classified by Riboud, et al. (2001), the leading six EU candidate countries in CEE hold the following ranks and value of the

---

3 For example, Hungary and to a lesser extent Slovakia privatized most state-owned enterprises in a way that assigned clear property rights. Poland and Slovenia proceeded slower, but both countries exposed state-owned enterprises to competition and a risk of financial failure. In all four economies there was also substantial creation of new private firms that contributed to growth. The Czech Republic is notable because it was similar to the four leading economies but it neglected to establish a functioning legal framework and corporate governance. The privatization experience of the Czech Republic, Russia, and Ukraine suggests that mass privatization in the absence of a functioning legal system has negative effects on performance.

employment protection index, respectively: Hungary (9; 1.7), Poland (10; 2.0), Czech Republic (11; 2.1), Slovakia (16; 2.4), Estonia (18; 2.6), and Slovenia (25; 3.5).

In terms of analytical and policy implications, if employment flexibility matters for a country's economic performance, we should observe better economic performance, *ceteris paribus*, in Hungary, Poland and Czech Republic than in Slovakia, Estonia and especially Slovenia. Yet, as may be seen from Figure 7.1, the labor market flexibility ranking of countries does not coincide with their ranking in terms of GDP growth during the 1990s, with Slovenia being the second fastest growing economy and the Czech Republic the slowest one. Factors other than labor market flexibility obviously affect GDP growth, but the lack of a tight relationship with labor market flexibility is notable.

Passive Labor Market Policies for the Unemployed

Already by the end of 1991, all the CEE countries had developed relatively well-functioning unemployment compensation and social security benefit schemes (principal pillars of their passive labor market policies). As they struggled to strike a balance between providing an adequate social safety net and reducing government intervention while controlling budget deficits, CEE governments gradually reduced the level of unemployment protection (Ham, Svejnar and Terrell, 1998). In particular, already by 1992-93 all the CEE countries required an individual to have a minimum period of previous employment in order to be eligible to collect unemployment compensation. Moreover, in all of the CEE countries, except Albania, the level of unemployment benefits was based on fixed replacement rates of previous wages and, except for Bulgaria and Poland; these replacement rates fell over the entitlement period. All the CEE countries, except Poland, also imposed a low maximum level of benefits (between 1.4 and 2.0 times the minimum wage). Finally, there was no indexation of benefits for inflation in any of the CEEs.

As was the case with employment protection, by the late 1990s the nature of passive and active labor market policies of the EU candidates started resembling policies pursued in the EU and diversity occurred across countries. Riboud, et al. (2001) show that the replacement ratio (the ratio of unemployment benefits to previous wage) is very low in Estonia (about 10 percent), relatively low in Poland (40 percent) and somewhat low in the Czech Republic (50 percent). In Hungary (64 percent), Slovakia (60 percent) and Slovenia (63 percent) the replacement ratio resembles the EU average of 60 percent. The duration of unemployment benefits is only 3-6 months in Estonia and 6 months in the Czech Republic. It rises to 6-12 months in Slovakia, 12 months in Hungary, 2-24 months in Slovenia, and a full 12-24 months in Poland. These figures compare to 6 months in the United States, 12 months in the UK, 24 months in Spain and no limit in Belgium. The coverage rate (the percentage of unemployed receiving unemployment benefits), which proxies for eligibility, also shows striking differences across countries, with the rate having been stable in the 1990s at about 40-50 percent in the Czech Republic and Estonia, and at 70-75 percent in Hungary. In contrast, the coverage rate fell continuously in the 1990s from 80 to 20 percent in Poland and Slovakia, and from 40 to 30 percent in Slovenia. Except for Poland, the CEE countries spend a much smaller share of GDP on unemployment compensation (passive policies) than the EU and OECD average, and all, including Poland, spend much less than the EU and OECD average in terms of GDP share per unemployed person.

Hence, if the generosity of unemployment benefits has a negative effect on a country's economic performance by reducing worker incentives to find and keep jobs, the countries that should have performed relatively well, *ceteris paribus*, are Estonia, the Czech Republic, and Slovakia, while performance should have been hindered in Hungary, Poland and Slovenia. However, as was the case with employment protection policies, the observed GDP growth outcomes in the 1990s (Figure 7.1) do not correspond to this ranking, thus suggesting that other more important factors have been at play as determinants of GDP growth.

Active Labor Market Policies

These policies cover many activities, including job search assistance, training of the unemployed and direct job creation. The overall spending as a percentage of GDP by the CEE countries on these policies is below that of the EU countries and is hence closer to that of the US. Within the CEE candidates for EU admission, Riboud, et al. (2001) find that both the share of GDP spent on active policies and share of GDP spent on active policies per unemployed person are very low in Estonia and the Czech Republic, while they are relatively high in Slovenia and to a lesser extent in Slovakia, Hungary and Poland. In examining these findings in relationship to Figure 7.1, it is clear that the relative economic performance of the CEE countries in terms of GDP growth since 1989 has been better in countries with higher expenditures on active labor market policies. This finding is interesting and goes in the right direction: countries that spend more on providing skills, jobs and matching of workers and jobs grow faster. The problem is that micro studies in transition economies have had a hard time identifying a positive effect of active labor market policies (Munich, Svejnar and Terrell, 1998). The question for future analytical research is therefore whether the benefits of active labor market policies exceed their costs and whether the net benefits are sizable enough to make a substantial difference in terms of GDP growth.

Trade Unions

While trade unions in the former Soviet bloc countries have changed from institutions of Communist party control and distributors of fringe benefits to becoming representatives of workers' economic interests, their power, especially in the private sector, appears not to be substantial. Riboud, et al. (2001) calculate union density to be about 60 percent in Hungary, Slovenia and Slovakia, and much lower in the Czech Republic (43 percent), Estonia (36 percent) and Poland (34 percent). This yields CEE average union density of 49 percent, which is somewhat higher than the EU average of 44 percent and the OECD average of 40 percent. Union coverage (the ability to extend union contracts to non-union workers) is low in the Czech Republic and Estonia, but it is higher in the other four EU candidate countries. In the multi-union context of the CEE countries, coordination among various trade unions is low in all the CEE countries, except for Slovenia. Overall, the values of the three measures of trade union power—density, coverage, and coordination—do not appear to be good predictors of the relative GDP growth of the CEE countries since 1989.

Payroll Taxes

The need to control budget deficits during the 1990s led most transition economies to impose relatively high payroll taxes. By the late 1990s, payroll taxes ranged from 33 percent in Estonia to 38 percent in Slovenia, 44 percent in Hungary, 47.5 percent in the Czech Republic, 48 percent in Poland, and 50 percent in Slovakia. These tax rates are well in excess of the EU average rate of 24 percent. While wages in the CEE countries were initially so low that the payroll tax rates often did not represent a major burden, the situation changed as real wages grew in the mid- and late 1990s. The fact that the two countries with the highest payroll tax rates (Poland and Slovakia) also have the highest unemployment rates points to a possible link between labor cost and (un)employment, a topic that I take up in the next section. However, as with the other measures of relative labor market regulations or institutional rigidities, the relative rate of economic growth of the CEE countries during the 1990s is not related in a simple way to the payroll tax burden.

In concluding this section, let me point out that in Russia and the other countries of the Commonwealth of Independent States, labor market regulations and institutional developments have been weaker than in CEE countries. Moreover, the official unemployment benefits were lower to start with and decreased dramatically in real terms over time—and some were not paid at all. The relatively poor economic performance of the transition economies further east (see Figure 7.1) has thus occurred with less rather than more labor market regulation and institutionalization.

Empirical Evidence

In this section, I provide a selective review of the conclusions that may be drawn from analytical studies of transitional labor markets. This evidence is a useful complement of the review of institutional and regulatory developments in the preceding section. For more in-depth reviews of analytical studies of the transitional labor markets, the reader is referred to Svejnar (1999) and Boeri and Terrell (2002).

Employment Adjustment and Wage Setting at the Firm Level

In most transition economies, employment declined by 15-30 percent in the 1990s. A continuous decline was observed in Russia, Slovakia, and Romania; an L-shape pattern was detected in Bulgaria, Hungary and Slovenia; a U-shape pattern appeared in Poland; and a sideways S-shape pattern in the Czech Republic. When combined with the GDP data in Figure 7.1, the employment data suggest that restructuring in the transition economies involved an initial decline in labor productivity as output fell faster than employment and a subsequent rise in productivity as output and employment stopped declining. But a note of caution is in order here. With production shifting from large to small firms, the decline in employment (and output) may be less pronounced than suggested by the official data, since small firms are harder to capture in official statistics.

State-owned enterprises in all the transition economies rapidly decreased employment and/or real wages in the early 1990s. In Central Europe, the greatest initial reduction in industrial employment occurred in Hungary (over 20 percent), followed by Slovakia (over 13 percent), Poland (over 10 percent), and the Czech Republic (9 percent). The downward adjustment in industrial wages in the early 1990s proceeded in reverse order and amounted to 24 percent in the Czech Republic, 21 percent in Slovakia and 1 percent in Poland. Hungarian real wages in industry actually rose by 17 percent (Basu, Estrin and Svejnar, 2000). In Russia and the rest of CIS, the transition brought a mixture of wage and employment adjustment (Desai and Idson, 2000) and the wage decline was more pronounced than in Central and Eastern Europe (Boeri and Terrell, 2002). While real wages in Central and East Europe have increased considerably after their initial decline, in Russia and a number of other CIS countries real wages declined until 1993 and stagnated or increased only moderately in the mid-to-late 1990s (Svejnar, 1999; EBRD, 2000). The trajectory of real incomes has thus been very different in the more and less advanced transition economies.

Basu, Estrin and Svejnar (1997, 2000) estimate that labor demand elasticities with respect to output and wages were significant in the more marketized pre-transition economies (Hungary and Poland) and that they rose rapidly in all of Central Europe as the transition was launched. The sharp decline in output at the start of the transition was hence reflected in the labor market, but depending on the institutional setting in a given country, it was absorbed more by employment or wage decreases. The empirical evidence on labor demand hence indicates that the labor markets were quite flexible from early on, but that the flexibility has different manifestations in different countries.

The empirical studies also indicate that, except for Poland, wages were set relatively independently of firms' performance under communism. During the transition, wages started to vary systematically with revenues per worker, suggesting that rent sharing has become a phenomenon in the CEE economies[4] Interestingly, evidence from Bulgaria suggests that the compensation of chief executives in not fully state-owned firms is positively related to labor productivity (Jones and Kato, 1997).

Firm ownership and legal form (type of registration and hence corporate governance) are not found to have a simple and uniform effect on employment or wages. In large samples covering the early transition period no uniform

4 This relationship is not found in some studies, however, when total revenue rather than revenue per worker is used as an explanatory variable.

employment effects appear, while in the smaller samples that extend further into the transition period, one finds some evidence that privatized firms may at first reduce employment and then increase it faster over time. Finally, foreign ownership appears to be increasing employment (and output). There is also some evidence that private firms tend to pay higher wages than other firms, but the evidence is not robust and relates only to some countries. Finally, unlike with data on individuals, within firm-level studies there is little evidence that wages are negatively related to local unemployment (wage curve effect).

Unemployment

As may be seen from Table 7.1, within two years after the start of the transition, unemployment rates rose from zero into double digits in most economies of Central and East Europe. For example, by 1993 the unemployment rate reached 16 percent in Bulgaria and Poland, 12 percent in Hungary and Slovakia, 10 percent in Romania, 9 percent in Slovenia, but only 3.5 percent in the Czech Republic. The high unemployment rates reflected high rates of inflow into unemployment as firms laid off workers, and relatively low outflow rates as the unemployed found it hard to find new jobs. The Czech labor market was an ideal model of a transition labor market, characterized by high inflows as well as outflows, with unemployment representing a transitory state between old and new jobs (Ham, Svejnar and Terrell, 1998, 1999; Svejnar, 1999; and Boeri, 2000). Unemployment rose more slowly in the Commonwealth of Independent States and the Baltic countries, as firms were slower to lay off workers and used wage declines and arrears as devices to hold on to workers (Boeri, 2000; Boeri and Terrell, 2002).

Over time, unemployment patterns have shown considerable differentiation. The Czech Republic was the only Central European country to enter recession in the second half of the 1990s and its unemployment rate correspondingly rose to 8 percent. The fast-growing economies of Poland, Hungary, Slovenia, and to a lesser extent Slovakia managed to reduce their high unemployment rates in the late 1990s. Conversely, the Commonwealth of Independent States and the Baltic countries experienced gradual increases in unemployment as their transition proceeded. A turning point occurred by 1999-2000 as the unemployment rate rose again in Bulgaria, the Czech Republic, Poland, Slovakia and Slovenia. It stabilized in countries such as Hungary, Romania and Russia. As may be seen from Table 7.1, with the exception of Hungary, Slovenia and Romania, transition economies have recently had unemployment rates that are at least as high, and often significantly exceed, those observed in the European Union.

In view of the high unemployment rates in all the CEE economies in the early to mid-1990s except for the Czech Republic, studies of unemployment in these countries have focused on the determinants of outflow from unemployment into employment and on the efficiency of matching the unemployed with vacancies. A particularly intriguing issue has been the difference in unemployment between the Czech Republic and the counterpart republic of Slovakia (and by implication the other CEE economies). Ham, et al.'s (1998, 1999) estimates of hazard models suggest that about one-third of the difference between the Czech and Slovak expected unemployment durations is brought about by differences in observable demand conditions, while the remaining two-thirds is brought about by different coefficient of the estimated hazards (proxying for different behavior of individuals, firms and labor market institutions). The second principal finding of the hazard estimates from several countries is that the generosity of the unemployment compensation scheme has only a moderate negative effect on efficiency in terms of lengthening an unemployment spell. Finally, the estimated coefficients on the demographic and demand variables indicate that minorities (e.g., Roma in the Czech and Slovak Republics or non-Slovenians in Slovenia), handicapped, the least educated, and often also the single and the old unemployed workers have a harder time obtaining jobs. The estimated effects of gender and marital status vary across countries and specifications. A number of studies find that the probability of moving from unemployment to employment is negatively related to local unemployment rate.

The results of the matching function studies indicate that great care must be taken in collecting, aggregating and adjusting the data, specifying the functional form and selecting the estimating procedure. In particular, there is some evidence that the usual assumptions of a Cobb-Douglas form and constant returns to scale may be rejected when these factors are carefully taken into account. The exceptionally low unemployment rate in the Czech Republic as compared to Slovakia and the other Central and East European economies appears to have been brought about principally by (1) rapid increases in vacancies along with unemployment in the Czech Republic, resulting in a balanced unemployment-vacancy situation at the aggregate as well as district level; (2) a major part played by vacancies and the newly unemployed in the outflow from unemployment; (3) a matching process with strongly increasing returns to scale throughout (rather than only in parts of) the transition period; and (4) an ability to keep long-term unemployment at relatively low levels. The matching function studies hence provide complementary evidence to the hazard estimates in that they identify local demand factors (vacancies) and the efficient behavior of agents and institutions (high returns to scale in matching) as being key to the low unemployment rates in the Czech Republic. Some, but not all, of the studies point to the importance of active labor market policies in increasing the efficiency of matching.

Job Destruction, Job Creation and Labor Mobility

The reduction in employment in the old state-owned firms, growth in unemployment, and establishment of new firms have brought about considerable destruction and creation of jobs, as well as mobility of labor. Contrary to the main models of the transition process, Jurajda and Terrell (2001) show that job creation in new firms is not necessarily tightly linked to job destruction in the old firms since many new jobs have been created even in economies (such as the Czech Republic) that experienced low rates of job destruction. They also show that in both the Czech Republic and Estonia more than half the labor force moved from old to newly created firms within a short period of 4-5 years. Sabirianova (2000) provides a related structural insight, that much of the labor mobility consisted of occupational rather than geographic change, with individuals moving from one occupation to another within regions, as jobs in old occupations were destroyed and opportunities in new occupations were created. Compared to the U.S. labor market, where individuals move more geographically than occupationally, the transition is a special phenomenon in that it has led to more occupational than geographic mobility.

Provision of Fringe Benefits

While data limitations prevent one from drawing strong conclusions about the provision of fringe benefits by firms in CEE countries, the Polish and Czech evidence suggests that benefits are more prevalent in state-owned and privatized firms than in newly established private firms. Moreover, the evidence from the Czech Republic and Romania suggests that firms that have restructured may be exploiting the incentive aspects of fringe benefits.

Returns to Human Capital

With the exception of East Germany and to some extent possibly men in Bulgaria, various studies indicate that returns to education increased during the transition. This suggests that education acquired under communism has a higher payoff during the transition but that a rapid introduction of a market economy and western wage scales, as happened in East Germany with the unification, may result in a decrease in the payoff to this human capital. The studies also indicate that women enjoyed a higher rate of return on education than men under communism and that the gap narrowed as the transition started. In several countries, there is evidence that return to experience obtained under communism fell during the transition.

Income Distribution

The communist countries had highly egalitarian income distributions. In central and east Europe, the Gini coefficients ranged from 20 in Czechoslovakia and Slovenia to 25 in Poland in the late 1980s. The 1988 Ukrainian Gini coefficient of 23 (based on survey data) and the 1991 Russian coefficient of 26 based on the registry wage data of the Russian Statistical Office (Goskomstat) suggest that income distribution was relatively egalitarian in the former Soviet Union as well. However, inequality increased during the 1990s, with the Gini coefficient reaching 26-34 in central and east Europe, 30 in Ukraine and 40 in Russia. These coefficients bring inequality in the transition economies into the range of capitalist economies from the relatively egalitarian Sweden to the relatively inegalitarian United States, and in line with developing countries such as India.

While the central and east European data seem to reflect reality, the Russian and Ukrainian data may well understate the extent of inequality. In particular, the Goskomstat data are based on wages that firms are supposed to be paying to workers, but many Russian firms have not been paying contractual wages (Desai and Idson, 2000). Inequality measures based on survey data from the Russian and Ukrainian longitudinal monitoring of households suggest that income inequality in Russia and Ukraine has reached much higher levels, corresponding to Gini coefficients of 47-50. This resembles the level of inequality found in developing economies with relatively inegalitarian distributions of income. The egalitarian structure of income distribution in central and eastern European countries has been brought about by their social safety nets, which rolled back inequality that would have been brought about by market forces alone (Garner and Terrell, 1998). Conversely, the Russian social safety net has been regressive: it has made the distribution of income more unequal than would otherwise have been the case (Commander, Tolstopiatenko and Yemtsov, 1999).

Overall, the income distribution data indicate that the regulatory and institutional frameworks of the transition economies have been flexible enough to give rise to wider income differentials. In Central and East Europe, the governments used social transfers to cushion the impact of market forces and reduce extreme inequalities in income and consumption.

Conclusions

Since 1989, most transition economies have experienced a period of sharp economic decline followed by slower than expected economic growth, a rise of the unemployment rate from zero to double digits, and the appearance of significant long-term unemployment. These developments have naturally raised concerns that insufficient labor market flexibility may be an important cause of these economic problems. My conclusion, based on the evidence reviewed in this paper, is that labor market flexibility is an issue, but it is not a major factor in comparison to imperfections and regulations in other areas (not explored in this paper) such as housing markets, transport infrastructure, capital markets, corporate governance, legal frameworks, and business environments.

At some level of abstraction, high unemployment rate is obviously a manifestation of labor market imperfections. For example, in a simple spot labor market there should be a low enough wage at which the market clears and observed unemployment is frictional. Bulgaria, Poland and Slovakia, with 2001 unemployment rates of 15-20 percent, are obviously above the frictional level of unemployment, as are arguably most other transition economies. However, the spot market model, while useful as a yardstick, misses important real-world phenomena even when minimum wages are very low. From a policy standpoint, it is therefore useful to ask whether labor markets in transition economies perform worse than those in well functioning market economies.

My assessment is that transition labor markets have been as flexible and functional as labor markets in wealthier market economies, and that the observed differences across transitional labor markets do not account for cross-country differences in economic performance. My conclusion is based on the following points.

First, the extent and effects of employment protection, labor market policies and unionization in the transition economies are similar to OECD and EU averages, and in some respects they resemble OECD economies with the most flexible labor markets.

Second, the transition economies with the least regulated and institutionally least rigid labor markets have not been uniformly the fastest growing economies, and vice versa.

Third, estimated labor demand elasticities quickly rose to western levels, indicating that firms started adjusting employment to output demand and wage shocks.

Fourth, substantial labor mobility took place from the old to the new firms, with some countries transferring over one-half of the labor force within four to five years.

Fifth, labor mobility appears to have been rational in that it has involved both quits and layoffs, with the resulting wage gains being higher on average for the quitters than the displaced workers. Workers have reacted to labor demand shocks by traditional as well as less-traditional (in the western context) responses, including massive occupational mobility.

Sixth, the return to education and other forms of human capital have risen substantially and wages have begun to play an equilibrating role.

From the policy standpoint, there are several important findings. First, the generosity of unemployment benefits has been found to have only modest negative effect on efficiency in terms of extending unemployment spells. This provides policy makers with latitude in setting the parameters of the compensation system so as to ensure popular support for the completion of the transition process. Second, economies with high unemployment rates tend to have fewer vacancies and estimated parameters that show less efficiency in matching the unemployed with vacancies and a lower probability (hazard) of the unemployed leaving unemployment for employment. The lack of vacancies points to low demand as a cause of unemployment, while the matching and hazard estimates suggest that these economies suffer from structural issues such as skill mismatch, inferior functioning of labor market institutions and active labor market policies, and less flexible behavior of employers and workers. Third, there are indications of rent sharing by workers, which may signal the presence of insider-outsider problems.

The above findings suggest that the principal reasons for the rapid but uneven rise in unemployment and the share of long-term unemployed in transition economies in the 1990s were (a) the enormous extent of transition-related restructuring, with labor demand falling dramatically in existing firms, (b) a major skill mismatch that took varying periods of time to alleviate, and (c) varying degrees of imperfections and regulations in other areas such as the housing markets, transport infrastructure, capital markets, corporate governance, legal frameworks, and the business environment.

The outstanding issue, however, is why there has been a significant resurgence of unemployment in some of the growing economies (Bulgaria, Poland, and Slovakia) but not in others in the late 1990s and early 2000s. These are presumably not brought about by sudden bouts of transition-related restructuring, skill mismatch and newly created imperfections outside of the labor market. Demographic forces (especially a recent baby boom-let) account for some of these developments, but further research is needed to clarify this issue.

References

Boeri, T. (2000), *Structural Change, Welfare Systems and Labor Allocation,* Oxford University Press, Oxford.

Boeri, T. and K. Terrell (2000), 'Institutional Determinants of Labor Reallocation in Transition', *Journal of Economic Perspectives*, Vol. 16, No. 2.

Commander, S., A. Tolstopiatenko and R. Yemtsov: (1999), 'Channels of redistribution: Inequality and poverty in the Russian transition', *Economics of Transition*, Vol. 7 (1), pp. 411-465.

Desai, P. and T. Idson (2000), '*Work without Wages: Russia's Nonpayment Crisis*', MIT Press, Cambridge, MA.

EBRD (1996 – 2001), *Transition Report*, London: European Bank for Reconstruction and Development.

Estrin, S., J. Svejnar and B. Swati (1997), 'Employment and wage behaviour of industrial enterprises in transition economies: The cases of Poland and Czechoslovakia', *Economics of Transition*, Vol. 5 (2), pp. 271-187.

Estrin, S., J. Svejnar and B. Swati (2000), 'Employment and Wages in Enterprises under Communism and in Transition: Evidence from Central Europe and Russia', *The William Davidson Institute Working Papers*, No. 114 b (1995, revised 2000).

Garner, T. and K. Terrell (1998), 'A Gini Decomposition Analysis of Inequality in the Czech and Slovak Republics During the Transition', *Economics of Transition*, Vol. 6 (1), pp. 23-46.

Ham, J., J. Svejnar and K. Terrell (1999), 'Women's Unemployment During the Transition: Evidence from Czech and Slovak Micro Data', *Economics of Transition*, Vol. 7 (1), pp. 47-78.

Ham, J., J. Svejnar and K. Terrell (1998), 'Unemployment and the Social Safety Net During Transitions to a Market Economy: Evidence from the Czech and Slovak Republics', *American Economic Review*, Vol. 88 (5), pp. 1117-1142.

Jones, D.C. and K. Takao (1997), 'The Nature and the Determinants of Labor Market Transitions in Former Communist Economies: Evidence from Bulgaria', *Industrial Relations*, Vol. 36 (2), pp. 229-254.

Jurajda, S. and K. Terrell (2001), 'Optimal Speed of Transition: Micro Evidence from the Czech Republic and Estonia', William Davidson Institute Working Paper No. 355, University of Michigan Business School.

Munich, D., J. Svejnar and K. Terrell (1998), 'Worker-Firm Matching in Transition Economies', *The William Davidson Institute Working Papers,* No. 107, University of Michigan Business School.

Riboud, M., C. Sanchez-Paramo and C. Silva-Jauregui (2002), 'Does Eurosclerosis Matter? Institutional Reform and Labor Market Performance in Central and Eastern European Countries in the 1990s', World Bank Working Paper No. 591.

Sabirianova, K. (October 2000), 'The Great Human Capital Reallocation: An Empirical Analysis of Occupational Mobility in Transitional Russia', *The William Davidson Institute Working Paper,* No. 309, University of Michigan Business School.

Svejnar, J. (1977), 'Pensions in the Former Soviet Bloc: Problems and Solutions', in Council on Foreign Relations, *The Coming Global Pension Crisis*, New York.

Svejnar, J. (1999), 'Labor Markets in the Transitional Central and East European Economies', Chapter 42 in Orley Ashenfelter and David Card (eds.), *Handbook of Labor Economics*, North Holland, Vol. 3B.

Svejnar, J. (2002), 'Transition Economies: Performance and Challenges', *Journal of Economic Perspectives,* Vol. 16, pp. 3-28..

Table 7.1 Unemployment rate (percent)

	1990	1991	1992	1993	1994	1995	1996	1997	1998	1999	2000	2001*
Czech Republic	0.7	4.1	2.6	3.5	3.2	2.9	3.5	5.2	7.5	9.4	8.9	8.2
Hungary	1.7	8.5	9.8	11.9	10.7	10.2	9.9	8.7	7.8	7.0	6.5	5.7
Poland	6.5	11.8	13.6	16.4	16.0	14.9	13.2	8.6	10.4	13.0	16.1	18.2
Slovak Republic	1.5	6.6	11.4	14.4	14.6	13.1	12.8	12.5	15.6	19.2	17.9	18.3
Slovenia	4.7	8.2	11.6	9.1	9.1	7.4	7.3	7.1	7.6	7.4	7.0	6.4
Estonia	0.6	1.5	3.7	6.5	7.6	9.7	10.0	9.7	9.6	10.3	13.6	12.6
Bulgaria	1.7	11.1	15.3	16.4	12.8	11.1	12.5	13.7	12.2	16.0	16.9	19.8
Romania	n.a	3.0	8.2	10.4	8.2	8.0	6.7	6.0	6.3	11.5	7.1	6.5
Russia	n.a	0.1	5.2	5.9	8.1	9.5	9.7	11.8	13.3	11.7	10.4	9.7
Ukraine	n.a	n.a	0.3	0.3	0.4	0.5	1.5	2.7	4.3	5.4	5.3	3.0
United States	5.6	6.8	7.5	6.9	6.1	5.6	5.4	4.9	4.5	4.2	4.0	4.8

* estimated

Source: William Davidson Institute based on EBRD Transition Report Update 2002, Datastream-EIU, and WDI staff calculations

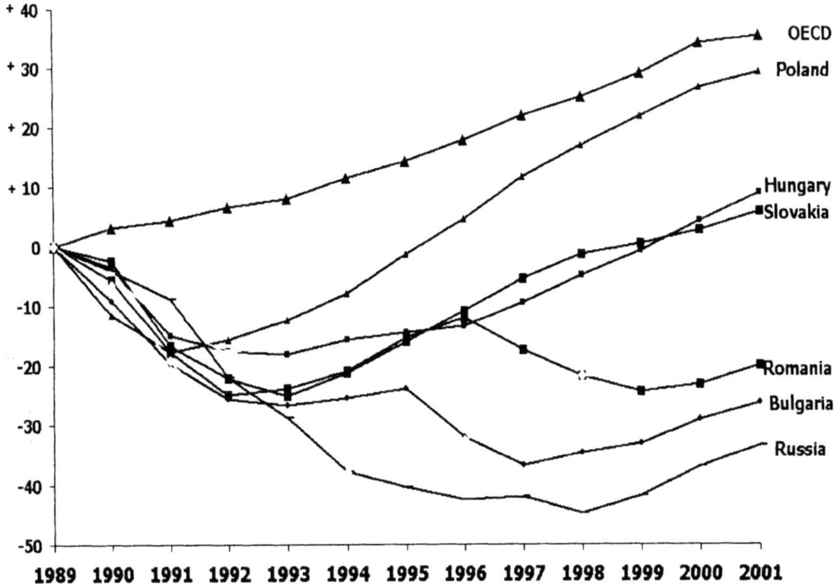

Source: William Davidson Institute based on various EBRD Transition Reports, OECD Economic Outlook Vol. 71 June 2002, and staff calculations.

Figure 7.1 Real GDP index (1989 base year)

Chapter 8

Labor Market Reform: Lessons from Spain

Juan Francisco Jimeno

Introduction

When discussing labor market issues in countries undergoing international economic integration, Spain is often singled out as an interesting case to study. Spain went through a political transition and a very intense process of economic reforms in the late 1970s and early 1980s to achieve EU accession in 1986. During this period the unemployment rate went from less than five percent in 1975 to almost 25 percent in the mid-1980s. Since then, continuous reforms have tried to improve the workings of the labor market without much success: the unemployment rate followed the business cycle and decreased to around 16 percent in 1991, to increase again to over 20 percent in the recession of the early 1990s. Only the second half of the 1990s have seen significant declines in the unemployment rate. While it had fallen to around 13 percent in 2001, this was still 5 percentage points higher than the average unemployment rate in the EU, although the gap keeps shrinking (see Figure 8.1).

Many pundits argue that there is something to learn from the Spanish experience, both regarding the causes of unemployment and the effectiveness of some labor market reforms. In particular, some Central and Eastern European Countries (CEECs, henceforth), which are candidates for EU membership in the near future, seem to face problems similar to Spain's in the late 1970s and early 1980s. To what extent can CEECs draw some lessons from the Spanish experience? In the proceeding part we argue that the Spanish approach for dealing with labor market reforms should not be taken as an 'example' to be followed by CEECs. There are both positive and normative foundations for this negative view. On positive grounds, Spain started from a less complex situation in which labor market reforms could be combined with increases in social expenditures to ease the burden of economic reshuffling. On the contrary, many CEECs have very large and inefficient social programs that need to be scaled down. On normative grounds, the implementation of continuous and marginal labor market reforms (the 'gradualist approach') has generated notorious distortions for the Spanish labor market.

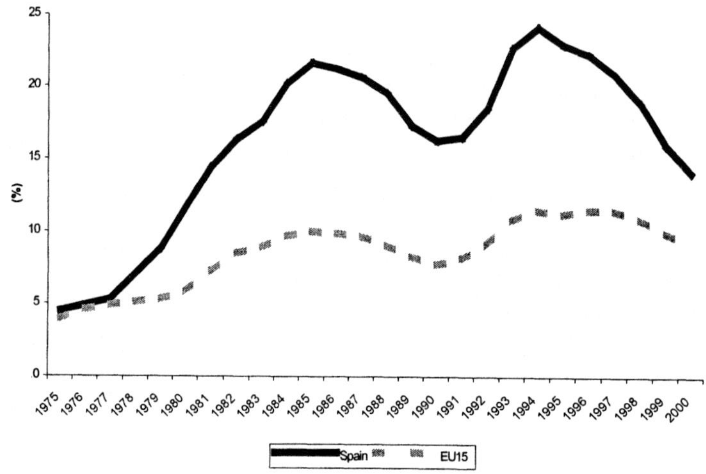

Source: Statistical Annex of European Economy, European Commission, Autumn 2001

Figure 8.1 Unemployment rate, Spain and the EU, 1975-2001

The structure of this chapter is as follows. In section 8.2 we take a closer look to the evolution of unemployment and inflation in Spain during the second half of the 1990s, to show the increases in structural unemployment during the 1980-1995 period and to assess the extent to which recent reductions in Spanish unemployment are structural or cyclical in nature. In Section 8.3 we describe the evolution of labor market reforms in Spain since the mid-1970s. Section 8.4 concludes with some comments that may be of some interest for the design of labor market policies in CEECs in light of the Spanish experience.

The Unemployment-inflation Trade-off in Spain, 1975-2001

Fluctuations in unemployment can reflect both cyclical and structural factors. Inflationary pressures are often indicative of which of the two factors are more relevant. Typically, unemployment increases (decreases) while inflation falls (rises) along the business cycle. However, if unemployment varies with a constant inflation rate, then structural factors are more likely to explain changes in unemployment.

Figure 8.2 shows the evolution of the inflation rate over the last quarter of the 20th century. Spain went through a gradual disinflation since the mid-1970s, as did the rest of the EU, but from higher levels. In the second half of the 1990s the Spanish inflation rate converged to the EU average, although over the last three years (1999-2001) there is a slightly growing gap. Since the early 1980s wage

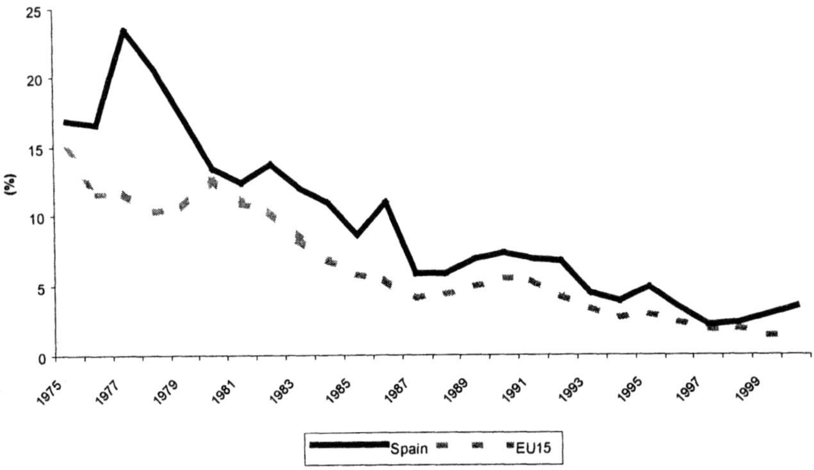

Source: Statistical Annex of European Economy, European Commission, Autumn 2001.

Figure 8.2 Inflation rate (as measured by the GDP deflator), Spain and the EU, 1975-2001

moderation has been noticeable, as in many other European countries.[1] During the second half of the 1990s, reductions in unemployment were achieved without being accompanied by accelerating inflation.[2] At first sight it could be argued that labor market reforms reduced structural unemployment. However, this conclusion would not be fully grounded.

It is true that Spanish labor market institutions have been in continuous turmoil during the 1980s and the 1990s. Labor market regulations changed frequently, but these changes were often marginal and contradictory. It is therefore difficult to point to fundamental reforms that increased labor market flexibility. The only significant difference between the current Spanish labor market institutions and those of the late 1970s and early 1980s is the introduction of 'flexible' (fixed-term) employment contracts in the mid-1980s. This eventually resulted in a segmented labor market with more than 30 percent of wage earners under fixed-term employment contracts. And it is not at all obvious that such a reform contributes to reducing structural unemployment.[3]

1 As documented, for instance, by the analysis of wage shares in Blanchard (1997).

2 During the 1995-2001 there were some methodological changes of the Spanish Labor Force Survey that explain to some extent the reduction in measured unemployment. Nevertheless, the acceleration of employment over this period is unquestionable.

3 See Dolado, Garcia-Serrano and Jimeno (2002) for a survey of studies on the effects of fixed-term contracts in Spain, and Blanchard and Landier (2002) for a model of fixed-term contracts applied to France.

Economic Transition and Labor Market Policies in Spain

In the mid-1970s Spain was a relatively backward economy, with an under-developed welfare state and a sclerotic labor market. GDP per capita and labor productivity were around 80 and 85 percent of EU averages, respectively. Agriculture accounted for over 22 percent of total employment in 1975, while self-employment was around 30 percent. Both pubic debt and social expenditures were below 15 percent of GDP. Labor market legislation was characterized by significant protectionism and government intervention in all areas of industrial relations, from dismissal procedures to collective bargaining agreements.

To prepare for EU accession, the Spanish labor market needed substantial restructuring, which was impeded by the rigidity of labor market institutions. Since the major elements of labor market regulation under the old regime were continued thanks to passage of a key piece of labor legislation in 1980 (the *Workers' Statute*), the need for sectoral reshuffling and labor reallocation had to be accommodated by alternative instruments. Thus, during the late 1970s and early 1980s growing social expenditures and a sequence of social pacts (1978-1984) were used to achieve the goals of restructuring and disinflation. For instance, the coverage and duration of unemployment benefits and participation in early retirement schemes were extended to provide income support for displaced workers. This eventually resulted in high long-term unemployment and a drastic fall in employment rates for the population close to the legal retirement age.

Soon after the introduction of the new labor legislation, it became clear that the combination of high dismissal costs, inefficient regulation of collective bargaining procedures, increasing social expenditures and social pacts achieved by means of government concessions in exchange for wage moderation, was not sustainable in the long-run. Public deficits were substantial and public debt surged. Moreover, the unemployment rate grew rapidly and surpassed 20 percent in the early 1980s, as firms continued to face strong obstacles in adjusting employment to changes in demand and technology. As overall reductions in dismissal costs were not politically viable, employment protection legislation was eased by the liberalization of fixed-term contracts, which entailed much lower dismissal costs that the regular employment contract. This measure eventually resulted in a dual labor market in which the proportion of employees working under fixed-term contracts exceeded 30 percent of all employees at the beginning of the 1990s. Although the introduction of flexibility at the margin promoted employment creation in the second half of the 1980s, it also had negative effects on trends in wages and productivity, and on wage inequality.[4] In other areas, collective bargaining legislation was not reformed. Eligibility requirements for unemployment benefits were eased while their replacement rates and duration grew throughout the 1980s. Despite strong job creation during the second half of the

4 On the effects of the liberalization of fixed-term employment contracts on employment growth over the second half of the 1980s, see Bentolila and Saint-Paul, (1992). As for evidence on other effects, see the survey by Dolado, Garcia-Serrano and Jimeno (2002).

1980s, unemployment rates remained high, with wide differentials across regions and population groups (see Table 8.1).

Table 8.1 Employment and unemployment rates in Spain, 1983-2001

Age	1983			1990			2001		
categories	All	Men	Women	All	Men	Women	All	Men	Women
Unemployment rates									
All	17.0	15.6	20.5	16.1	11.8	24.4	13.1	9.2	19.0
16-24	37.6	33.7	43.7	30.1	23.2	39.7	24.7	19.4	31.4
25-54	11.5	11.5	11.6	13.1	9.3	20.6	11.5	7.6	17.1
55-64	7.4	8.8	2.9	8.1	8.4	7.2	8.6	7.6	11.1
Employment rates									
All	49.5	71.7	27.6	51.1	71.0	31.6	57.1	71.9	42.5
16-24	35.9	45.2	25.9	38.3	47.4	28.7	36.0	42.3	29.4
25-54	56.1	83.6	29.4	61.1	85.5	37.2	68.7	85.4	52.3
55-64	41.3	65.2	19.7	36.8	57.2	18.1	38.6	57.3	21.5

Source: OECD, *Employment Outlook*, (several years).

More recently, there have been three labor market reforms (in 1994, 1997, and 2001) aimed at undoing the liberalization of fixed-term contracts in 1984 and reducing the proportion of employees under fixed-term contracts. In 1994 employment protection legislation was changed, easing restrictions on 'fair' dismissals and restricting conditions for the use of temporary contracts. In 1997 the employer confederation (CEOE) and the two major unions (UGT and CC.OO.) reached an agreement to reform the employment contract system and the structure of collective bargaining. The main novelty of the reform was the introduction of a new permanent employment contract with lower costs in case of unfair dismissals (33 days of wages per year of seniority, with a maximum of 33 months of wages). This new contract could be used for most new hires, with the exception of males 30-45 years of age with unemployment spells below one year. This amounted to a significant reduction in dismissal costs (it was the first time that Spanish unions conceded to this type of reduction), which was thought necessary to promote employment creation, and above all to reduce temporary employment. The government supported this agreement by heavily subsidizing hiring under the new permanent contracts and the conversion of temporary contracts into permanent ones. The subsidies took the form of rebates to social security contributions in the range of 40-60 percent over a period of two years, depending on the individual characteristics of the employee. These new contracts were to be in effect until May 2001. In March 2001, after further negotiations between the trade unions and employer confederations about labor market reforms, the government unilaterally extended the coverage of these new permanent contracts to other groups of workers and authorized the use of these contracts further into the future.

Thus, a brief summary of the process of labor market reforms in Spain over the last two and a half decades can be as follows. Since Spain had some of the most rigid employment protection legislation in the EU and since the collective bargaining system favored insiders, flexibility 'at the margin' was introduced in 1984 by easing the use of temporary contracts for non-seasonal reasons while keeping the protection of permanent contracts. As the proportion of temporary jobs surged, labor market reforms during the 1990s tried to 'balance' the situation between the two types of contracts, both by restricting the use of temporary contracts and by reducing dismissal costs under permanent contracts. However, although recent labor market reforms have attempted to reduce the proportion of workers under temporary contracts, this share still remains above 30 percent. By contrast with the reforms in employment protection legislation, the regulation of the wage bargaining system introduced in 1980 remains more or less unchanged,[5] while unemployment benefits, extended in the 1980s, were cut after 1992-1993.

But even under these conditions, the Spanish economy underwent dramatic structural changes. By 1985, the share of agriculture employment had fallen by almost 5 percentage points, and, despite restrictive employment protection legislation, high job destruction rates were observed in declining sectors. Social expenditures, particularly unemployment benefits and old-age and invalidity pensions, were increased substantially to ease workers' resistance to displacement. This allowed Spain to embark on a path of rapid modernization and technological upgrading, and therefore high labor productivity growth. These structural changes took place under a fairly rigid institutional framework and during times of negative supply and demand shocks. Not surprisingly, unemployment surged.[6] Some features of the institutional framework (increasingly long-lasting unemployment benefits, strong insiders' bargaining power in wage determination, employment segmentation between permanent and temporary workers) also contributed to the persistence of unemployment (Dolado and Jimeno, 1997) and to an unequal distribution of unemployment among groups, increasing relative unemployment rates of young and female workers (Jimeno and Rodriguez-Palenzuela, 2001). The fact that unemployment mostly affected second earners in the household, the role of the extended family as an additional provider of insurance (Bentolila and Ichino, 2000), and the rise in social protection expenditures, explain why unemployment could remain at such high levels during so long.

---

5 For a comprehensive survey of recent labor market reforms in Spain, see Segura (2001). For a description of collective bargaining in Spain, the need for its reform, and the resistance it encounters, see Bentolila and Jimeno (2002).

6 On this point, the comparison with Portugal is very illustrative (see Jimeno et al., 2000). Portugal adopted a sort of labor-intensive broad-based growth strategy, with more flexible labor institutions that delivered lower labor productivity and wage growth, but higher employment rates.

Some Lessons for the CEECs

The economics literature on the relationship between labor market institutions and labor market performance suggests some possible 'culprits' of bad labor market performance.[7] Although these findings are not completely robust, there are some general lessons to bear in mind.

Labor market institutions matter for labor market performance. Excessively rigid labor legislation that constrains (rather than arranging or coping with) structural change is bound to fail: it will impede growth and will not prevent employment destruction.

Institutions matter, not only in themselves, but also in terms of their interactions with one another and with demand and supply shocks. Moreover, their effects may change over time. For example, collective bargaining regulation becomes virtually irrelevant if dismissal costs are non-existent. An excessively rigid institutional framework may convert temporary shocks in permanent ones by generating hysteresis in unemployment dynamics.

Apparently small differences in institutions matter. Countries with similar institutional features (Belgium and Holland, the US and Canada, the UK and Ireland, Spain and Portugal) have shown dissimilar labor market performance.

There is no a unique set of institutions that generate efficient labor markets delivering high employment rates. For instance, atypical work (part-time employment contracts) have helped reduce unemployment in Holland but less so in Spain. Active labor market polices are managed differently across countries also with contrasting results.

In contrast with unemployment, there are institutions that unambiguously deliver lower wage dispersion. Flexible, less-regulated labor market adjusts to shocks through changes in relative wages. A centralized wage determination system, as used to be the case in Scandinavian countries, reduces wage inequality.

Economic agents react to institution by shifts in their labor demand and supply, and by changes in labor demand and labor supply elasticities. Decisions about investment in human capital, participation in the labor market, retirement, and the like are very much affected by the incentives implicit in social norms and labor market institutions.

Besides these general lessons, the Spanish experience with labor market reform may be of some relevance for CEECs undergoing structural reforms, although the level of economic development and the international macroeconomic scenario are now very different with respect to the situation prevailing in the late 1970s and early 1980s. Some broad conclusions can be drawn from the Spanish experience.[8]

---

7 Just to cite three of the most recent ones, see Nickell and Layard (1999), Blanchard and Wolfers (2000), and Bertola, Blau, and Kahn (2002).

8 Similar conclusions are also in Boeri, Bruckner, et al. (2001).

First, as regards employment, a flexible labor market helps accommodate better the labor reallocation required by shifts to different specialization patterns, modernization, and technological upgrading. The Spanish case shows that restrictive employment protection legislation does not prevent intense labor shedding during re-industrialization and changes in the sectoral composition of employment. It also shows that, when combined with increasing provision of long-lasting unemployment benefits, restrictive employment protection legislation augments hysteretic labor market features. Eventually, labor market reforms easing employment protection legislation are needed. In this case, two-tier institutional reforms may result in a dual labor market, where not only equity, but also efficiency is negatively affected. As for equity, temporary employees (mainly young and female workers first entering the labor market) suffer the burden of the adjustment, while the insider power of workers under permanent contracts strengthens. As for efficiency, investment in human capital, training, and subsequently productivity growth are discouraged by the resulting employment segmentation.

Second, as far as distribution is concerned, the demand for social protection increases during times of structural reforms. The challenge is to accommodate this demand in a stable macroeconomic policy framework while designing social protection schemes that do not impede labor market participation and employment creation. As far as fiscal balance is concerned, here the situation of some CEECs seems more problematic than the Spanish situation in the early 1980s. In the latter, increasing unemployment benefits and other social protection expenditures helped promote labor reallocation and cushion the effects of rising unemployment. By contrast, in some CEECs unemployment has risen sharply while room for augmenting social protection expenditures is more limited. This makes the design of social programs involving the proper labor supply incentives especially relevant. For instance, in-work benefits seem superior to long-lasting unemployment benefits. Experience-rated unemployment benefits, as in the US, may prevent excessive labor shedding instead of using them, as happened in Spain, as an incentive for firms to reshuffle their labor force. Active labor market policies should be targeted, well designed, properly evaluated and not used for the extension of unemployment benefits. And the abuse of early retirement schemes to ease labor force adjustments and to enhance youth employment is a non-starter. Youth employment rates often fail to increase as a result of reductions in the supply of adult labor. Moreover, in countries with rising life expectancy and declining fertility, the financial viability of unfunded/pay-as-you-go social security schemes calls for delaying retirement, not the contrary. The Spanish experience is very illustrative in this regard.

References

Bentolila, S. and G. Saint-Paul (1992), 'The macroeconomic impact of flexible labour contracts: An application to Spain', *European Economic Review*, 36.

Bentolila, S. and A. Ichino (2000), 'Unemployment and Consumption: Are Job Losses Less Painful near the Mediterranean?' CEMFI Working Paper 0010.

Bertola, G., F. Blau and L.K. Kahn (2002), 'Comparative Analysis of Labour Market Outcomes: Lessons for the US from International Long-Run Evidence' in A. Krueger and R. Solow (eds.), *The Roaring Nineties: Can Full Employment Be Sustained?*, New York: Russell Sage.

Blanchard, O. (1997), 'The Medium Run', *Brookings Papers on Economic Activity*, 2, pp. 89-158.

Blanchard, O. and J. Wolfers (2000), 'Shocks and institutions and the rise of European unemployment. The aggregate evidence', *Economic Journal*, 110 (1), pp. 1-33.

Blanchard, O. and A. Landier (2002), 'The perverse effects of partial labour market reform: fixed duration contracts in France' *The Economic Journal*, 112, June.

Boeri, T., H. Bruckner, et al. (2001), 'The Impact of Eastern Enlargement on Employment and Labour Markets in the EU Member States', European Integration Consortium (DIW, CEPR, FIEF, IS, IGIER), mimeo.

Dolado, J.J., C. Garcia-Serrano and J.F. Jimeno (2002), 'Drawing Lessons from the Boom of Temporary Jobs in Spain', *The Economic Journal*, 112, June.

Dolado, J.J. and J.F. Jimeno (1997), 'The Causes of Spanish unemployment: A structural VAR, Approach', *European Economic Review*, 41, pp. 1281-1307.

Jimeno, J.F., O. Canto, A.R. Cardoso, M. Izquierdo and C.F. Rodrigues (2000), 'Integration and Inequality: Lessons from the Accessions of Portugal and Spain to the EU' in *Background papers: Making Transition Work for everyone*, The World Bank.

Jimeno, J.F. and D. Rodriguez-Palenzuela (2001), 'Youth unemployment in the OECD: demographic changes, labour market institutions, and macroeconomic shocks', FEDEA and ECB, mimeo.

Nickell, S. and R. Layard (1999), 'Labour Market Institutions and Economic Performance', en O.C. Ashenfelter y D. Card (eds.), *Handbook of Labour Economics*, Vol 3C, North-Holland, Amsterdam.

Segura, J. (2001), 'La reforma del mercado de trabajo espanol: un panorama', *Revista de Economia Aplicada*, Vol. IX, No. 25, pp. 157-190.

Chapter 9

Designing Labor Market Institutions

Olivier Blanchard

Introduction

> Western Europe suffers from too many labor market rigidities, from excessively generous unemployment insurance, high employment protection, and high minimum wages. It is essential that countries putting in place new institutions do not commit the same mistakes.

The quote is made up. But it is, I believe, a fair representation of the opinions of many experts and many organizations, from *The Economist* to the OECD.

I am more skeptical, or at least, more open. Labor markets are far from textbook competitive markets. They are rife with information problems, and have ample room for market power and for bargaining. They do not function well without proper institutions. And these institutions, from unemployment insurance to the minimum wage, came into being in response to clear market failures, from the exploitation of workers in company towns in the nineteenth century, to the extreme suffering of the unemployed during the Great Depression.

That labor market institutions developed in response to market failures surely does not imply that the institutions we have today are optimal in any sense. Their design may have been poor to start with; circumstances and the economic environment have surely changed; what was needed or appropriate then may not be so today. Political economy considerations give institutions a life and a shape of their own: employment protection creates a constituency for employment protection, and so on. Still, it is clear that simple slogans will not do. Economists owe countries in transition clear analysis of what institutions are needed today, how they should be designed, and how existing institutions should be reformed.

This is a difficult task. Labor markets are complex. What follows below is a presentation of my own reflections on this topic, which are largely the result of on-going research with Jean Tirole on the optimal design of labor market institutions. They are an attempt to identify the issues, and some preliminary insights as to the shape of potential institutional solutions.

Some Facts

Western European labor market institutions are surely not the world's best, but their adverse effects are in fact not so easy to identify.

For example, GDP per hour worked in the private sector is actually quite similar on both sides of the Atlantic. As Table 9.1 shows, France and Germany are clearly within sight of US productivity levels. During the 1990s, their growth performance, in terms of labor productivity growth, was actually slightly higher than that of the US.

Table 9.1 PPP GDP per hour worked, private sector

Country	US	Germany	France
Level, 2001	100	85	95
Growth rate, 1990s	1.6%	1.8%	1.8-2.0%

Notes: US level normalized to 100. Germany growth: 1992-99.

Source: McKinsey, MGI, 2002.

Obviously, these numbers do not prove that labor market institutions have no adverse effect on efficiency and output. Maybe with different labor market institutions, Europe would be far ahead of the United States. But these numbers also show that pictures of doom, either about the level or the growth rate of GDP, are wide of the mark.

What about unemployment? Unemployment increased a lot in Western Europe in the 1970s and the 1980s. It is still high today, around 8 percent for the European Union as a whole. But the high average number hides a lot of diversity across countries. In 2001, the unemployment rate stood at 2.5 percent in the Netherlands, 4.7 percent in Sweden, and 4 percent in Portugal—three countries that clearly have 'European style' labor market institutions.

This is not to say that different labor market institutions yield similar outcomes. If one looks not just at unemployment but at flows of job creation and destruction, and at the flows of workers through the labor market, then clear differences emerge (see Table 9.2). Reallocation is lower in Europe than in the United States. Even at the same unemployment rates over the last twenty years, flows are lower in Portugal than in the United States.

Quarterly rates of job creation and destruction are substantially lower in Portugal than in the US. The difference goes away when looking at annual rates (which is in line with findings from other European countries). The fact that numbers look similar at annual or longer frequencies suggests that lower reallocation may not actually impede very much the churning process required for growth. What it seems to impede is the higher frequency reallocation, the ability of firms to quickly adjust their labor force in response to temporary shocks.

Table 9.2 Reallocations of jobs in Portugal and the US

Country	Portugal	United States
Jobs, quarterly creation	3.6%	5.4%
annual creation	11.1%	10.6%
Workers, quarterly inflows	4.1%	11.1-14.1%

Source: Blanchard and Portugal (2001).

Flows of workers are substantially lower (less than half) in Portugal than in the United States (the replacement of a worker by another on a given job gives rise to a worker flow, but not to a job flow. This is why measures of worker flows exceed measures of job flows). One interpretation of this fact is that the matching of workers and jobs is less efficient in Portugal than in the US: More workers stay in jobs they do not like; more firms keep workers they are not very happy with.[1]

If unemployment rates are similar, but flows of workers are lower, then it follows that unemployment durations are longer in Europe. This is indeed the case. For an individual, being unemployed means something very different on both sides of the Atlantic. In the US, it means remaining unemployed for three months on average before finding another job; in Europe it means remaining unemployed on average for close to a year. For those who are unemployed, a group which often disproportionately includes the young and the old in Europe, being unemployed is likely to be much more traumatic in Europe than in the US. A long unemployment spell is much more likely to lead to a loss of skills, a loss of hope and self-confidence; indeed these effects have been well documented in Europe. Here, different labor market institutions look very much like a potential culprit.

In much of my work on unemployment, I have explored how specific labor market institutions may be responsible for these various aspects of the labor market. Here, the approach is normative. We pose the question: If we started from scratch, which labor market institutions would we want to put in place?

Unemployment Insurance

I take it as nearly self-evident that, left to itself, the labor market provides too little unemployment insurance.[2] The question is why, and what can the state do that the private sector cannot?

Self-insurance—the accumulation of private funds for a rainy day—can only play a limited role. For many workers, unemployment comes too early in their working life to allow them to accumulate sufficient funds. Its duration may be too

1 This is not the only interpretation. Another, less pessimistic interpretation is that European firms and workers are organized differently from US firms and workers. They invest more in their employment relationship, and so, having done the investment, tend to stay together longer.

2 To be convinced, I think one only has to read about the fate of the unemployed in the Great Depression.

uncertain to be reasonably sure that they will not run out of funds. The state may and probably should provide fiscal and other incentives for workers to save more for such a contingency. Some countries have put such incentives in place. These are highly desirable since, as we shall see below, other solutions come with a number of their own problems. But it is unrealistic to expect self insurance to provide sufficient insurance for workers. So one has to look for insurance by others.

Insurance by the firms themselves runs into a number of problems. First, there is the moral hazard problem often associated with insurance of any kind. If they receive unemployment insurance, workers have less of an incentive to search for and accept jobs. Monitoring the search effort of its laid off workers is extremely hard for an individual firm. Indeed, the firm may have a hard time simply finding out whether the worker is still unemployed or has taken another job. This sharply limits the amount of insurance it can offer.

Insurance by firms also runs into what economists refer to as 'a lack of deep pockets'. Layoffs typically are high when a firm does poorly, or when it goes bankrupt. The problem may then be the same as for self insurance: the funds will not be there when they are needed. Alternatively, the firm may be able to pay, but, as a consequence, suffer serious liquidity problems. This may lead in turn to inefficiently low investment and production.

What about insurance by *private insurance companies*? The deep pockets problem will be less severe: only in the case of large aggregate shocks would insurance companies be unable to pay. The monitoring problem may also be alleviated: economies of scale may allow insurance companies to do a better job than individual firms. But a new problem emerges: monitoring of firms and workers. Layoffs trigger payments from the insurance company, which in turn strengthens incentives to lay off workers.

Is there then *a role for the state* to provide unemployment insurance? The answer is yes, for two reasons. Because it has an administrative infrastructure that already covers the country, the state can monitor workers' status, if not search effort, more easily. And it has deeper pockets than private insurance companies. Even in the event of an economy-wide recession, workers do not have to worry about receiving their unemployment benefits.

Negative Income Taxes

However the state cannot solve the problem of fully monitoring the search efforts of the unemployed. Here, recent reforms (the Blair reforms in England, the PARE in France) that typically offer more generous benefits but reduce or end them if workers keep turning down jobs for which they qualify suggest that traditional unemployment insurance systems can be improved upon, in terms of both incentives and insurance.

But, even in the best designed system, monitoring is likely to remain far from perfect. And all this is more relevant for low-skill workers. Their marginal product and wage may be barely above what is considered a minimum socially acceptable standard of living. If unemployment insurance is to provide that minimum, what incentive do they have to look for work?

The solution is clearly not to increase the minimum wage. On this, basic economic theory must be right: higher minimum wages in this case will simply eliminate low skill jobs. Nor can the solution be to pay unemployment payments below the minimum standard of living: this would be inconsistent with its basic purpose. The only solution is therefore to increase the take home pay of low skill workers so they have an incentive to work, without increasing their cost to firms. This is typically done through a negative income tax. The generosity of the tax must depend on the relationship between the productivity of the lowest skilled workers and what is perceived to be the socially acceptable minimum standard of living. This relationship is likely to vary across countries.

Severance Payments and Employment Protection

The other problem faced by any third party provider of unemployment benefits, whether for private companies or the state ones, is the effect it has on the decision to layoff.

Assuming that the decision to layoff is privately efficient, layoffs will occur when the productivity of the worker is less than his/her reservation wage (the wage at which the worker is indifferent between working and not working). The reservation wage is clearly an increasing function of unemployment benefits. This implies that the provision of unemployment benefits will lead, from a social point of view, to too many layoffs: Some workers, who would have had low but positive productivity will be unemployed, and thus producing nothing at all.

The solution, from both a conceptual and practical point of view, is to offset this distortion by a tax paid by firms when they lay off a worker. How large should the tax be? The answer is straightforward: It should be equal to the expected value of unemployment benefits that will be paid to the worker. In this case, the tax will exactly offset the subsidy to layoffs implicit in the payment of unemployment benefits to the worker, and lead to a socially optimal layoff decision.

This result looks like a happy coincidence from a fiscal viewpoint. Layoff tax payments from firms to the state will equal the expected value of unemployment benefits. Payments from the state to workers will be equal to the actual value of unemployment benefits. Given the law of large numbers, the state should roughly balance its accounts.

But this argument is not quite right. Firms' lack of deep pockets that prevents them from directly paying for unemployment insurance also means that some firms will not be able to make the necessary tax payments either. Thus, the unemployment insurance system is likely to—and should—run a deficit. Since most layoffs are not associated with bankruptcies but take place in firms, which are on-going, most firms should be able to pay the tax. This suggests that the deficit is likely to be small.[3]

This description pertains to a system in which the state runs the unemployment insurance system, and collects taxes from firms when they layoff workers. But there are many alternative ways of achieving the same (or nearly the same) result. While they may look different, they have essentially the same properties.

For example, firms may pay these taxes not when they lay off workers, but each month, at a rate corresponding to the probability that they will lay off workers—more realistically, at a rate corresponding to the historical layoff rate of the firm. This is not unlike the US system (except for the cap on contributions by firms in the US). The implications and caveats will be very similar.

By contrast, the state may just play the role of monitor, and delegate the running of the system to private insurance companies or other private entities that collect contributions from firms and pay benefits to the unemployed as the state would. The state may still have to come in case of aggregate shocks, and to finance the deficit.

The system can also be run with a combination of unemployment benefits and severance payments. Part of the present value of benefits may be given to laid off workers directly by firms in the form of severance payments. The rest, including the insurance component, can then be provided by a scaled down unemployment insurance system run by the state, with smaller contributions from firms, and smaller unemployment benefits going to workers. Workers in firms that go bankrupt and cannot pay will be worse off (they will not receive severance payments, and will receive the same unemployment benefits as workers who receive severance payments), but otherwise the system will very much resemble our original system.

This last description suggests a justification for employment protection in the form of severance payments. It does not provide a justification for the administrative and judicial steps that typically characterize employment protection in most continental Western European countries, and are seen by firms as the major cost of employment protection legislation. Given the rules on severance payments, the decision should be left to the firm, and there is no reason for a judge to intervene.

Can one think of an economic rationale for such administrative and judicial interventions, in addition to severance payments? The argument I have developed suggests one potential rationale. Instead of using a tax in order to reduce the layoff rate to its efficient level, this role could be played by a smart and fully informed judge, who would make sure that only those layoffs which are socially efficient are allowed to take place. Stating the argument shows its logic, but also, I believe, its dangers. Judges are unlikely to know much about the firm and, given

---

3 If bankruptcy allows firms to avoid paying layoff taxes, large firms will have an incentive to subdivide, so as to escape the tax as often as possible by invoking bankruptcy of the subsidiary. This in turn will make the deficit larger. My guess is that this induced effect is unlikely to be large.

their discretionary powers, have many reasons to achieve objectives other than efficient layoffs. Taxes, or a combination of taxes and severance payments, are clearly the better way to go.

Job Destruction Versus Job Creation

One would hope that the provision of insurance benefits by firms, either directly or indirectly through the state, would lead workers to accept lower wages while employed. Indeed, one might argue, the very provision of insurance, and thus reductions in the risk faced by workers, should reduce overall labor costs, including not only wages but also the payment of unemployment contributions and severance payments by firms.

In fact, just the opposite is likely to happen. Both the provision of unemployment insurance, and the taxes associated with layoffs are likely to increase the wage, thus leading to both a direct (through the payment of taxes and severance pay), and indirect (through the higher wage) increase in labor costs for firms. This is because wages in the labor market reflect the relative bargaining power of firms and workers. And both unemployment benefits and layoff taxes or severance payments improve the bargaining position of workers.

The wage may be viewed as a weighted average of what the worker is worth is to the firm (the marginal product of the worker) and the reservation wage of the worker (the wage at which the worker is indifferent between working in the firm or becoming unemployed), with the weights reflecting the relative bargaining power of both sides. Then, higher unemployment benefits increase the reservation wage of workers (as they can now more easily survive unemployment), and so increases the wage. Higher severance payments have the same effect. In thinking about whether to keep a worker or lay him/her off and replace the worker by another, the firm now has to take into account the cost of severance payments to be paid to the first worker. This in turn strengthens the worker's bargaining position, again increasing the wage. The presence of unemployment insurance, and its associated financing, is likely to increase labor costs, and in so doing, decrease job creation.

This adverse effect can be avoided, at least conceptually, if the state gives subsidies to firms so as to offset the increase in labor costs. But the limits of such a solution are obvious. The subsidies may induce the creation of fly-by-night firms that collect the subsidies and then declare bankruptcy to avoid paying layoff taxes or severance payments. The subsidies have to be substantial, as they have to cover not only the direct but also the indirect increase in cost to firms. And for the state to finance them requires raising revenues and presumably creating distortions elsewhere in the economy. It may be more realistic to simply rule out such subsidies. In this case, we are confronted with a clear trade off: the provision and financing of unemployment insurance is likely to harm job creation, and thus increase unemployment.

There is no clean or elegant solution; the state must do the best it can, subject to this constraint. This implies that the state provides a bit less unemployment insurance than it otherwise would, that it reduces unemployment contributions/ severance payments by firms, and that it accepts some increase in unemployment. How much of each depends on such factors as the degree to which the unemployed are self-insured, the characteristics of the job destruction and job creation processes, their elasticity with respect to the cost of labor, and so on. This suggests that different countries may want to choose different combinations of labor market institutions.[4]

Ex Post-bargaining and the Minimum Wage

The fact that wages are likely to reflect the relative bargaining power of firms and workers has implications that go far beyond the effect we just discussed. At times, firms or workers may find themselves with overwhelming bargaining power. This may lead to very low or very high wages, with both distributional and efficiency implications.

Designing labor market institutions so as to avoid such extreme outcomes raises a whole new set of issues. For the most part, there is not a lot the state can do, except for setting rules on collective bargaining: an important set of issues that I do not want to take on here). I want however to focus on a case where the state can do something: the case in which the firm holds most of the bargaining power. The standard example is that of the nineteenth-century company town, where workers had no alternative and thus could be forced to accept very low wages. But, short of this extreme case, there are clearly circumstances in which firms may be in a position to pay a very low wage. Few other jobs may be available in the immediate proximity, or moving costs may rule out the option of relocating elsewhere. In this case, what is to prevent the firm from offering a very low wage, or in the limiting case no wage at all?

Unemployment benefits are one such constraint. No worker will accept work at a wage below his/her reservation wage, so unemployment benefits put a floor on how low the wage can fall. But this level may still be very low, or the worker may not qualify for benefits. And this is where there is a case for a minimum wage. This in effect puts a floor on the wage that firms can offer. It is a rough instrument. Ideally, its object is to push the wage closer to (but not above) the marginal product, to reduce the rents going to the firm without making hiring the worker unprofitable for the firm. In practice, any minimum wage is likely to have some employment cost. The important point is that it should be used to eliminate the worst cases of exploitation of workers by firms, not to reshape wage

---

4 One fascinating fact about Continental Europe is the inverse relation between the degree of employment protection and the generosity of the state unemployment insurance system across countries. One potential explanation is that these may be two different ways of addressing the same failures, each one more appropriate to the circumstances of the given country. Another is that one system (high unemployment benefits and low employment protection) is much less distortionary than the other, but the existence of the other is explained by political economy considerations: the demand for employment protection is higher if unemployment benefits are low.

and income distributions. For that reason, the minimum wage should be set at low levels, probably lower than most minimum wages are today in Western Europe. If this wage is too low to live on, the right tool is the negative income tax, not the minimum wage.

Conclusions

My purpose has been to identify the central imperfections that characterize labor markets, and to think about the proper institutions. The above analysis suggests a set of institutions, consisting of a mix of tax incentives for self-insurance together with a state-provided unemployment insurance system, a mix of layoff taxes or unemployment contributions by firms, together with severance payments to workers, a negative income tax, and a low minimum wage.

Much remains to be done in characterizing the exact menu of institutions, and how the menu might vary across countries. And even if we were to get the general conceptual structure and the general menu right, the devil is, as many reforms have shown, likely to be largely in the details. But much also remains to be done in improving the political dialogue on these issues. It is time to go beyond the slogans, to avoid blaming 'labor market rigidities' for the ills of our economies (I would gladly get rid of the term altogether). Starting from the position that these institutions are in fact needed but probably need to be reformed is likely to facilitate and improve the dialogue among social partners, be it business organizations, unions, or the state.

References

Blanchard, O. and P. Portugal (2001), 'What Hides Behind an Unemployment Rate: Comparing Portuguese and U.S. Labor Markets', American Economic Review, March, Vol. 91, Issue 1, March.

McKinsey Global Institute (MGI) Report (2002), 'Reaching Higher Productivity Growth in France and Germany'.

Chapter 10

Tax Systems in Transition

Pradeep Mitra and Nicholas Stern

Introduction

The transition economies which most successfully resumed growth and made progress towards a market economy by the end of the first decade of transition (i) imposed market discipline on the enterprise sector and (ii) established an investment climate conducive to the creation of new firms. These firms became the most dynamic sector of the economy and they flourished without special favors dispensed by the state. Countries such as Hungary, the Czech Republic, Poland, Lithuania and Latvia, which witnessed a quick return to growth following the 'transitional recession' which affected all countries, were those where small enterprises (defined as those employing fewer than 50 workers) provided—by the end of the 1990s—over half of all employment and value added generated in the economy (World Bank, 2002a). Moreover, imposition of market discipline and creation of an attractive investment climate must go hand in hand: Figure 10.1 shows that countries where budget constraints on enterprises were softened, usually through tax exemptions, fiscal and financial subsidies and tolerance of arrears on payments of taxes and energy bills to utility companies, and which thereby created barriers to exit for unviable firms, also saw a low share of aggregate employment in small enterprises (see World Bank, 2002a).

What implications do these findings have for tax systems in the transition countries of Eastern Europe and the former Soviet Union? And, looking ahead, on which reforms in tax policy and administration should attention be focused? These are the issues with which this chapter is concerned.[1] Section 10.2 outlines changes in levels of public expenditures and their current structure in order to provide a background for the tax analysis that follows. Section 10.3 sets out the stylized facts regarding tax systems in transition and relates them to the characteristics of public

---

1 An earlier version of this chapter was prepared for a conference on 'Beyond Transition: Development Perspectives and Dilemmas', April 12-13, 2002. We thank Daniel Daianu, Yegor Gaidar and Alari Purju, who were the discussants at the conference, for their comments, Jit Gill for a written communication on tax administration in transition countries, Andriy Storozhuk for putting together the tax revenue data for the transition countries and for his invaluable assistance to us with the data, calculations, and charts and Lodovico Pizzati, Afsaneh Sedghi, Giedre Tarbuniene and Ekaterina Vashakmadze for compiling the public expenditure data base for the transition countries. Views expressed are the authors' and do not necessarily represent those of the World Bank.

expenditures noted in Section 10.2. Section 10.4 appeals to comparative evidence to suggest the combinations in which different tax instruments might be used to finance public expenditure without introducing serious distortions in the private sector.

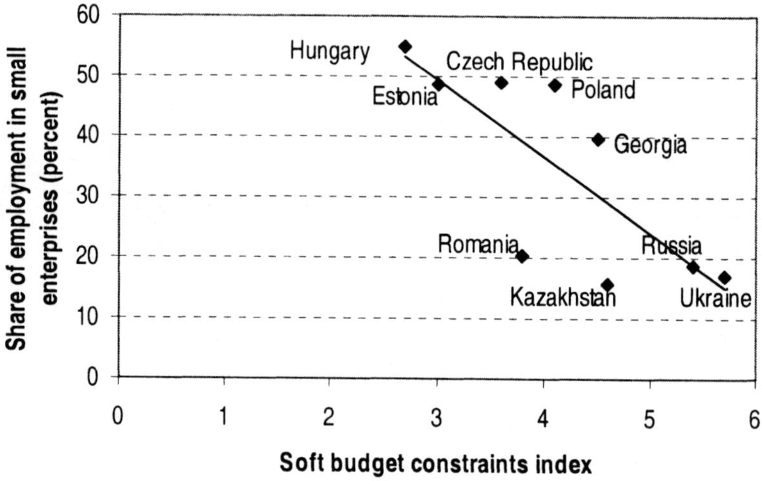

Source: EBRD (2000); World Bank database on SMEs.

Figure 10.1 Soft budget constraints and employment in small enterprises, 2000

Section 10.5 reviews the impact of tax systems on the investment climate in transition economies. Section 10.6 contains a brief review of outstanding issues in the reform of tax administration. Section 10.7 considers foreign direct investment. Section 10.8 concludes by bringing together the questions raised by the whole analysis.

Public Expenditure in the Transition Countries

The purpose of taxation is to raise resources to finance government expenditures on key public goods (such as a stable macroeconomic environment and legal and judicial systems to secure property rights) and the provision of basic social services. Taxation and expenditures should ideally be analyzed together.

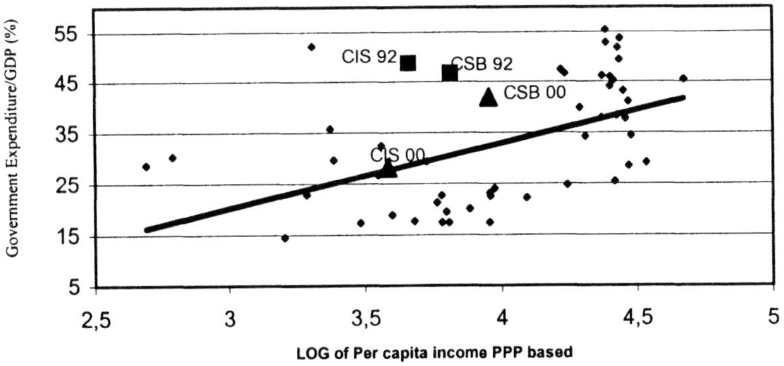

Trendline: Y=12.7 X - 18.0 , with R^2=0.3 , Based on a sample of 49 developed and developing countries with comparable fiscal data.

* CSB refers to Central and Southeastern Europe and the Baltics and includes: Albania, Bosnia, Bulgaria, Croatia, Czech Republic, Estonia, Hungary, Latvia, Lithuania, Macedonia, Poland, Romania, the Slovak Republic and Slovenia; CIS refers to the Commonwealth of Independent States and includes: Armenia, Azerbaijan, Belarus, Georgia, Kazakhstan, Kyrgyz Republic, Moldova, Russian Federation, Tajikistan, Turkmenistan, Ukraine and Uzbekistan.

Source: Alam and Sundberg (2002).

Figure 10.2 Public expenditures and income level per capita, 2000

Figure 10.2, reproduced from Alam and Sundberg (2002), plots countries' shares of government expenditure in GDP against the log of their per capita income (adjusted for purchasing power parity) across a sample of developed and developing countries for which comparable fiscal data were available in 2000. The figure allows the following two points to be made.

First, the magnitude of expenditure adjustment during the 1990s was much greater in the CIS countries. Starting from levels of 50 percent or more in the pre-transition years (Tanzi, 1991) and between 45 to 50 percent in 1992 (which were comparable to those in the industrial countries), the share of government expenditure in the CIS countries fell to levels comparable to those in countries at similar per capita income levels. In contrast, the share of government expenditure in the CSB countries was almost a third higher than the figures for countries at similar per capita income levels. This does not necessarily imply, pending further analysis, that public spending in the CSB countries is excessive, since the size of government here, as elsewhere, is shaped, *inter alia*, by both views about the role of the state and the costs of the tax systems needed to support public expenditures at different levels.

Second, the size of government rises with the level of income per capita. Public expenditure as a proportion of GDP is on average 29 percent in the CIS countries, a group of countries with a PPP-based per capita GDP of USD 3,850 that have made limited progress with transition to a market economy, compared with just under 41 percent in the CSB countries, a group of countries with a PPP-based per capita GDP of USD 9,350 that are further advanced in the transition. These may be compared with an average of 42 percent in the high-income OECD countries.[2 3]

However, it should be noted that these numbers do not include spending that was moved out of the budgetary arena in the form of implicit and contingent liabilities which softened budget constraints (see examples in World Bank, 2000a).

Table 10.1 displays the functional structure of public expenditure both as a share of GDP and as a share of total public expenditure in these groups of countries: the high-income OECD, the CSB and the CIS countries. Social security and welfare account for over a third of public expenditure in the high-income OECD and CSB countries and for roughly a quarter of public expenditures in the CIS countries. Public expenditures on health and education make up a quarter of public expenditure in the high-income OECD and CSB countries and a little under 22 percent in the CIS countries. They are split roughly evenly between health and education in the OECD and EU accession countries, but health expenditures are around twice as much as those for education in the CIS countries. Altogether expenditures on education, health and social protection account for nearly 60 percent of public expenditures in the high-income OECD and CSB countries and nearly a half in the CIS countries. It will be recollected however that both GDP and the share of public expenditures in GDP are significantly lower in the CIS countries, so that public expenditures on education and health, for example, have each fallen to USD 10 per capita or less in the poorest CIS countries such as the Kyrgyz Republic and Tajikistan.

2 Simple averages are used to arrive at figures for country groups.

3 The high income OECD countries include Australia, Austria, Belgium, Canada, Denmark, Finland, France, Germany, Greece, Iceland, Ireland, Japan, Luxembourg, New Zealand, Netherlands, Norway, Portugal, Spain, Sweden, Switzerland, United Kingdom and the United States of America.

Table 10.1a Functional structure of public expenditures: country groups (1999-2000 average; in percent of GDP)[a]

											Economic Affairs and Services					
	GDP per capita in 2000 (PPP USD)	Total Expenditure[c]	General Public Service	Defense	Public Order & Safety	Education	Health	Social Security & Welfare	Housing & Community Amenities	Recreational, Cultural, & Religious Affairs	Fuel & Energy	Agriculture, Forestry, Fishing, & Hunting	Mining, Manufacturing, & Construction	Transportation & Communication	Other Economic Affairs & Services	Interest	Other Expenditures
High-Income OECD[2]	26,200	42.4	2.9	1.6	1.2	5.3	5.4	15.6	1.5	0.8	0.2	0.8	0.3	2.2	1.0	4.6	-0.9
CSB [3]	9,300	41.9	2.9	1.9	2.3	4.8	5.2	14.0	1.8	1.0	0.2	1.2	0.3	2.3	1.2	2.7	0.0
CIS[4]	3,850	29.1	1.8	1.7	1.5	4.3	2.2	7.8	1.3	0.6	0.5	1.5	0.6	1.5	0.5	1.9	1.3

Table 10.1b Functional structure of public expenditures: country groups (1999-2000 average; in percent of total expenditures)[a]

											Economic Affairs and Services					
	GDP per capita in 2000 (PPP US$)	Total Expenditure[c]	General Public Service	Defense	Public Order & Safety	Education	Health	Social Security & Welfare	Housing & Community Amenities	Recreational, Cultural, & Religious Affairs	Fuel & Energy	Agriculture, Forestry, Fishing, & Hunting	Mining, Manufacturing, & Construction	Transportation & Communication	Other Economic Affairs & Services	Interest	Other Expenditures
High-Income OECD[b]	26,200	100.0	6.8	3.9	2.7	12.5	12.7	36.7	3.4	1.9	0.5	2.0	0.7	5.1	2.3	10.8	-2.1
CSB[c]	9,300	100.0	7.0	4.5	5.5	11.6	12.3	33.3	4.2	2.4	0.5	2.9	0.7	5.6	2.8	6.8	0.1
CIS [d]	3,850	100.0	6.3	5.7	5.1	14.9	7.6	26.9	4.5	2.2	1.8	5.3	2.2	5.1	1.6	6.4	4.5

Notes to Table 10.1a and Table 10.1b

[a] Consolidated budgetary, extra budgetary and social security accounts of central, state/provincial and local governments. For High-Income OECD countries years of observations vary;
[b] Austria, Belgium, Denmark, Finland, France, Germany, Greece, Ireland, Italy, Luxembourg, Netherlands, Portugal, Spain, Sweden, United Kingdom, Australia, Canada, Iceland, Japan, New Zealand, Norway, Switzerland, United States;
[c] Albania, Bosnia, Bulgaria, Croatia, Czech Republic, Estonia, Hungary, Latvia, Lithuania, Poland, Romania, Slovak Republic, Slovenia, Yugoslavia. For purposes of expenditure, the CSB excludes Macedonia where a comparable disaggregation into functions was not available and included Yugoslavia, for which the data pertains to 2001;
[d] Armenia, Azerbaijan, Belarus, Georgia, Kazakhstan, Kyrgyz Republic, Moldova, Russian Federation, Tajikistan, Turkmenistan, Ukraine, Uzbekistan;
[e] Excluding grants and transfers between budgets of different levels.

Source: IMF Staff Reports.

Tax Systems in Transition

What are the characteristics of the tax systems that raise resources to finance those public expenditures? This section sets tax systems in transition countries in comparative international perspective.

Cross Sectional Comparisons

We begin by comparing features of the tax systems in the CIS countries with those in the CSB countries and the high-income OECD countries. Four stylized facts emerging from such a comparison at the end of the first decade of transition, 1999-2000, as follows (see Table 10.2 and Figure 10.3).

First, the share of tax revenue in GDP raises from 22 percent in the CIS countries through 33 percent in the CSB countries to 37 percent in the high-income OECD countries.

Second, the share of direct taxes, viz., personal and corporate income taxes plus social security contributions-cum-payroll taxes, in total tax revenue rises from 43 percent in the CIS countries through 54 percent in the CSB countries to 63 percent in the high-income OECD countries. While the share of personal income taxes in total tax revenue increases, that of corporate income taxes falls sharply, reflecting in part the integration of personal and corporate taxes, with collection at the corporate level counting as advance payment for the personal income tax. It should also be noted that the share of social security contributions-cum-payroll taxes in total tax revenue is significantly higher in the CSB countries at the end of the decade compared not only to the high-income OECD countries but also to the European Union where social security contributions are higher than in the non-EU countries of the high-income OECD group.[4]

Third, the share of domestic indirect taxes, viz., VAT/sales/turnover taxes and excises in total tax revenue decreases from 44 percent in the CIS countries through 38 percent in the CSB countries to 30 percent in the industrial countries. With the share of excises remaining broadly unchanged, this reflects a decline in VAT/sales/turnover taxes.

Fourth, trade taxes are relatively unimportant in transition countries and their contribution to tax revenue is negligible in the industrial countries.

4 It may be noted that social security in the USA generally refers only to pensions whereas social security in Europe covers the area called social protection in the USA.

Table 10.2a Tax structure of industrial and transition countries[1] (in percent of GDP)

	Total Revenue & Grants	Tax Revenue	Other Revenue & Grants	Taxes on Income, Profits, and Capital Gains			Social Security & Payroll tax	Domestic Taxes on Goods & Services: of which General sales, turnover			International Trade Taxes			Wealth & Property Taxes	Other Tax Revenues
				Total	Of which Individual	Of which Corporate		Total	VAT	Excises	Total	Of which Import duties	Of which Export duties		
High-income OECD	42.9	36.6	6.3	14.4	10.1	2.6	8.9	10.7	6.1	3.1	0.1	0.1	0.0	1.8	0.7
European Union[2]	45.2	39.4	5.8	14.3	9.6	2.6	10.8	11.9	6.7	3.7	0.0	0.0	0.0	1.5	0.9
CSB (early transition)	40.8	35.0	5.8	9.7	5.3	4.3	11.2	11.0	8.4	2.2	2.0	2.0	0.0	0.3	0.8
CSB (late transition)	37.7	33.0	4.7	7.4	5.2	2.1	10.6	12.4	8.7	3.4	1.3	1.3	0.0	0.4	0.7
CIS (early transition)	29.3	24.4	4.9	8.0	1.7	6.2	6.2	9.0	6.2	2.5	0.7	0.5	0.1	0.2	0.3
CIS (late transition)	25.5	22.2	3.2	5.3	2.0	3.1	4.5	9.7	6.1	2.5	1.2	1.1	0.1	0.8	0.6

Table 10.2b Tax Structure of industrial and transition countries [1] (in percent of tax revenue)

	Total Revenue & Grants	Tax Revenue	Other Revenue & Grants	Taxes on Income, Profits, and Capital Gains			Social Security & Payroll tax	Domestic Taxes on Goods & Services: of which			International Trade Taxes			Wealth & Property Taxes	Other Tax Revenues
					Of which			General sales, turnover				Of which			
				Total	Individual	Corporate		Total	VAT	Excises	Total	Import duties	Export duties		
High-income OECD	117.4	100.0	17.4	39.6	28.2	7.6	23.3	29.6	16.8	8.9	0.5	0.4	0.0	5.3	1.8
European Union[2]	114.9	100.0	14.9	36.0	24.2	7.0	26.6	31.3	17.8	10.0	0.0	0.0	0.0	3.9	2.2
CSB (early transition)	117.7	100.0	17.7	27.5	14.7	12.6	31.5	31.7	24.0	6.5	6.2	6.2	0.0	0.7	2.4
CSB (late transition)	114.9	100.0	14.9	22.5	15.6	6.5	31.6	37.9	26.6	10.3	4.3	4.3	0.0	1.3	2.4
CIS (early transition)	126.8	100.0	26.8	33.1	7.7	24.6	23.9	37.0	28.1	9.7	3.2	2.4	0.3	0.8	2.1
CIS (late transition)	115.3	100.0	15.3	23.9	9.8	12.6	19.4	44.0	31.0	11.6	5.9	5.4	0.4	3.3	3.4

Notes:

[1] Consolidated General Government unless indicated otherwise. For those latter indications, see Appendix Tables 1 to 6.

[2] Austria, Belgium, Denmark, Finland, France, Germany, Greece, Ireland, Italy, Luxemburg, Netherlands, Portugal, Spain, Sweden, United Kingdom.

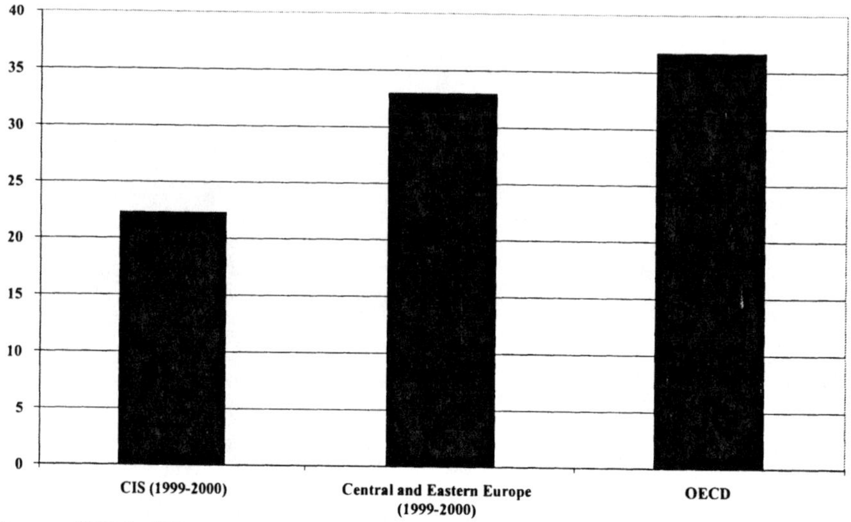

Source: IMF Staff Reports.

Figure 10.3 Tax revenues in developed and transition economies as percent of GDP, 1999-2000

Comparisons over Time

These stylized facts involving a comparison both in levels and in composition of tax systems in the CIS, CSB and industrial countries from the lowest to the highest levels of GDP per capita, are broadly similar to those observed in comparisons of developing with industrial countries (Burgess and Stern, 1993). However, in understanding why tax systems in transition countries look the way they do now, it is also necessary to compare the evolution of tax structures of the CIS countries as well as those of the CSB countries from the early years of transition to those prevailing at the end of its first decade. The stylized facts emerging from this comparison may be summarized as follows (see Table 10.2)

First, the share of tax revenue to GDP *fell* from 24 percent to 22 percent in the CIS countries and from 35 percent to 33 percent in the CSB countries between the beginning and end of the 1990s, paralleling the reduction in public expenditures noted in Section 10.2. This left the CSB countries and, *a fortiori,* the CIS countries in 1999-2000 with a *lower* tax revenue to GDP ratio than the 37 percent prevailing in the high-income OECD countries.

Second, the share of direct taxes, viz., personal and corporate income taxes plus social security contributions-cum-payroll taxes in total tax revenue *fell* from 56 percent to 43 percent in the CIS countries and from 59 percent to 54 percent in the CSB countries. This left the transition countries with a share of direct taxes in total tax revenue in 1999-2000 much *lower* than the 63 percent obtaining in industrial countries. The decline was primarily due to a sharp fall in the share of the corporate income tax — from 25 percent to 13 percent in the CIS countries and 13 percent to 7 percent in the CSB countries — and reflected the elimination of a captive source of revenue, viz. taxes on profits of publicly owned enterprises. This more than offset an increase in the share of the individual income tax in total tax revenue in both groups of transition countries. The share of social security contributions-cum-payroll taxes to total tax revenue *fell* in the CIS countries to levels *below* that in the high-income OECD economies but remained broadly unchanged in the CSB countries.

Third, the decline in the share of direct taxes is reflected in growth in the share of domestic indirect taxes, viz., VAT/sales/turnover taxes plus excises, which *rose* from 37 percent to 44 percent in the CIS countries and from 32 percent to 38 percent in the CSB countries. There was an increase in the share of both VAT/sales/turnover taxes as well as excises. This left the CIS and, *a fortiori*, the CSB countries in 1999-2000 with shares of domestic indirect taxation to GDP *higher* than the corresponding share of 30 percent in the industrial countries. Moreover, this observation applied equally to the shares of both VAT/sales/turnover taxes and excises in total tax revenue.

Graphing the Tax Transition

A visual perspective on how the composition of tax revenue varies between high-income OECD, CSB and CIS countries in cross section and over time is provided, following Burgess and Stern (1993), by Figure 10.4. With trade taxes accounting for a very low proportion of total tax revenue, the figure focuses on the shares of income tax, social security contributions-cum-payroll taxes and domestic indirect taxes in non-trade tax revenue (total tax revenues less trade tax revenue). The points A, B, and C in the triangle represent 100 percent of (non-trade) tax revenue from personal and corporate income taxes, 100 percent from social security contributions cum-payroll taxes and 100 percent from domestic indirect taxes, respectively. A point on the line BC corresponds to a zero level of income taxes, while a point on the line AC corresponds to a zero level of social security contributions-cum-payroll taxes, and a point on the line AB corresponds to a zero level of domestic indirect taxes.

The high-income OECD countries are on average closer to the income tax corner and towards the axis AB compared to the transition countries. The CIS countries are on average closer to the domestic indirect tax corner and towards the axis AC compared to the industrial and CSB countries. The CSB countries are closer to the social security contribution - cum-payroll tax corner and towards the axis BC compared to the CIS countries.

Figures 10.5 and 10.6 compare the characteristics of tax system in the CSB and CIS countries between the early years of transition and the end of its first decade. They show that, on average, the CSB and CIS countries in 1999-2000 were further away from the income tax corner and closer to the domestic indirect tax corner than they were in early transition. This was a movement *away* from the composition found in high-income OECD countries. The share of social security contributions-cum-payroll (non-trade) tax revenue remained broadly unchanged in the CSB, so that the points representing the CSB countries in early transition and 1999-2000 are equally far away from the AC axis. But the CIS countries moved away from the social security contributions-cum-payroll tax corner during the first decade of transition.

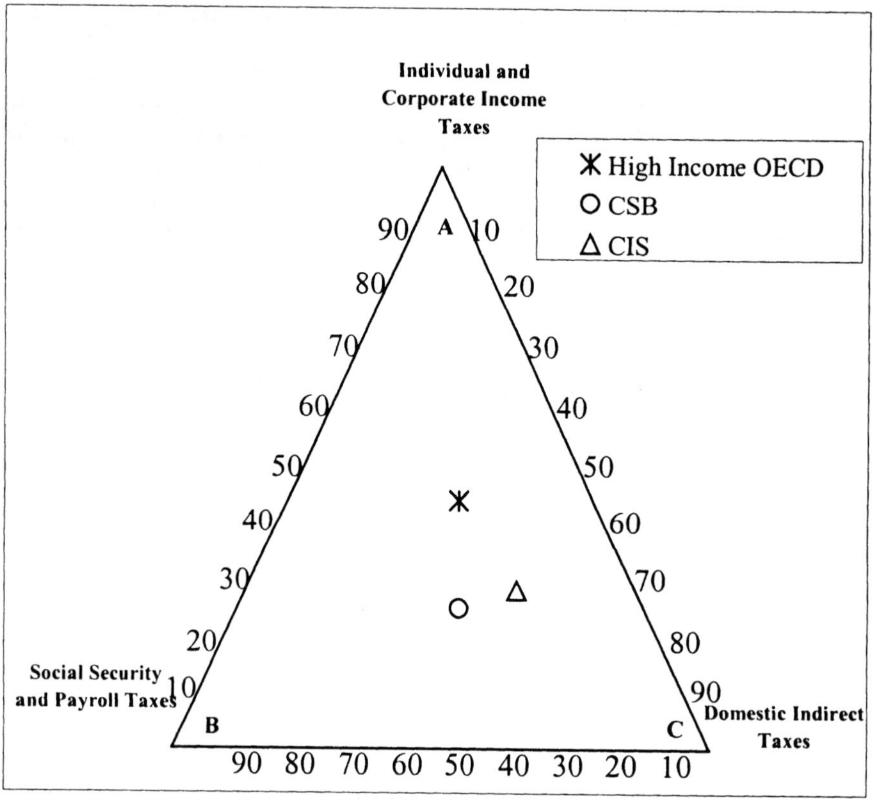

Figure 10.4 Breakdown of non-trade tax revenue by type: High-income OECD, CSB, and CIS economies (unweighted group averages)

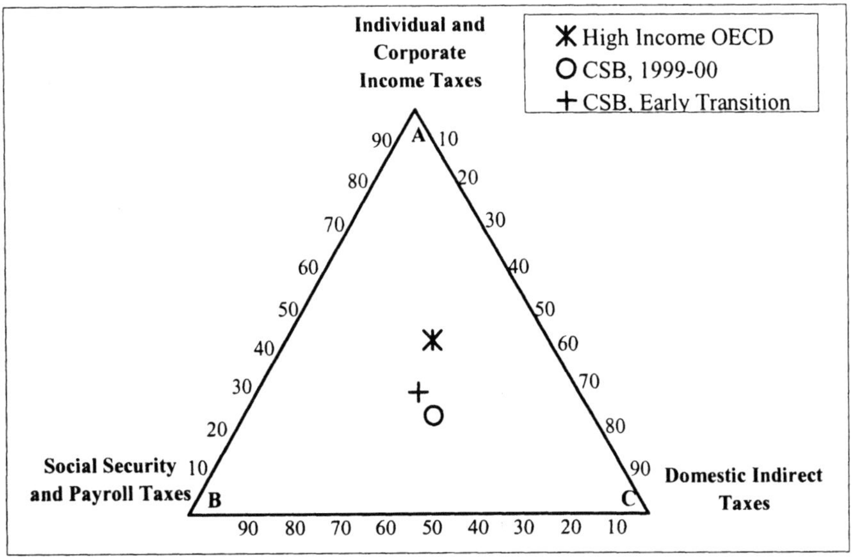

Figure 10.5 Breakdown of tax revenue by type: High-income OECD and CSB economies during Early transition and in 1999-2000 (unweighted group averages)

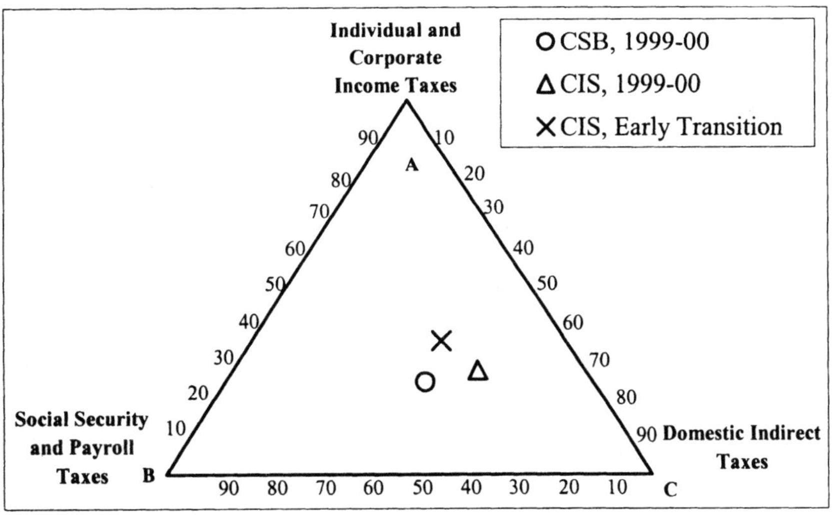

Figure 10.6 Breakdown of non-trade tax revenue by type: CSB and CIS economies during early transition and in 1999-2000 (unweighted group averages)

The results of these comparisons, in cross-section between the CIS, CSB and the high-income OECD countries, and for two time periods for the CSB and the CIS themselves, illustrate the challenges that transition countries face in developing a tax system appropriate for a market economy. The opposing movements in key ratios describing levels and composition of taxes (i) between the onset of transition and the end of its first decade in the transition countries and (ii) in cross-section compared to the industrial countries at end-decade suggest that the evolution of tax systems in transition countries is 'U-shaped', with regard both to the share of tax revenue to GDP and the shares of major taxes in tax revenue.

The comparison across the same subgroups of transition countries between the onset of transition and the end of its first decade, *inter alia*, reflect two sets of developments. First, the loss of traditional profit, turnover and payroll tax revenues from erstwhile captive state enterprises rendered uncompetitive by price liberalization and either downsized by hardening budget constraints or kept afloat by tax exemptions and a tolerance of tax and other arrears. Secondly, the inability to institute quickly a well-administered tax system covering a broad base with low rates that would encourage tax compliance among new and restructured enterprises rather than driving them underground. Both considerations illustrate a key aspect of transition, viz. a movement from a system where the government exercised a preemptive claim on output and income before citizens had access to the remainder to one with a greatly diminished role for the public sector, where the government needs to collect revenue in order to spend.

These developments manifested themselves in a number of areas. These included a fall in the tax revenue-to-GDP ratio, a significant part of which was accounted for by declines in revenue from the corporate income tax due to losses of revenue from profits of publicly-owned enterprises. The ratio of public expenditures to GDP also fell, due to the need to reduce fiscal deficits in order to stabilize inflation. The importance of income taxes declined, mainly because of the fall in the share of corporate income taxes. The importance of social security contributions-cum-payroll taxes in the CIS countries fell, while the share of individual income taxes in these countries rose. Domestic indirect taxes (both VAT/sales/turnover taxes and excises) became much more important elements of tax revenue—reflecting in part the decline in the role of direct taxes.

What needs to be done? The cross-sectional and intertemporal comparisons between the CIS, the CSB and the high-income OECD countries show that, viewed from the perspective of taxation, outcomes often associated with the unraveling of command economies in the early transition differed from the outcomes that subsequently occurred, which were analogous to those seen in poor countries. With the exception of the welcome increase in the importance of personal income taxation, the developments that actually occurred need to be reversed in order to move towards a market economy. However, this needs to be done not by reclaiming the traditional bases and instruments of central planning, but by accessing tax bases in the emerging private sector and using the apparatus of a modern tax system, viz., a personal income tax, a corporate income tax with deductions for the costs of generating those incomes, social security contributions and payroll taxes, a value added tax levied on consumption, excises on items such as tobacco, alcoholic beverages and petroleum and low customs tariffs—all of which needs to be implemented by a rule-based tax administration. These reforms are needed to boost the shares of tax revenue in GDP, direct taxes in tax revenue, and personal income taxes in direct taxes. They are also needed to reduce the share of revenue earned from domestic indirect taxes and from trade taxes.

Suggested Levels and Composition of Tax Revenue

Could current levels of public expenditure in the transition countries arrived at in part through socio-political judgments about the role of the state, be financed by these taxes without creating significant distortions in the private sector? The following considerations are relevant in answering this question.

First, the value added tax (a very successful innovation in tax practice) raises on average around 7 percent of GDP in the high-income OECD countries. Empirical evidence from these countries suggests that in all countries where the VAT collects more than 7 percent of GDP, there is a clear tradeoff between a higher tax rate and a broader tax base. Countries facing such a tradeoff have rates of 14 to 22 percent on bases of 40 to 60 percent of GDP. The evidence also suggests that the longer a VAT has been in place, allowing taxpayers and administrators more time for improved compliance and enforcement, the higher is the rate of compliance with the tax (Agha and Haughton, 1996; IMF, 2001). It therefore seems reasonable to suppose that transition countries, which have limited experience with the VAT, could not, for the next few years, expect to raise more than 6 to 7 percent of GDP (depending on the quality of their tax administration) without encountering problems with compliance or introducing significant distortions into their economies. The other major item of indirect taxation, viz., excises, which are generally levied on alcohol, tobacco and petroleum, can be expected to yield 2 to 3 percent or so of GDP. With trade taxes becoming less important, the share of indirect taxes in GDP can thus be expected to yield roughly 8 to 10 percent of GDP.

Second, income taxes average around 15 percent of GDP in the high-income OECD countries. Within the income tax category, personal income tax revenues are usually about three to four times as large as corporate income tax revenues in the industrial countries. Corporate taxes typically account for 2 to 3 percent of GDP, partly reflecting the fact that well-functioning tax administrations reduce the need to use income taxes on corporations as a withholding device for collecting personal income taxes. Furthermore, a high corporate income tax rate can discourage investment in a world where capital is very mobile across national boundaries. The base for income taxation is assumed to be roughly half of non-agricultural income. The latter as a share of GDP ranges from below 50 percent in Albania to over 90 percent in the Central European countries (depending on the country's per capita income level), yielding a range of 25 and 45 percent for the tax base. With average income tax rates in the range of 20 to 25 percent, and taking into account tradeoffs between a higher tax rate and a broader tax base, it may then be expected that the income tax could eventually raise between 6 and 9 percent of

GDP (depending on a country's per capita income), with the share of personal taxes (relative to corporate taxes) increasing with the level of economic development and the quality of the tax administration.

Third, social security contributions and payroll taxes as a share of GDP average 11 percent both in the EU and CSB countries (despite the significantly lower per capital income in the latter). This reflects in part the CSB countries' socialist legacy, and in part the successful use of social expenditures to cushion the impact on the poor of downsizing in the early years of transition.[5] In fact, payroll taxes in the EU accession countries range from 33 percent in Estonia to 50 percent in Slovakia, while Italy, Spain and Sweden have rates about 30 percent and in no case higher than 40 percent (Riboud, Sanchez and Silva, 2002). Evidence from a recent empirical analysis of Slovakia, where the unemployment rate averaged 19 percent in 2001, suggests that while the unemployment insurance, social assistance and social support schemes have been effective in alleviating poverty, they have exerted significant disincentive effects on labor supply. Reforms of the benefit program designed to 'make employment pay' rather than penalizing unemployment have the potential to reduce double digit unemployment and lower social spending, thereby making possible an eventual reduction in payroll taxes.[6] This is broadly consistent with the findings from other OECD countries, and argues for reforms in social expenditures and reductions of the distortions arising from payroll taxes. The situation is however quite different in the CIS countries, where social security contributions average less than 5 percent of GDP. Turning to the role of these taxes in an overall revenue package, with the wage bill in the formal sector of the economy as a share of GDP ranging from 20 to 50 percent (or more) across the region, a payroll tax rate averaging 20 to 30 percent could yield 6 to 10 percent of GDP.

On the basis of these broad efficiency considerations and consistency with comparative evidence on public expenditure shares for countries at comparable income levels, it is suggested (see Table 10.3) that the transition countries, depending on their stage of development, aim for a tax revenue-to-GDP ratio in the range of 22 to 31 percent or so, comprising revenues from VAT (6 to 7 percent), excises (2 to 3 percent), income tax (6 to 9 percent), social security contribution-cum-payroll tax (6 to 10 percent), and other taxes such as on trade and on property (2 percent).[7]

---

5 For a further discussion of this point, see World Bank (2000)

6 The analysis is reported in World Bank (2001)

7 A similar analysis for China is presented in Hussein and Stern (1993)

Table 10.3 Suggested levels and composition of tax revenue

Tax	Base, % of GDP	Rate in %	Yield, % of GDP
VAT	40-60	12-22	6-7*
Income tax	25-45	20-25	6-9
Social Security contribution cum payroll tax	20-50	20-30	6-10
Subtotal			18-26
Excises (tobacco, alcohol, petroleum)			2-3
Other taxes (trade, property, etc.)			2
Total tax revenue			22-31

*Adjusted downward by one percentage point from 7-8 percent for inexperience with the tax

While the upper end of this suggested range is lower than the 33 percent of GDP that tax revenue represented in the CSB countries in 1999-2000, it is close enough to the expenditure to GDP ratio of 33 percent, typical of countries at comparable per capita income levels. This difference can be financed by non-tax revenues, which usually account for roughly 2 to 3 percent of GDP. In any event, most EU accession countries, as part of their 2000-2004 pre-accession economic programs, sought to cut taxes on the order of 2 percent of GDP and incur incremental expenditures on the order of 3.5 percent of GDP to comply with the requirements of the EU's *acquis communautaire*, while at the same time improving budget balance by around 0.5 percent of GDP (Funck, 2002). These ambitious goals can only be accomplished through a sharp reduction in the share of regular public expenditures to GDP, together with a tight prioritization within that envelope. This requires a thorough going reappraisal of the role of the state in the economy.

The lower end of the 22 to 31 percent range for tax revenue to GDP is equal to the average for the CIS countries. However, the average tax revenue to GDP ratio for the low-income CIS countries that face the most acute development challenges (Armenia, Azerbaijan, Georgia, the Kyrgyz Republic, Moldova, Tajikistan and Uzbekistan) is only 18 percent. Raising this share in order to finance public expenditures, especially in the social sectors where they have fallen to extremely low levels in those countries (for example, on education USD 4 per capita in Tajikistan, USD 9 per capita in the Kyrgyz Republic and USD 11 per capita in Armenia in 1999, compared to USD 180 per capita in the EU accession countries, and on health USD 1 per capita in Tajikistan and USD 7 per capita in the Kyrgyz Republic and Georgia in 1999, compared to USD 176 per capita in the EU accession countries) together with appropriate prioritization of those expenditures, is an important policy priority.

Taxation and the Investment Climate

Small enterprises employing fewer than 50 workers, many of them *de novo* but also some firms spun off from state enterprises, have been key to generating employment and creating wealth in transition economies. A major policy-cum-institutional challenge facing governments across the region has been the creation of an attractive and competitive investment climate in which restructured and new enterprises have incentives to absorb the labor and assets rendered redundant by the downsizing of old and unviable enterprises, as well as invest in expansion. This challenge includes reducing excessively high marginal tax rates, simplifying regulatory procedures, establishing security of property rights, and providing basic infrastructure, while maintaining a level playing field among old, restructured, and new enterprises.

The Business Environment and Enterprise Performance Survey, covering a large number of enterprises in over 20 transition economies, and conducted jointly by the European Bank for Reconstruction and Development and the World Bank in 1999 (see EBRD, 1999), unbundled factors influencing the investment climate into microeconomic variables (including taxes and regulations), macroeconomic variables (including policy instability, inflation and exchange rates) and law and order (including the functioning of the judiciary, corruption, street crime, disorder, organized crime, and mafia). According to the respondents, taxes and regulations were consistently among the most important impediments to expansion by new enterprises.

Table 10.4 reports the number of taxes and the average rates that are imposed on businesses.[8] The number of national taxes—profit tax, VAT/sales tax, income tax and social security taxes (in the form of payroll taxes, the latter of which is treated as one tax), together with turnover taxes to support various special funds—which is shown in column 5 of the table, is a rough indicator of the complexity of the tax system.[9] By this measure, Poland and Hungary have the least complex national tax systems, as contrasted with Belarus, Turkmenistan, and Uzbekistan. However, the last four columns of Table 10.4 also report the extent to which countries attempt to relieve the burden on small firms through tax breaks or simplified arrangements.[10 11]

---

8 We thank Kjetil Tvedt for producing Table 10.4, which updates Table 8.3 in EBRD (1999). Definitions on SMEs and micro businesses are those used in national tax codes.

9 Column (4) of the table also reports the maximum rate of personal income tax since businesses registered as sole proprietors and often subject to personal income tax.

10 The 'tax incentive for new start-ups/investments' column emphasizes tax breaks either in favor of or against SMEs. The latter include all incentives promoting large investments. Tax breaks for FDI are interpreted as discrimination against SMEs, on the assumption that foreign investors normally faces some initial obstacles in form of administrative problems or lack of information that generate fixed costs which are more significant for small start-ups firms.

11 General SME tax breaks here are understood as cases when SMEs face lower profit tax rates because of their size. A simplified tax in form of a gross turnover tax or lump sum tax may reduce the tax burden as well. However, the impact of simplification on the tax

Whatever the merits of rules and legislation, arbitrary bureaucratic harassment to which the administration of taxes and business licensing gives rise continues to be a significant problem. For example, a survey of some 2000 predominantly small and medium enterprises (with a mean firm size of 22 workers and a median firm size of 10 workers) done in Russia in March-April 2002 by the Center for Economic and Financial Research (CEFIR) and the World Bank found that in 2001, 5 to 21 percent of those who had been in business before and after the passing of legislation designed to improve the investment climate were visited between 2 and 3 times each by sanitary, police and fire safety inspectors, which is in excess of that prescribed by the law (CEFIR and World Bank, 2002).

While steps to improve the investment climate are important, the hardening of budget constraints on all enterprises has also been key to the resumption of growth in successful transition economies. The experience of the 1990s suggests that a sharp and early decline in aggregate employment preceded the rapid growth of new firms. This made assets cheaply available to new enterprises, which was useful when financing was not readily available and new investment was not forthcoming. When the proportion of employment in small firms reached a threshold of around 40 percent, the sector evolved from being a passive receptacle for absorbing resources into an active competitor, rapidly increasing its share of employment. In countries where aggregate employment picked up, it did so after the recovery of aggregate output. When the threshold was not reached, people remained 'unemployed on the job' as in the CIS and some countries in southeastern Europe. Aggregate employment started to fall only later in the process. These observations suggest a sequence where hard budget constraints are imposed and the old sector declines before the new sector can grow. The complementarity between hardening budget constraints and improving the investment climate has been extremely important.

This discussion suggests that major elements of the agenda of tax reform should therefore include eliminating tax exemptions, which reflect governance problems in tax administration rather than being equity-enhancing. In Georgia, for example, it is estimated that an additional 2 percent of GDP could be collected from excise taxes on petroleum products and cigarettes (World Bank, 2002b). Likewise, simplifying tax regimes for small businesses, in order to relieve the administrative and reporting burden on the taxpayer and minimize contact between the tax authorities and the taxpayer, should also be a priority. The use of tax exemptions and tax relief for such firms is, however, not recommended, in part because potentially 50 percent or more of value added that is generated by small firms in successful transition economies would then escape taxation. This would significantly worsen the government's fiscal position without addressing such key issues as insecure property rights or inadequate infrastructure that impede the development of small firms.

---

burden is often not clear, and such procedures are never interpreted as an SME tax discount.

Table 10.4 SME taxation

Country	GENERAL TAXATION				TAXATION RELATED TO SMEs				
	Standard profit tax	Standard VAT	Max. personal Income tax	Number of national taxes	VAT turnover threshold (US$)	Tax incentives for new start-ups/investments		General SME tax break	Simplified tax for SMEs and sole proprietors (lump sum or presumptive)
						Favoring SMEs	Favoring large firms		
Albania	25%	20%	25%	5	57000	No	No	No	Lump sum or gross turnover tax[1]
Armenia	20%	20%	20%	4	17200	No	Yes[2]	No	Lump sum[3]
Azerbaijan	27%	18%	35%	4	6400	No	No	No	Gross turnover tax[4]
Belarus	30%	20%	30%	8[5]	6000	No	No	Yes[6]	Lump sum[7]
Bosnia & Herzegovina	30%	24% sales tax	50%	4	No	No	Yes[8]	No	No
Bosnia & Herzegovina (Rep)	20%-10% (regressive)	18% sales tax	25%	5	No	No	Yes[9]	No	No
Bulgaria	23.5%	20%	29%	4	33000	No	No	Yes[10]	Lump sum[11]
Croatia	20%	22%	35%	4	6000	No	Yes[12]	No	Lump sum
Czech Republic	31%	22%	32%	4	91000	No	Yes[13]	No	Lump sum
Estonia	26%	18%	26%	4	No	No	No	No	No
Georgia	20%	20%	20%	5	11000	No	No	No	Lump sum[14]
Hungary	18%	25%	40%	4	No	Yes[15]	No	No	No
Kazakhstan	30%	16%	30%	4	25000	No	No	No	Lump sum or gross turnover tax
Kosovo	20%	15%	20%	4	92000	No	No	No	Gross turnover tax[16]
Kyrgyzstan	20%	20%	20%	6	2100	No	No	No	Gross turnover tax[17]
Latvia	22%	18%	25%	4	16000	No	Yes[18]	Yes[19]	No
Lithuania	15%	18%	33%	4	2600	No	No	Yes[20]	Presumptive tax[21]
(FYR) Macedonia	15%	19%	18%	4	76000	No	Yes[22]	No	Lump sum
Moldova	25%	20%	35%	4	No	Yes[23]	Yes[24]	No	Lump sum[25]
Poland	28%	22%	40%	4	9000	No	No	No	Lump sum
Romania	25%	19%	40%	6	1500	Yes[26]	Yes[27]	No	Gross turnover tax[28]
Russia	20-24%	20%	13%	5 (4 from 2003)	No	No	No	No[29]	Gross turnover tax
Slovak Republic	25%	23%	38%	4	16000	No	Yes[30]	No	Lump sum
Slovenia	25%	20%	50%	4	20000	No	No	No	No
Tajikistan	30%	20%	20%	N.A.	N.A.	N.A.	N.A.	N.A.	N.A.
Turkmenistan	25%	20%	25%	6	Small-scale firms exempt.	No	Yes[31]	Yes[32]	Lump sum[33]
Ukraine	30%	20%	40%	5	11500	No	No	No	Gross turnover tax[34]
Uzbekistan	26%	20%	36%	6	Small firms are exempt.	No	Yes[35]	No	Gross turnover tax or lump sum[36]
FRY Montenegro	20%	8-17% sales tax	40%	4	No	N.A.	N.A.	N.A.	N.A.
FRY Serbia	20%	20% sales tax	20%	4	No	Yes[37]	No	No	No

Notes

Albania

[1] Lump sum for micro businesses = annual turnover under 2 million leks (US$14000), 4 percent gross turnover tax for small businesses = annual turnover 2-8 million leks (US$57000).

Armenia

[2] FDI over ADM 500 million (US$ 860,000).

[3] Fixed payment for small scale activities such as hairdressers, gas stations, commercial fishing, and trading activities conducted in locals with trading area less than 30 square meters.

Azerbaijan

[4] 2 percent gross turnover tax when turnover less than 300 times the minimum tax-exempted wage (US$ 6400).

Belarus

[5] In addition to the standard 4, there is Road tax, Chernobyl fund, Public housing fund, and R&D fund.

[6] 50 percent discount on profit tax for small enterprises = profit less than 5,000 MMW (5000*BYR3600=US$10,000) and having number of staff as mentioned below; for industries - less than 200 people; in science and scientific services - less than 100 people, for construction and other productive sectors up to 50 people; for non-productive sectors up to 25 people.

[7] Lump sum tax for stores that are single owned and total trading space less than 25 square meters, plus public catering enterprises, and at markets and sales exhibitions.

Bosnia & Herzegovina (Federation)

[8] profit generated by foreign capital.

Bosnia & Herzegovina (Republic)

[9] profit generated by foreign capital.

Bulgaria

[10] 20 percent profit tax for small businesses defined by taxable profit less than BGN 50,000 (US$22,200).

[11] for sole traders.

Croatia

[12] Newly established companies qualify for reduced tax rates and the reduction is higher for larger investments.

Czech Republic

[13] for inv. over CZK 350 million (US$ 10 million).

Georgia

[14] for enterprises with turnover less than GEL 24,000 (US$ 11,000).

Hungary

[15]SMEs can write off its tax by interest on loan used for investment in assets.

Kosovo

[16] 3 percent gross turnover tax for SMEs = turnover under 200,000 DEM (US$ 92,000).

Kyrgyzstan

[17] SMEs (total revenue up to 3 million soms or approximately US$63 000) may pay from 5 to10 percent gross turnover tax instead of all national taxes above (apparently SMEs find this system unfavorable and rather use the general system). Individual entrepreneurs can optionally get a patent and pay a monthly gross turnover tax, i.e. in retail trade – 4 percent.

Latvia

[18] For inv. over US$ 16 million.

[19] 20 percent profit tax for SMEs meeting at least two of the following three conditions: book value of tangible assets – 70 000 lats (EUR 123 700); net turnover – 200 000 lats (EUR 353 400); average number of employees – 25 persons.

Lithuania

[20] 13 percent profit tax for small businesses with less than 11 employees and a gross annual income less than LTL 500,000 (US$ 130,000).

[21] Optional for firms with gross income less than 100,000 LTL (US$ 26,000).

Macedonia (FYR)

[22] tax holiday for tax generated by foreign capital.

Moldova

[23] SMEs may benefit from a 35 percent discount on profit tax for two years.

[24] 50 percent tax discount given the first five years if foreign investments exceeds US$ 250,000.

[25] Individual entrepreneurs can buy patent which involve a monthly fee.

Romania

[26] for reinvested profit.

[27] for large FDI.

[28] micro-enterprises with less than 10 employees and an annual turnover less than Euro 100,000.

Russia

[29] Planned from 2003; Small enterprises with annual turnover of 10 million roubles (US$320,000) and up to 20 employees will be entitled to choose between 8 percent turnover tax or 20 percent profit tax (standard 24 percent).

Slovak Republic

[30] 5 years tax holiday for FDI over EUR 5 million.

Turkmenistan

[31] Tax breaks subject to negotiations. It is assumed that large firms have more negotiation power.

[32] 20-24 percent profit tax, depending on nature of activity, for small legal entities defined by annual turnover less than TMM 72 million (US$ 14,000), or less than 50 persons in producing firms, or less than 10 persons in trading firms, or less than 25 persons in all other types of firms.

[33] Lump sum license for entrepreneur without a legal entity and with annual turnover less than 72 million manats (US$14,000).

Ukraine

[34] Firms with up to 50 employees and turnover less than UAH 1 million (US$ 190,000) can pay a 6 percent gross turnover tax which does not exempt actor from VAT, or 10 percent gross turnover tax which do exempt firms from VAT.

Uzbekistan

[35] for FDI

[36] Optionally, small trading enterprises can pay 25 percent and small production enterprises can pay 10 percent tax of gross turnover instead of entire set of national taxes. Lump sum tax for individual entrepreneurs without a legal entity.

FRY Serbia

[37] tax discount amounting 30 percent of new investments for SMEs (in comparison to 10 percent of new investments for non-SMEs).

Administering the Tax System

The fundamental changes that tax policy has undergone in transition as a result of changing bases and instruments require a tax administration capable of implementing those policies in countries where such institutions were not present. While many countries now have modern tax legislation on their books, the development of the tax administration has lagged behind. This reflects not only a greater focus on changes in policy rather than administration in the early years of transition, but also the fact that demands on administration arising from changes in tax policy usually precede the development of supporting institutions.

While tax administration in transition countries shares many problems with those in developing countries (Bird and Oldman, 1990; Gillis, 1989), there are several unique features of the post-communist legacy. These include a culture of mutual mistrust between taxpayers and the tax authorities, and the absence of traditions of voluntary compliance with tax legislation, of appeals to the courts against the decisions of the tax authorities (which, by enhancing trust in the fairness of the tax administration, could encourage voluntary compliance), and of self-assessment, which shift the burden of appraisal to the private sector and reduce the administrative demands on the tax authorities.

This implies that much attention has been paid not only to strengthening enforcement but also to developing taxpayer education and services in order to improve compliance, and to maintain an appropriate balance between the two. The former has involved, *inter alia*, (i) making potential taxpayers aware of the general concept of taxation and why they should pay their taxes; (ii) providing assistance (not readily available to any but large taxpayers in the private sector in transition countries) to taxpayers who wish to comply voluntarily; and (iii) reducing compliance costs through simplification of procedures. Strengthened enforcement is also an important factor in improving tax compliance. By way of example, the use of information technology to detect non-filers and those that have not paid the full amounts due, and to notify them of the need to comply, sends a signal to delinquent taxpayers of the tax authorities' capacity to detect and punish evasion. Another example is the compilation of databases from third party information from multiple public sources (registrars of companies, land transactions etc.) and cross-checking of information between the VAT, income tax and excise tax authorities, as well as from private sources (sellers of luxury cars, banks and financial institutions etc.) about taxable transactions. These help provide independent checks on the veracity of tax returns and identify cases where taxes may have been evaded. Yet another example is the selection of cases for auditing so as to target scarce auditing and investigation resources where they can be most effective. International constraints that impinge on tax administration require additional skills, such as the implementation of tax treaties with other countries and the ability to detect transfer pricing that shifts income from high-tax to low-tax locations.

Most transition countries have set up large taxpayer units to focus on those taxpayers from whom the vast bulk of tax revenue would be derived. These units, which have the most qualified staff, have proved to be important in maintaining revenue collections while the rest of the tax administration is being modernized.

Evidence from the first decade of transition shows that SME sectors (made up of firms employing fifty or fewer workers) are the most dynamic part of transition economies. As noted above, taxation is among the most prominent difficulties in the business climate facing these firms. Tax policy and its associated administrative requirements for such firms must therefore be simplified in order to improve the investment climate while minimizing interactions between them and the tax authorities.

While many weaknesses in tax administration may be addressed through technical solutions, the development of civil society and political will is critically important for effective tax administration. Tax compliance will grow *pari passu* with the development of civil society, which is much further along in the CSB than in the CIS countries. Political will is required on two fronts. First, political support for harder budget constraints is essential in order to allow large taxpayer units to go after the most prominent tax debtors. Second, a strong political commitment to a level playing field for small enterprises is essential to simplifying the tax regime applicable to these enterprises. This sends a clear signal to foreign and domestic investors that the authorities are serious about creating an attractive investment climate. Revenue-sharing rules with subnational governments should also be structured so as to generate incentives for the latter to encourage the creation of small and new firms, instead of focusing on old enterprises that are kept afloat through tolerance of tax arrears. Political commitment to the effective implementation of tax policy should be distinguished from the use of the tax administration for political ends, such as selectively enforcing tax discipline on large taxpayers. Politicization of the tax administration should be avoided.

Taxation and Foreign Direct Investment

During 1996-99 more than USD 70 billion in foreign direct investment (FDI) flowed to the region, nearly 70 percent of it to the CSB countries (Table 10.5, which also presents gross domestic investment as a percent of GDP for comparison). In the CIS countries FDI has been largely confined to the energy-rich countries, with Azerbaijan, Kazakhstan and Russia receiving 75 percent of the total. Russia's share of FDI in GDP was even lower than that of several of the CIS countries, despite its considerable resource endowment.

Much foreign direct investment was driven by the sales of assets to strategic foreign investors; indeed, cumulative FDI is highly correlated with cumulative privatization revenues (EBRD, 2000). FDI brought with it two key advantages: first, technology and skills and, in some cases, the governance capacity and standards of the home country; and second, a source of foreign financing which, compared to bond and equity capital flows, was less prone to volatility in international capital markets.

Table 10.5 Main recipients of Foreign Direct Investment, 1992-1995 and 1996-1999

	1992-95			1996-99		
Country	USD millions	Percent of GDP	Memo item Gross Domestic Investment as a percent of GDP	USD millions	Percent of GDP	Memo item Gross Domestic Investment as a percent of GDP
CSB	**21,091**	**0.5**	**19.3**	**50,558**	**3.3**	**24.7**
Czech Republic	4,821	2.9	29.4	10,104	4.6	31.5
Estonia	647	3.9	26.9	1,050	5.2	28.2
Hungary	9,399	5.7	20.5	6,979	3.8	28.3
Poland	2,540	0.6	17.9	17,096	2.9	24.8
CIS	**8,272**	**1.0**	**26.2**	**22,001**	**2.5**	**20.8**
Azerbaijan	237	4.2	15.1	3,222	20.9	30.8
Kazakhstan	2,357	2.7	25.0	4,971	6.4	15.1
Russia	3,965	0.3	28.1	8,412	0.7	19.6
Turkmenistan	427	3.5	-	334	3.0	43.5*

Notes: Shares of GDP are period averages of medians for the group.
* Averages of 1997-1999

Source: World Bank staff estimates and country statistical offices.

Figure 10.7 shows that higher cumulative foreign direct investment, often a good proxy for a more attractive investment climate in the host country (see World Bank, 2002c), is associated with a higher share of aggregate employment in small enterprises.

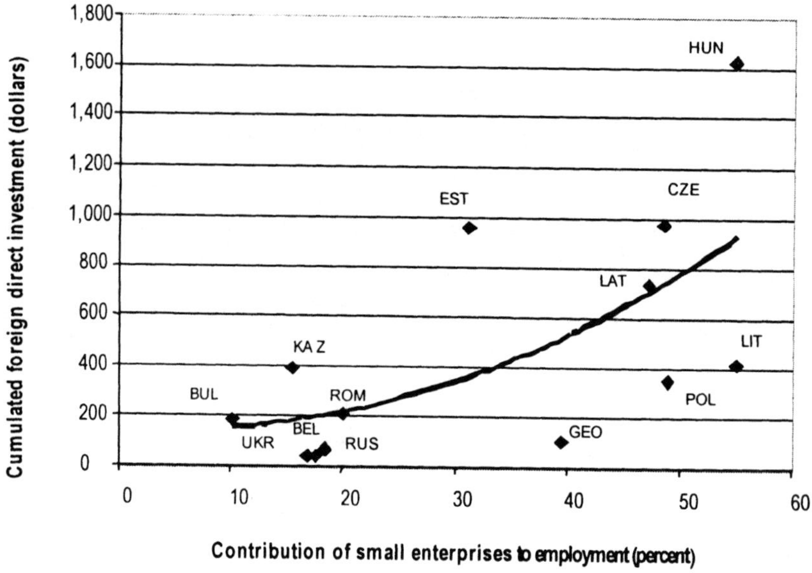

Source: EBRD (2000); World Bank database on SMEs.

Figure 10.7 Cumulative Foreign Direct Investment per capita and employment in small enterprises, 1998

Improving the investment climate for domestic and foreign investment remains an important issue for the CIS countries and those in southeastern Europe. In the advanced reformers where few large privatizations are left, devising an investment climate that can attract inflows of FDI into greenfield ventures and cross-border acquisitions of private sector assets, together with the associated entrepreneurial experience—without undermining the country's fiscal position through the provision of tax incentives—is a major challenge facing policy makers. Many countries—Bulgaria, Estonia, the Czech Republic, Hungary, Romania and Slovakia—have offered tax incentives, employment subsidies and special economic zones to attract foreign investment. In fact, the provision of generous investment incentives in the Czech and Slovak Republics in 1996 and 1997 respectively was associated with a doubling of non-privatization-related FDI in those countries.

Recent empirical studies in developed countries suggest that the location of investment, its modes of financing and associated tax avoidance respond more strongly to tax changes than had been previously thought.[12] Moreover, both EU accession countries, and some member countries of the EU (such as Ireland), have successfully engaged in tax competition to attract FDI within their borders. In such a situation, countries with high corporate tax rates face the prospect of reduced FDI inflows and profit-shifting to lower tax locations through transfer pricing by multinationals. They may, therefore, be tempted to engage in a race to the bottom through competitive reductions in tax rates. Caution is, however, warranted here. The tax system, although important, is but one ingredient of an attractive investment climate. The interaction of tax and non-tax incentives on investment is a subject that has not yet been adequately explored in recent empirical work. Hence, if particular regions of a country experience stubbornly high double-digit unemployment as is the case in Central Europe, the solution may lie, not in a rush to tax holidays, accelerated depreciation and the like, but instead in directly addressing the sources of the problem, which could include the provision of relevant educational opportunities to match skills with labor demand, reducing disincentives to labor supply arising from overly generous social expenditures, cutting effective labor costs by lowering payroll taxes, and removing impediments to labor mobility arising from infrastructure bottlenecks. While this may still leave role for tax policy, governments should avoid the temptation to pick winners and engage in activist industrial policies. That route can lead to poor choices, subsidized inefficiency, and corrupt seeking after government favors.

Conclusions

This chapter raises the following important questions. First, what are the levels and composition of tax rates and revenues that raise enough resources to finance public expenditures without introducing excessive distortions in the private sector? Is tax revenue as a share of GDP 'too high' in the CSB countries and 'too low' in the CIS countries?

Second, must hardening budget constraints for all firms and improving the investment climate to promote the creation of new firms and stimulate entrepreneurship, without the state dispensing special favors, go hand in hand?

Third, what is the appropriate tax treatment for small firms, which have been the key to growth and employment generation? What political strategies are available to eliminate tax exemptions that benefit powerful special interests, and to lower tax rates and simplify tax administration, which would benefit and encourage compliance by small firms?

Fourth, are the right partnerships in place or being constructed between the government, private sector, and civil society in order to foster a culture of voluntary tax compliance in transition economies?

12 Hines (1999) provides on useful survey.

Fifth, how important is the use of corporate tax regimes in transition countries to compete for foreign direct investment, as compared to harmonizing taxes and focusing on broader reform of the investment climate?

References

Agha, A. and J. Haughton (1996), 'Designing VAT Systems: Some Efficiency Considerations', *Review of Economics and Statistics (U.S.)*, Vol. 78, pp. 303-8, May.

Alam, A. and M. Sundberg (2002), 'A Decade of Fiscal Transition', World Bank memo.

Bird, R. and O. Oldman, (1990), *Taxation in Developing Countries*, Baltimore: John Hopkins University Press.

Burgess, R. and N. Stern (1993), 'Taxation and Development', *Journal of Economic Literature (U.S.)*, Vol. 31, pp. 762-826, June.

Center for Economic and Financial Research and the World Bank, (2000), *Monitoring of Administrative Barriers to SME Development in Russia.*

EBRD (1999), *Transition Report.*

EBRD (2000), *Transition Report.*

Funck, B. (2002), *The Expenditure Policies towards EU accession*, World Bank.

Gillis, M. (1989), *Tax Reform in Developing Countries*, Durham, Duke University Press.

Hines, J. (1999), 'Lessons from Behavioral Responses to International Taxation', *National Tax Journal (U.S.)*, Vol. 52, pp. 305-22, June.

Hussein, A. and N. Stern (1993), 'The Role of the State, Ownership, and Taxation in Transitional Economies', EF No. 1, Development Economies Research Program, London School of Economics.

International Monetary Fund (2001), *The Modern VAT.*

Riboud, M., C. Sanchez and C. Silva (2002), 'Does Eurosclerosis Matter? Institutional Reform and Labor Market Performance in Central and Eastern European Countries', in B. Funck and L. Pizzati (eds.), *Labor, Employment and Social Policies in the EU Enlargement Process*, World Bank.

Tanzi, V (1991), 'Fiscal Issues in Economies in Transition', in V. Corbo, F. Coricelli, and J. Bossak (eds.), *Reforming Central and Eastern European Economies*, World Bank.

World Bank (2000), *Making Transition Work for Everyone: Poverty and Inequality in Europe and Central Asia.*

World Bank (2001), *Slovak Republic: Living Standards, Employment and Labor Market Study.*

World Bank (2002a), *Transition: The First Ten Years: Analysis and Lessons for Eastern Europe and the Former Soviet Union.*

World Bank (2002b), *Georgia: Public Expenditure Review.*

World Bank (2002c), *Global Development Finance.*

Chapter 11

Tax Reforms in the Baltic States

Alari Purju

Introduction

All the Baltic States introduced tax reforms as an important part of their transitions from planned to market economies. Tax reforms played an important role in the adoption of responsible fiscal policies in the 1990s. Starting in the late 1990s, the EU accession process has also influenced the development of the tax system in the Baltic States, through screening and harmonization procedures. However, several critical issues of tax harmonization remained unfinished in mid-2003. Those problems are also discussed in this chapter.[1]

Main Features of Tax Systems

Table 11.1 shows that tax rates as of 2003 were quite similar in the Baltic States, with the largest differences affecting the subjects who are obliged to pay the social insurance tax. Important differences in corporate income tax rates and regulations are also present.

Table 11.1 Tax rates in the Baltic States in 2003

Country	Personal income tax	Payroll tax	Corporate income tax	Value added tax
Estonia	26%	33%	26%	18%
Latvia	25%	33%	22%	18%
Lithuania	33%	34%	15%	18%

Sources: Ministry of Finance of the Republic of Estonia, Latvian Development Agency, Lithuanian Development Agency.

---

1 This analysis of tax systems in the Baltic states is based on Ginevicius and Tvaronaviciene (2001), Kaulina (2000), Kerem and Randveer (2001), Kerem (2000) and Zvidrina (2000). General procedures for evaluating different tax systems follow OECD Tax Policy Studies (2000).

Estonia

The first wave of tax reforms introduced a progressive personal income tax (PIT) with rates ranging from 16 to 33 percent. Those rates were replaced in 1994 by a flat PIT of 26 percent. The corporate income tax (CIT) rate was reduced in 1994 from 35 to 26 percent. The initial idea of tax reform was therefore to apply the same flat tax rate for personal and corporate earnings, simplifying in this way the system and signaling to taxpayers the authorities' neutrality concerning the taxation of corporate and non-corporate forms of economic activity. Starting from January 2000, a new income tax law introduced several new regulations regarding personal and corporate income taxes, the most controversial of which was the exemption of undistributed profits from the CIT (see subsection 11.2.4).

The payroll tax was introduced at the rate of 33 percent, which reflected levies for social insurance (20 percent) and health insurance (13 percent), paid by employers. This framework was subsequently modified to facilitate pension reform and the transition to a three pillar pension system. The second pillar of the reformed pension system is partly financed from the redistributed 20 percent social-insurance part of a payroll tax, and partly from additional voluntary contributions, with the remainder financed through a two percent increase in the regular payroll tax.

The value added tax (VAT) was originally introduced with a 10 percent rate, which was raised to 18 percent in 1992. The tax base is relatively wide with only few exemptions. These include preordered periodicals, textbooks and other teaching materials, electricity produced using water or wind power (which is taxed at a zero rate), thermal energy sold to physical persons, housing cooperatives, and churches and institutions financed from state or local budgets. The Estonian government has promised to harmonize most of remaining differences in VAT when EU membership will come into force, by adopting a lower five percent tax rate for preordered periodicals and textbooks.

The issue of untaxed electricity produced using water or wind power was brought up by the government in its accession negotiations with the EU. The government sought to negotiate a transition period in harmonizing the VAT for those items until end of 2006, basing its case on other EU accession precedents and environmental arguments. The EU position was that the VAT system in the single market requires the application of the same tax rate for the same product or service. Other contested issues included the VAT for thermal energy (a transition period was requested by the Estonian government for social reasons), a minimal level of turnover for purpose of VAT registration (EUR 16,025 in Estonia comparing to EUR 5,000 according to the relevant EU directive), and duty-free trade on ships between Estonia and Scandinavian states, primarily Finland.[2]

The European Commission allowed Estonia to maintain the reduced VAT rate on heating until end of 2007. All acceding countries, including Estonia, can maintain a turnover that exceeds the thresholds for VAT exemption for SMEs that

2 For negotiation details see http://spunk.mfa.ee/euro/liitumine.htm.

are specified in the *aquis communautaire* (Report on the results of the negotiations…, 2003, p. 29). No exceptions were allowed on the issue of duty-free trade on ships between Estonia and Scandinavian states. By contrast, Finland during its EU membership negotiations managed to maintain tax-free status for its mainly Swedish speaking autonomous region.

Latvia

The PIT rate is fixed at 25 percent, and the standard VAT rate is 18 percent. In the mid-1990s the payroll tax was divided between employers (37 percent of the wage bill) and employees (one percent). The employer's part was reduced by one percentage point in 2000 and by another one percentage point in 2001. Starting from 2002, social insurance expenditures are financed by contributions of 16.5 percent paid by employer and another 16.5 percent paid by the employee (Kaulina, 2000).

The CIT law adopted in 1995 introduced a flat rate of 25 percent, with exemptions for investment spending. A 40 percent reduction (effective until 2004) is applied to investments related to research and development. The CIT rate in 2002 was reduced to 22 percent, and a further reduction (to 15 percent) is anticipated in 2004. (Latvian Development Agency 2003, http://www.lda.gov.lv)

Lithuania

Corporate tax regulations have undergone more changes in Lithuania than in Estonia and Latvia, due perhaps to Lithuania's more frequent changes in government. Lithuania also retained special tax exemptions for foreign investment longer than Estonia or Latvia.

A flat PIT rate of 33 percent has been applied since 1994. Income earned from employment with a foreign company is taxed at a rate of 20 percent.

The rate for social security contributions is set at 34 percent, with employers paying 31 percent and employees 3 percent since 2000. The VAT is charged at base rate of 18 percent. The CIT was introduced in 1990 with a 35 percent rate, which was reduced to 29 percent in 1991. In 1993, a reduced 10 percent rate has been applied to reinvested profits.

Between 1993 and 1997, Lithuania applied various tools for stimulating foreign investment. During the second half of 1993 the income tax for foreign companies was reduced by 70 percent for five years and by 50 percent for the next three years. A 50 percent reduction for six years was in place from January 1994 until August 1995. No requirements concerning minimal amount of foreign capital were applied. From August 1995 until March 1997, investors received a three-year CIT exemption from the moment profit was received, and a 50 percent reduction for another three years if the foreign capital invested exceeded USD 2 million. Taxation on reinvested profits by both domestic and foreign companies was completely lifted in March 1997. In January 2000, the overall CIT rate was reduced to 24 percent, and the tax-free status was retained for reinvested profits (Ginevicius and Tvaronaviciene, 2001, p.131).

The Law on Tax on Profit was adopted at the end of 2001, and has been applied since January 2002. Lithuanian entities and permanent establishments of foreign entities face a 15 percent CIT rate. Dividends and other distributed profits are also taxed at 15 percent. A zero percent rate applies to companies manufacturing agricultural products and to specialized agricultural service enterprises if such companies derive more than 50 percent of their receipts from such activities. (Lithuanian Development Agency, 2003, http://www.lda.lt).

Case Study: Estonia's Corporate Income Tax

Special CIT exemptions for new foreign investments were abolished in January 1994. In October 1997, Parliament amended the income tax law to allow the government to grant tax concessions according to a specific formula for investments in specific regions. Companies can also deduct expenses to acquire or upgrade fixed assets from taxable income. The intention was to promote investment in Estonia's less-developed regions. In practice, all regions except Tallinn and surrounding Harju county received preferential treatment. Despite this, more than half of total investment still went to Tallinn and Harju county. This law was in force until the end of 1999.

From January 2000, resident companies and permanent establishments of foreign entities (including branches) are subject to taxes on actual and estimated incomes. The tax is payable on the distribution of profits, and on transactions that could be treated as hidden distributions of profits. These include fringe benefits for employees, gifts and donations, and transfer pricing adjustments. The CIT rate is 26 percent of taxable payments and expenses.

Under current Estonian law, income is treated as profit withdrawn from an enterprise where the beneficiary is either a physical or legal person. In the case of physical person, the shareholders will later pay correspondingly smaller personal income taxes, because the dividends have already been taxed when the company distributed them as profit (i.e., distributed profits are only taxed once).

In the case of legal persons, dividends paid to Estonian resident companies are exempt from further tax. Dividends paid to non-resident shareholders are subject to a withholding tax of 26 percent. Non-resident persons also pay income tax of 26 percent on capital gains from the sale of shares in an Estonian company if at least 10 percent of the shares and 75 percent of the company assets sold (comprising real estate or buildings) are located in Estonia. In negotiations with the EU, this differential taxation of non-residents and residents was judged to be discriminatory and in conflict with the Code of Conduct for Business Taxation.

The European Commission has been granted Estonia a transitional arrangement until 31 December 2008 to ensure full compliance with Directive 90/435/EEC, a 'Parent-Subsidiary' directive (Report on the results of the negotiations…, 2003, p. 30).

Comparisons with General Trends

In the Baltic States, the share of tax revenues in GDP (Table 11.2) differs somewhat from the regional trends presented in Chapter 10. The share of total budget revenue in Estonia's GDP actually increased from 37.2 percent of GDP in 1991-92 to 38.7 percent of GDP in 1999-2000, and tax revenue increased during this time from 34.4 to 36.1 percent, respectively. In Latvia, the share of total revenues increased from 36.6 to 38.7 percent, but the share of tax revenue decreased from 33.7 to 32.7 percent. This was due in part to the fact that infrastructure privatization in Latvia was conducted later than in Estonia.

In Lithuania, by contrast, the share of total revenue in GDP dropped from 39.9 percent in 1990-1991 to 31.2 percent in 1999-2000, and tax revenues decreased from 35.5 to 29.4 percent. Lithuania's lower tax burden results in part from smaller social security and payroll taxes. In 1999-2000, payroll tax contributions represented 12.2 percent of GDP in Estonia and 11.8 percent in Latvia, but only 7.0 percent in Lithuania.

Other tendencies in the Baltic States have been quite similar to those described in the Chapter 10. The share of the PIT in total tax revenues has increased in all the Baltic States. The share of the CIT in total tax revenues has fallen sharply, with Lithuania and Estonia being the leaders in the race to bottom.

Trends in taxes on domestic goods and services in Estonia and Lithuania have also differed from the general picture described in Chapter 10. In all the Baltic States, the shares of those taxes in total tax revenues increased. In Estonia, VAT revenues increased together with revenue from excises. In Latvia and Lithuania, the proportion of tax revenue from the VAT decreased, but this was more than offset by increased revenues from excise taxes. A very clear determination in Estonia, but also Lithuania and to a lesser degree Latvia, to redistribute the general tax burden more towards indirect taxes in order to reduce the burden of the CIT, is a major factor behind this shift. Improvement in tax administration capacity, together with the adjustment of excise tax rates toward minimal EU levels (a process that is not yet finished) also made significant increases in tax revenues possible.

On the whole, the Baltic States, and particularly Estonia, are quite close to the levels of different taxes recommended by Mitra and Stern in Chapter 10. They may even be trying to go too far in increasing the role of indirect taxation, with its undesirable regressive qualities.

Table 11.2 Tax structure of the Baltic States compared with Central and Eastern Europe, CIS and OECD (average 1999-2000, in percent of GDP).

Country	Total budget revenue	Tax revenue	Other revenues	PIT	CIT	Social security (payroll) taxes	VAT/ sales tax	Excises	Trade taxes	Other taxes
Estonia	38.7	36.1	2.6	8.3	1.6	12.2	9.1	3.5	0.0	1.4
Latvia	38.7	32.7	6.0	6.1	2.1	11.2	8.0	3.8	0.4	1.1
Lithuania	31.2	29.4	1.8	8.2	0.8	7.0	7.9	3.6	0.4	1.2
C&E Europe	37.7	33.0	4.7	5.2	2.1	10.6	8.7	3.4	1.3	1.1
CIS	25.5	22.2	3.2	2.0	3.1	4.5	6.1	2.5	1.2	1.4
EU_{95-99}	45.2	39.4	5.8	9.6	2.6	10.8	6.7	3.7	0.0	2.4
Other $OECD_{95-99}$	38.5	31.5	7.0	11.1	2.6	5.3	4.9	2.2	0.4	2.8

Note: Figures for groups of countries represent unweighted averages.

Sources: IMF country reports and IMF and World Bank estimates (cited from Chapter 10).

Conclusions

Tax reforms in the Baltic States have been quite successful in managing to avoid large budget deficits. Lithuania has had the largest fiscal shortfalls, but due to the reformed tax system the budgetary situation seems to be sustainable. Estonia and Latvia had some critical years with budget deficits, but trends in these countries now seem under control, as is apparent in the relatively low levels of state debt.

Tax reforms in the Baltic States have been very much targeted toward creating a competitive market environment. This is particularly apparent in the general business friendliness in the new CIT regimes and tax systems.[3] However, as several studies have demonstrated, tax burden is not the sole element of competitiveness and attractiveness for the FDI. Better administration of existing taxes and harmonization with EU requirements are the next important tasks.

Small companies do not receive special support in these countries' tax systems, except for the minimal level of turnover needed to register for the VAT purposes. One option for the future development of the tax systems is to consider some possibilities for supporting small companies. Some activities in this field have been already realized in other areas of business support (credits, consultancy, business incubators).

References

Funke, M. (2001), 'Determining the Taxation and Investment Impacts of Estonia's 2000 Income Tax Reform', *BOFIT Online*, No. 15.

Ginevicius, R. and M. Tvaronaviciene (2001), 'Comparative Analysis of Tax Systems in Lithuania, Latvia and Estonia'. In: K. Liuhto (eds.), *Ten Years of Economic Transformation*, Volume III: *Societies and Institutions in Transition*, Lappeenranta University of Technology, Studies in Industrial Engineering and Management, No. 16. pp. 127-145.

Kaulina, G. (2000), 'Tax policy in Latvia', In: B. Lesser (eds.), *BALT-ECON 2000. Economic Policy and Reform in Estonia, Latvia and Lithuania, 1992 to 2000 and Beyond*, Halifax: BEMTP, pp. 68-70.

Kerem, K. (2000), 'Fiscal Policy and Economic Growth: The Estonian Case', in B. Lesser (eds.), *BALT-ECON 2000. Economic Policy and Reform in Estonia, Latvia and Lithuania, 1992 to 2000 and Beyond*, Halifax: BEMTP, pp. 89-99.

Kerem, K. and M. Randveer (2001). 'The Impact of Fiscal Policy on Business Environment in Estonia', In: V. Vensel and C. Wihlborg (eds.), *Estonia on the Threshold of the* European *Union: Financial Sector and Enterprise Restructuring in the Changing Economic Environment*, Tallinn: Department of Economics at Tallinn Technical University, pp. 361-383.

Latvian Development Agency (2003), http://www.lda.gov.lv.

Lithuanian Development Agency (2003), http://www.lda.lt.

---

3 The new CIT arrangements have been in force for too short a period of time to learn their full effects. Funke 2001 estimated the long-run impact of the new CIT regime in Estonia at 6 percent of GDP (Funke, 2001). The large amounts of FDI that Estonia received in 2001 can be seen as evidence of the positive effect of reform.

Report on the results of the negotiations on the accession of Cyprus, Malta, Hungary, Poland, the Slovak Republic, Latvia, Estonia, Lithuania, the Czech Republic and Slovenia (2003), Brussels: European Commission, pp. 29-30.

Tax Burdens (2000), 'Tax Burdens: Alternative Measures', *OECD Tax Policy Studies*, No. 2.

Zvidrina, S. (2000). 'Fiscal Review by Budgets: Latvia', in: B. Lesser (ed), *BALT-ECON 2000. Economic Policy and Reform in Estonia, Latvia and Lithuania, 1992 to 2000 and Beyond*, Halifax: BEMTP, pp. 79-88.

Chapter 12

Weak Institutions, Fiscal Policy, and Low Equilibria

Daniel Daianu and Radu Vranceanu

Introduction

Highlighting the role of institutions in economic life is not of recent vintage. There is even a school of economic thought, *institutional economics*, with its older and newer versions, which focuses on the institutional underpinnings of economic processes.[1] Arrow (1971) in a very insightful and precious small book remarked that trust, loyalty, truth telling, etc., are quasi-public goods, which oil the economic machinery of society. In his influential writings, Olson (1996, 2000) also put forward the positive role of state institutions in protecting individuals entering the voluntary exchange against abuses and fraud on growth and prosperity.[2] On empirical grounds, several studies, such as those surveyed by Aron (2000), tend to indicate a positive correlation between the quality of public and private economic institutions and growth. This message is strongly reinforced by the World Development Report of the World Bank (2001).

In transition economies, which are plagued by congenital institutional fragility, the institutions/economic performance nexus has aroused increasing interest. As a matter of fact, in recent years there has not been any major conference or seminar in the economics of transition, which did not underline the key role of institutions in determining economic performance. Kozul-Wright and Rayment (1997) have stressed the impossibility of conducting successful 'orthodox' reforms in economies lacking of basic institutions that, in Western Europe, are the outcome of a long-term social evolution. In a very influential speech, Stiglitz (1999) criticized what he perceived as the overdone emphasis on macroeconomic stabilization in transition economies and called attention to the need to build solid market institutions as a precondition to successful economic reforms. Rodrik (1999) also emphasized that, although relative prices matter a lot for development policy, the shortcomings of the focus on price reform during the 1990s were increasingly evident. He put forward the argument that economists were generally inclined to take for granted the existence of important institutions such as a clearly delineated system of property rights, a regulatory apparatus

1 The major contribution of Douglas North (1981) should be acknowledged here.

2 This line of reasoning was buttressed by social writers such as Putnam (1993) and Fukuyama (1995) in recent years.

curbing the worst forms of fraud and anti-competitive behavior, as well as the social and political bodies deemed to mitigate and manage social conflicts. Unfortunately, these features are generally absent in poor countries, and this major drawback seems to explain the failure of many stabilization policies. Finally, Arrow (2000) points out that abrupt deregulation of the planned economy may be counter-productive in a world where the intermediate institutions and instruments that allow individuals to exchange among themselves are absent.

The role of the state in the context of transition to a market economy is obvious: enforcing contracts, guaranteeing property rights, providing public services like education and health care, social security and basic infrastructure (telecommunication, transportation, etc.) and, last but not least, setting up effective legal and regulatory frameworks. In the absence of such institutions, external financial assistance is in danger of being diverted toward rent-seeking activities, and the impact of this assistance on economic development is therefore limited.[3] Moreover, much-needed structural reforms would be considerably slowed down, or could not be implemented, as unregulated economic agents would find ways to avoid the constraints intended to make their activity compatible with the public interest. Of course, the actions of the state institutions must be predictable, transparent, and accountable.

This chapter[4] builds on two simple models inspired by the economic context of (the less advanced) transition economies, which challenge, to some extent, the standard approach to policy reform in these countries. It emphasizes the lack of well-functioning institutions as a source of major economic disruption and failure of conventional fiscal policies. The first model develops a simple analysis of firm-strategic behavior in a transition economy, where the state is able to provide public services enhancing the output of the representative firm. It is shown that in the absence of adequate institutions to monitor firms, the decentralized equilibrium might not be Pareto optimal. Under certain circumstances, it may be rational for a firm to unilaterally 'misbehave': to refuse to pay taxes, not respect contracts, and so on. Decisions of rational individual firms are non-coordinated. In the Nash equilibrium, all firms misbehave and the global output collapses together with investment and saving ratios; in the end, this may become a development trap.[5] It is true that firms differ as to their ability to pay taxes and their behavior varies but this fact does not alter the prominence of conditions that can lead to a vicious cycle of non-payment. An important policy implication is that external support should be directed toward institution building and enforcement of state regulatory and legal activities. This recommendation should be seen in the wider context of the need to

3 In the last years, an impressive number of papers analyzed the impact of state official corruption on economic performance. See the survey by Bardhan (1997).

4 An earlier version of the paper was published by Oeconomica, Acta Oeconomica and the William Davidson Institute. We thank Valentin Lazea for useful comments. The authors also benefited from the comments of the participants of the 6th EACES Conference, Barcelona, 7-9 September 2000 on an earlier draft.

5 An alternative explanation builds on the structural inability to pay of a large number of firms (Daianu 1994, 1998).

work out effective public policy in transition economies as a means for fostering development (*catching-up*).

At variance with the previous set-up, in the second model, it is assumed that the state possesses an efficient tax collection institution, thereby ruling out free-rider behavior by firms. From the very beginning of the reform process in Central and Eastern Europe, the international financial institutions have pushed for a drastic reduction of public deficits as a prerequisite for price stability and credible monetary policies. This objective has often been achieved not by reduced spending, but by increased tax burdens. Romania provides a glaring example in this respect. Although tax rates in this country are not higher than in other Central and Eastern European economies, the social insurance tax (paid by employees and employers) has reached a staggering level (around 65 percent) of wages, suggesting a clear presence on the right side of the Laffer Curve. It is shown that in the specific context of transition economies, the objective of increasing tax incomes may conflict with the first-best optimum of output maximization. The quest for large tax receipts comes with the hidden risk of pulling too many firms out of the market, which may cause excessive unemployment and would harm human and organizational capital. Of course, this is not a plea in favor of deficits, but a call for a more careful assessment of policy tradeoffs and of the means for controlling the budget deficit (control of spending) consistent with a first-best taxation policy. This statement can also be interpreted as an argument in favor of a *sui generis* industrial policy, which would help the restructuring of potentially viable companies as an inherently gradual process (Flemming, 1993).

Both models suggest that reform effectiveness in transition economies may have been partially affected by perverse mechanisms stemming from the characteristic features of these economies, which sometimes may have been neglected by international advisory agencies. A careful analysis of the experience of the past ten years is thus necessary, in order to improve policies and avoid further wasting of resources. Simple models like those developed here may shed some light on various policy episodes, which can be illustrated by the Romanian experience.

Free-rider Behavior and the Cost of a Weak State

Main Assumptions and Optimal Decision of the Firm

The economy is made up of $n+1$ identical firms, all producing a homogeneous output. Each firm has to pay a lump-sum tax, denoted by t. A given firm i may choose either to pay the tax or not: $t_i = (0, t)$.

The state collects the tax and uses it to produce a public service/good in quantity D with a linear technology. Public service refers to the functioning of the judicial system that protects property and enforces contracts, education, public health, but also infrastructure related to different networks (telecommunications, transportation, energy and water distribution). Institutions in charge of tax collection themselves may be seen as an element of this public service. Formally, we write $D = \alpha + \gamma \sum_{i}^{n+1} t_i$, where $\alpha \geq 0$ is a minimum level of the public service, which will be provided independent of the tax collection and γ is a positive parameter related to the technology of producing the public services and the relative price of the input utilized for this production. As the main conclusions do not depend on this parameter, we set γ=1.

The representative firm produces the final goods by means of a 'private input' (like capital assets) that is bought by the firm in the marketplace at a predetermined price. The quantity of private input utilized by the firm i is denoted by x_i. Production also increases with the public good provided by the state. In a simple framework, the production function is multiplicative in the two factors:

$$f(x_i, D) = x_i^{0.5} D$$

In keeping with the standard neoclassical assumption, this function exhibits decreasing marginal returns with respect to the private input. However, we assume constant marginal returns with respect to the public service, a reasonable assumption in the context of developing countries (in fact, given the low initial endowment, marginal returns to D could even be increasing). We also have $f_{xD}>0$, that is, increases in the available quantity of one factor increase the marginal productivity of the other factor.

To simplify, we assume that the price of the final good is normalized to one. Then, the (real) profit function is:

$$\pi_i = f(x_i, D) - px_i - t_i \qquad (12.1)$$

where p is the price of the private input.

Profit equation 12.1 can be rewritten in the alternative form:

$$\pi_i = x_i^{0.5}(\alpha + t_i + nt_j) - px_i - t_i, \text{ with } j = (1, \ldots, i-1, i+1, \ldots, n+1) \qquad (12.2)$$

where t_j indicates the tax paid by every other firm in the economy (i.e., n firms without the firm i).

The profit maximizing amount of the private factor can easily be inferred from the first order condition $d\pi_i/dx_i=0$:

$$x_i^* = \left(\frac{\alpha + t_i + nt_j}{2p} \right)^2 \qquad (12.3)$$

By placing equation 12.3 into 12.1 we obtain the maximum profit as a function of the tax only:

$$\hat{\pi}_i = \frac{[\alpha + t_i + nt_j]^2}{4p} - t_i \qquad (12.4)$$

The Strategic Decision of the Firms

We can now analyze the strategic decision that will be made in a decentralized framework. Two cases should be considered:

a) When all firms pay the tax: $t_i = t_j = t$, then the maximal profit of the firm i is:

$$\hat{\pi}_i^{t,t} = \frac{[\alpha + (1+n)t]^2}{4p} - t \tag{12.5}$$

b) In the case where the firm does not pay the tax, while the other do, t_i=0, t_j>0, $j = (1, \ldots, i\text{-}1, i\text{+}1, \ldots, n\text{+}1)$, the 'deviating' firm would obtain the profit:

$$\hat{\pi}_i^{0,t} = \frac{[\alpha + nt]^2}{4p} \tag{12.6}$$

A firm i will have an incentive to deviate (that is, not to pay its taxes) if the profit for the individual firm of not paying taxes—while all other firms pay them—is higher than in the case when it pays taxes. So, a firm would unilaterally deviate if:

$$\hat{\pi}_i^{0,t} > \hat{\pi}_i^{t,t} \tag{12.7}$$

that is, if: $\dfrac{[\alpha + nt]^2}{4p} > \dfrac{[\alpha + (1+n)t]^2}{4p} - t$ or:

$$p > 0.5\alpha + 0.25t + 0.5tn \tag{12.8}$$

For a predetermined tax, the condition for 'deviant behavior' is more likely to be fulfilled if the price of the private input is high (in this case, the left hand term in equation 12.8 is relatively large) or the number of firms is low (in this case, the right hand term in equation 12.8 is relatively small).

To interpret this condition, it should be noted that a marginal productivity of each factor is increasing in the available quantity of the other factor. Thus, a reduction in the amount of private input x would decrease the marginal productivity of the public good and this, in turn, would reduce the marginal productivity of the private input. Ceteris paribus, a high p induces the firm to use less x. In turn, this reduces the contribution of D to output, which gives less incentive to the firm to pay the tax so as to increase D.

In order to bring more intuition to the theoretical construct, let us take D as a project to build a public highway and x as the capital assets of a transportation firm, e.g., trucks. The cost of operating one truck depends on the price of the truck and the interest rate or, if the firm does not owns the trucks, on the rental cost of one truck. A high rental cost would make it too costly for firms to run large numbers of trucks, thereby diminishing their use of the highway. This would make firms less eager to pay the tax for building the highway. Similar reasoning applies to a small number of firms. The smaller their number, the smaller the total tax income. That prevents the proper level of D from being provided. This reduces the productivity of capital and results in a lower than optimal level of x than would otherwise be the case, again reducing the marginal productivity of the public good.

Of course, if condition of equation 12.8 is fulfilled, not only one, but all firms would deviate: $t_i = t_j = 0 \;\; \forall j$. The resulting non-cooperative Nash equilibrium is clearly inefficient from a social point of view, in that the global output will be lower than in the cooperative configuration. Unfortunately, transition economies suffer—to a greater or lesser extent—from this kind of free-riding behavior. At several decision levels, firms 'misbehave', because such a decision is individually rational.

The model can be extended to analyze the case of free entry of firms into the market. To deal with this complication, the profit function would need to be slightly modified. For instance, let us assume that, in addition to taxes and capital costs, each firm bears a cost $c(n)$ that rises with increases in the number of firms in the market. Such a form may be justified by the congestion effect. Under plausible assumptions, profit in the representative firm could be expected to be higher in the cooperative equilibrium than in the non-cooperative one.[6] Given that free entry implies zero profits in the long run, a larger number of firms (each producing more) will be present in the cooperative than in the non-cooperative equilibrium.

The Case of the Well-intended Excessive Tax Burden

General Formulation

At variance with the previous section, we now assume that the government has established an efficient tax collection institution and uses all the tax income to provide a public good (service). Firms cannot follow free-rider strategies by refusing to pay the tax. In this context, there is a risk that the government will pursue a 'second best' policy of tax revenue maximization, so as to deliver the largest amount of public service. It will be shown that this policy may lead to a lower than optimal number of firms in the economy.[7]

Let us denote by n the number of firms in the economy. In a first step, each firm has made optimal microeconomic choices: it has fixed all choice variables under its control in such a way as to maximize profits. In this case, the production function will determine output only according to those variables that are beyond the firms' control, e.g., taxes and the number of firms.

Production in a firm depends on its upstream input supply relationships. In a developed economy, these inputs are by and large traded on the global marketplace given low transaction costs. In transition economies, markets are segmented and less developed, so that production in one firm depends largely on the survival of its

6 This would occur for not a too high price of the private input. $\pi^{t,t} > \pi^{0,0} \Leftrightarrow p < 0.25[(1+n)(2\alpha + (1+n)t)]$. That this condition is consistent with equation 12.8; i.e., there is a range in which p satisfies both inequalities.

7 Such an outcome implies limited rationality on the part of the government, which is not aware of the economy's true characteristics, and proceeds by trial and error through successive tax increases until tax revenue is maximized.

traditional suppliers (Calvo and Coricelli, 1992; Blanchard, 1997; Blanchard and Kremer, 1997). To bring this feature into the picture, we assume that the production of one firm depends on the total number of firms in the economy. As in the former model, the state delivers a public good/service proportional to the total amount of taxes collected, which also has a favorable impact on output (this public service may be interpreted as in the former model). Therefore, the production function of the representative firm may be written as $y = f(n, T)$, with $f_1>0$, $f_2>0$ where y stands for output, n for the total number of firms and T for total tax revenues collected by the state. The form of $f(n, T)$ encompasses the optimal choice of other inputs by the firm.

By assumption, each firm that makes positive profits has to pay a lump-sum tax t. In contrast to the previous model, firms are not strictly identical. While all firms produce the same amount of output, they are not all equally solvent. The number of surviving firms is a decreasing function of the tax rate: for a low tax, more firms stay in the market, for a high tax only a few firms are profitable enough to survive. We can write this assumption as: $n=n(t)$, with $dn/dt<0$.[8] Finally, the total tax revenue is $T=tn$, as result of the tax rate and a number of surviving (efficient) firms.

Under these assumptions, it can be shown that the tax rate maximizing total tax receipts is 'too high'. The proof is as follow. Let us write total output Y as a function of the tax: $Y = nf(n, T) = n(t)f[n(t), tn(t)]$

If one wishes to plot this function, the study of the first derivative is useful:

$$dY/dt = n'f + nn'f_1 + nf_2(dT/dt) \tag{12.9}$$

At a point t^* where output is maximized, we also have $dY/dt=0$, therefore:

$$\left(\frac{dT}{dt}\right)_{t=t^*} = -\frac{n'(f + nf_1)}{nf_2} > 0 \tag{12.10}$$

that is, increasing t above t^* would increase the total tax revenue.

Conversely, the tax rate which maximizes total tax revenue should fulfill $dT/dt=0$. Let us denote the solution of this condition by $\hat{t}$. Turning back to equation 12.9, it is also clear that:

$$\left(\frac{dY}{dt}\right)_{t=\hat{t}} = n'(f + nf_1) < 0 \tag{12.11}$$

that is, reducing the tax rate below $\ddot{t}$ contributes to increasing overall output by allowing more firms to operate; over time this may, eventually, even raise total tax revenue by expanding the tax base.[9]

---

8 With a lump-sum tax, firm heterogeneity could be modeled explicitly by introducing a fixed cost c per firm and a statistical distribution of c across firms. A more realistic assumption would consider that corporate taxes are proportional to company profits. However, the model would not change much if we assume that firms that systematically make zero profits exit the market.

9 This effect should be distinguished from the supply-side argument, according to which a lower tax rate enhances the propensity of firms to pay taxes. A more powerful model would combine the two effects.

A Numerical Example

To obtain some more intuition, let us introduce the simple linear functions: $n(t) = a - bt$ and $f(n,T) = \lambda[(a - bt) + t(a - bt)]$, where a, b and λ are positive parameters. Of course, $0<t<a/b$, or else no firm would survive.

From the first order condition, the output maximizing tax is $t^* = \frac{1}{3}\frac{a-2b}{b}$ (it can be checked that for this value the second derivative is $-2b\lambda(a+b) <0$). (Hereafter we assume that $b<0.5a$, such that an internal solution exists.)

The output-maximizing tax does not maximize total tax revenue. This can be verified by evaluating the derivative dT/dt for this value: $\left(\frac{dT}{dt}\right)_{t=t^*} = \frac{a+4b}{3} > 0$. The maximum tax income is obtained at $\hat{t} = \frac{a}{2b} > t^*$.

The conflict of objectives is self-evident in Figure 12.1 which represents the number of firms, total tax revenue, and total output as a function of the tax, for a=1, b=0.25 and λ=1.

In this theoretical context, a government that pursues the immediate objective of maximizing tax revenues—very likely to be related to the more general aim of providing the largest supply of public goods—might pull an overly large number of firms out of the market, thereby harming welfare and future growth.

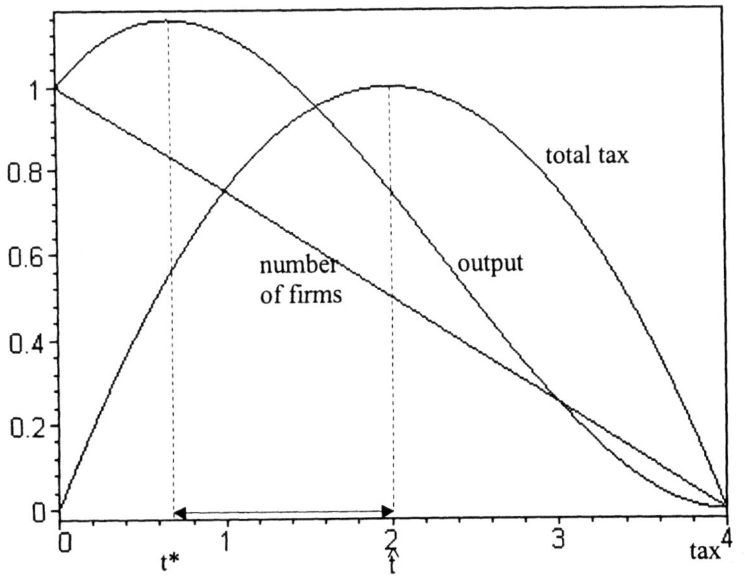

Figure 12.1 The fiscal policy dilemma

Conclusions

In transition economies, reforms face the challenge of distorted economic relationships and particular constraints. Against the background of intense strain and disorganization (Blanchard, 1997; Daianu, 1998), we have proposed two highly stylized models that emphasize unconventional responses of the economic system to orthodox reform programs, focusing on tax related issues.

In the first part, we argue that the main challenge for the government is to find appropriate ways to enforce the cooperative equilibrium. Clearly, setting up the institutions needed to enforce the law (for example, to collect taxes) is costly. But a vicious cycle comes into play. If non-cooperation initially leads to a bad equilibrium, no taxes are paid and the state has no resources to build the required institutions or enforce rules and regulations. In this case, taxes will not be levied (or collected) in the future. This self-sustained bad equilibrium may not be broken without external intervention. Our simple model puts forward a justification for directing an important fraction of external support toward institution building.

In the second part, we show that the goal of a balanced budget may come with the risk of excessive taxation, in that the revenue maximizing tax implies a lower than optimal number of firms and reduced output. In this context, the tax system should take into account the firm's financial viability, since sound firms may be endangered if financially weak firms exit the market at once.[10] This should not necessarily be interpreted as an argument in favor of blanket state support for weaker companies (although a case-by-case approach should not be ruled out), but as a suggestion to focus on the spending side of the budget when imbalances become unsustainable.

The two models complement each other by stressing the complexity of optimal taxation in transition economies, which should reconcile the demand for public goods and services with the need to avoid excessive tax burdens on firms when there is a scarcity of suppliers in the production chain.

Whether Central and Eastern European countries will manage to fill the institutional gap in a short period of time remains to be seen. Their decision to join the European Union started a process of quick replication of the European regulations and laws 'summarized' by the 80,000 pages of the *acquis communautaire*. Although this should set up the basis for modern institutions, their efficient functioning is not automatic. Many years may elapse before western institutions become a part of the civil society of these countries. In the meantime, efficient economic policy reform should take into account institutional shortages.

References

Aron, J. (2000), 'Growth and institutions: a review of the evidence', The World Bank Research Observer, Vol. 15, No. 1, pp. 99-135.

Arrow, K.J. (2000), 'Economic transition: speed and scope', Journal of Institutional and Theoretical Economics, Vol. 156, No. 1, pp. 9-18.

Arrow, K.J. (1971), The Limits of Organization, Norton, New York.

Bardhan, P. (1997), 'Corruption and development: a review of issues', Journal of Economic Literature, 35 (3), pp. 1320-46.

Blanchard, O. (1997), *The Economics of Transition*, Oxford, Clarendon Press.

Blanchard, O. and M. Kremer (1997), 'Disorganization', Quarterly Journal of Economics, 112, pp. 109-126.

Calvo, G. and F. Coricelli (1992), 'Stagflationary effects of stabilization programs in reforming socialist countries: enterprise-side and household-side factors', World Bank Review, Vol. 6, No. 1, pp. 71-90.

Daianu, D. (1994), 'Arrears in a post-command economy', IMF Working Paper 94/54.

Daianu, D. (1998), *Transformation of Economy as a Real Process*, Aldershot, Ashgate.

Flemming, J. (1993), 'Relative price shocks and unemployment: arguments for temporarily reduced payroll taxes or protection', mimeo, EBRD, London.

Fukuyama, F. (1995), *Trust. The Social Virtues and the Creation of Prosperity*, New York, Simon and Schuster.

Kozul-Wright, R. and P. Rayment (1997), 'The institutional hiatus in economies in transition its policy consequences', Cambridge Journal of Economics, 21, pp. 641-661.

North, D. (1981), *Structure and Change in Economic History*, Norton, New York.

Olson, M. (1996), 'Big bills left on the sidewalk: why some nations are rich and others poor?', Journal of Economic Perspectives, Vol. 10, No. 2, pp. 3-24.

10 The impact of excessive taxation is analogous to that of high real interest rates, when the increases in the latter strain balance sheets of indebted companies.

Olson, M. (2000), *Power and Prosperity. Outgrowing Communist and Capitalist Dictatorships*, New York, Basic Books.

Putnam, R. (1993), *Making Democracy Work*, Princeton, Princeton University Press.

Rodrik, D. (1999), 'Institutions for high-quality growth: what they are and how to acquire them', Paper prepared for the IMF Conference on 'Second Generation Reforms', Washington, October 14.

Stiglitz, J. (1999), 'Whither Reform? Ten Years of Transition', Annual World Bank Conference on Development Economics 1999, in B. Pleskovic and J. Stiglitz (eds.), The World Bank, Washington DC, 2002.

World Bank Development Report (2001), The World Bank, Washington DC.

Chapter 13

Privatization and Corporate Governance

Simon Johnson

Introduction

Privatization is at the top of the political agenda in Asia. In China, the state sector has failed to wither and continues to consume a large amount of state resources (Steinfeld, 1998, 2000). In Korea, the state has acquired substantial banking assets through bailout programs and now faces the serious issue of how to dispose of these assets (Chopra, et al., 2001). In Malaysia, there is the beginning of a real discussion about how best to manage the relationship between the state and previously state-owned enterprises (Gomez and Jomo, 1998). Throughout Asia, strong interest is developing in whether further privatization will help speed the economic recovery and sustain growth.

The early appeal of privatization, however, has worn off since the 1980s and there is a general feeling of caution. Recent experience, particularly in Eastern Europe and the former Soviet Union, has demonstrated that simply privatizing is often not enough. As a result, there is a new emphasis on various complementary measures, such as stimulating competition. These complementary measures are often quite distinct from privatization itself and require separate political initiatives. In this chapter we focus on one important issue that has emerged over the past decade: corporate governance of privatized firms.

Privatized firms with weak corporate governance have repeatedly demonstrated weak performance and have frequently been 'tunneled' by their management. In the Czech Republic, management of newly privatized firms conspired with the managers of investment funds to strip assets and siphon off cash flow (Coffee, 1999b). Belated attempts by the Czech authorities to control this process have proved difficult. The lesson from post-communist countries is that effective investor protection measures need to accompany privatization.

But how exactly should corporate governance be implemented? In particular, is it necessary or even helpful for the government to pass and enforce laws or legal regulations? Or can the private sector achieve all its desired outcomes by simply relying on private contracts, in which case all the government needs to do is ensure that such contracts can be enforced?

Ronald Coase (1960) explained the conditions under which individuals and private firms should be able to make contracts as they please. As long as the enforcement costs of these contracts are nil, individuals do not need statutory law or can find ways to contract around the law. There remains strong support in both law and economics for three important Coasian positions: law does not matter; law matters, but other institutions adapt to allow efficient private contracts; and finally, while law matters and domestic institutions cannot adapt enough, firms and individuals can write international contracts that achieve efficiency.

Coasian arguments have had great influence on discussions about corporate finance, and in this chapter we focus on this literature, emphasizing points that seem particularly relevant for thinking about privatization. In the spirit of this general position, Easterbrook and Fischel (1991) argue that firms wishing to raise external finance can commit themselves to treat investors properly through a variety of mechanisms. Law may restrict the scope of these mechanisms, but firms and investors can always reach efficient arrangements. If this view is taken to the extreme, all countries that have a good judicial system should be able to achieve similar and efficient financial arrangements for firms. In this view, all privatization needs to do is to transfer property rights to private investors and the market will take care of the rest.

Also in the Coasian spirit, Berglof and von Thadden (1999) argue that civil law countries in Europe have developed institutions that allow companies to enter enforceable contracts with investors. In their view, law may matter and have shortcomings, but the political process and firm-specific actions can generate other ways of providing effective guarantees to investors, for example through mandating certain forms of government intervention or establishing a particular ownership structure and dividend policy. As a consequence, they argue that bringing US-type institutions into Europe would not be helpful and could even be disruptive. In this view, the arrangements may differ across countries, but in many cases firms should be able to access external finance. The implication is that while privatization should be accompanied by institution building in some form, it does not necessarily need US-style investor protection in order to be effective.

Even among the scholars who are convinced that legal rules matter, there is Coasian skepticism about whether changing rules can have large effects. Coffee (1999a, 1999b) argues that while US firms derive important advantages from the US legal system, other countries are not converging through changing their rules, presumably because this is politically difficult. Instead, there is a process of 'functional' convergence, through which firms choose to adopt US-type private contracts with their investors, for example by issuing American Depositary Receipts (ADRs). In this view, corporate governance of privatized firms can be assured through the issue of ADRs or through otherwise listing in a stock market with a high level of investor protection.

These Coasian arguments are extremely powerful. However, they are rejected by the data. Recent research shows that the legal rules protecting investors matter in many ways, that other institutions cannot adapt sufficiently, and that changing domestic legal rules can have a big impact. We are also moving closer to a theoretical understanding of why exactly these Coasian positions are not correct, and what this implies for standard models of economics and finance. The implication is that unless privatization is accompanied by enforceable investor protection, it will not improve firm performance and will likely be accompanied by severe agency problems, including various forms of expropriation or 'tunneling' by management.

There is now overwhelming evidence that legal rules matter. Protection for minority shareholders is weaker in countries with a civil law tradition. In many countries, the judiciary cannot be counted on to enforce contracts between investors and firms. Countries with less protection for minority shareholders have smaller equity markets, other things being equal (La Porta, Lopez-de-Silanes, Shleifer, and Vishny (hereafter LLSV), 1997a). Firms in countries with less investor protection use less outside finance (LLSV, 1997a) and have higher debt-equity ratios, making them more vulnerable to collapse (Friedman, Johnson and Mitton, 2001). Countries and companies with weak corporate governance can also suffer larger collapses when hit by adverse shocks (Johnson, Boone, Breach and Friedman, 2000; Mitton, 2002; Lemmon and Lins, 2001). Countries with weaker institutions have experienced greater output volatility over the past 40 years (Thaicharoen, 2001) and have suffered larger exchange rate crises (Pivovarsky and Thaicharoen, 2001).

Other domestic institutions can adapt to some extent but not enough to offset weak legal protection. The government has only limited ability to act directly to compensate for weak investor protection. Private companies in civil law countries have developed various mechanisms to improve their investor relations, but these mechanisms are far from perfect. In many civil law countries there are significant loopholes through which value can be 'tunneled' legally out of a company (Johnson, La Porta, Lopez-de-Silanes and Shleifer, 2000.) An important complement of effective privatization is the effective legal protection of investors.

Laws and other institutions providing investor protection are persistent and hard to change. But this does not mean that legal reform is ineffective. Among the countries with relatively strong legal systems, there is a move to establish stronger investor protection for important segments of the stock market. Germany leads the way in this regard (Goyer, 1999; Johnson, 1999); other European countries are following. Among countries with relatively weak legal systems, the evidence indicates that strong stock market regulation can to a large degree act as an effective substitute for judicial enforcement of contracts. However, as Glaeser, Johnson and Shleifer (2001) point out, there is a theoretical danger that a strong regulator will act in a capricious manner and undermine economic freedom. But Poland provides a clear example of conditions under which a strong independent regulator can create a well-functioning stock market, despite a weak judiciary. In all successful cases of capital market development and privatization through public sale of shares, good legal rules are of paramount importance.

Shleifer and Vishny (1997) review the literature on corporate governance before the recent wave of findings from comparative research. LLSV (2000a) describe the first wave of this research, which constitutes about 20 papers written through the early fall of 1999. However, the pace of research activity in this area is accelerating. We cover about 30 new papers not included in either of these previous surveys.

Sections 13.2, 13.3, and 13.4 review the evidence against each of the Coasian positions, with particular emphasis on recent experience with privatization. Section 13.5 reports recent theoretical analysis based on this evidence. Section 13.6 concludes.

Law Matters

The strongest Coasian position is that law does not matter. If this were true, we should expect to see no significant correlation between legal rules and economic outcomes around the world. The evidence decisively rejects this hypothesis.

Investor Protection

The new literature on the importance of law begins with LLSV (1997b, 1998), who show there are systematic differences in the legal rights of investors across countries. An important explanatory factor of these differences is the origin of the legal system.

LLSV (1998) propose six dimensions to evaluate the extent of protection of minority shareholders against expropriation by insiders, as captured by a commercial code (or company law). First, the rules in some countries allow proxy voting by mail, which makes it easier for minority shareholders to exercise their voting rights. Second, the law in some countries blocks the shares for a period prior to a general meeting of shareholders, which makes it harder for shareholders to vote. Third, the law in some countries allows some type of cumulative voting, which makes it easier for a group of minority shareholders to elect at least one director of their choice. Fourth, the law in some countries incorporates mechanisms that give minority shareholders who feel oppressed by the board the right to sue or otherwise seek relief from the board's decision. In the United States, this oppressed minority mechanism takes the very effective form of a class action suit, but in other countries there are other ways to petition the company or the courts with a complaint. Fifth, in some countries, the law gives minority shareholders a preemptive right to new issues, which protects them from dilution by the controlling shareholders who could otherwise issue new shares to themselves or to friendly parties. Sixth, the law in some countries requires relatively few shares to call an extraordinary shareholder meeting, at which the board can presumably be challenged or even replaced, whereas in other cases a large equity stake is needed for that purpose. LLSV (1998) aggregate these 6 dimensions of shareholder protection into an anti-director rights index by simply adding a 1 when the law is protective along one of the dimensions and a 0 when it is not.

The highest shareholder rights score in the LLSV (1998) sample of 49 countries is 5. Investor protection is significantly higher in common law countries, with an average score of 4, compared with French-origin civil law countries, with an average score of 2.33. There is significant variation within legal origin, however. In the LLSV (1998) data, there is no association between a country's level of economic development and its anti-director rights score, but a strong association between the score and the size of its stock market relative to GNP.

LLSV (1998 and 1999) also find that the legal enforcement of contracts is weaker in countries with a civil law tradition. For example, the efficiency of the judicial system is on average 8.15 in English-origin countries (on a scale of 1-10, where 10 means more efficient), but only 6.56 in French-origin countries. Legal origin therefore affects investor protection both through the rights available in the laws and the ease of enforcement of these rights.

Glaeser, Johnson and Shleifer (2001) look in more detail at Poland and the Czech Republic, which were not included in the original LLSV (1998) sample. They find that the Polish commercial code protected investors more than did the Czech code, but the most important difference was in the design and implementation of securities law. As Pistor (1995), Coffee (1999a) and Black (2000) also argue, protection under the commercial code is complementary to protection under securities law.

Slavova (1999) has extended the LLSV work to 21 formerly communist countries of Eastern Europe and the former Soviet Union. Rather than looking directly at the laws, she uses a survey to ask local legal professionals what specific rules are in place and how they are enforced. Her work confirms the analysis of LLSV on the general relationship between shareholder protection and stock market development. It also confirms the detailed assessment of Glaeser, Johnson and Shleifer (2001) on Poland and the Czech Republic. For post-communist countries, privatization has proved much more effective where capital markets have also developed at least to some extent.

Recent research has focused on some additional determinants of investor protection (Bebchuk and Roe, 1999; Roe, 2000, 2001; Stulz and Williamson 2001). Rajan and Zingales (2001) maintain that there is an important underlying political process. Berkowitz, Pistor and Richard (1999) argue that the way in which legal systems were transplanted to other countries is more important than legal origin. However, Acemoglu, Johnson and Robinson (2001) confirm that legal origin has explanatory power with respect to current institutions. They find that additional explanatory power lies with the way, in which countries were colonized, and particularly whether the disease environment favored early settlers, but legal origin remains important. Using the pattern of colonization to generate a set of plausible instrumental variables, they show that institutions have a major impact on GDP per capita today.

Outcomes

Measures of investor protection matter for economic outcomes. Investor protection directly effects the development of external capital markets. Both stock markets and debt markets have developed less in French origin countries (LLSV, 1997a). This is evident both in outside capitalization (measured as market capitalization owned by outsiders relative to GNP), domestic listed firms per capita, and initial public offerings per capita. For a sample of the largest firms in each country in 1996, LLSV (1997a) find that French legal-origin countries have significantly lower market capitalization relative to sales and to cash flow.

Subsequent work has found that lower stock market development can reduce growth (Levine and Zervos, 1998), that financial development is correlated with growth (Beck, Levine and Loayza, 2000) and that the availability of external finance determines whether a country can develop capital intensive sectors (Rajan and Zingales, 1998). Wurgler (2000) finds there is a better allocation of capital to industries in countries with more financial development.

There is also evidence that countries with weaker investor protection suffer greater adverse effects when hit by a shock. Johnson, Boone, Breach and Friedman (2000) present evidence that the weakness of legal institutions for corporate governance had an adverse effect on the extent of depreciations and stock market declines in the Asian crisis. Corporate governance provides at least as convincing an explanation for the extent of exchange rate depreciation and stock market decline as any or all of the usual macroeconomic arguments. These results hold more generally for exchange rate crises and output volatility over the past 40 years (Pivovarsky and Thaicharoen, 2001; Thaicharoen, 2001).

Firm-level evidence supports this view. Mitton (2002) looks at the five Asian countries most affected by the 1997-98 crisis, and finds that firms with larger inside ownership and less transparent accounting suffered larger falls in stock price. He also finds more diversified firms suffer a greater fall, particularly if they have more uneven investment opportunities (measured in terms of Tobin's Q). This is consistent with (although it does not prove) the view that firms with weaker corporate governance faced a larger loss of investor confidence. It may also be the case that more diversified firms are less able to allocate investment properly due to internal politics, as suggested by Scharfstein and Stein (1998), and that these political problems become worse in a downturn.

Nalbantoglu and Savasoglu (2000) find similar results for Turkey in the late 1990s. Lemmon and Lins (2001) confirm Mitton's (2002) findings using the separation of control and cash flow rights to measure the extent of agency problems. Firms in which controlling shareholders had less cash flow rights suffered larger stock price declines in the Asian crisis. Over longer periods of time, Lins and Servaes (1999) also find a discount for diversified firms in seven emerging markets. Claessens, et al. (1999) find a diversification discount for East Asian firms and worse performance for conglomerates during the East Asian crisis.

Other Institutions

The second Coasian view is that even if legal rules matter and are weak in some countries, other governmental or private institutions should adapt to protect investors. The political process can produce investor protection or it may be the outcome of reasonable private negotiation between firms and investors. Three main mechanisms have been suggested.

First, the government may pressure firms to treat investors properly, even though the law does not require it. If firms expropriate investors, they can lose other rights, such as favorable tax treatment or even the right to operate. This is the argument made by Berglof and von Thadden (1999) for many European countries.

The government could try to ensure that firms behave by directly owning and running banks. In fact, government ownership of banks is significantly higher in French origin legal systems (LLSV, 2002a).

This approach requires an honest and effective government, but this is itself an endogenous outcome partially affected by legal institutions. LLSV (1999) show that countries with a civil law tradition are likely to have more corruption and less effective government administration. Governments may also say that they want to protect investors, but in a sharp downturn find that they would rather protect entrepreneurs. This is one interpretation of what happened recently in some Asian countries, for example Malaysia (Johnson and Mitton, 2003).

Second, ownership may develop in a different way from in the US and the UK. In particular, concentrated outside ownership may allow more effective control over management. In fact, most civil law countries have concentrated ownership. La Porta, Lopez-de-Silanes and Shleifer (1999) show that groups of connected firms are much more usual than stand-alone firms in most countries. These groups typically control at least one company that is publicly traded or otherwise used to raise funds from outside investors, and a number of other companies that are privately held without any outside investors. Some valuable assets are usually kept private.

This type of organization is particularly common in 'emerging markets' where legal protection for minority shareholder rights and creditors is weaker (LLSV, 1998). With the exception of Chile, the other Latin American countries for which data are available have higher than average ownership concentration (La Porta and Lopez-de-Silanes, 1998.) Concentrated ownership also plays an important role in some European countries. For example, Gorton and Schmid (1999) find that firms are more highly valued when large shareholders own more shares in Germany. In 18 emerging markets, Lins (1999) finds that large blockholders generally increase firm value.

The trouble with this approach is that there are still small minority shareholders in most countries with stock markets (see LLSV, 1997a, Table 2). If large shareholders actually control management, small shareholders are not protected from expropriation. In fact, what happened in the Czech Republic over the past decade suggests that in an environment of weak legal protection, it is easy to gain control over a privatized firm and then strip it of value (Coffee, 1999b; Glaeser, Johnson and Shleifer, 2001). Hellwig (1999) explains clearly the deficiencies of protection for small shareholders in Germany and Switzerland.

Third, there may be some reputation building by firms. For example, by paying higher dividends, companies in civil law countries could establish a reputation for treating shareholders properly. In principle, repeated interaction between managers and shareholders could establish that management can be trusted, and this should increase their ability to raise more capital.

Theoretically, this argument has an important weakness. Managers may be happy to treat shareholders well when the economy is growing fast, but this does not imply anything about how they will be treated in a downturn. It is very easy to expropriate shareholders for a few years, and then return to the capital markets. Not surprisingly, the empirical evidence does not support the view that there is more reputation building through dividend policy in civil law countries. In fact, LLSV (2000b) show that companies in common law countries pay higher dividends.

Legal Reform

Coffee (1999a) argues that there is an important movement towards 'functional convergence', through which firms around the world are adopting US-type mechanisms to protect investors. There is certainly a move towards issuing ADRs, and these seem to improve access to external capital markets. Lins, Strickland, and Zenner (1999) show that the sensitivity of investment to cash flow falls when an ADR is issued by a company from a country with a weak legal system and a less-developed capital market (as defined by LLSV, 1997a). Reece and Weisbach (1999) show that companies in civil law countries are more likely to list ADRs on an organized exchange in the US, thus committing themselves to greater disclosure. All of this work supports the third Coasian view that international contracts can get around some of the deficiencies of domestic investor protection. The implication is that while law may matter and domestic institutions cannot adapt, domestic legal reform is irrelevant.

The trouble with this argument is that ADRs may help companies opt into a regime of greater disclosure, but they do not stop expropriation as long as it is disclosed. The substitutes for the law thus do not work perfectly. For example, privatized Italian companies over the past decade have often issued ADRs, but there is an active debate about whether this has proved effective.

There are important legal reform processes at work in many countries, and the evidence suggests that some of these efforts have important effects on investor protection and the financing of firms. We can divide reforms into two groups: those in countries with strong legal systems, and those in countries with weak legal systems. In both cases, legal reform has proved strongly complementary to privatization.

Strong Legal Systems

The stock markets in many European countries do not attract initial public offerings. This may slow the development of new high technology firms. Despite a debate about how to address this issue, the main problem is that established firms like the status quo (Hellwig, 1999). It enables them to raise capital on favorable terms, in part because they do not have to compete with new firms. Established firms also have strong relationships with some financial institutions, such as banks. Germany, however, has experimented successfully since 1997 with a new segment of the stock market designed for start-ups. This is part of a broader process of corporate governance reform that was prompted, in part, by the desire to privatize assets such as Deutsche Telecom.

The Neuer Markt represents a significant change in the rules protecting minority shareholders in Germany. The two most important changes are greater disclosure (in English) and requiring the introduction of US generally accepted account practices (GAAP) or international accounting standards (IAS) for company accounts. Management of the exchange emphasizes the importance of clear and regular disclosure, including briefings for analysts. They enforce a system of disclosure, so that companies that list on this market know that they have to disclose a good deal and investors know that this will actually happen. It also helps that investment banks play the role of friendly enforcer by being 'designated sponsors'.

The established markets, on the other hand, retain German accounting principles and the old culture of non-disclosure and non-transparency, which is considered more favorable to creditors than shareholders. All German stock markets are governed by the same law (i.e. primarily the commercial code, securities law, and insider trading prohibitions). But the Neuer Markt offers new legal rules, in the form of a private contract, to those who agree to participate. Establishing these rules has had a significant effect on the ability of young technology-based companies to raise capital through public offerings in Germany. The success of the Neuer Markt in promoting IPOs of technology companies is helping encourage broader changes in the legal protection of shareholders in Germany (Balz, 1999).

Changes are also underway in France, and it appears that newly privatized companies generally have better corporate governance than well-established family-run firms (Goyer, 1999). Japan is lagging but there is definite pressure for change, particularly from international investors (Matsui, 1999). Other industrialized countries with strong legal systems are adopting measures similar to those in Germany.

Weak Legal Systems

In countries with weak legal systems, the expropriation of outside investors takes place through relatively open forms of outright theft, transfer pricing, related lending, failure to disclose relevant information when issuing securities, failure to report earnings properly. What can prevent this when the courts are weak? Recent work suggests that in such financial markets a strong regulator can protect the property rights of outside investors and thereby improve welfare. This may be particularly important where privatization is being attempted.

The idea of focusing the regulation of securities markets on intermediaries is sometimes credited to James Landis, a contributor to the 1933 and 1934 Securities Acts in the United States (McCraw, 1984). Landis reasoned that the US Securities Commission by itself could monitor neither compliance with disclosure, reporting and other rules by all listed firms, nor the trading practices of all market participants. Rather, the Commission would regulate intermediaries, such as brokers, the accounting firms, the investment advisors, etc., who would in turn attempt to assure compliance with regulatory requirements by the issuers and the traders. Moreover, by maintaining substantial power over the intermediaries through its administrative relationships, including the power to issue and revoke licenses, the Commission could force them to monitor market participants.

Glaeser, Johnson and Shleifer (2001) find that the stringent—and stringently enforced—regulations in Poland, expressed in both company and securities laws, have stimulated rapid development of securities markets, and enabled a large number of new firms to go public. It has also greatly facilitated the privatization of state-owned firms. The expropriation of investors has been relatively modest, and qualitative evaluations of the Polish market have been very positive as well. In contrast, the lax—and laxly enforced—regulations in the Czech Republic have been associated with the stagnation of markets, the delisting of hundreds of privatized companies from the stock exchange, and no listing of new private companies. The expropriation of investors has apparently been rampant, and has acquired a new Czech-specific name: tunneling. Consistent with these concerns, the qualitative assessments of the Czech market have been poor. Starting in 1996, the Czech Republic has sharply tightened its regulations. These findings suggest that even countries with relatively weak legal systems can improve the protection of investors, and that this improvement will help firms to obtain external finance.

Poland also demonstrates the value of regulating intermediaries, particularly investment funds and brokers. When these organizations are tightly regulated, it is possible to suspend or revoke their licenses for inappropriate actions. These intermediaries then have a strong interest in ensuring both internal compliance and external vigilance. It is helpful that everyone involved with the securities market watch out for the misbehavior of others.

Theory

The Coasian argument seems extremely powerful. Why does it fail? How does this affect standard models of finance? What is the right way to model firms in countries with weak legal institutions?

Law and Regulation

The Coasian argument, in all three versions reviewed here, relies on the crucial assumption that the judiciary is able to enforce both existing property rights and efficiency-enhancing contracts. But what if the courts are not efficient enough to perform this role, because they are underfinanced, unmotivated, unfamiliar with the economic issues, or even corrupt? At the least, it may be necessary to provide a detailed legal framework to facilitate the work of the courts. In some cases, it may be necessary to go further and create a regulatory framework that empowers a regulator to provide and enforce rules that promote more efficient outcomes. This case for regulation is stronger when the government is more interested in public welfare than in catering to incumbent firms. Glaeser, Johnson and Shleifer (2001) and Glaeser and Shleifer (2000) discuss incentives to enforce alternative laws and regulations more generally.

It is quite possible for a country to get stuck in equilibrium with weak law enforcement. For example, Johnson, Kaufmann and Shleifer (1997) argue that many countries in the former Soviet Union drove firms underground with high taxation, corruption, and regulation. This undermined the tax base and made it harder to provide reasonable rule of law. Without the rule of law, there is much less incentive to become a registered firm and pay taxes. Thus, most of the former Soviet Union, but not the better parts of Eastern Europe, is trapped with weak law enforcement, a large unofficial economy, and a low tax base. In this environment, it proved very difficult to privatize without creating widespread possibilities for tunneling.

Tunneling, Propping and Debt

While the evidence reviewed above suggests that expropriation of shareholders is endemic, it is not the case that there is a zero cost of stealing in most countries. In fact, we need to understand how standard finance results are modified as the cost of stealing varies.

The original model of expropriation by managers is Jensen and Meckling (1976). Burkhart, Gromb and Panunzi (1998) introduce the assumption that most diversion by management is costly, for example because it involves legal maneuvers. LLSV (2002) show how to think about the cost of stealing across countries in a simple static framework. This approach has been developed further by Johnson, Boone, Breach and Friedman (2000) and more recently by Friedman, Johnson and Mitton (2001).

Johnson, Boone, Breach and Friedman (2000) present a new theoretical explanation for the effects of corporate governance on macroeconomic outcomes. If stealing by managers increases when the expected rate of return on investment falls, then an adverse shock to investor confidence leads to increased theft and to lower capital inflow and greater attempted capital outflow for a country. These, in turn, translate into lower stock prices and a depreciated exchange rate.

The model in Friedman, Johnson and Mitton (2001) puts ideas from Jensen (1986), Myers (1977) and LLSV (2002b) into a dynamic setting. The key assumption is that entrepreneurs can not only take from the firm, but they can also give. There is substantial evidence that in moments of crisis, entrepreneurs in some legal systems prop up their firms in order to keep them going (Hoshi, Kashyap and Scharfstein, 1991).

Friedman, Johnson and Mitton (2001) find that the presence of some debt is generally optimal because it reduces theft and induces propping in some states of the world. Thus debt can serve the role proposed by Jensen (1986) in reducing agency costs, even if there is no enforceable debt contract (i.e., effectively no collateral). However, in other states of the world, a debt overhang may induce entrepreneurs to loot the company. Thus there can develop an 'overhang' of debt with the negative features analyzed by Myers (1977). When the legal system is weaker, Friedman, Johnson and Mitton (2001) show that the debt-equity ratio will usually be higher, even though this increases the probability that the firm will collapse. In weaker legal systems, entrepreneurs also make investments that increase the cost of renegotiation, because this raises the cost of defaulting on a loan and thus increases the feasible amount of debt.

In this model, weaker legal institutions lead to fewer projects being financed. But weak legal institutions can also contribute to economic crises. Having weak protection of investor rights does not make shocks more likely, but it does mean that negative shocks have larger effects on the overall economy. Institutions matter for a particular aspect of volatility—whether countries can suffer large collapses. Reasonable capital structures in a weak legal environment can lead to bimodal distributions of outcomes.

The data are broadly supportive. Friedman, Johnson and Mitton (2001) show that Asian firms with weaker corporate governance were more highly indebted before the financial crisis of 1997-98. Kim and Stone (1999) find that countries with more corporate debt suffered larger falls in output during the Asian crisis of 1997-98. Other work suggests both that aggregate corporate debt is higher in countries with weaker corporate governance (Demirguc-Kunt and Maksimovic, 1999) and that it was higher within Asian countries for firms with weaker corporate governance. Lee, Lee, and Lee (1999), for example, demonstrate that corporate leverage was higher for chaebol companies than for non-chaebol, and highest for the top few chaebol.

More work is needed to link the debt findings more precisely to corporate governance and macroeconomic outcomes. Caballero and Krishnamurthy (1999) is one early attempt to formalize these ideas, emphasizing implications of underinvestment in appropriate collateral that occurs due to legal problems in some countries.

This research is part of a broader movement looking at the macroeconomic implications of institutions. Blanchard (1999) argues that labor market institutions in Western Europe were appropriate, but could not handle the shocks they received in the 1970s and 1980s. In his view, a functional set of institutions became dysfunctional because of a particular set of shocks. More generally, Blanchard (2000) argues that macroeconomic dynamics may depend on institutional structures: 'Institutions also matter for short-run fluctuations, with different mechanisms across countries (...) Identifying the role of differences in institutions in generating differences in macroeconomic short- and medium-run evolutions is likely to be an important topic of research in the future' (p. 1404).

Conclusions

A great deal of research suggests that privatization can be helpful for economic development. But the effectiveness of privatization is greater when corporate governance works well. This chapter has reviewed recent evidence showing that effective laws are an important requirement for corporate governance. Without enforceable investor protection, privatization is less likely to succeed.

Law definitely matters. Countries with better investor protection have better developed financial markets and more growth. The determinants of law are complex, but the origin of the legal system is an important factor.

Legal origin is not destiny. Other institutions can adapt to some extent. Civil law European countries have become rich with more government ownership and more concentrated ownership than is seen in common law countries. But it is a fallacy to infer that compensating institutions develop always and everywhere.

Legal reform works. Countries as diverse as Chile, Germany, Poland and South Korea have all made progress recently with changing the rules for investor protection. There are many different ways to change the rules, and the required changes vary by country. But investor protection is advancing in many countries, precisely because people have learned that it matters for economic development.

We are not arguing that all countries could or should become just like the United States. But in important dimensions we see countries around the world adopting investor protection measures that are modeled on US law. The evidence suggests that when these measures are implemented in an enforceable way, they can change both the extent of investor protection and the ability of firms to obtain external finance. Properly designed US-type innovations can work even in countries with quite different legal origins, such as Germany and Poland.

By giving us a clear framework to think about contracts, Ronald Coase shed a great deal of light on many issues, including international corporate governance and privatization. It is an indication of the power of his approach that research is now advancing by trying to reject Coasian arguments about how firms are financed around the world. The Coasian idea that private contracts can attain efficient outcomes is powerful and in many instances correct. The right question is how to make it easier for the private sector to write its own efficient contracts. In many cases, this can only be achieved through changing the broader legal rules that underpin capital and other markets.

References

Acemoglu, D., S. Johnson. and J.A. Robinson (2001), 'The Colonial Origins of Comparative Development: An Empirical Investigation', *American Economic Review*, December, Vol. 91, No. 5, pp.1369-1401.

Balz, M. (1999), 'Corporate Governance in Germany', manuscript, presented at the OECD Conference on 'Corporate Governance in Asia: A Comparative Perspective', Seoul, March.

Bebchuk, L.A. and M.J. Roe (1999), 'A Theory of Path Dependence in Corporate Ownership and Governance', *Stanford Law Review*, Vol. 52, pp. 127-170.

Beck, T., Levine R. and N. Loayza (2000), 'Finance and the Sources of Growth', *Journal of Financial Economics*, Vol. 58, No. 1-2, pp. 261-300.

Berglof, E. and E.L. von Thadden (1999), 'The Changing Corporate Governance Paradigm: Implications for Transition and Developing Countries', manuscript, SITE, Stockholm School of Economics.

Berkowitz, D., K. Pistor and J.F. Richard (1999), 'Economic Development, Legality, and the Transplant Effect', manuscript, Pittsburgh and Max Planck Institute for Foreign and Comparative Private Law.

Black, B.S. (2000), 'The Legal and Institutional Preconditions for Strong Stock Markets', manuscript, Stanford Law School, January.

Blanchard, O. (1999), 'European Unemployment: The Role of Shocks and Institutions', manuscript, MIT.

Blanchard, O. (2000), 'What do we know about macroeconomics that Fisher and Wicksell did not?', *Quarterly Journal of Economics*, Vol. 115, November, pp. 1375-1410.

Burkhart, M., D. Gromb and F. Panunzi (1998), 'Why higher takeover premia protect minority shareholders', *Journal of Political Economy*, Vol. 106, pp. 172-204.

Caballero, R. and A. Krishnamurthy (1999), 'Emerging Markets Crises: An Asset Markets Perspective', manuscript, MIT.

Chopra, A., Kang K., M. Karasulu, H. Liang, H. Ma and A. Richards (2001), 'From Crisis to Recovery in Korea: Strategy, Achievements and Lessons', Asia and Pacific Department, International Monetary Fund, May 14.

Claessens, S., S. Djankov, J. P. H. Fan and L.H.P. Lang (1999), 'The Benefits and Costs of Internal Markets, Evidence from Asia's Financial Crisis', World Bank manuscript.

Coase, R. (1960), 'The Problem of Social Cost', *Journal of Law and Economics*, Vol. 3, pp. 1-44.

Coffee, J.C. Jr. (1999a), 'The Future as History: The Prospects for Global Convergence in Corporate Governance and its Implications', *Northwestern University Law Review*, Vol. 93, pp. 631-707.

Coffee, J.C. Jr. (1999b), 'Privatization and Corporate Governance: the Lessons from Securities Market Failure'. manuscript, Columbia University Law School.

Demirguc-Kunt, A. and V. Maksimovic (1999), 'Institutions, Financial Markets, and Firms Debt Maturity', *Journal of Financial Economics*, Vol. 54, pp. 295-336.

Easterbrook, F.H. and D.R. Fischel (1991), *The Economic Structure of Corporate Law*, Harvard University Press, Cambridge, MA.

Friedman, E., Johnson S. and T. Mitton T. (2001), 'Corporate Governance and Corporate Debt in Asian Crisis Countries', manuscript, MIT, Rutgers and Brigham Young University, May.

Glaeser, E., Johnson A. and A. Shleifer (2001), 'Coase versus The Coasians', *Quarterly Journal of Economics*, Vol. 116, Issue 3, pp. 853-900, August.

Glaeser, E. and A. Shleifer (2000), 'Legal Origins', manuscript, Harvard.

Gomez, E.T. and K.S. Jomo (1998), *Malaysia's Political Economy: Politics, Patronage and Profits*, Cambridge University Press.

Gorton, G. and F. Schmid (2000), 'Universal Banking and the Performance of German Firms', *Journal of Financial Economics*, Vol. 58, No. 1-2, pp. 29-80.

Goyer, M. (1999), 'Boards, bankers, and bureaucrats: The evolution of corporate governance in France and Germany', working paper, Wissenschaftszentrum Berlin.

Hoshi, T., Kashyap A. and D. Scharfstein (1991), 'Corporate Structure, Liquidity, and Investment: Evidence from Japanese Industrial Groups'. *Quarterly Journal of Economics*, Vol. 106, pp. 33-60.

Hellwig, M. (1999), 'On the Economics and Politics of Corporate Finance and Corporate Control', manuscript, University of Mannheim.

Jensen, M.C. (1986), 'Agency Costs of Free Cash Flow, Corporate Finance and Takeovers', *American Economic Review*, Vol. 76, pp. 323-29.

Jensen, M.C. and W.H. Meckling (1976), 'Theory of the Firm: Managerial Behavior, Agency Costs and Ownership Structure', *Journal of Financial Economics*, Vol. 3, pp. 305-360.

Johnson, S. (1999), 'The Neuer Markt', manuscript, MIT, October.

Johnson, S., P. Boone, B. Breach and E. Friedman (2000), 'Corporate Governance in the Asian Financial Crisis', *Journal of Financial Economics*, Vol. 58, pp. 141-186.

Johnson, S., D. Kaufmann and A. Shleifer (1997), 'The Unofficial Economy in Transition', *Brookings Papers on Economic Activity*, Vol. 2, pp. 159-239.

Johnson, S., R. La Porta , F. Lopez-de-Silanes and A. Shleifer (2000), 'Tunneling', *American Economic Review*, Vol. 90, No. 2, pp. 22-27, May.

Johnson, S. and T. Mitton (2003), 'Cronyism and Capital Controls: Evidence from Malaysia' Vol. 67 (2), pp. 351-382.

Kim, S.-J. and M. R. Stone (1999), 'Corporate Leverage, Bankruptcy, and Output Adjustment in Post-Crisis East Asia', *IMF Working Paper*, WP/99/143.

La Porta, R. and F. Lopez-de-Silanes (1998), 'Capital Markets and Legal Institutions', in S. Burki and G. Perry (eds.), *Beyond the Washington Consensus: Institutions Matter*, World Bank.

La Porta, R., F. Lopez-de-Silanes and A. Shleifer (1999), 'Corporate Ownership around the World', *Journal of Finance*, Vol. 54, pp. 471-517.

La Porta, R., F. Lopez-de-Silanes, A. Shleifer and R.W. Vishny (1997a), 'Legal determinants of external finance', *Journal of Finance*, Vol. 52, pp. 1131-1150.

La Porta, R., F. Lopez-de-Silanes, A. Shleifer and R.W. Vishny (1997b), 'Shareholders Rights: Appendix', unpublished appendix to LLSV 1998.

La Porta, R., F. Lopez-de-Silanes, A. Shleifer and R.W. Vishny (1998), 'Law and Finance', *Journal of Political Economy*, Vol. 106, pp. 1113-55.

La Porta, R., F. Lopez-de-Silanes, A. Shleifer and R.W. Vishny (1999), 'The Quality of Government', *Journal of Law, Economics and Organization*, Vol. 15, pp. 222-279.

La Porta, R., F. Lopez-de-Silanes, A. Shleifer and R.W. Vishny (2000a), 'Investor Protection and Corporate Governance', *Journal of Financial Economics*, Vol. 58, Nos. 1-2, pp. 3-28.

La Porta, R., F. Lopez-de-Silanes, A. Shleifer and R.W. Vishny (2000b), 'Agency Problems and Dividend Policies around the World', *Journal of Finance*, Vol. 55, pp. 1-33, February.

La Porta, R., F. Lopez-de-Silanes, A. Shleifer and R.W. Vishny (2002a), 'Government Ownership of Banks.' *Journal of Finance*, February, Vol. 57, pp. 265-302.

La Porta, R., F. Lopez-de-Silanes, A. Shleifer and R.W. Vishny (2002b), 'Investor Protection and Corporate valuation' *Journal of Finance*, Vol. 57, pp. 1147-1170.

Lee, J.-W., Y. S. Lee and B.-S. Lee (1999), 'The Determination of Corporate Debt in Korea', manuscript, Harvard, Hankuk Aviation, and Columbia University.

Lemmon, M.L. and K.V. Lins (2001), 'Ownership Structure, Corporate Governance, and Firm Value: Evidence from the East Asian Financial Crisis', manuscript, University of Utah.

Levine, R. and S. Zervos (1998), 'Stock Markets, Banks, and Economic Growth', *American Economic Review*, Vol. 88, pp. 537-58.

Lins, K. (1999), 'Equity Ownership and Firm Value in Emerging Markets', manuscript, University of North Carolina.

Lins, K. and H. Servaes (1999), 'Is Corporate Diversification Beneficial in Emerging Markets?', manuscript, University of North Carolina.

Lins, K., D. Strickland and M. Zenner (1999), 'Do non-US firms issue stock on US equity markets to relax capital constraints?', manuscript, University of North Carolina and Ohio State University.

Matsui, K. (1999), 'Corporate Governance: Progress Report', Japan Strategy Flash, Goldman Sachs.

McCraw, T.K. (1984), *Prophets of Regulation*, Cambridge, MA: The Belknap Press of Harvard University Press.

Mitton, T. (2002), 'A Cross-Firm Analysis of the Impact of Corporate Governance on the East Asian Financial Crisis.' *Journal of Financial Economics*, Vol. 64, pp. 215-242

Myers, S.C. (1977), 'Determinants of Corporate Borrowing', *Journal of Financial Economics*, Vol. 5, pp. 147-175.

Nalbantoglu, O. and S. Savasoglu (2000), 'Impact of Corporate Governance and Foreign Trading on Firm Returns During Crises: the Case of Turkey', manuscript, Harvard University, April.

Pistor, K. (1995), 'Law Meets the Market: Matches and Mismatches in Transition Economies', manuscript.

Pivovarsky, A. and Y. Thaicharoen (2001), 'Institutions and the Severity of Currency Crises', manuscript, MIT and Harvard, May.

Rajan, R.G. and L. Zingales (1998), 'Financial Dependence and Growth', *American Economic Review*, Vol. 88, No. 3, pp. 559-586.

Rajan, R.G. and L. Zingales (2001), 'The Politics of Financial Development', manuscript, University of Chicago.

Reece, W.A. Jr. and M.S. Weisbach (1999), 'Protection of Minority Shareholder Interests, Cross-listings in the United States, and Subsequent Equity Offerings', manuscript, University of Illinois and Tulane.

Roe, M.J. (2000), 'Political Foundations for Separating Ownership from Corporate Control', *Stanford Law Review*, Vol. 53, December.

Roe, M.J. (2001), 'The Quality of Corporate Law Argument and its Limits', *Columbia Law and Economics Working Paper*, No. 186, February 15.

Scharfstein, D.S. and J.C. Stein (1998), 'The Dark Side of Internal Capital Markets: Divisional Rent-Seeking and Inefficient Investment', mimeo, MIT.

Shleifer, A. and R. Vishny (1997), 'A Survey of Corporate Governance', *The Journal of Finance*, Vol. 52, No. 2, pp. 737-783.

Slavova, S. (1999), 'Law and Finance in Transition Economies', manuscript, London School of Economics.

Steinfeld, E.S. (1998), *Forging Reform in China*, Cambridge University Press.

Steinfeld, E.S. (2000), 'AMCs in China', CLSA Emerging Markets: China Research, October.

Stulz, R.M. and R. Williamson (2001), 'Culture, Openness, and Finance', *Dice Center Working Paper*, No. 2001-02, March.

Thaicharoen, Y. (2001), 'Institutions and Output Fluctuations', manuscript, MIT, May.

Wurgler, J. (2000), 'Financial Markets and the Allocation of Capital', *Journal of Financial Economics*, Vol. 58, pp. 187-21.

Chapter 14

Growing Irrelevance of Corporate Governance

Peter Mihalyi

Introduction

Starting from the second half of the 1990s, the new wave of the corporate governance literature has developed an interesting sub-stream concerning the privatization process in the post-communist transition. The bulk of this literature[1] begins and ends with the same three-point tenet:

- effective privatization requires enforceable investor protection,
- investor protection rests on legal foundations,
- good laws need to be created, if they do not already exist.

These points leave little room for disagreement. Economists can subscribe to them without any reservation. However, after a closer scrutiny, the message of this literature is less compelling than these three unquestionable points suggest.

This chapter will criticize this literature from two angles. First, many authors seem to pay little attention to the definition of their own key terms. In advancing their argumentation, they do not clearly delineate the borders between corporate governance—as a specific term concerning the relationship between investors and managers—and the legal system in general that regulates the economic and political matters of a given country. They speak of 'weak' and 'strong' legal systems, 'high' and 'low' levels of corruption without properly defining what these terms might mean in different countries. We can ask, for example, whether the Chinese legal system can be viewed as 'strong' because corruption and embezzlement in that country are mortal sins, while in most European countries the death sentence was abolished long time ago. In a similar fashion, we may ask whether corruption can be regarded as endemic in a country like Hungary, where bribing policemen on the street has become an everyday practice. Or alternatively, one can perhaps argue that the US economy is plagued

1 For a detailed survey of the literature, see Shleifer et al. (1997), and Chapter 13.

more by corruption, as evidenced by the recent 'Enron *cum* Arthur Andersen,[2] scandal that reached the highest political levels.

Section 14.2 sets out the theoretical background and concludes that corporate governance as usually understood is rapidly becoming irrelevant in transition economies. Section 14.3 examines this rather provocative statement from an East European perspective. Section 14.4 argues that privatization should be assessed from the viewpoint of the types of investors that dominate the markets in transition economies. The literature often assumes that the typical investors are US-type managed funds, which is not the case. Section 14.5 enumerates the differences between the small Central and East European markets and the potentially vast Russian and Chinese markets. Section 14.6 concludes by suggesting that the smaller Central and East European countries will never develop full-fledged capital markets of their own. If these countries soon join the European Union, such markets will not even be needed.

On the Concept of Corporate Governance

What corporate governance means in narrow, scientific terms can be defined in several ways, but the most frequently used definitions do not greatly differ from one another in the substance.

- 'Corporate governance deals with the ways in which suppliers of finance to corporations assure themselves of getting a return on their investment' (Shleifer and Vishny, 1997).

- 'Corporate governance is the system by which business corporations are directed and controlled. The corporate governance structure specifies the distribution of rights and responsibilities among different participants in the corporation, such as, the board, managers, shareholders and other stakeholders, and spells out the rules and procedures for making decisions on corporate affairs. By doing this, it also provides the structure through which the company objectives are set, and the means of attaining those objectives and monitoring performance' (OECD, 1999).

It is customary in the corporate governance literature to begin the analysis with a direct reference to Coase's (1960) seminal paper and/or to the *principle-agent paradigm*. First, it is taken for granted that good corporate governance is the solution to the principle-agent problem, which is correct. This leads to the conclusion that good corporate governance is important, because the agency problem is *the* greatest impediment to successful privatization policies both in the transition economies and other non-American markets. This is where I have strong doubts. A few years ago an EBRD (1997) report summarized this view, as follows: '*The main factors governing growth are the same for both transition economies and market economies*'. Let me try to show what is wrong in this argument.

2 As a British newspaper ironically noted, Fortune magazine voted Enron 'the most innovative company of the year' for 2000, which was not meant to be a joke at that time (*The Economist*, 9 March 2002).

Historically, the discovery of the importance of the agency problem (Berle and Means, 1933) meant a direct criticism of the neoclassical paradigm. In light of this new critique, the firm was not seen anymore as a profit-maximizing black-box entity. Berle and Means noticed that firms were simultaneously controlled by two distinct groups of utility maximizing individuals and the interests of these two groups diverged. Investors are single-minded. They are typically concerned only with the return on and the safety of their original investments, while managers are guided by different and sharply conflicting objectives (e.g. high salary, job security, luxurious work conditions, risk avoidance, pet projects, asset stealing, etc.). Later, the paradigm was enhanced by the recognition of the fact that the relationship of investors and managers is additionally burdened by *asymmetric information*.

Quite clearly, the two corporate governance definitions quoted above fit the world of publicly traded companies quite well, at least as they have been existing in the United States since the 1930s and some major international stock markets since the 1980s. Already ten years ago institutions held 46 per cent of American public stock (Harvard Business Review, 1991). Since then, the figure has probably grown. These companies regularly raise funds from institutional and private external investors, making unfair treatment or even the expropriation of these outside investors a real possibility. Who are these outside investors? The description applies primarily to large US-type pension funds and similar saving vehicles. For them corporate governance does matter in five interrelated areas: (1) shareholder rights; (2) equitable treatment of shareholders; (3) the role of stakeholders; (4) disclosure and transparency obligations; and (5) the responsibilities of the board.[3]

Box 14.1 The loose interpretation of corporate governance

Unfortunately, the term 'corporate governance' is often used in broad, journalistic fashion. E.g., 'Corporate governance is about promoting corporate fairness, transparency and accountability' J. Wolfensohn, President of the World Bank, as quoted by an article in *Financial Times*, 21 June 1999. In other cases, the term is used as an euphemism for private ownership, democracy, law and order. The following statement is quoted from an official OECD document that actually carries the term 'corporate governance' in its title: 'Good corporate governance ensures that companies use their resources more efficiently and leads to better relations with workers, creditors, and other stakeholders. Most importantly for a transition economy like Romania, good corporate governance enhances the confidence of domestic and foreign investors'. (OECD, 2001, p. 6).

Beyond the black-box approach, however, the neoclassical paradigm had two other weak points that are not addressed by the principal-agency model: (1) the

3 This list corresponds exactly to the terminology and grouping used in OECD (1999).

assumption of constant return to scale; and (2) the assumption of single-layer company operation.

Let us recall that it was first the Marxist and then the Keynesian critique of the standard neoclassical model that emphasized the importance of *increasing returns* (Marx, 1867; Marshall, 1890, Appendix H; Young, 1928; Kaldor, 1967). In a different context Kornai (1971) also used this argument, as a first-line criticism of his comprehensive attack on general equilibrium theory (Walras, 1874; Arrow and Debreu, 1954; Debreu, 1959). But only Kornai identified the second weakness of the neoclassical paradigm. In criticizing the Walrasian model, he rightly pointed out that large modern firms are typically multi-layer organizations, with headquarters at one location and subordinated entities in many other parts of the world.[4]

Once the concept of increasing returns is introduced, differentiation among companies by size follows inescapably. *Size matters*. Even if we exclude from our analysis very small service-type companies (which is usual in the comparative privatization literature) there still remains a long continuum between middle-size domestic companies at one end and multi-billion trans-national companies (TNCs) on the other. Crucially, size goes hand-in-hand with institutional complexity. Modern corporations have multi-level structures because they are large.

The issue of size its consequences are often completely ignored. It is simply assumed that all companies, be they American, German, Hungarian or Malay, are large, unconnected publicly traded companies. It is assumed that these publicly traded companies generate the bulk of GDP in each and every country, therefore the quality of the corporate governance regimes of these respective countries determine growth, financial stability and living standards. This is simply not true. In most parts of the world, including Central and Eastern Europe, as well as the so-called emerging markets, non-public companies generate the vast majority of output, where the majority owner has industry-specific knowledge and directly controls the firm.

The East European Perspective

From the perspective of the transition economies much more can be said about the importance of the scale problem.

If we stay within the neoclassical paradigm, transition economics becomes a cookbook. Buy the book and learn how the former state owned enterprises (SOEs) can transform themselves into an IBM or a Siemens. Only a few macro- and microeconomic conditions need to be fulfilled. Macroeconomic stability needs

4 Legal distinctions between subordinated entities, legally independent joint stock companies, limited companies or branch offices is not important here.

to be established and maintained; a state-of-the-art corporate governance regime needs to be introduced; and managers of the former SOEs need to be taught how to find optimal combinations of inputs and how to apply state-of-the-art management techniques.

Although, it may sound simplistic and cynical to summarize in this manner the advice that was initially given to the governments of transition economies, I believe that the above description correctly reflects the essence of the early debates in the transition literature on privatization, stabilization and sequencing. It should have been clearly stated in 1989, however, that Central and Eastern Europe's 5,000-10,000 middle-size and large SOEs did not have the slightest chance of becoming TNCs, or of competing with already existing TNCs. It should also have been publicly acknowledged that the viability of privatized SOEs did not depend on the right combination of inputs, their capacity to innovate and learn modern sales methods, or their willingness to harden the budget constraint. The truth was that already in 1989 Central and East European companies were hopelessly disadvantaged against the existing TNCs in the worldwide size competition.[5] This was and remains the crux of the problem. The suggested and often implemented round-about ways OF 'fixing' this shortcoming by creating privatization intermediaries, and supporting cross-ownership with banks,[6] solved little at best and caused irreparable harm at worst.[7]

Size matters not only for manufactured exports. From the very beginning of the transition, large TNCs could easily penetrate and capture the traditional domestic markets of the former SOEs. In some countries, the penetration took place first on the traditional industrial markets, while services, including the financial sector were taken over later. In other countries, e.g. in the former GDR, the three Baltic countries or Hungary, the insurance and banking sectors were conquered at an early stage.[8]

Where the scale effect is important, unit costs are considerably lower for TNCs, which is a big advantage. Larger size also implies stronger financial positions, which in turn can be used as a collateral for bank loans in supporting capital formation, new projects and research. Larger companies are more attractive to the best new labor market entrants, who are offered higher salaries and more

---

5 Politically, of course, such a message would have been difficult to embrace. However, it was quite visible already at that time that the former SOE managers had intuitively understood all this. Many of them resisted privatization, precisely because they new that their firms, be they big and powerful on the protected domestic market, were all ridiculously small in comparison with their international competitors. As the president of Hungary's largest company said at one point: 'The oil multies of the world are bigger by three orders of magnitude than the largest East European oil company. At some point, the multies will "hoover up" us all'.

6 This was explicitly recommended in an important study of the EBRD (Phelps *et al.*, 1993).

7 Recent economic history knows only one counter-example: Nokia.

8 For a recent overview of developments, see the proceedings of a series of UNCTAD conferences under the title *Privatization and Greenfield FDI in Central and Eastern Europe: Does the Mode of Entry Matter?* in Kalotay (2001).

promising career paths. Established trademarks, such as Coca Cola or Citibank, greatly increase the chances of success in marketing and public relations.

The fate of the banking sector is particularly instructive. In the former East Germany, West German banks took over 100 per cent of the market literary on the very first day of economic transition (i.e., with the introduction of the D-Mark on 1 July 1990). In the Baltic countries, it took 3-4 years for the Nordic neighbors to settle themselves. In Eastern Europe, the first post-communist Hungarian government resisted for four years selling banks to foreigners and only the costly and painful lessons of multiple recapitalizations forced the second government to allow the foreign domination of the Hungarian banking sector. After the Hungarian 'capitulation' in 1995, the Czech and the Polish governments followed, while the former Yugoslav republics, Bulgarian and Romania remained temporarily behind.

Practice has also shown that, once the penetration of TNCs begins in a certain market segment, it is difficult to find a 'right' balance between TNCs and domestic firms. In the case of the banking sector, for example, the point of no return was quickly achieved when clients had to decide with whom they wanted to bank in the future. Would they keep their accounts with a domestic bank and risk another bank failure, or would they rather they switch to an AAA-rated OECD-country bank, where the mother company will guarantee their deposits under all circumstances? For enterprises, this tendency was further strengthened by the fact that manufacturing TNCs prefer to bank with the same bank worldwide. By this logic, local management preference for banking with a locally owned bank simply does not make sense.

The importance attached to corporate governance in transition economies hinges crucially on the neoclassical assumption about single-layer company operation. If this is the case, the interest of investors and managers can be harmonized by ways that are described in the corporate governance literature. But the fact is that the privatized Central and East European companies are typically not self-contained single level entities. They are merely subordinated units of a TNC, headquartered somewhere else in the world. From the perspective of the TNCs, these Central and East European operations are not full-fledged companies or profit maximizing entities. Although well-defined goals are set for these entities—typically in terms of production and/or distribution, sometimes in terms of research and development—they are not expected to develop a complete set of enterprise activities. Another consequence of the multi-level character of TNCs is that within these Central and East European companies, the principle-agent problem—i.e., conflicts between investors and managers—does not manifest itself at all. There is no need for governing bodies (board of directors, supervisory board) either. One or two designated managers directly represent the interest of the foreign owner.

Table 14.1 Largest 20 Hungarian non-financial companies ranked by 2000 net revenue

Rank	Name	Net revenue in € mln	Method of establishment	Present ownership form	Type of ownership	Listed on the BSE?	Nationality of top executive
1	**MOL Hungarian Oil and Gas Rt.**	**4,271**	**SOE partitioned**	**JSC**	**Financial investors**	**Yes**	**Hungarian**
2	Audi Hungaria Motor Kft.	3,753	Greenfield	LLC	Strategic TNC	No	German
3	Philips Hungary Kft.	2,665	Greenfield	LLC	Strategic TNC	No	Dutch
4	IBM Storage Product Kft.	2,633	Greenfield	LLC	Strategic TNC	No	German
5	Matav Rt.	1,858	SOE partitioned	JSC	Strategic TNC	Yes	Hungarian
6	Hungarian Electricity Works (MVM) Rt.	1,415	SOE partitioned	JSC	State-owned	No	Hungarian
7	**Panrusgaz Rt.**	**1,209**	**Greenfield**	**JSC**	**Diversified 49% owned by [1]**	**No**	**Russian**
8	Flextronics International Kft.	1,021	Greenfield	LLC	Strategic TNC	No	USA
9	Metro Holding Hungary Kft.	841	Greenfield	LLC	Strategic TNC	No	Hungarian
10	GE Hungary Rt.	774	SOEs merged	JSC	Strategic TNC	No	USA
11	Opel Hungary Kft.	745	Greenfield	LLC	Strategic TNC	No	German
12	Hungarian State Railways (MÁV)	739	SOE unchanged	JSC	State-owned	No	Hungarian

Table 14.1 continued

13	Dunaferr Danube Steel Works Rt.	721	SOE unchanged	JSC	State-owned	No	Hungarian
14	**Tisza Chemical Works (TVK) Rt.**	**653**	**SOE unchanged**	**JSC**	**Diversified majority owned by [1]**	**Yes**	**Hungarian**
15	Westel Rt.	638	Greenfield	JSC	100% owned by [5]	No	Hungarian
16	Budapest Electricity Work (ELMÜ) Rt.	569	SOE partitioned	JSC	Strategic TNC	No	Hungarian
17	Tesco Global Department Stores Rt.	527	Greenfield	JSC	Strategic TNC	No	UK
18	Magyar Suzuki Rt.	525	Greenfield	JSC	Strategic TNC	No	Japan
19	Hungarotabak - Tobaccoland Tobacco Trade Rt.	520	SOE unchanged	JSC	Strategic TNC	No	German
20	Shell Hungary Trade Rt.	493	Greenfield	JSC	Strategic TNC	No	Hungarian

Notes: LLC—limited liability company; JSC—joint stock company; TNC—trans-national corporation; SOE—state-owned enterprise; BSE—Budapest Stock Exchange. **Bold** typeface indicates companies for which the diversified ownership structure justifies complex corporate governance methods. Some companies were first listed on, then were delisted from, the BSE.

Source: Budapest Business Journal, Book of Lists, 2001-2002, p. 142, and author's own research.

Table 14.2 Largest 100 Hungarian non-financial companies ranked by 2000 net revenue

Ranking	1-20	21-40	41-60	61-80	81-100	Total (1-100)
Method of establishment						
- SOE	4	14	16	13	16	63
- SOEs partitioned or merged	5	0	0	2	1	8
- Greenfield investment	11	6	4	5	3	29
Present ownership form						
- Joint stock company	14	11	17	12	12	66
- Limited liability company	6	9	3	7	8	33
- Other	0	0	0	1	0	1
Type of ownership						
- TNC - strategic investor	15	15	12	12	9	63
- Financial investors	1	0	2	0	2	5
- State or municipal ownership	3	3	2	1	1	10
- Other	1	2	4	7	8	22
Listed on the BSE or elsewhere	3	1	9	2	2	17
Nationality of top local executive						
- Hungarian	10	11	13	12	16	62
- Other	10	9	7	8	4	38

Notes and sources: see Table 14.1.

Tables 14.1 and 14.2 show that, out of the largest 100 Hungarian non-financial companies, 63 are directly owned by a large TNC. The legal form of operation itself shows the irrelevance of corporate governance, as these companies are not corporations, but only limited liability companies. Of the top 100 largest companies, 66 are in joint stock form, while in the other 34 there are only owners, but no shareholders. This, of course, excludes the possibility of public trading with the shares. Even if trading is technically possible, only 17 of the largest 100 firms were—at some point in their history—actually traded on the Budapest Stock Exchange or elsewhere.[9] Table 14.3 completes the Hungarian picture by listing commercial banks. While all these banks are joint stock companies (the law does not permit any other legal form), there are only three banks in which the ownership structure may require sophisticated corporate governance measures.

Another aspect of the multi-layered character of modern firms is reflected in foreign trade. In contrast to the neoclassical paradigm, a firm's capability to produce 'high quality, low price' goods is not a guarantee that it will find markets. Central and East European companies have virtually no chance to sell their products on world markets if they remain specialized in end-products. World trade in manufactures consists largely of intra-industry trade. For the small Central and East European firm the only choice is to integrate itself into RNC production and supply chains.[10]

Following the literature's customary logic, one can argue that good corporate governance is important for transition economies even if it applies only to domestically owned middle-size companies. This argument can be developed further in three ways.

First, good corporate governance may also good for the health and stability of domestically owned companies. On closer inspection of the evidence, however, the reverse argument appears equally logical. That is, the strength and viability of *private*[11] middle-sized domestic firms reflect their abilities for non-formalized, quick decision-making, in which the business instinct of a single decision-maker prevails over collective deliberations. Such domestic companies are as a rule extremely secretive towards all stakeholders, with the important

9 This complicated formulation is required, because there is a growing number of delisting from the Budapest Stock Exchange. In addition, there is a growing number of 'dormant' shares that do not trade at all.

10 Hungary was able to choose this strategy in part because this option had been publicly discussed well before the transition period began (Mihalyi, 2000/2001, 2001).

11 The word 'private' is emphasized here to differentiate between *de nouvo* created private firms and privatized SOEs that are still *de facto* state owned in one way or another. In Central and Eastern Europe there are many ways in which state ownership is hidden behind the veil of municipal ownership, cross-ownership, ownership chains, differentiation among shareholders' class, etc. Unfortunately, the poor performance of these quasi-privatized firms is often falsely interpreted in the literature. Instead of uncovering the 'devil' of state ownership behind the veil, foreign observers explain everything in the context of *internal* and *external* control.

exception of banks. There is little official communication beyond the legal minimum,[12] company managers refuse to talk to the press about substantive matters, and even employees are not informed about company matters. On the other hand, these companies maintain close and open relationship with their banks, because they have to. This is where financing comes from. All other stakeholders are unimportant.

In abstracto, a second version of the same argument can be pulled out of our sleeves. Even the domestic firms would be better off if they rely on equity rather than loan financing. Unfortunately, the scale effect argument creeps back again. The unit costs associated with an initial public offer and maintaining a subsequent presence on the stock market are prohibitive for many domestic firms in Central and East European countries.

A third argument in favor of transparent corporate governance is to look at the motivation of domestic financial investors. This proposition was discussed at the beginning of the transition (Kornai, 1990; UN ECE 1994, p. 16.), and the conclusion was that foreign investors would not enter the Central and East European markets *until* they see that the domestic investors are fairly treated and well protected. Actual developments have showed the reverse to be the case. In the Czech Republic, Hungary and in other places, domestic investors were unwilling to move until the foreign funds appeared. In retrospect, the explanation is quite simple. Only the very large foreign funds were able to generate sufficient liquidity for the stocks and thus relative stability to the market as a whole. Without the participation of foreign funds, domestic stock exchanges are bound to be extremely volatile.

The economic success of the Baltic countries illustrates another interesting point. Due to the particularities of their post-1990 transition paths, the very smallness of these three countries almost equally affected their equity, government securities, and foreign exchange markets (Sutela, 2002). There is almost nothing to invest in. These countries inherited zero debt from the USSR, central government fiscal balances have been quite good, and the pattern of foreign investment has favored long-term strategic investors (as opposed to financial investors). The Baltic example reminds us of the fact that asset markets are horizontally integrated, which is another consideration missing from the neoclassical paradigm. In other words, the lack of sizeable bond and foreign exchange markets reduces the motivation of foreign investors to participate actively in equity markets, even if these latter markets are perfectly liberalized and transparent (as it happens to be the case in the Baltics).

---

12 In Hungary, the company law requires that a copy of the annual tax report be deposited with the court of registry within 30 days after the closing of the tax reports. Many companies deliberately break this law year after year, preferring to pay a fine instead.

Table 14.3 Largest banks in Hungary ranked by unconsolidated total assets in 2001

Rank	Name	Unconsolidated assets € mln	Established in Hungary	Largest shareholder(s)	Listed on the BSE?	Nationality of top executive
1	**OTP Bank**	**8,860**	**1949**	**Institutional (80%) and small investors (20%)**	**Yes**	**Hungarian**
2	K&H Bank	4,708	1986	Belgian and Dutch Banks (99%)	No	Canadian
3	MKB	3,764	1950	Bayerische Landesbank group (99%)	No	Hungarian
4	CIB Bank	3,153	1979	IntesaBci S.p.A. (100%)	No	Hungarian
5	HypoVereinsbank	2,250	1993	HypoVereinsbank group	No	German
6	Raiffeisen Bank	1,934	1986	Raiffeisen Banking Group (96.3%)	No	Hungarian
7	Postabank	1,513	1988	State-owned	No	Hungarian
8	Hungarian Development Bank	1,427	1991	State-owned	No	Hungarian
9	AEB	1,340	1922	Gazprom group (100%)	No	Russian
10	Budapest Bank	1,321	1988	GE Capital (100%)	No	US
11*	Citibank	1,309	1986	Citibank group (100%)	No	US
12	Erste Bank	1,135	1986	Erste Bank (99.3%)	No	Hungarian
13	**Inter-Europa Bank**	**723**	**1981**	**Italian banking groups (84%), other investors (15%)**	**Yes**	**Italian**
14	Commerzbank	607	1993	Commerzbank AG (100%)	No	German
15*	ING Bank	597	1991	ING Bank N.V. (100%)	No	Dutch
16	Takarekbank	573	1989	DG Bank (72%), Hungarian savings cooperatives (23%), Allianz Hungaria Insurance (5%)	No	Hungarian

Table 14.3 continued

17	Eximbank	470	1990	State owned	No	Hungarian
18	Volksbank	421	1991	Volksbank group (100%)	No	German
19	BNP Paribas	359	1990	BNP Paribas (100%)	No	Hungarian
20	Konzumbank	346	1986	State owned	No	Hungarian
21*	WestLB	321	1993	Westdeutsche Landesbank (100%)	No	German
22	Deutsche Bank	283	1995	Deutsche Bank (100%)	No	Hungarian
23	Merkantilbank	248	1988	Directy owned by [1]	No	Hungarian
24	Credit Lyonnais	193	1992	Credit Lyonnais (100%)	No	French
25	Daewoo Bank	173	1989	Daewoo Securities (100%)	No	Korean
26	Hungarian Land Credit and Mortgage Bank	147	1997	State owned	No	Hungarian
27*	Rabobank	107	1995	Rabobank group (100%)	No	Dutch
28	Cetelembank	86	1996	Cetelem (99%)	No	French
29	Opelbank	78	1996	General Motors	No	Finnish
30*	Societe Generale	59	1998	Societe Generale (100%)	No	French
31	Hanwha Bank	51	1990	Hanwha group (99%), Hungarian Education Ministry (1%)	No	Korean
32	IC Bank	48	1993	Malaysian individuals (100%)	No	Hungarian
33	Credigen Bank	41	1999	Sofinco (100%)	No	French

Notes: * 2000; other notes – see Table 14.1

Source: see Table 14.1 and daily press reports

The Western Perspective

Looking at Central and Eastern Europe with a neoclassical eye, the behavior of transnational foreign investors could be easily misinterpreted, which can then lead to wrong forecasts. At the beginning of transition it was assumed that privatization would automatically trigger a 'pull' effect—the supply of investment possibilities would create its own demand. As said before, the neoclassical vision of firm behavior did not pay attention to economies of scale, or to variations in scale effects from sector to sector. In reality, FDI flows have always been concentrated in those few sectors where scale effects are largest (telecommunication, energy, information technology, pharmaceuticals, banking, etc.). In other sectors, everything—including the relatively low price of assets, well-functioning R&D capacities that were created during the last two decades of socialism, traditional East European trade marks—were totally disregarded.

Another mistake, which almost inevitably followed from the previous one, is the underestimation of geographical considerations. *Geography matters.*[13] As the eye moves eastwards on the map of Europe, the appetite of TNCs weakens. Several factors are at work here: increasing transportation costs, language and cultural differences. Landlocked countries have an additional disadvantage. In sum: bad location is a big handicap that even perfectly implemented corporate government reforms can not fully counterbalance.

Scale and location effects often reinforce one another. The Central and East European experience shows that it matters a lot, which country is chosen first as an investment opportunity. Once a major investment takes place, say in the Czech Republic, it makes little sense for the same TNC or even for a competitor of this TNC to start business in the neighboring Slovakia.

Geography matters in another sense as well. In analyzing the dangers of expropriation, the term 'investor' is used without distinguishing between domestic and cross-border investments. In reality, the dangers that threaten cross-border investors are not those of minority shareholder positions. They are: country risk, exchange rate risk, and regulatory risk.

To make matters even more complicated, the first two types of risks have to be considered in a regional, if not worldwide, perspective. Financial investors display herd behavior, which is a cause and consequence of the contagion of crisis from one market to another.[14] Regulatory risk is important, because TNCs concentrate their activities in network industries (which in turn reflects increasing returns). Network industries, however, are usually regulated by national

---

13 The importance of geography was strongly emphasized by J. Sachs at an October 1999 CASE conference 'Ten Years After: Transition and Growth in Post-Communist Countries'.

14 To make the matter even more complicated, recent evidences suggest that herding behavior itself is itself a variable in the equation. In 1998, the Russian bond market crisis had far reaching contagion effects, but three years later a disaster of major magnitude in Argentina sent much smaller shock waves around the world.

governments and/or supranational organizations.[15] If these regulations are not neutral, or for any other reason severely constrain the freedom of the investor, this can do much more harm than a lack of sophistication in corporate governance.

Russia, China, and Other Monopolistic Markets

The above argumentation needs to be qualified when it is extended to the two largest former communist economies, Russia and China. Potentially both countries possess large markets, where size in itself is not a growth constraint for domestic companies. In theory, domestic companies in these countries have a chance to reach dimensions comparable to those of established TNCs and can argue that this long process of capital concentration presupposes a well-regulated capital market and good corporate governance for the participating companies.

The Russian case illustrates the strengths and the weaknesses of this line of thinking. Large Russian corporations have emerged, some of which are already measurable by international standards. But it is noteworthy that all the large Russian companies are built on raw materials, chiefly gas and oil (e.g. Gazprom, LUKOil, Yukos). If we add that, for historical reasons, these mining and processing companies were already large during the Soviet times, we can conclude that competitive Russian markets (to the extent that such exist) did not support the rise of giants. This implies that financial success of these already existing very large companies depends more on the caprice of world market prices then on governance and management. Indeed, Russia's very large companies are extremely vulnerable. In the financial crisis of 1998, the capital base of Russia's largest private banks melted like snow within weeks.[16]

The case of China is less clear. While the size of the market is potentially even bigger than in Russia, for historical and cultural reasons it is less likely that the Chinese capital market will really be opened soon for US-type foreign managed funds. If the recent past is any guide to the future, it seems more likely that mainland China will continue to attract capital from Hong Kong, Taiwan or Singapore along ethnic lines, rather than along purely commercial considerations based on relative factor prices and capital affordability.

15 The importance of national price and tariff controls are only the trivial examples in the energy and telecommunication sectors, but the WTO, ITU, and BIS are also important in determining profit-generating possibilities in the pharmaceutical, broadcasting, and banking sectors, respectively.

16 This argument can be extended to those Central and East European economies that were or potentially are able to develop a sizeable tourist industry on their seashores or mountains. Prospects for these enterprises depend more on natural endowments, country risk, and exchange rate risk than on good corporate governance.

Conclusions

This chapter presents a provocative statement about the irrelevance of corporate governance for the transition economies. It shows that, if the term 'corporate governance' is understood in a strict, specific manner pertaining to the set of rules defining the operation of publicly traded, large shareholding companies, then the relevance of this doctrine is rapidly diminishing. This is reflected first and foremost in the fact that, taken individually, the markets of Central and Eastern Europe are too small and are thus not conducive for the emergence of truly large companies. As it happened, the privatization process in this region has been dominated by large transnational companies that directly own and control the local companies. For this simple reason, the agency problem hardly appears, if at all.

Another way of summarizing the lessons of the Central and East European transition process is to include the question of regional integration into the analysis. The fate of former East Germany, once the most developed socialist country, is instructive here. As it is well known, East Germany was legally integrated into what used to be West Germany through constitutional changes introduced in a single day. In this newly created legal environment, the former East German SOEs had no time to adopt western type corporate governance structures. The companies themselves were simply 'swallowed' by their hungry competitors.

The three Baltic countries occupy the middle of this continuum. In a way, Estonia, Latvia and Lithuania did not seek from the very beginning to establish a full set of domestic markets, but instead pursued integration by becoming regions in the fully-established North-Western Europe (Sutela, 2002). The Czech Republic, Hungary and Poland have been aspiring to European Union membership since the collapse of communism. While in the euphoria of the first transition years the authorities of all three countries were strongly dedicated to the development of stock markets and widespread popular stock ownership, first then the other two countries accepted that the majority of their large companies would become subsidiaries and/or branch offices of transnational corporations. And once the Central and East European countries join the European Union, the relevance of national corporate governance regimes will largely vanish without a trace.

References

Arrow, K.J. and G. Debreu (1954), 'Existence of an equilibrium for a competitive economy', *Econometrica*, Vol. 22, pp. 265-290.

Berle, A.A. and G.C. Means (1933), *The Modern Corporation and Private Property*, New York: Macmillan.

Coase, R. (1960), 'The problem of social cost', *Journal of Law and Economics*, Vol. 3, pp.1-44.

Debreu, G. (1959), *Theory of Value*, New York: Wiley.

EBRD (1997), Transition Report, European Bank for Reconstruction and Development, London.

Financial Times, 21 June 1999.

Harvard Business Review (1991), November-December.

Kaldor, N. (1967), *Causes of the Slow Rate of Economic Growth of the United Kingdom*, Cambridge: Cambridge University Press.

Kalotay, K. (eds.) (2001), *Privatization and Greenfield FDI in Central and Eastern Europe: Does the Mode of Entry Matter?*, Special issue of *Transnational Corporations*, Vol. 10, No. 3, December.

Kornai, J. (1971), *Anti-Equilibrium*. Amsterdam: North Holland.

Kornai, J. (1990), *The Road to a Free Economy. Shifting from a Socialist System: The Example of Hungary*, New York: W. W. Norton.

Marshall, A. (1890), *Principles of Economics*, London: Macmillan.

Marx, K. (1867), *Das Kapital*, Berlin: Dietz Verlag.

Mihalyi, P. (2001), 'The evolution of Hungary's approach to FDI in post-communist privatization', in Kalotay (2001), pp. 61-74.

Mihalyi, P. (2000/2001), 'Foreign direct investment in Hungary – the post-communist privatization story re-considered', *Acta Oeconomica*, Vol. 51 (1), pp. 107-129.

OECD Ad Hoc Task Force on Corporate Governance (1999), *OECD Principles of Corporate Governance*.

OECD (2001), Corporate governance in Romania.

Phelps, E., R. Frydman, A. Rapaczynski and A. Shleifer (1993), 'Needed mechanisms of corporate governance and finance in Eastern Europe', *EBRD Working Papers*, No. 1, March.

Shleifer, A. and R.W. Vishny (1997), 'A survey of corporate governance', *The Journal of Finance*, Vol. 52, pp. 737-783.

Sutela, P. (2002), 'Managing capital flows in Estonia and Latvia', *International Center for Economic Growth European Center Working Papers*, No. 8.

The Economist, 9 March 2002.

UN ECE (1994), 'Overview of transition economies in 1993-1994', *Economic Survey of Europe in 1993-1994*, UN Economic Commission for Europe, UN, New York, pp. 155-187.

Young, A. (1928), 'Increasing returns and economic progress', *Economic Journal*, December.

Walras, L. (1874), *Elements d'economie politique pure; ou theorie de la richesse sociale*, Lausanne: L Corbaz.

Chapter 15

Links between Privatization and Other Policies

Irena Grosfeld

Introduction

Privatization policies in transition economies are receiving mixed reviews. Twelve years after the beginning of transition, the attempt to disentangle the effect of privatization on firm performance turns out to be a complex endeavor. Recent experience provides fertile ground for testing various hypotheses concerning the impact of privatization on corporate performance but the results of several empirical studies are ambiguous (for a recent survey see Djankov and Murrell, 2002).

Careful reading of this literature suggests that two main problems make the results difficult to interpret. The first problem in the empirical work using firm level data is the issue of endogeneity. Interrelations between ownership, firm characteristics and corporate performance are usually studied in a cross-sectional context where ownership is treated as exogenous. But ownership and performance may be endogenously determined by exogenous and partly observed changes in the firm's environment. In order to test whether ownership is an important determinant of firm behavior, we need panel data allowing testing for this relationship in a dynamic framework.

The second problem is the issue of complementarity. There is an increasingly wide consensus that privatization requires appropriate institutional reform in order to be effective. But if we move away from such a general claim, the unanimity disappears. What is really important? Competition? Corporate governance? The legal system?

Johnson in Chapter 13 stresses the role of the law. He argues that the effectiveness of privatization depends on the quality of the legal system, which is viewed as the main determinant of corporate governance. This is certainly an important argument. However, in order to empirically identify the causality effect between law and performance, we need a study based on cross-country longitudinal data. Moreover, extensive heterogeneity in firm performance within countries and even within industries remains puzzling. Obviously, this heterogeneity cannot be explained by the quality of legal and regulatory environment. Other aspects of corporate governance related to firm specific characteristics might play a role. Ownership structure is one of the main corporate governance mechanisms potentially affecting firm value.

A number of observers underline the importance of product market competition. According to an early view, competition may substitute for privatization. It was even argued that competition was more important than ownership and should have been put in the center of the transformation strategy from the very beginning (Stiglitz, 1999). The argument strongly relied on the weakness of corporate governance arrangements due to the dispersed ownership structure that mass privatization programs were supposed to generate. Recent empirical work shows, however, that the ownership structure emerging from the mass privatization programs is quite concentrated (see, for instance, Grosfeld and Hoshi, 2003). Other work suggests that that strong complementarities exist between privatization (or corporate governance) and product market competition (see Grosfeld and Tressel, 2002).

In what follows we start with a discussion of the definition of corporate governance, in order to bring into focus a specific dimension of corporate governance, namely, the ownership structure. We then discuss the issue of the ambiguous, possibly non-linear relationship between ownership concentration and performance. We also briefly review various strategies of transition according to the importance attributed to corporate governance. In the last section we report some of the results of our empirical work focusing on the interaction between product market competition and ownership concentration. Finally, we give some tentative conclusions concerning the relationship between corporate governance and firm performance.

The Focus of Corporate Governance: Shareholders or Stakeholders?

Before considering in more detail the role of ownership concentration, let me say a few words about the recently debated issue on what should be the real focus of corporate governance. According to the classical view, corporate governance deals with the ways in which suppliers of funds '*assure themselves of getting a return on their investment*' (Shleifer and Vishny, 1997). The objective is seen as maximizing shareholders value. Recently, however, it has been suggested that a broader definition of corporate governance should be adopted. What matters is not only the interest of shareholders but also the welfare of other stakeholders having an interest and long term relationship with the enterprise, such as employees, suppliers, or even consumers in general (see Tirole, 2001; Stiglitz, 1999; Berglof and von Thadden, 2000; Allen and Gale, 2000). Sometimes it is even argued that a firm should be responsible not only for the protection of those with whom it has a contractual relationship, but that it should also behave in an 'ethical' way, i.e. refraining from bribing officials or from polluting. This is indeed the idea of a stakeholder society.

The main argument for such a view could be traced back to the change in the theory of the firm. According to an older view, tangible assets were considered as critical resources of the firm. Human capital was tied to inanimate assets. Legal claims, or the ownership of assets, were considered as the most important source of power. Each claim on the firm had a pre-determined payoff, except for the claims of shareholders. Having a comparative advantage in diversifying risk, shareholders accepted a residual payoff. Therefore, the maximization of shareholders' value led to maximization of the value of the enterprise.

The new view of the firm emphasizes the role of human capital relative to that of inanimate tangible assets. The firm can no longer be defined by the common ownership of assets. Knowledge, not tangible assets, has become the main source of economic advantage. The boundaries of economic organizations have become less well defined. Consequently, all contracts, not only those of shareholders, should be considered as incomplete: all stakeholders can at some point be residual claimants. What are the consequences of this change for corporate governance? According to Rajan and Zingales (1998), instead of studying mechanisms stimulating the maximization of shareholders' value, corporate governance should be concerned with the mechanisms giving the firm the power to provide incentives to human capital.

The arguments in favor of stakeholders' society are quite strong. However, focusing on shareholder value may still appear as a second best solution. It would be extremely difficult indeed to devise an incentive scheme for managers taking into account various stakeholders' interests. Tirole (2001) argue in particular, that if managers had to maximize the sum of various stakeholders' interests, they should also be rewarded on the basis of some measure of aggregate welfare of all stakeholders. Such measure, an equivalent of the stock market value of assets, is not easy to find. Eventually, managers left with and arbitrating between contradictory objectives would be in a position to capture important rents.

Ownership Concentration: a Solution to Corporate Governance Problem?

Until recently the thinking about corporate governance issues has been dominated by the early concern of Berle and Means, who stressed the negative consequences of dispersed equity holdings. The separation of ownership and control and the agency conflict between shareholders and managers were viewed as the main impediments to the provision of external finance to firms. When equity is widely dispersed, shareholders do not have appropriate incentives to monitor managers, who, in turn, can expropriate investors and maximize their own utility instead of maximizing shareholder value. Concentration of ownership stakes was often seen as a potential solution to this problem of divergent interests.

However, it is increasingly recognized that concentrated ownership structure does not always have a positive impact on firm performance. Recent empirical and theoretical work suggests that the impact of ownership concentration on performance may be more ambiguous than initially expected.[1]

---

1 Similarly, the impact of managerial equity ownership, often viewed as another way of alleviating the agency costs within the firm (Jensen and Meckling, 1976), has been shown to be ambiguous. Managerial share ownership may increase managerial opportunism, lead

A number of papers show a significant and negative relation between ownership concentration and firm value, productivity or profitability. Demsetz and Lehn (1985) find no significant positive relationship between ownership concentration and accounting profit rate. In Nickell et al. (1997) control by a financial company improves performance whereas control by a non-financial company tends to be negatively correlated with productivity growth. Leech and Leahy (1991) do not get clear-cut results; they show that the correlation between performance and concentration depends on the concentration variable chosen. Bianco and Casavola (1999), using a panel of Italian firm data, find a negative correlation between ownership concentration and profitability.

Looking at economic theory to find some help in interpreting these results we find that it is difficult to describe *a priori* the characteristics of 'good' ownership structures. As Morck (2000) puts it, '*economic theory provides equally ample resources for* constructing *models in which concentrated corporate ownership is either good or bad*'. The usual explanation of the non-monotonic relationship between ownership concentration and firm performance is expropriation hypothesis. La Porta et al. (1998) argue that if the presence of controlling shareholders alleviates the problem of monitoring, it may also be responsible for the expropriation of minority shareholders. Other works provide, although not always explicitly, different explanations of the non-monotonic relationship. According to Demsetz and Lehn (1985) or Heinrich (2000), concentrated ownership may be costly for large shareholders because it limits diversification and reduces the owners' tolerance for risk. This, in turn, may affect investment decisions. Interpreting Aghion and Tirole (1997) we may say that concentrated ownership provides incentives to control management, but it also reduces the manager's initiative or incentives to acquire information. In this perspective, Burkart et al. (1997) view dispersed ownership as a commitment device ensuring that shareholders will not exercise excessive control, which might hinder managerial activism. Managerial initiative and competence is particularly valuable when the firm operates in an environment characterized by high degree of uncertainty. In such a situation a concentrated ownership structure may turn out to be costly.[2] Finally, dispersed ownership implies higher stock liquidity, which, in turn, improves the informational role of the stock market (Holmstrom and Tirole, 1993). The generation of information by the stock market is particularly valuable in

---

to entrenchment and allow the manager to pursue other aims than profit-maximization. Some empirical evidence suggests that the relationship between managerial shareholdings and firm value is non-linear: low levels of shareholdings may align manager and shareholder interests and increase firm value, but beyond some threshold management becomes entrenched and the firm value may decline (see, for instance, Morck, 2000; Shleifer and Vishny, 1988).

2 In the context of transition characterized by high degree of uncertainty about what should be produced and how, the competence of those who manage and control the firm, and their initiative, seems to be the most important factor of success. Recognizing the trade off between monitoring and initiative suggests that leaving some degree of control in the hands of managers may be desirable. See Grosfeld and Hoshi (2003) for the discussion of the relationship between risk and ownership concentration.

an uncertain environment (Allen, 1993), or when it is essential to ensure that the management of underperforming firms changes hands. The concentration of ownership may make control insufficiently contestable, hampering the selection of controlling individuals.

Overall, in some circumstances with which high degrees of uncertainty are associated, the separation of ownership and control may turn out to be optimal for shareholders (see Allen and Gale, 2000). On the other hand it is important that dispersed ownership not preclude the formation of controlling blocks when needed (see Bolton and von Thadden, 1998).

Corporate Governance in Transition

When comparing transformation strategies in different transition countries, it appears that the problem of corporate governance arrangements emerging from the process of privatization clearly got unequal treatment.

In Poland, the design of the privatization strategy was dominated by the classical concern of the separation of ownership and control and the conflict between managers and shareholders. The main objective was to find a 'real' owner, somebody with the ability and incentive to control management. Mass privatization programs implemented in other countries were usually seen as inefficient because of the dispersed ownership structure they were thought to create. Consequently, special programs were elaborated with the objective of putting in place concentrated ownership structures providing adequate incentives and tools for monitoring. The National Investment Funds were created o avoid the dispersion of control rights resulting from the transfer of several hundreds of firms to the population. Therefore, a concentrated ownership structure was imposed on the firms and the funds were to be managed by highly experienced western specialists.

In other countries, such as the Czech Republic and Russia, concerns about specific corporate governance arrangements were practically absent during the development of voucher schemes. In the Czech Republic privatization was understood as the precondition for the process of radical institutional change and was supposed to generate important spillover effects. Consequently, the main concern was the speed of the process and less attention was paid to the emerging ownership structure. In Russia, the whole process of free distribution of assets to the population was dominated by political considerations: the objective was to overcome resistance to reforms, to create a constituency in favor of reforms, and to ensure their irreversibility.[3]

A couple of years later, it turns out that the actual evolution of the ownership structure followed quite similar pattern in several countries. In the Czech Republic, starting from a highly dispersed ownership structure, the large majority of companies have found a dominant owner. In Poland, starting from a uniform ownership structure imposed by the mass privatization program, the

---

3 Such was at least the initial understanding of and the motivation for the privatization process.

majority of companies involved in the scheme have also found dominant owners, some ten per cent of them being foreign investors. So the deliberate search for 'good' ownership structure notwithstanding, the ownership structure has become strongly concentrated, probably in response to various pressures and constraints characterizing firms' environment.[4]

This is really what the spiritual fathers of mass privatization schemes expected. It should be noted, however, that the conditions for the reallocation of property rights were quite different in the two countries. Poland is usually given as an example of good regulatory strategy for other countries in transition (see Glaeser et al., 2001) while the Czech Republic is blamed for the weakness of its regulatory framework. The fact that the extent of ownership concentration is similar in the two countries characterized by important differences in shareholder protection is puzzling if we consider, following Johnson (see Chapter 13), that concentration of ownership is a response to the poor legal framework and weak protection of minority investors.

Competition and Ownership Concentration: Complements or Substitutes?

A recent study of firm performance in transition provides evidence of a non-linear effect of ownership concentration on performance. In Grosfeld and Tressel (2002) the data on the non-financial firms listed on the Warsaw Stock Exchange were used to analyze the ways in which competition and corporate governance affect firm performance.[5] First, we studied the separate effects of competition and ownership concentration on productivity growth at the firm level. Competition turns out to have a positive influence on productivity growth. This suggests that product market competition may be an effective mechanism for ensuring efficient restructuring and productivity growth during the transition, as claimed by many economists today. Concerning the effect of ownership concentration, which turns out to be quite high in Poland, we found a U-shaped relationship with performance. Firms with relatively dispersed ownership (no shareholder with more than 20 per cent of voting shares), and firms in which one shareholder has more than 50 per cent of voting shares, show higher productivity growth than firms with intermediate levels of ownership concentration. This correlation between concentration of ownership and productivity growth is not explained by the identity of controlling shareholders. When the CEO, a bank, or a National Investment Fund controls the firm, the type of the controlling shareholder has an independent negative effect on performance.

Finally, we studied the relationship between product market competition and ownership concentration. How do they interact when affecting firm productivity? The question was whether competition and corporate governance

4 For the firms listed on the Warsaw Stock Exchange the mean of the largest voting block is 38 per cent (see Grosfeld and Tressel, 2002).

5 By using panel data and GMM estimators we take care of the crucial problems of heterogeneity and endogeneity of explanatory variables.

(proxied by ownership concentration) reinforce each other (are complements), or whether they should rather be considered as substitutes? The substitution effect would mean that, when corporate governance is weak, competition plays an important disciplinary role, forcing managers to improve performance and reducing slack. If, on the contrary, agency costs or other problems of corporate governance are not too severe, the role of competition in stimulating managerial efficiency may be more limited. On the other hand, if competition and corporate governance were complementary, the effectiveness of corporate governance would be enhanced by market competition, and vice-versa.

The results in Grosfeld and Tressel (2002) strongly support the idea that the impact of product market competition depends on the ownership structure of the firm. Competition has no significant impact on productivity growth in firms with 'poor' governance; it has a significant and positive effect in the case of firms with 'good' corporate governance. So, competitive pressure, at least in the case of the Polish listed firms, did not compensate for the weakness of corporate governance mechanisms. Therefore, competition and corporate governance appear as complements rather than substitutes. This result can be considered as evidence that competition policies and ownership changes should be promoted simultaneously. Transformation strategies focusing solely on competition may not be successful if they are not accompanied by efficient ownership changes.

Conclusions

If we take ownership structure as the main characteristic of corporate governance, it turns out that the impact of ownership concentration on firm performance is ambiguous. Therefore, it appears difficult to define *a priori* optimal ownership structure. This depends on a number of firm specific characteristics and may endogenously adjust in response to firm specific needs, pressures of the environment, etc. It may be that what really matters for successful firm restructuring is less the particular corporate governance arrangements than the possibility of their flexible adaptation.

Privatization seems necessary for such an evolution to occur. Trying to make sense of the recent experience of transition, privatization of the state assets does indeed appear to be a necessary precondition for the emergence of appropriate corporate governance arrangements.

The institutional infrastructure that is set up in transition should promote such flexible adjustment of corporate governance. Only then can privatization as such effectively be welfare improving.

This brings us to a more general view of the process of institutional change, or the relationship between the law and the market. Is the law something that stands apart from the market and should be dealt with separately (as Joseph Stiglitz claimed), or should legal and regulatory frameworks be considered in relation with the privatization process (as Andrei Shleifer argued at the beginning of the 1990s)? In the latter perspective institutions (law and regulations) appear as to some extent endogenous to the privatization process, adapting themselves to new opportunities. Privatization is viewed as a precondition facilitating the process of institutional change. The experience of the last twelve years of transition provides powerful arguments in favor of both views. Carefully discriminating between them remains a challenge for economists.

References

Aghion, P. and J. Tirole (1997), 'Formal and real authority in organizations', *Journal of Political Economy*, Vol. 55, pp. 1-27.

Allen, F. (1993), 'Stock markets and resource allocation', in C. Mayer and X. Vives (eds.), *Capital Markets and Financial Intermediation*, Cambridge: CEPR and Cambridge University Press.

Allen, F. and D. Gale (2000), *Comparing Financial Systems*, Cambridge: MIT Press.

Berglof, E. and E.L. von Thadden, (1999), 'The changing corporate governance paradigm: Implications for transition and developing countries', mimeo.

Bianco, M. and P. Casavola (1999), 'Italian corporate governance: effects on financial structure and firm performance', *European Economic Review*, Vol. 43, pp. 1057-1069.

Bolton, P. and E.L. von Thadden (1998), Blocks, Liquidity and Corporate Control, *The Journal of Finance*, February.

Burkart, M., D. Gromb and F. Panunzi (1997), 'Large shareholders, monitoring and the value of the firm', *Quarterly Journal of Economics*, Vol. 112, pp. 693-728.

Demsetz, H. and K. Lehn (1985), 'The structure of corporate ownership: causes and consequences', *Journal of Political Economy*, Vol. 93, pp. 1155-1177.

Djankov, S. and P. Murrel (2002), 'Enterprise restructuring in transition. A Quantitative survey', *Journal of Economic Literature*, Vol. 40, pp. 1202-1214.

Glaeser, E., S. Johnson and A. Shleifer (2001), 'Coase versus the Coasians', *Quarterly Journal of Economics*, Vol. 116, pp. 853-899.

Grosfeld, I. and T. Tressel (2002), 'Competition and ownership structure: substitutes or complements? Evidence from the Warsaw Stock Exchange', *Economics of Transition*, Vol. 10, pp. 525-551.

Grosfeld, I. and I. Hoshi (2003), 'Mass privatization, corporate governance and endogenous ownership structure', The William Davidson Institute Working Paper No. 596.

Heinrich, R.P. (2000), 'Complementarities in corporate governance: Ownership concentration, capital structure, monitoring and pecuniary incentives', *Kiel Working Paper*, No. 968.

Holmstrom, B. and J. Tirole (1993), 'Market liquidity and performance monitoring', *Journal of Political Economy*, Vol. 101, pp. 678-709.

Jensen, M.C. and W.H. Meckling (1976), 'Theory of the Firm: Managerial behavior, agency costs and ownership structure', *Journal of Financial Economy*, Vol. 3, pp. 305-360.

La Porta, R., F. Lopez-de-Silanes and A. Shleifer (1998), 'Corporate ownership around the world', *NBER Working Paper*, No. 6625.

Leech, D. and J. Leahy (1991), Ownership structure, control type classifications and the performance of large British companies. *The Economic Journal*, Vol. 101, pp. 1418-1437.

Morck, R. (2000), *Concentrated Corporate Ownership*, Chicago and London: The University of Chicago Press.

Nickell, S.J., D. Nicolitsas and N. Dryden (1997), 'What makes firms perform well?', *European Economic Review*, Vol. 41, pp. 783-796.

Rajan, R. and L. Zingales (1998), 'Power in the theory of the firms', *Quarterly Journal of Economics*, Vol. 63, pp. 387-432.

Shleifer, A. and R. Vishny (1988), 'Management Ownership and Market Valuation: An Empirical Analysis', *Journal of Financial Economics*, Vol. 20, pp. 293-315.

Shleifer, A. and R. Vishny (1997), 'A survey of corporate governance', *Journal of Finance*, Vol. 52 (2), pp. 737-783.

Stiglitz, J. (1999), 'Whither reform? Ten Years of transition', paper prepared for the Annual Bank Conference on Development Economics, Washington D.C., April 28-30.

Tirole, J. (2001), 'Corporate governance', *Econometrica*, Vol. 69 (1), pp. 1-35.

Chapter 16

The EU Enlargement: Consequences for the CIS Countries

Anders Aslund and Andrew Warner

Introduction

Within a few years, ten former communist countries are supposed to become members of the European Union (EU). The question immediately arises what this enlargement of the EU will mean to the twelve former Soviet countries of the Commonwealth of Independent States (CIS). The effects will be many and multifaceted, both qualitative and quantitative.

A substantial literature has dealt with the effects of EU enlargement on the ten East-Central European (CEE) accession countries and the EU members (notably Baldwin et al., 1997; Buch and Piazolo, 2001). However, the literature on the CIS members of exclusion is relatively thin, and it tends to focus on individual countries (e.g. Hoffman and Mollers, 2001).

This chapter[1] is concerned with the impact of the current EU enlargement on the CIS countries, particularly in terms of GDP growth, trade, and the impact on the overall economic system. As we are discussing profound long-term changes, the time perspective should be at least a decade.

Economic Output and Growth

The effect of accession of an adjacent group of states on growth of the CIS states is of course not immediate. Nevertheless we can outline possible indirect effects. The clearest way forward is to outline the factors that probably will be important for CIS growth and then to examine the extent to which EU accession of neighboring countries will influence them.

To start, it is important to bear in mind that transitional issues dominate current growth in CIS countries and that these issues, while important today, are likely to recede in importance in future years. The major transition is the massive movement of resources from state industries or at least communist-dictated sectors

1 Caroline McGregor has kindly provided research assistance, compiling the tables and tracing references. We would like to thank the participants of the CASE conference on 'Beyond Transition' for their many comments and especially Michael Emerson and Daniel Gros.

to new and sometimes unknown sectors. In practice there is often no movement of resources at all, rather simply a decline of the older sectors resisted by entrenched elites and a slow creation of entirely new structures and industries.

The major economic reality in the CIS states is that the industries inherited from communist planning are outdated and sometimes perverse vis-à-vis the economic endowments of the countries. The importance of structural change makes the growth determinants somewhat different for post-communist countries than for other countries. It requires attention to things that facilitate structural change such as the elimination of remaining subsidies for outdated factories, labor market flexibility, anti-monopoly policy and facilitating new entry and start-up enterprises.

The post-communist countries vary considerably in terms of the rates at which they have eliminated barriers to structural change. Labor markets were quite flexible in many countries almost from the beginning of transition. Subsidies (both implicit and explicit) were eliminated gradually as part of the inflation stabilization of the 1990s. More recently, there has been a concerted effort in several countries to reduce administrative barriers to start-up enterprises, through increased attention to the problems of small and medium sized enterprises. The financial system remains an issue in most countries. It is usually impossible to get venture capital and the formal financial system has little patience with new enterprises asking for financing with little or no collateral. The good news is that the importance of formal financial structures may be overrated. Informal financial arrangements are flourishing in several countries. The recent Bulgarian recovery from the financial crisis of 1996-7 must have been financed without formal financing because the banking statistics do not show any significant increase in credit.

Although there has been considerable progress, the CIS countries still lag behind Eastern Europe in structural change. Table 16.1 shows a composite structural reform index, consisting of 73 per cent liberalization and 27 per cent privatization (De Melo et al., 1997). While a normal market economy would attain the index value 1, nine CEE countries had achieved 0.88 in 2000 and the CIS countries only 0.63. This means that transitional growth is not over in many of the former Soviet economies.

How will EU accession affect this? If there is any effect at all, it will be primarily a demonstration effect, raising support for further reform. In the previous ten years of transition, a reliable empirical regularity has been that countries with faster and deeper reforms have grown faster; and countries on the border with Europe have had faster and deeper reforms. In other words, greater proximity to Europe has been conducive to greater acceptance of market reforms, and this has propelled growth. As the border of European economic institutions shifts further to the east, we can expect this to bolster reforms and transition in the CIS states.

However, as the transition matures and as the remaining barriers to structural change diminish, traditional determinants of growth will become more prominent. At the risk of oversimplification, we can list three broad categories. One is factor accumulation, including physical capital, skills and knowledge capital; a second is openness to external trade, foreign investment and the inflow of

Table 16.1 Structural reform index

Country	**1990**	**1991**	**1992**	**1993**	**1994**	**1995**	**1996**	**1997**	**1998**	**1999**	**2000**
Bulgaria	0.19	0.62	0.86	0.66	0.63	0.61	0.57	0.67	0.79	0.79	0.85
Czech Rep.	0.16	0.79	0.86	0.90	0.88	0.82	0.82	0.82	0.90	0.90	0.93
Estonia	0.20	0.32	0.64	0.81	0.83	0.77	0.78	0.82	0.90	0.93	0.93
Hungary	0.57	0.74	0.78	0.82	0.83	0.82	0.82	0.87	0.93	0.93	0.93
Latvia	0.13	0.29	0.51	0.67	0.71	0.67	0.74	0.74	0.86	0.86	0.82
Lithuania	0.13	0.33	0.55	0.78	0.79	0.71	0.74	0.74	0.82	0.82	0.86
Poland	0.68	0.72	0.82	0.82	0.83	0.79	0.79	0.81	0.86	0.86	0.86
Romania	0.22	0.36	0.45	0.58	0.67	0.65	0.64	0.66	0.76	0.82	0.82
Slovakia	0.16	0.79	0.86	0.83	0.83	0.79	0.79	0.77	0.90	0.90	0.89
EU Acc. AVG	0.27	0.55	0.70	0.76	0.78	0.74	0.74	0.77	0.86	0.87	0.88
Belarus	0.04	0.10	0.20	0.33	0.42	0.50	0.44	0.37	0.37	0.37	0.43
Moldova	0.04	0.10	0.38	0.51	0.54	0.64	0.64	0.64	0.76	0.76	0.75
Russia	0.04	0.10	0.49	0.59	0.67	0.64	0.71	0.72	0.64	0.64	0.64
Ukraine	0.04	0.10	0.23	0.13	0.33	0.54	0.57	0.59	0.65	0.65	0.68
Georgia	0.04	0.22	0.32	0.35	0.33	0.50	0.61	0.66	0.79	0.79	0.79
Armenia	0.04	0.13	0.39	0.42	0.46	0.54	0.61	0.61	0.76	0.76	0.72
Azerbaijan	0.04	0.04	0.25	0.31	0.33	0.40	0.44	0.51	0.61	0.61	0.65
Kazakhstan	0.04	0.14	0.35	0.35	0.42	0.50	0.64	0.66	0.79	0.72	0.71
Kyrgyzstan	0.04	0.04	0.33	0.60	0.71	0.71	0.67	0.70	0.82	0.79	0.79
Tajikistan	0.04	0.11	0.20	0.26	0.42	0.40	0.40	0.39	0.55	0.58	0.61
Turkmenistan	0.04	0.04	0.13	0.16	0.29	0.27	0.27	0.36	0.36	0.36	0.35
Uzbekistan	0.04	0.04	0.26	0.30	0.50	0.57	0.57	0.54	0.57	0.50	0.49
CIS AVG	0.04	0.10	0.29	0.36	0.45	0.52	0.55	0.56	0.64	0.63	0.63

Source: De Melo, et al., 1997a; Havrylyshyn and Wolf (1999), p. 34; Aslund (2002).

foreign ideas and practices; and a third is institutions, meaning especially property rights to protect investments and efficient legal mechanisms for solving disputes.

For more specific empirical evidence on which variables have been reliably correlated with growth during the past forty years we can turn to Doppelhofer, Miller and Sala-I-Martin (2000). Their list includes: initial income; openness to international trade from Sachs and Warner (1995); life expectancy; primary schooling enrollment rates and primary export intensity (inversely correlated with growth). Earlier studies found evidence that smaller governments and less corruption help growth, although these studies did not include many controls (see Barro and Sala-I-Martin, 1995; Mauro 1995). The existence of some effect on both counts is plausible, although the size of the effect is under considerable doubt.

Most discussions of the effects of EU enlargement tend to focus on trade and finance or exchange rate issues. We use the discussion above to take a broader approach, reviewing some quantitative assessments that have been made and discussing the relative importance of various effects. Of the factors listed in the previous two paragraphs, accession is most likely to have an impact on growth through its effect on future trade and integration of the CIS countries, and to a lesser extent on capital accumulation through its effects on financial flows. We list five areas for discussion:

1. Trade will be most obviously affected. These effects are usually divided into trade creation or trade diversion. The static allocation effects are comparatively easy to assess, but it is the accumulation effects, or the long-term dynamic effects, that are most important. The countries that become members of the EU will benefit greatly from trade creation on large and open export markets, while the non-members might suffer from less access, though they may also gain from the unification of their major export market.
2. EU accession will also influence international financial flows. The new EU members will receive net direct EU financing. They are also likely to obtain more foreign direct investment, as EU membership will guarantee them steady trade access to the whole common market; EMU membership will follow and eliminate the currency risk; the acceptance of the *acquis communautaire* and all EU institutions also provides substantial institutional guarantees. But what does this mean for the CIS countries?
3. The political dimensions of migration are discussed more often the economic dimensions. After several years of membership, the new EU members will become part of a free common labor market. That will probably encourage labor migration, and as a consequence wages are likely to rise more in the accession countries than otherwise would be the case. How will the CIS countries be affected?
4. Systemic consequences of membership in (or exclusion from) the EU are more esoteric but possibly the most important in the long term. The new EU members will be compelled to adopt a full range of EU institutions and policies. They will also be encouraged to conform to other non-compulsory institutions of their EU peer countries. Non-members, by contrast, will be on their own. This will allow the CIS countries choose institutions and policies in quite another fashion.
5. A fifth effect on the accession countries will be the introduction of the EMU and the permanent fixing of their exchange rates. On the one hand, the euro will eliminate the exchange rate risk and make it more attractive to invest in the accession countries. On the other hand, if inflation does not converge rapidly to European levels, the permanent exchange rate involves the risk of overvaluation, as is most obvious in East Germany.

Table 16.2 shows that GDP per capita is very low in the transition countries compared with the EU level, only 40 per cent in 1998 even when measured in purchasing power parity (PPP) terms. The CIS countries, in turn, have a GDP per capita in PPP that is only 40 per cent of that of the EU accession countries,[2] though Russia is actually wealthier than four of the accession countries (Bulgaria, Romania, Latvia and Lithuania). This should offer the CIS countries the opportunity to grow faster *ceteris paribus* than the EU accession countries, given their large underutilized human capital (Barro, 1991). Yet such an effect was not apparent during the first decade of transition (Berg et al., 1999).

The critical issue is clearly trade, on which the next section will focus.

Trade

The nature of EU trade policy and how it might change after accession are major issues in understanding trade prospects for the CIS countries. There is currently a sharp difference in export performance between the CIS countries in comparison with the CEE countries. What explains this difference and what, if anything, do these explanations imply for the future?

The data show that while exports to the European Union from the CEE countries have grown towards normal levels, exports from CIS countries remain depressed, especially to the major regional market, the European Union. Most CIS exports to Europe are still chiefly related to natural resources. Natural resources were exported to the west under communism; hence this trade simply continues pre-existing patterns. Furthermore, natural resource trade does not compete with European products and is less politically sensitive. The crux of the matter lies in the causes of the low levels of exports to Europe in agriculture and manufactures. How much of this missing trade is explained by geographic barriers, poor conditions in the CIS countries themselves, or protectionism from the European Union? Are there significant trade barriers in Europe for CIS goods?

We address the question of possible European protectionism from a number of angles. We test whether CIS/CEE status explains the share of exports to Europe of each country after controlling for the distance of each former communist country from Brussels and the EBRD reform rankings. We also look at the issue from the vantage point of Europe and focus on so called sensitive goods such as agriculture, steel and chemicals. We examine whether the European import share of these goods specifically is lower for CIS than for CEE countries.

Before looking at the econometric evidence, it is worth asking whether CIS trade with the EU is lower than it should be based on international standards.

2 Throughout this chapter, we use unweighted averages, as our purpose is to illustrate the relative position of various countries.

Table 16.2 GNP per capita (PPP), 1999

Country	USD	% of EU average
Bulgaria	4,683	22.2
Czech Rep.	12,197	57.8
Estonia	7,563	35.8
Hungary	9,832	46.6
Latvia	5,777	27.4
Lithuania	6,283	29.8
Poland	7,543	35.7
Romania	5,572	26.4
Slovakia	9,624	45.6
Slovenia	14,400	68.2
CEE AVG	**8,347**	**39.6**
Belarus	6,314	29.9
Moldova	1,995	9.5
Russia	6,180	29.3
Ukraine	3,130	14.8
Georgia	3,429	16.2
Armenia	2,074	9.8
Azerbaijan	2,168	10.3
Kazakhstan	4,317	20.5
Kyrgyzstan	2,247	10.6
Tajikistan	1,041	4.9
Turkmenistan	2,550	0.1
Uzbekistan	2,044	9.7
CIS AVG	**3,124**	**13.8**

Source: World Bank (2000).

A large number of calculations have been made with help of gravity models concerning the plausible geographical distribution of trade that would obtain if free trade and markets prevailed. Gravity models predict trade on the basis of GDP and distance.[3] For example, Susan Collins and Dani Rodrik (1991, p. 134) estimated that 58 per cent of the then Soviet Union's exports should have gone to the soon-to-be 15 EU countries in 1989, when the actual share was only 33 per cent. However, the actual numbers have been approximately constant, and even in 2000 only 31 per cent of the exports of the CIS countries went to the EU countries (see Table 16.3).

By contrast, the EU accession countries have increased the average share of their exports to the EU from a low of 53 per cent in 1993 to 67 per cent in 2000, which compares favorably even with the EU members' mutual trade of 63 per cent of their total trade in 1993. This grand expansion has occurred in part because the

3 For its econometric specification, see Matyas (1997; 1998) and Egger (2000).

EU phased out all tariffs on industrial goods from the CEE (Baldwin et al., 1997, pp. 130-2). It does not much matter what assessment is used (see Hamilton and Winters, 1992; Havrylyshyn and Al-Atrash, 1998). A distortion in the order of one quarter of total exports of the CIS countries results.

Table 16.3 Exports to the EU as share of total exports (in per cent)

Country	1992	1993	1994	1995	1996	1997	1998	1999	2000
Bulgaria	46	46	40	38	29	36	50	51	51
Czech Rep.	..	47	46	43	58	60	64	68	69
Estonia	87	48	48	55	51	49	57	65	84
Hungary	62	56	64	65	65	73	73	76	69
Latvia	40	35	39	44	44	49	57	63	65
Lithuania	89	39	30	36	33	33	38	50	48
Poland	62	69	70	70	66	64	71	71	70
Romania	35	41	48	55	53	56	67	67	64
Slovakia	..	27	35	37	41	55	56	59	59
Slovenia	..	63	66	68	65	64	65	65	64
CEE AVG	**59***	**53**	**55**	**55**	**57**	**60**	**65**	**68**	**67**
Belarus	32	32	13	12	8	7	7	9	9
Moldova	3	3	6	12	10	10	12	21	20
Russia	48	44	33	32	31	32	31	32	35
Ukraine	10	14	7	13	11	12	17	18	16
Georgia	5	35	1	5	9	8	35	28	21
Armenia	1	11	28	29	21	28	34	46	36
Azerbaijan	15	7	13	15	9	11	22	46	60
Kazakhstan	30	42	16	22	19	26	31	23	23
Kyrgyzstan	37	36	6	14	4	5	41	38	34
Tajikistan	38	58	53	46	34	33	43	36	28
Turkmenistan	81	52	19	8	6	6	13	15	19
Uzbekistan	51	74	..	..	..	..	..	..	..
CIS AVG	**40**	**39**	**27**	**27**	**26**	**26**	**27**	**28**	**31**

* includes Czechoslovakia.

Source: IMF (1996; 2001).

What about growth of trade to all countries, not just the EU? The post-communist transition has brought the liberalization of foreign trade to nearly all countries in the region. As a result, exports have almost tripled from 1992 to 2000 for the region as a whole. Strangely, there is little difference between EU accession countries and the CIS countries in this respect. The former increased their exports in this period by 183 per cent in current USD, whereas the latter boosted theirs by 162 per cent (see Table 16.4).

Table 16.4 Total Exports (USD million)

Country	1992	1993	1994	1995	1996	1997	1998	1999	2000
Bulgaria	*2,495*	*2,363*	3,947	5,359	6,602	5,323	4,299	3,964	4,810
Czech Rep.	..	13,205	16,230	21,686	21,916	22,746	26,418	26,832	29,018
Estonia	*355*	805	1,313	1,838	2,077	2,924	3,131	2,936	3,133
Hungary	10,680	8,918	10,689	12,439	12,652	18,628	22,958	24,950	28,007
Latvia	*774*	963	991	1,305	1,443	1,672	1,811	1,723	1,865
Lithuania	*689*	2,025	2,029	2,705	3,355	3,860	3,711	3,004	3,810
Poland	13,324	14,143	17,042	22,895	24,440	25,751	27,191	27,397	31,651
Romania	4,363	4,892	6,151	7,910	8,085	8,431	8,300	8,505	10,367
Slovakia	..	5,451	6,709	8,595	8,823	8,254	10,721	10,226	11,885
Slovenia	..	6,083	6,828	8,316	8,312	8,372	9,048	8,604	8,733
CEE TOTAL	**43,990***	**58,848**	**71,929**	**93,048**	**97,705**	**105,961**	**117,588**	**118,141**	**133,279**
Belarus	*1,053*	*757*	2,510	4,707	5,652	7,301	7,070	5,909	7,331
Moldova	*470*	*484*	619	739	805	890	644	*668*	*805*
Russia	42,040	44,297	67,542	81,096	88,599	88,288	74,888	74,663	104,836
Ukraine	8,045	7,817	10,305	13,317	14,441	14.232	12,637	11,582	*14,579*
Georgia	*774*	*124*	156	151	199	240	192	*381*	*330*
Armenia	*774*	*156*	216	271	290	233	221	232	294
Azerbaijan	*1,571*	*993*	638	637	631	781	606	929	*1,745*
Kazakhstan	*244*	*788*	3,231	5,250	5,911	6,497	5,436	5,598	9,140
Kyrgyzstan	*76*	*112*	640	409	505	604	514	454	*502*
Tajikistan	*29*	*124*	492	749	772	803	597	689	784
Turkmenistan	*64*	*324*	1,162	1,881	1,693	751	593	1,187	2,505
Uzbekistan	*162*	*611*	1,991	2,718	1,620	2,896	2,312	1,952	2,126
CIS TOTAL	**55,302**	**56,587**	**89,502**	**111,925**	**121,118**	**123,516**	**105,710**	**104,244**	**144,977**

* includes Czechoslovakia.

Source: IMF (1996; 2001) unless italicized. Italicized figures are Direction of Trade Statistics (DOTS) numbers.

The small and interconnected CEE countries could be expected to have very high export ratios to their GDP, at 38 per cent of GDP at current exchange rates in 1999. However, the CIS countries are barely lagging behind with exports amounting to 28 per cent of their GDP (see Table 16.5). A major caveat is that the apparent high foreign trade intensity of the CIS countries is explained by their depressed real exchange rates. If we make the same calculation in PPP terms, exports were 15 per cent of GDP for CEE, but only six per cent of GDP for the CIS countries, indicating very low levels of exports in the CIS countries.

Empirical Tests

This section shows empirical tests of the determinants of exports of former socialist countries. It is worth bearing in mind that the statistical problems are considerable. The United Nations and the WTO compile the most authoritative trade statistics, but these are released with a delay of several years. The IMF does produce a lot of statistics relatively fast, and we shall make use of them, but they are not sufficiently detailed, nor is trade a major focus of the IMF. The EBRD and various UN agencies also reproduce some trade statistics produced by others. Most

Table 16.5 Total exports as percentage of GDP, 1999

Country	Current exchange rate	PPP terms
Bulgaria	32	10
Czech Rep.	51	20
Estonia	56	24
Hungary	52	22
Latvia	28	11
Lithuania	28	12
Poland	18	8
Romania	25	6
Slovakia	52	18
CEE AVG	**38**	**15**
Belarus	22	9
Moldova	58	8
Russia	19	7
Ukraine	30	7
Georgia	14	3
Armenia	13	3
Azerbaijan	23	4
Kazakhstan	35	8
Kyrgyzstan	36	4
Tajikistan	37	Na
Turkmenistan	37	7
Uzbekistan	11	13
CIS AVG	**28**	**6**

Sources: IMF (2001) and World Bank (2001).

governments in the region offer very poor trade statistics, which are neither accurate, comparable, nor particularly accessible. We use these only in so far as they are reported, and therefore implicitly sanctioned, in statistical annexes of reports from IMF missions. The European Commission does offer a lot of commodity-specific trade statistics, but the Commission does not offer a comparative global picture. The trade statistics for the last year of communism and the first year of transition are particularly poor.

Bearing these points in mind, Table 16.6 presents regression estimates of the determinants of the share of exports destined to Europe in total exports of post communist countries. The table shows results from a number of cross section regressions, one for each year during the 1994-2000 period. The explanatory variables are a dummy variable taking the value one for CIS countries (used to test discrimination against CIS countries), the distance in kilometers between the capital city of each country and Dusseldorf (used as a rough estimate of the economic center of Europe), and the two-year lagged value of the economic reform index released by the EBRD (used as a control for country-specific policies that affect exports).

Table 16.6 Cross section regressions testing for the roles of distance from Europe, reform, and CIS membership in explaining the share of total trade to Europe

Year of Regression	Dummy Variable for CIS Countries	Distance of Capital city from Brussels	EBRD reform index lagged two years	N	R^2
1993	-15.24	0.01	27.02	20	36
	-1.01	2.46	0.92		
1994	-24.65	0.00	20.54	20	56
	-1.87	0.32	0.70		
1995	-21.43	0.00	31.72	20	63
	1.41	0.36	1.58		
1996	-20.49	0.00	44.51	20	74
	-2.54	-0.34	2.17		
1997	-27.12	0.00	42.83	20	72
	-3.26	-0.14	1.42		
1998	-29.52	0.00	67.21	20	79
	-4.78	1.97	3.25		
1999	-22.34	0.00	67.43	20	77
	-3.21	0.20	3.00		
2000	-22.35	0.00	67.92	20	80
	-3.13	-0.44	3.07		

Notes: T-ratios appear below the coefficients. The sample is 20 Central European and CIS countries. Azerbaijan was excluded from the regressions due to the special nature of its oil exports but this does not affect the substantive conclusions.

Source: HIID database.

After preliminary analysis of the data, it emerged that Azerbaijan and Latvia were statistical outliers in these regressions. We tested whether the results depended on the inclusion of these countries and found little sensitivity. Nevertheless since Azerbaijan's exports are so dominated by a single commodity, namely oil, the regressions we report exclude Azerbaijan.

The results generally show that both reform and CIS status but not distance were significant factors explaining exports to Europe. The unimportance of distance is a telling fact because it confirms that market forces such as transport costs are not particularly important in explaining trade of the region. This result is also reasonable since natural resource trade tends to be dictated by who has the resources rather than transport costs.

The unimportance of distance can be illustrated by referring back to Table 16.3. Among the EU accession countries, the EU share of their exports ranged from 48 per cent to 84 per cent in 2000, while this share varied from 9 per cent to 36 per cent among the CIS countries (ignoring oil-exporting Azerbaijan). Among the CIS countries, inverse gravity appears to be at work. Moldova, arguably most adjacent to the EU, managed to sell only 20 per cent of its exports to the large EU market, although it has undertaken almost as much structural reform as Latvia, with 65 per cent of its exports directed to the EU (Table 16.3). Ukraine, which is about as close to the EU, sells only 16 per cent of its exports to the EU, while Russia, Armenia and Kyrgyzstan deliver about 35 per cent of their exports to the EU. Distant Azerbaijan manages to send no less than 60 per cent of its exports to the EU.

The variable in these regressions to test for possible European protectionism is the dummy variable for CIS status. The regressions show that this is significantly negative. The point estimates imply that the shares of exports to Europe for CIS countries are 20 to 29 percentage points lower than the shares for CEE countries. A noteworthy point about this estimated effect is that it does not decline over time, and after 1996 it is consistently statistically significant. This provides preliminary evidence that some common EU policy towards the CIS group is responsible for the export shortfall. The CIS countries as a group have significantly lower export shares to European markets. Moreover, these are commodity exports. If we excluded natural resources, the estimated CIS shortfall would be larger since they have a higher share of natural resources in their EU export than the CEE countries.

A country's own performance also matters. Regressions show that exports to Europe are affected by the country's overall economic reform performance. This variable is lagged two years to give a chance for the reforms to have an effect. The length of the lag however does not importantly affect the results. Although this variable does not measure specific policies that facilitate exports, it is nonetheless a rough proxy for a number of background reforms that are important for exporting. This variable is usually statistically significant giving the overall picture that there is a positive effect.

In summary, the EU export shares of the CIS countries are significantly lower than those of the accession countries, and this fact is not eliminated by controls for reform or distance from the EU market. Moreover, the commodity structure of CIS exports is dominated by natural resources (see Table 16.7). Azerbaijan is so successful on the EU market because it exports oil. So does

Russia, while Kyrgyzstan exports gold and Armenia diamonds, probably the least sensitive commodities to protectionist measures. By contrast, exports of agricultural goods, textiles and clothing from the CIS countries are remarkably small, and large steel exports from Russia, Ukraine, and Kazakhstan are going to other countries.

There are other possible explanations for the significant dummy variable for CIS countries in the previous regressions. Note, however, that any such explanation would have to be sharply different between the two groups of countries to explain the regression result. One possibility is continued implicit export barriers of CIS, perhaps a hidden legacy from older communist practices. However, overt export quotas have declined dramatically and although there is some holdover from previous practices, it is hard to believe that these are significant enough to fully explain the large differences in exports to Europe.

Table 16.7 Main exports of selected CIS countries

Country	Year	Sector	Share of Total Exports in %
Azerbaijan	2000	Oil and refined products	90
Kazakhstan	2000	Oil and refined products	39
		Ferrous metals and refined products	15
		Manufactured goods	13
		Copper and refined products	11
Kyrgyzstan	2000	Nonferrous metals	47
		Electrical energy	16
		Machine building	10
		Light industry	9
		Agriculture	9
Tajikistan	2000	Aluminum	50
		Electricity	23
		Cotton	12
Russia	2000	Oil and refined products	35
		Metals	17
		Natural gas	17
		Machinery	9
		Chemicals	7
Ukraine	1999	Metals	39
		Food and agriculture	11
		Chemicals	11

Sources: Statistical Appendices to IMF Country Reports.

Another explanation would be that CIS countries as a group have suffered a larger destruction of their export capacity than CEE countries, through the brain drain, or lack of connections with European markets. But again, it seems implausible that this would be so starkly different between the two groups of counties to account for the estimated effect of a 20-29 percentage point shortfall in exports to the EU.

The trade shortfall of CIS countries to Europe would be less serious if CIS exports to Europe were growing and thereby closing the gap with the CEE countries. If this were the case we would see the estimated CIS effect decline over time, but the estimated coefficients show no such decline. We would also expect to see direct evidence of recent faster growth of CIS exports, but as we show below, there is little evidence for this on a commodity-by-commodity basis. Table 16.8 shows that while CEE exports to the EU skyrocketed by 220 per cent from 1992 to 2000 (from 26 to 83 billion USD) CIS exports to the EU, on the contrary, rose by only 102 per cent (from 22 to 44 billion USD), while CIS exports to other parts of the world surged by 201 per cent. EU imports from the CEE increased at an annual rate of 19.2 per cent between 1993 and 1997, while imports from the CIS grew at 12.3 per cent (Allen, 1999).

What about CIS exports to non-European destinations? Did they grow faster than European exports? Statistics on total exports of transition countries to non-transition countries are hard to trace, but the EBRD has compiled the share of total trade with non-transition countries, essentially from 1994 to 1999. In that period, the EU accession countries' trade with non-transition countries rose from 64 per cent to 75 per cent, while that of the CIS countries increased from 41 per cent to 52 per cent, although Belarus and Tajikistan went in the opposite direction (see Table 16.9). Although the CIS countries should have gone through a greater reorientation of their external trade, it did occur with the rest of the world but not with the EU.

A second test for a group effect with respect to the CIS countries is to take the vantage point of the European market and ask whether CIS-sourced imports are lower, or have grown more slowly, than other imports. We consider the specifics of the European market in the next section.

Differences in EU Trade Regime towards CEE and CIS Countries

One reason of this very diverse development of exports to the EU from the CEE and the CIS countries, respectively, has been totally different trade regulations. The EU has developed an elaborate hierarchy of trade treaties, reflecting the graduation of countries from the status of trading partner to full member-state (Messerlin, 2001, p. 4). As countries on the way to be full members, the CEE countries greatly benefit, while the CIS countries remain minor trading partners.

The EU offered favorable Europe Agreements to the CEE early on, which committed all parties to eliminate tariff and non-tariff barriers on industrial products by the end of a ten-year period, which ended in 2001 or 2002. The reductions in protection were asymmetric, to the benefit of CEE.

Table 16.8 Exports to the EU (million USD)

Country	1992	1993	1994	1995	1996	1997	1998	1999	2000
Bulgaria	1,144	1,089	1,564	2,013	1,913	1,942	2,137	2,035	2,463
Czech Rep.	..	6,268	7,480	9,273	12,760	13,557	16,976	18,172	19,905
Estonia	308	389	628	1,006	1,060	1,424	1,788	1,894	2,623
Hungary	6,644	4,982	6,818	8,077	8,234	13,603	16,782	18,927	19,263
Latvia	310	334	389	568	628	815	1,025	1,078	1,206
Lithuania	610	780	610	984	1,096	1,256	1,409	1,505	1,824
Poland	8,221	9,794	11,929	16,039	16,248	16,553	19,285	19,338	22,154
Romania	1,536	2,027	2,970	4,388	4,271	4,752	5,522	5,723	6,630
Slovakia	..	1,493	2,340	3,208	3,645	4,540	5,970	6,076	7,017
Slovenia	..	3,847	4,539	5,648	5,369	5,321	5,917	5,625	5,577
CEE TOTAL	**25944***	**31,003**	**39,267**	**51,204**	**55,224**	**63,763**	**76,811**	**80,373**	**88,662**
Belarus	335	245	315	579	457	495	522	526	689
Moldova	12	13	39	86	78	90	79	137	164
Russia	20,227	19,672	22,411	26,051	27,189	27,998	23,073	24,022	36,881
Ukraine	806	1,120	671	1,716	1,599	1,762	2,135	2,130	2,362
Georgia	37	44	1	7	17	20	67	106	68
Armenia	4	17	61	79	62	66	76	107	107
Azerbaijan	228	70	83	94	59	88	131	423	1,054
Kazakhstan	72	331	515	1,145	1,127	1,708	1,711	1,284	2,074
Kyrgyzstan	28	40	41	57	19	30	213	173	171
Tajikistan	11	72	259	347	266	269	259	248	220
Turkmenistan	52	169	216	142	101	48	75	174	471
Uzbekistan	83	452	..	..	..	..	..	..	..
CIS TOTAL	**21,895**	**22,245**	**24,612**	**30,303**	**30,974**	**32,574**	**28,341**	**29,330**	**44,261**

* includes exports from Czechoslovakia.

Source: IMF (1996; 2001).

Agricultural products are subject to preferential treatment under tariff quotas. On January 1, 1998, the EU lifted quantitative restrictions on imports of textiles and clothes from CEE (WTO, 2000, pp. 32, 54).

To the CIS countries, by contrast, the EU offered limited Partnership and Cooperation Agreements, which were little but a codification of WTO principles for non-WTO members. Unlike the Central European economies, the major CIS countries are not members of the WTO. The first CIS country to become a member of the WTO was Kyrgyzstan in 1998, and to date Georgia, Moldova, Armenia have entered, while Russia, Ukraine and Kazakhstan remain non-members.

The CEE countries are considered market economies by the EU, which means that any anti-dumping investigation is based on their own prices and not on a hypothetical country's prices. The CIS countries, on the contrary, are labeled 'economies in transition' by the EU. In practice, this means that they are subject to potentially biased calculations based on another country's prices and not the actual prices.

Table 16.9 Share of total trade with non-transition countries, 1991-1999 (percentage of total trade)

Country	1991	1992	1993	1994	1995	1996	1997	1998	1999
				Central Europe					
Poland	83.2	84.4	87.7	86.3	82.3	79.3	75.5	77.4	79.3
Czech Republic	..	..	..	68.6	68.1	71.3	72.1	74.3	73.9
Slovakia	..	..	39.5	44.9	45.6	49.4	54.2	62.0	62.0
Hungary	82.3	80.6	78.2	79.1	77.7	77.0	81.2	84.3	87.9
				South-East Europe					
Romania	65.8	74.8	84.4	86.2	88.8	88.9	86.5	88.0	89.5
Bulgaria	80.0	85.1	84.2	76.1	65.4	66.2	72.0	76.9	80.4
				Baltics					
Estonia	..	..	54.8	54.5	61.6	59.5	73.1	64.3	76.3
Latvia	..	46.8	43.6	46.4	49.5	50.0	56.7	66.4	..
Lithuania	..	..	..	35.0	43.0	38.8	54.6	46.6	50.9
				CIS					
Russia		..	..	66.6	68.2	67.0	65.4	66.9	70.5
Belarus		..	..	28.5	20.5	19.0	19.3	17.3	22.6
Ukraine		..	..	38.7	40.3	45.5	57.1	53.6	57.4
Moldova		..	..	8.9	16.5	15.4	19.4	29.2	40.3
Armenia		..	..	34.3	52.4	55.5	55.4	60.0	62.0
Azerbaijan		..	..	58.4	58.3	53.1	43.8	43.7	..
Georgia		..	..	33.3	33.1	27.6	35.7	58.7	70.0
Kazakhstan		..	..	33.2	39.9	41.7	52.4	47.3	58.7
Kyrgyzstan		.	..	40.2	17.6	19.4	33.5	57.7	55.7
Tajikistan			..	75.6	58.9	52.7	28.2	27.6	23.6
Turkmenistan			..	23.3	31.8	32.4	38.8	72.6	61.0
Uzbekistan	..		..	45.6	34.9	47.3	38.2	47.4	53.5

Source: EBRD (2000).

On the whole, this means a world of difference in EU treatment of the CEE and CIS countries, respectively. The CEE countries are about to become EU members, while the CIS countries have no associate status, customs union or free trade arrangement. Largely, they are not even members of the WTO or recognized as market economies by the EU. In short, they have a trade status reminiscent of'open season'. These differences in status are reflected quite consistently in very many regards.

The total effect of these different trade arrangements adds up to something significant. The CEE countries with their regional trade agreements get 80 per cent of lines duty free, while the CIS countries obtain 54 per cent of lines duty free as GSP beneficiaries (WTO 2000, p. xix). GSP (Generalized System of Preferences) applies to developing countries, but they are not very beneficial. For very sensitive goods—textiles, metals, and many agricultural goods—most-favored nation (MFN) duty rates are reduced by only 15 per cent, and for sensitive goods—chemicals, many agricultural goods, footwear, plastics, rubber, leather goods, wood, wood products, paper, glass, copper, etc.—MFN tariffs are reduced by 30 per cent. Only non-sensitive goods, which tend to be not very significant, are duty-free (WTO, 2000). Moreover, the GSP regime suffers from many weaknesses. The supposed beneficiaries do not conclude any contract and therefore have no recourse to any dispute settlement conflict. The rules of origin are onerous, while special simplified agreements have been reached with CEE. Tariff reductions are less than for the EU accession countries (Stevens and Kennan, 2000).

Patrick Messerlin (2001) has assessed EU protection by industry in 1999. He puts the level of overall protection for the whole of the EU economy at almost 12 per cent in 1999. EU protection however varies by commodity, with rates of overall protection exhibiting wide differences by sector, and the differences have remained stable. Messerlin has included ordinary customs tariffs, major border non-tariff barriers (quantitative restrictions and antidumping measures), while he has ignored all the non-border barriers, that is, an array of norms and standards.

The simple nominal average of all existing EU tariffs on goods was 7 per cent in 1999. It is important to stress that EU tariff levels are not very high by global standards, and certainly not when compared to other highly protectionist countries during the past thirty years. However, the commodity structure of protection is important. Protection is higher for certain goods that the CIS countries might be expected to export. A second issue is that even small barriers can have important restrictive effects on the exporting countries if two potential exporters are otherwise similar. If other costs in the CIS countries are similar to CEE countries, then moderate barriers can effectively preclude imports from the CIS countries. The CIS countries generally have a cost advantage compared to the CEE countries due to lower wages, but this is counteracted by higher transport and other costs. Even small differences in protection make all the difference when the overall competitive situation without tariffs is similar.

EU trade policy is in other respects more restrictive than simple nominal average tariffs would indicate, because of a lack of transparency. For instance, about half the EU tariffs are expressed in euros per physical unit of output and not in *ad valorem* terms (WTO, 2000). The non-tariff barriers include variable levies in agriculture, voluntary export restraints in industrial sectors (notably in textiles and clothing), quotas on imports from centrally planned economies (to which the EU includes the CIS countries) and antidumping measures. The peaks of overall protection are very high, with maximum tariffs exceeding a prohibitive 200 per cent for certain agricultural goods (WTO, 2000).

We turn now to a comparison of EU imports from CIS and CEE countries. Unlike the earlier regression estimates, these comparisons do not control for other factors affecting trade, but they have the advantage of focusing on specific commodities. We focus on agriculture, steel, textiles, clothing, and chemicals as particularly important sensitive products.

EU measures against CEE countries are persistently milder than for CIS countries. One example is antidumping measures. The number of antidumping cases that the EU instigated against the CEE countries from 1990-99 was 42—admittedly almost equal to the 41 initiated against the CIS countries. However, the duties imposed against the CIS countries were about twice as high as those levied on the CEE countries (Messerlin, 2001, p. 353).

EU agriculture is particularly well protected. While the simple nominal average tariff is estimated at 17.3 per cent (WTO, 2000, p. xix), the actual effective protection is often prohibitive for the CIS countries because of variable levies and technical standards. In addition, the EU is reluctant to give any preferences for farm goods from temperate countries and food products (Messerlin, 2001, p. 28). EU minimal market access commitments in cereals under the Uruguay round prompted bilateral agreements on a duty-free quota of 300,000 tons of wheat essentially from the CEE, while the major grain producers in the CIS, who were not WTO members, were left without access (Messerlin, 2001, p. 302). The CEE countries are allowed to export meat, fruit and vegetables to the EU, and the EU has reciprocal protection through bilateral agreements with Bulgaria, Hungary and Romania, the main wine producers in CEE (WTO, 2000, pp. 87, 91).

The results are reflected in Table 16.10 below. Although EU agricultural imports from the 13 candidate members remain small because of severe EU protectionism, they at least increased from 1995 to 1998. EU imports of agricultural goods from the CIS countries actually declined somewhat, although this was a time when they were recovering, indicating extraordinary EU protectionism. The country that is suffering the most from this EU protectionism is Moldova, which primarily exports agricultural goods. Although it is located just beside the EU and its accession countries, only 20 per cent of its exports go to the EU. Moldova is Europe's poorest country today, but it is refused access to the vital EU market. Ukraine also has major comparative advantages in agriculture, but only 11 per cent of its total exports originate from that sector, and its agricultural exports are—like Moldova's—primarily directed to Russia.

EU steel imports are subject to moderate protection. The GATT-bound tariff of 4.8 per cent and the antidumping protection of 16.3 per cent lead to an overall protection of 21.9 per cent. The Europe Agreements initially abolished EU tariffs on steel exports from CEE, but a regime of tight monitoring of steel imports from the region prevails, and it can lead to antidumping actions. For the CIS countries that are major producers and exporters of steel (Russia, Ukraine and Kazakhstan), restrictive EU import quotas were imposed from 1995. These have become ever more cumbersome as steel capacity has recovered swiftly, while domestic demand has plummeted. In addition, antidumping measures remain a severe and permanent threat (Messerlin, 2001, pp. 278, 282; WTO, 2000, p. 55). Russia, Ukraine and Kazakhstan are far greater producers and exporters of steel than the CEE countries, and they have obvious comparative advantages in this sector. Even so, they have barely managed to increase their exports to the EU, and CEE exports to the EU remained twice as large in 2000 (see Table 16.11). The open-ended threat of anti-dumping provisions discourages investments in capacity to export to Europe.

The trade regime for chemicals is similar to that for steel. The average MFN tariff on industrial chemicals is moderate at 5.7 per cent, but antidumping measures are common and severe with an average antidumping rate of 24.5 per cent (Messerlin, 2001, pp. 22-23). The major CIS producers are Ukraine and Russia. The CIS has not been able to catch up with the CEE countries in this highly protected product group, but they have seen a slight decline in their exports to the EU, and CEE exports to the EU remain more than twice as large (see Table 16.12).

Table 16.10 EU imports of agricultural goods, billion euros

Direction of Import	1995	1996	1997	1998
From 13 candidate countries	4.5	4.7	5.1	5.1
From 12 CIS countries	1.5	1.6	1.5	1.3
Difference	3.0	2.9	3.4	3.9

Source: EU Trade Directorate.

Table 16.11 EU imports of steel, billion euros

Direction of Import	1998	1999	2000
From 13 candidate countries	3.5	3.0	4.0
From 12 CIS countries	1.5	1.4	2.2
Difference	2.3	2.1	1.8

Source: EU Trade Directorate.

Table 16.12 EU imports of chemical goods, billion euros

Direction of Imports	1995	1996	1997	1998
From 13 candidate countries	3.8	3.8	4.2	4.3
From 12 CIS countries	2.0	1.6	1.8	1.8
Difference	1.9	2.4	2.3	2.4

Source: EU Trade Directorate.

Differences in trade regimes for textiles and clothing are great. In January 1998, the EU lifted quantitative restrictions on imports of textiles and clothes from all CEE countries, and they account for more than one-tenth of CEE exports to the EU. All the candidate members are considered to have comparative advantages in this sector. The CIS countries, on the contrary, are subject to low quotas unilaterally imposed by the EU. As most of the CIS countries are not members of the WTO, these are inspired by but go beyond the Uruguay Agreement on Textiles and Clothing, which succeeded the Multi-Fiber Agreement. In addition, antidumping actions are common for textiles (Messerlin, 2001, pp. 289-292; Allen, 1999). WTO membership is the responsibility of the CIS countries; but the preferential access given by the EU to the accession countries puts the CIS countries at a great competitive disadvantage.

Table 16.13 Sensitive goods as share of total exports, 1997

Direction	Food[1]	Chemicals	Iron & Steel	Textiles[2]	All Sensitive Goods
from Albania, Bulgaria, Czech Republic, Hungary, Poland, Romania, and Slovakia					
to the EU	6.1	5.5	4.1	14.1	29.8
to the World	7.2	8.3	6.4	10.9	32.8
from Estonia, Latvia, Lithuania, Russia, Ukraine, Moldova, and Belarus					
to the EU	3.2	6.7	2.6	5.2	17.7
to the World	5.5	9.6	11.9	3.8	30.8

Notes:
[1] all food items, including beverages, tobacco and edible oils and seeds;
[2] exports of textile fibers, textile yarn and fabrics, and clothing.

Source: UNCTAD (2000).

Oil and natural gas are usually considered freely traded commodities, but this is not necessarily the case. In the early 1990s, the EU negotiated an Energy Charter with the CIS countries. For many reasons, the Russian Duma will never ratify this agreement. It does not comply with current Russian energy policy. The same is true of Norway. However, the EU demands that Russia ratify this treaty before major energy projects are undertaken, thus restricting Russian energy exports to the EU. The Energy Charter is an issue in its own right; nevertheless, a by-product of the deadlock on the Charter is that CIS energy exports are restricted.

EU protection tends to be concentrated in so-called sensitive goods, especially agricultural goods, textiles, steel and chemicals. Do CIS exports of these goods do worse in Europe than in the rest of the world? To examine this, we review the share of these goods in exports to all countries and to the EU specifically from two slightly different groups: the seven Central European countries and the European former Soviet countries (see Table 16.13).[4] The Central Europeans export about the same to Europe as to other countries. While the share of sensitive goods in their exports to the EU amounts to 30 per cent, it is only slightly larger - 33 per cent - in their total exports. By contrast, the seven European former Soviet republics (including the Baltics) have only 18 per cent sensitive goods in their exports to the EU, compared with 31 per cent in their total exports. In particular, the EU appears more protectionist than the rest of the world with regard to steel. The share of foods in total exports is remarkably low for all these countries, although Moldova and Ukraine should be major exporters of agricultural goods.

Apart from the lack of equal treatment for imports from the CIS countries, a potentially more serious issue would be that European protection tends to be high for precisely those goods for which the CIS countries have a comparative advantage. Comparative advantage is difficult to assess before the fact, but an important clue is what products the CIS countries already exports (refer back to

4 The different categorization depends on UNCTAD statistics.

Table 16.7). It appears plausible that Ukraine has an underutilized comparative advantage in textiles and apparel; Moldova and Ukraine in food products; and Ukraine, Russia and Kazakhstan in steel. A large share of EU imports from countries, such as Ukraine and Moldova, pertain to these sensitive categories, but that is exactly as it should be, if those countries' comparative advantages are concentrated to sensitive products. That is very likely, since the sensitive goods tend to be labor-intensive and the CIS countries are less than half as wealthy as the EU accession countries.

Another relevant measure is the share of raw materials and labor-intensive goods, respectively, in exports. In a quantitative analysis of Ukraine's exports to the EU Wolfgang Quaisser and Volkhart Vincentz (2001) find that these exports consist of very few products—steel, metal scrap, clothes and oil seeds, all sensitive goods. While the EU accession countries succeeded in switching their exports to the EU to labor-intensive products early on, Ukraine only saw a rise in these in the mid-1990s. This could be a reflection of slow domestic reforms, effects of outside protectionism or a combination of both.

EU advocates argue that these countries should raise the degree of processing of their export goods in order to avoid EU barriers. However, it is difficult to jump one stage in processing. One common pattern is that exports take off with raw materials and intermediary goods, such as steel and chemicals, which function as cash cows for investment for the next stage of processing. If this is the EU stance, they are cutting off the CIS countries from a common strategy of export development. A recent survey of enterprises in Ukraine found that export orientation and especially orientation of sales towards non-CIS markets drive enterprise restructuring (Akimova, 2001).

Given economic geography—the location of the CIS countries, transportation routes and the relative size of adjacent economies—the EU is their all-dominant potential export market. If they are not allowed to export to the EU, they might have no alternative customer, as transportation costs are crucial for bulky goods. The end result may be that potential EU export goods will never be produced. Thus, rather than looking upon the limited CIS trade with the EU as trade diverted elsewhere, we may consider the lacking exports lost production. Obviously, cumulative effects are strong. Interestingly, Peter Christoffersen and Peter Doyle (2000) find that the growth of potential export markets has been one of the most important determinants of growth in the transition countries.

Furthermore, in each transition country, the interests of progressive exporters, pushing for more progressive market reforms, tend to take over after a few years. External protection means that it takes longer for the progressive exporters to acquire the critical weight, which delays systemic reform.

The question that is posed is whether the CIS countries will benefit or suffer from the EU enlargement in terms of trade and real income. The broader point being brought out by these statistics, however, is that the effect of EU enlargement on future EU trade policy towards the CIS countries is the crucial issue. The EU has been surprisingly successful in accommodating the CEE trade interests. When CEE has well acceded to the EU, the Union will be able to deploy substantial analytical and policy-making resources to focus on the problems of the

CIS countries. This change in perspective and the freeing up of policy-making capacity are likely to greatly improve the economic prospects for the CIS countries. Therefore, the CIS countries may benefit considerably from the completion of the current EU enlargement in a roundabout and unanticipated fashion.

References

Akimova, I. (2001), 'Export Orientation and Its Impact on Enterprise Restructuring in Ukraine', in Hoffman and Mollers (2001) *Ukraine on the Road to Europe*, pp. 181-205.

Allen, T. (1999), 'Trade of Central European Countries', Eurostat, Statistics in Focus: External Trade, Theme 6, February.

Aslund, A. (2002), *Building Capitalism: The Transformation of the Former Soviet Bloc*, New York: Cambridge University Press.

Baldwin, R.E., J.F. Francois and R. Portes (1997), 'The Costs and Benefits of Eastern Enlargement: The Impact on the EU and Central Europe', *Economic Policy*, No. 24: pp. 127-176.

Barro, R.J. (1991), 'Economic Growth in a Cross Section of Countries', *Quarterly Journal of Economics*, Vol. 106, No. 2, pp. 407-443.

Barro, R.J. and X. Sala-i-Martin (1995), *Economic Growth*, MIT Press.

Berg, A., E. Borensztein, R. Sahay and J. Zettelmeyer (1999), 'The Evolution of Output in Transition Economies: Explaining the Differences', *IMF Working Paper*, No. 99/73.

Buch, C.M. and D. Piazolo (2001), 'Capital and Trade Flows in Europe and the Impact of Enlargement', *Economic Systems*, Vol. 25, pp. 183-214.

Christoffersen, P. and P. Doyle (2000), 'From Inflation to Growth: Eight Years of Transition', *Economics of Transition*, Vol. 8, No. 2, pp. 421-451.

Collins, S.M. and D. Rodrik (1991), *Eastern Europe and the Soviet Union in the World Economy*, Washington D.C.: Institute for International Economics.

De Melo, M., C. Denizer and A. Gelb (1997), 'From Plan to Market: Patterns of Transition', in M.I. Blejer and M. Skreb (eds.), *Macroeconomic Stabilization in Transition Economies*, New York: Cambridge University Press, pp. 17-72.

Doppelhofer, G., R.I. Miller and X. Sala-i-Martin (2000), 'Determinants of Long-Term Growth: A Bayesian Averaging of Classical (Bace) Approach', *NBER Working Paper*, No. 7750, June 17.

Egger, P. (2000), 'A Note on the Proper Econometric Specification of the Gravity Equation', *Economic Letters*, Vol. 66, pp. 25-31.

EBRD (1999), *Transition Report 1999*, London: European Bank for Reconstruction and Development.

EBRD (2000), *Transition Report 2000*, London: European Bank for Reconstruction and Development.

EBRD (2001), *Transition Report 2001*, London: European Bank for Reconstruction and Development.

EBRD (2002), *Transition Update 2002*, London: European Bank for Reconstruction and Development.

Hamilton, C.B. and L.A. Winters (1992), 'Trade with Eastern Europe', *Economic Policy*, No. 14, pp. 77-116.

Havrylyshyn, O. and H. Al-Atrash (1998), 'Opening Up and Geographic Diversification of Trade in Transition Economies', IMF Working Paper, No. 98/22.

Havrylyshyn, O. and T. Wolf (1999), 'Growth in Transition countries, 1990-1998: The Main Lessons', in O. Havrylyshyn and S.M. Nsouli (eds.), *A Decade of Transition: Achievements and Challenges*, Washington, D.C.: International Monetary Fund, pp. 83-128.

Hoffman, L. and F. Mollers (eds.) (2001), *Ukraine on the Road to Europe*, Heidelberg: Physica-Verlag.

IMF (1996), *Direction of Trade Statistics Yearbook* (DOTSY), Washington, D.C.: International Monetary Fund.

IMF (2001), *Direction of Trade Statistics Yearbook* (DOTSY), Washington, D.C.: International Monetary Fund.

Matyas, L. (1997), 'Proper Econometric Specification of the Gravity Model', *World Economy*, Vol. 20, pp. 363-368.

Matyas, L. (1998), 'The Gravity Model: Some Econometric Considerations', *World Economy*, Vol. 21, pp. 397-401.

Mauro, P. (1995), 'Corruption and Growth', *Quarterly Journal of Economics*, Vol. 110, pp. 681-712.

Messerlin, P.A. (2001), *Measuring the Costs of Protection in Europe: European Commercial Policy in the 2000s*, Washington, D.C.: Institute for International Economics.

Quaisser, W. and V. Vincentz (2001), 'Integrating Ukraine into the World Economy: How, How Fast and Why?' in Hoffman and Mollers (2001), pp. 79-91.

Sachs, J.D. and A. Warner (1995), 'Economic Reform and the Process of Global Integration', *Brookings Papers on Economic Activity*, Vol. 25, No. 1, pp. 1-118.

Stevens, Ch. and J. Kennan (2000), 'Analysis of EU Trade Arrangements with Developing and Transition Countries', Institute of Development Studies, August.

UNCTAD (2000), *Handbook of Statistics*, U.N. Conference on Trade and Development, Geneva: United Nations.

World Bank (2000), *World Development Indicators*, CD-ROM.

World Bank (2001), *World Development Indicators*, CD-ROM.

WTO (2000), *Trade Policy Review: European Union*, Vol. I, Geneva: The World Trade Organization.

Chapter 17

Russia's Relations with the EU: Problems and Prospects

Vladimir Mau

Introduction

External economic relations are at the top of Russia's economic policy agenda. The Russo-European summit in May 2002 was as important landmark in this process, as both parties used this venue to state their intention to establish a Common European Economic Space (CEES). This put an end (at least on paper) to discussions on the geopolitical vector of Russia's development that had dominated Russia's first post-communist decade. The European direction was clearly identified as a priority.

However, the confirmation of Russia's European identity is only a starting point for this movement, rather than its final destination. The concept of the CEES has so far been formulated in a very general manner, and a lot of work—both intellectual and political—is needed to give it real content. In addition, the attitudes of Russia's European partners are far from straightforward: influential elements in the European business community and in Brussels take a dim view of prospects for economic rapprochement with Russia. Moreover, unlike the Central and Eastern European countries, which are on course for complete integration into the EU, Russia has the opportunity to elaborate such a European policy that would allow it to take advantage of the benefits of European integration without denying itself close relations with other regions of the world, particularly North America and the Asia-Pacific region.

In 2002 the debate on relations between the EU and Russia intensified significantly, and is now being conducted at the political, business, academic and expert levels. The overview below[1] outlines some aspects of Russian-EU relations that, in my view, are central to progress towards creating a common economic space and, eventually, a real 'Europe from the Atlantic to the Urals' (or, perhaps a 'Europe from the Atlantic to the Pacific').

1 The author is grateful to Eric Brunat, Olga Kuznetsova and Vadim Novikov for assistance in preparing this paper.

Historical Background

> Prospects for creating a free trade zone between the EU and Russia were first addressed in the Partnership and Cooperation Agreement (PCA) that was signed in Corfu in June 1994 and came into effect December 1997. The partnership sought 'to create the necessary conditions for the future establishment of a free trade area between the Community and Russia covering substantially all trade in goods between them, as well as conditions for bringing about freedom of establishment of companies, of cross-border trade in services and of capital movements'. A study examining the question of whether the time was ripe for beginning talks on a free trade agreement (FTA) was to commence in 1998.

The goal of '*Russia's integration into a common economic and social space*' was also stated in the EU's Common Strategy on Russia (June 1999), which mentions the '*establishment of an EU-RF free-trade area*' and the subsequent creation of the CEES as a result of gradual harmonization of laws and standards.

Many points still need to be further spelled out and clarified in these proposals. Europe already has the European Economic Area (EEA), which includes EU member countries as well as Norway, Iceland and Liechtenstein. These last three countries and Switzerland are also part of the European Free Trade Area (EFTA). Participation in the EEA implies not only establishment of a 'common market' but also substantial progress in legal harmonization. Participation in the EEA actually means adoption by member countries of EU legislation and standards, although it does not require establishment of supranational bodies (other than dispute settlement mechanisms).

However, for all the existing vagueness and lack of detail, as well as the technical and legal problems that practical implementation of this idea would be bound to encounter, the importance of the declaration on establishing a common economic area can hardly be over estated. In effect, we are talking about development of key institutional guidelines for Russia's socio-economic transformation, a sort of keystone of post-communist reform. For the first time since the collapse of communism, Russian society may come to recognize and formulate its own long-term development path. The common economic area is also directly related to the problem of Russia's accession to the WTO, as movement towards a common economic area and the WTO must move along the same lines at the current stage. The common economic area can also be seen as a station along the way to the creation of a single enlarged European market.

Goals to Be Achieved by Russia in Its Relations with the EU

Formulating and implementing a *catching-up development strategy* under the conditions of the post-industrial world should be a fundamental goal of Russia's economic policy, and should be reflected in relations with the EU (Mau 2002). This goal is without precedent in history, as there is no experience to draw on. The world's most developed countries are pioneers in the process; they did not have to accomplish the task of catching-up development. At the same time countries, which have experienced economic growth miracles during recent decades (South Korea, Taiwan, China), did so while making a transition from traditional (agrarian) to industrial societies. The problems they had to address were qualitatively different from those faced by Russia.

The experience of the second half of the 20th century showed that open economies were more successful in accomplishing catching-up development (Sachs and Warner, 1995). Policy makers should keep this in mind in developing the strategy of Russia's socio-economic development, especially in addressing the problems of external economic policy.

A post-industrial breakthrough emphasizes the need for flexibility and adaptivity in the economic system, the ability of economic agents to meet challenges promptly and appropriately. Adaptivity is much more important than formal indicators of economic performance as measured by per capita GDP.

Post-industrial societies differ from industrial societies in that the share of services becomes predominant in GDP and employment. Movement in this direction has become discernible in present-day Russia, but it should be made more determined and consistent. A breakthrough (as opposed to repetition) strategy should focus on accelerating the development of the service sector, with an emphasis on high-tech services (although further concretization would be dangerous).

As regards 'industrial' policy (or structural policy), under no circumstances should it focus on 'picking winners' or even 'selection of winners'. Both approaches would mean preserving the existing structural framework. A strategy of *permanent structural adjustment,* under which the authorities use policy instruments (including foreign policy) to flexibly protect actors who succeed in international competition, is much more important. Negotiations on WTO accession, and subsequently on establishment of CEES should be aimed at securing a post-industrial breakthrough, rather than at the primitive 'protection of domestic producers'. Policy should focus on helping viable companies secure access to international markets for high-tech services, rather than protecting inefficient industries.

Such an approach implies fundamentally different motives for WTO accession than those that are commonly described today. This is apparent, for example, in the post-WTO accession prospects for the agricultural sector. Russian agriculture can be competitive on world markets, if the necessary additional infrastructure is put in place. The Institute for the Economy in Transition (IET) has proposed that Russia launch a radical rapprochement with countries with low levels of agricultural protectionism, including Australia and New Zealand.

Of course, an emphasis on the service sector need not mean neglect of other sectors that have good prospects in Russia. These include, for example, the automotive and aircraft industries. However, it should be understood that—despite their political, technological, and social importance—these sectors are unlikely to provide the basis for a post-industrial breakthrough.

The liberalization of foreign trade, especially as part of the integration between Russia and the EU, is important for Russia, particularly from the perspective of the institutional processes that are currently on going in the Russian economy. This is particularly the case in terms of the strengthening of financial-industrial groups (FIGs), which may have a mixed impact on economic development. On the one hand, FIGs can lower transaction costs and boost investment in Russia (see Dynkin and Sokolov, 2001, p. 13). On the other hand, they tend to pursue the policy of 'privatization of profits and nationalization of losses', which requires certain measures for this trend to be neutralized. The liberalization of foreign trade and the opening of domestic markets could become instrumental in dealing with this problem.

Intensified cooperation with the EU, in terms of market access and acquiring modern technologies through capital imports, is very important in this respect. The experience of the Central and East European countries provides convincing evidence that access to the markets of more advanced countries is essential to sustainable growth.[2]

Areas of Cooperation

The establishment of the CEES could be beneficial for Russia in a number of critical respects, many of which would be beneficial for the EU as well. These include: (1) Russia's use of EU's institutional experience in establishing market economy institutions in Russia; (2) the mutual opening of Russian and EU markets, starting perhaps with a free trade zone, to be followed by the free movement of capital and labor; and (3) the resolution of specific sectoral or regional problems (energy, transport, regional cooperation, the Kaliningrad region in the context of EU enlargement, etc.).

These are separate problems but they are also interrelated. The adaptation of EU-type institutions in Russia can promote the establishment of a common economic space and may also facilitate the resolution of problems in specific sectors, such as energy and transport. There are also trade-offs between the institutional and sectoral topics: attempts to resolve the former may result in endless legal and political debates, while an emphasis on the latter may deprives relations of their appropriate political framework.

The issue of *institutional rapprochement* between Russia and the EU did not spring up over night. While the debate did focus on this issue during 2001–2002, movement towards European institutions began much earlier, at the outset of transition. In fact, the first step in this direction was taken with elaboration in 1992 of the reform program under the guidance of then Deputy Prime Minister Yegor Gaidar. However, only the groundwork for a market democracy was laid at that

2 P. Bauer (1998, p. 246) was quite right pointing to this factor already at beginning of the 1990s. In his view, access to the market is more important to transition countries than financial aid: '*There are several things that West can do to promote economic advance in Eastern Europe. First and foremost, Western countries should reduce their trade barriers. Eastern Europe would benefit because international trade acquaints people with the market system; helps to allay suspicions about its operation; and promotes market-oriented attitudes, habits, and conduct, which would emerge only from direct experience.*' (See also Chapter 16 of this volume.)

stage, and claims that an explicitly West European development vector had taken shape then would have been premature. The institutions that were being set up in the 1990s were European in the historic and cultural sense of the word, rather than specifically EU-oriented.

The next step was made with the preparation of the 2000 program, whose proposed measures of institutional and structural policy were oriented to the system of EU institutions (although this was not discussed formally). The influence of EU practices is apparent in such areas as deregulation (streamlining of red tape), proposals on reforming the financial market, and, partly, in proposals to reform the natural monopolies (especially the railway and electricity sectors).

In 2001 the problem of institutional (in fact legislative) convergence was officially put forward, and discussions around this question began. Although official documents, as a rule, mention convergence between the institutions of Russia and the EU, everyone understands this refers to the adoption of European institutions by Russia. This seems to be justified: Europe represents much more developed and stable socio-economic systems and does not seek their substantial and comprehensive reform. By contrast, Russia is in the midst of reform process and the establishment of new market economy institutions. In addition, changes in the 'rules of the game' within the EU are an extremely complicated process requiring lengthy coordination of positions of all member-countries (Mau and Novikov, 2002).

The *Acquis Communautaire* and Russian Legislation

The argument that European standards should be applied in Russia as strategic reference points requires some qualification, in a number of respects. *First*, the use of these standards as parameters should not be identified with the goal of EU accession. The latter is a political issue, which Russian society is not yet ready to discuss. *Second*, these parameters are still quite vague today. Further work is needed to adapt the Maastricht and Copenhagen criteria, as well as special reports of the European Commission (evaluating the degree of preparedness of individual countries) for more detailed targets for Russia. *Third*, all the criteria should be applied to Russian realities and practices. There should also be no formal alignment of Russian institutions with European ones if this were to impair Russia's competitive advantages. *Fourth*, standards need to be developed in Russia and for Russia. There can be no question of parameters being developed under the control of European entities. Russia should determine its own targets and goals rather than formalize its desire to join the EU.

Remaining within the economic framework, adaptation of European standards should be undertaken primarily in the following areas: creating a functioning market economy; guaranteeing effective competition (via deregulation and the establishment of competitive conditions, legislative stability and fiscal transparency); implementing structural reforms to protect property rights, making bankruptcy legislation and the tax system more effective, and promoting the stability of the banking and financial sectors; promoting the monetary and fiscal policies needed for steady growth; and establishing administrative and government institutions in line with European standards.

The criteria for financial convergence as set forth in the Maastricht agreement (for entry into the EU's Economic and Monetary Union) are: (1) price stability (annual inflation should not exceed 1.5 percentage points above the three best performing EU countries); (2) the general government deficit should not exceed 3 per cent of GDP; (3) total outstanding public debt should not exceed 60 per cent of GDP; (4) exchange-rate stability (for at least 2 years prior to entry, the exchange rate vis-à-vis the Euro must remain within 'normal' fluctuation margins (as envisaged by the European Exchange Rate Mechanism); and (5) average nominal long term interest rate should not exceed 2 percentage points above the average rate in the three countries with the lowest inflation rates.

Fulfilling the criteria associated with establishment a functioning market economy, guaranteeing effective competition and the operation of market forces, structural reform, and the adaptation of the EU's technical standards to Russian realities seem of special importance today. Administrative reform is also of interest, to the extent that it is not focused on procedures directly related to EU accession. The Maastricht-related macroeconomic goals are not, of course, unimportant; but for Russia they have become much less serious in recent years. With respect to some of the Maastricht criteria Russia now displays better performance than EU membership requires (e.g., fiscal policy) or may even have 'rules of the game' that are more conducive to economic growth than in the EU. This makes Russian legislation potentially attractive to European countries. Of course, as long as the socio-economic situation in Europe is fairly stable, the EU is unlikely to turn to Russian experience in practice.[3]

Regardless of what the future may or may not hold in store, Russia now needs to determine the role of European legislation in the further implementation of institutional reforms. The right-wing critics of the Euro-enthusiastic approach to reforms point out that European legislation is overly socialist (or, rather, social) in its orientation, placing too heavy a burden on the government and hence, is not the most conducive for accelerated economic growth. This concern is not unjustified.[4] However, a distinctive feature of Russia's transformation is that—unlike the EU candidate countries—it can adopt European rules to the extent that they promote growth in Russia, and refuse economically doubtful standards. The *acquis communautaire* can in fact be divided somewhat roughly into four groups: (1) chapters unrelated to the economic sphere, going beyond the scope of a common economic space; (2) chapters with which Russia already complies; (3) chapters whose implementation would be useful and advisable for Russian economic development; and (4) rules whose implementation would be counterproductive for Russia's economic development.

3 However, since nothing is impossible in economic life, we do not rule out future situations in which West European countries will adopt Russian institutions.

4 The mixed effect of the *acquis communautaire* on economic growth in the candidate countries of Central and Eastern Europe has been pointed out by, among others, Aslund and Warner (2002).

Although the full demarcation of the *acquis communautaire* as it might pertain to Russia would require a separate analysis, as a first approximation the following differentiation of the *acquis* could be proposed. Rules pertaining to the free movement of goods and services, the regulation of capital flows, legislation on banks and financial services, corporate law, bankruptcy law, and regulation of natural monopolies are worthy of adaptation in the Russian context. The unification of standards and the use of EU legislation on standardization could be another important area of cooperation. Elements of the *acquis* that should not be transferred to Russia lie in the areas of social and labor legislation, consumer rights protection, the common agricultural policy, the tax system, and budget deficit targets.

Stages and Practical Steps

Questions about the establishment of a free trade zone, a customs union, or eventually an economic and monetary union between Russia and the EU are matters of strategic importance for the two partners. The current status of relations between Norway and the EU offers some guidance in this respect, although such parallels should not be drawn without reservation. Although Norway is not a formal EU member, it is part of the European common market.[5] Norway has therefore opted for the full adoption of the *acquis communautaire*, which (as mentioned above) is hardly appropriate in Russia's case. The only steps that Russia is taking towards European institutions are associated with WTO and OECD accession (a formal application for OECD accession was filed in 1996).

It is hard to say now when Russia's accession to the single European market might become possible. Russian business concerns about competition from European producers do not seem to be the main barrier here. Indeed, Russia's experience with the EU and European businesses suggests that our Western partners are much more concerned about the penetration of Russian goods into their markets (see Chapter 16). Many European businesses opposed granting Russia 'market economy' status, suggesting that the interests of European producers prevail over those of European consumers. However producers, as is well known, are organized much better than consumers, even if overall efficiency of the economy suffers. The situation is paradoxical indeed. On the one hand, everybody points to the weakness of the Russian economy, claiming that its integration with the EU is impossible in the foreseeable future. On the other hand, the Europeans are clearly concerned about competition from Russian producers.

Without analyzing the comparative positions of individual sectors and their prospects for access to the European and Russian markets, I would like to tentatively propose a radical breakthrough in relations between Russia and the EU, regarding the CEES. Instead of discussing the situation in individual industries and sectors, the parties could agree on the mutual opening of market for goods and services, including for financial and insurance services. This would be an effective

---

5 For details of relations between Norway and EU see Emerson, et al. (2002).

and efficient solution. It would contribute to raising the overall level of competition on our market and promote economic growth, including drastic improvements in financial services. In such a situation, the crucial issue to negotiate would be the date of the mutual opening of the market (which, of course, cannot happen overnight) as opposed to a meticulous comparison of the positions of individual sectors. Then it would be businessmen themselves, who would be eager to go into the issues of their competitiveness improvement. Many would think this idea absolutely unrealistic at the moment. However, until recently, the idea of a common economic area had not been seriously discussed, either.

Kaliningrad as a 'Region of Cooperation'

Relations between Russia and the EU concerning the Kaliningrad region are a kind of flashpoint for relations between the two parts of Europe concerning a specific issue of utmost importance to people. These relations could be based on a comprehensive framework agreement and a series of secondary arrangements on specific issues. Ensuring the stability of Kaliningrad is a crucial political and economic challenge for the Russian government, which starting in 2001 adopted a new approach to developing this region.

In the first years of post-communist transformation, the Kaliningrad region's main problems were seen as providing for people's survival, particularly in terms of supplying required resources (primarily consumer goods) to the region. This led to the establishment of a free economic zone in Kaliningrad, and the preferential terms for importers that came with it led to sharp increases in exports with adverse effects on domestic production. By contrast, the Kaliningrad Region's Concept of Social and Economic Development, which was approved in 2001, emphasizes investment and domestic production. This implies that import concessions should be abolished and better conditions for investment should be created. Today's agenda focuses on the implementation of special deregulation measures, the further simplification of the tax regime, and provision of additional guarantees to investors. There should be a special focus on development of export-oriented production in the region. In sum, the Kaliningrad region should move away from being an 'unsinkable aircraft carrier' toward becoming an 'unsinkable assembly plant' of Europe (Kuznetsova and Mau, 2002).

Progress in this direction requires closer cooperation with the EU, since Kaliningrad will become a Russian enclave within the EU following the Union's eastern expansion. In addition to purely political problems (first and foremost, the problem of visas for Russian citizens to travel through Lithuania), there are some economic issues that the EU addresses using special instruments (funds). The Kaliningrad Region's potential access to these funds, which are now open only to EU member and candidate countries, is a crucial problem to be resolved.

The following issues are likely to be at the heart of the Russo-EU dialogue concerning Kaliningrad:

Visa regime The standard EU border and visa regimes associated with the Schengen agreement create difficulties both for Kaliningrad residents and the Russian government, which seeks to implement constitutional guarantees concerning the equality of all Russian citizens in their political and economic activities. Solutions need to be found that reflect both EU rules and procedures and Russia's interest. This problem could be dealt with in two steps. First, before Poland and Lithuania become signatories to the Schengen Treaty, accelerated visa procedures could be introduced for Kaliningrad residents. Following Poland's and Lithuania's accession to the Schengen regime, multiple national Schengen visas could be issued, allowing entry only to the country that has issued the visa.

Extending EU regional cooperation programs to Kaliningrad The goals of the European Investment Bank (EIB) include promoting integration and cooperation with non-EU countries. Russia is not on the list of countries covered by the Bank's mandate, so affording Russia access to EIB programs would require negotiations with the EU leadership. EU assistance in developing Kaliningrad's automotive transport infrastructure, and its integration into the European road system, would be beneficial for all parties. So would establishing a system of control over transportation of hazardous loads. In maritime transport, bringing the Russian system of vessel control and identification by flag and port of registry into compliance with European standards should be considered. The development of Kaliningrad's port infrastructure is another important and interesting issue. EU activities in this area focus on transforming ports from budget-financed entities into commercial businesses. The European Regional Development Fund, the Cohesion Fund, and the EIB finance the development of the transport sector, while for candidate countries finance is provided via pre-accession funds. Currently Russia does not have access to these funds, but this could be negotiated with the EU.

Telecommunications Market entry is the main point of interest for the EU in this sector. This involves the licensing of both fixed and mobile network operators (at least three Russian GSM operators are attractive to EU companies). Investments in mobile communications are financed by the EIB in third countries, such as Brazil and Mozambique, so this could be extended to Russia as well. The issue of local television broadcasting should be considered in the context of switching over from analogue to digital television. The European Commission is lobbying for DVD-T(errestrial) standards when specific countries opt for the system of terrestrial broadcasting.

Agriculture The EU recommends establishing administrative and control systems in the veterinary and phitosanitary fields, as well as a unified system of livestock registration and identification. This requirement is imposed on the EU candidate countries as part of improvement of veterinary control. Bringing dairy and meat production facilities into compliance with EU hygienic standards should also be considered. In the area of horticulture, the issue of producer registration could be considered. Prospects for equipping border posts with instruments meeting European standards for supervising cross-country movement of agricultural products require study. The EU through a special fund provides finance for such initiatives.

Fisheries Russia has signed a bilateral fisheries agreement with the EU, in line with which the introduction of satellite control over fishing vessels could be considered. The EU has a special instrument for fisheries finance, which could be devoted to quality controls for fishery products. The EU has claimed that more financial aid should be provided to developing countries that are parties to special agreements, in order to help them meet food safety requirements. The EU is also developing a strategy for and integrated coastal management system.

Environmental issues These could be addressed through joint projects, dealing in part with the Kaliningrad region's energy problems. The adoption of EU standards for protecting water resources could also be considered, particularly in the area of agricultural runoff (nitrate content) and urban drinking water systems. In the field of Baltic water protection, Russia is already a member of the commission established under the Helsinki convention (HELCOM), which deals with issues of industrial waste, air pollution, and the like. The pulp and paper plant in the Kaliningrad region is a candidate for attention. The issue of air pollution by motor vehicles has the potential for extensive cooperation. There are separate standards for trucks and cars; additional limits have been imposed on sulfur content in diesel and aviation fuel. The EIB is one of the banks financing activities in this area. There is also the LIFE program with a 640 million Euro budget for 2000–2004. This program provides grants to non-EU countries with access to the Mediterranean and Baltic Seas. Extension of environment budget funds is the responsibility of the European Commission.

Technical assistance for harmonizing standardization and certification systems Russia is bringing its standardization laws into compliance with EU legislation. The Kaliningrad region could become a pilot for refining and introducing the new system, especially voluntary standards for Russian companies oriented to production for European markets.

EU assistance for science and education in the Kaliningrad region, with an emphasis on introducing EU methods into higher and secondary professional education. A European business school could be established (to train top managers who would be ready to work with EU partners). TACIS could be a source of funds.

While most of these proposals could apply to Russia as a whole, the use of the Kaliningrad region as a 'bridge' between Russia and the EU (or as a bridgehead for new relations between the parties) has many advantages. In signing agreements on these matters with the EU, the Russian side could establish a preferential visa regime for foreign investors and citizens employed by Kaliningrad businesses, provide investment guarantees, and could pledge to gradually change over to European quality and environmental standards. Such commitments will only be of interest to the EU if the Kaliningrad region is really attractive to European investors—which is far from evident at this point. Otherwise, the EU will only be interested in neutralizing instability coming from its problem-plagued (and therefore dangerous) neighbor.

For practical purposes, a rapprochement between Russia and the EU regarding the Kaliningrad region could be carried out in two directions simultaneously. The first would involve legislative convergence (including regional legislation) and support for the adaptation of standards for regional products (primarily exports). Second, the specific problems of the Kaliningrad region's development (visa regime, energy, transportation) need to be addressed. It would be wrong to condition the solution to specific problems on the resolution of fundamental institutional and legal issues.

Conclusions

Thus, in developing its policy of rapprochement with the EU, Russia should seek to address two groups of problems. It should seek to remove barriers to the movement of goods, services, labor and capital, and to draw on the EU's institutional experience in creating conditions for sustainable growth. Solutions to both groups of problems would promote Russia's convergence with the most developed Western countries. In doing this, the Russian government faces three key tasks. First, the government needs to consistently and unilaterally liberalize the economy, particularly in terms of foreign economic relations, by developing and implementing the appropriate reforms. Second, the government must negotiate a change in the EU's external economic regime vis-à-vis Russia. Third, it must assess the impact of these measures on various social groups, in order to build coalitions in support of these measures.

We believe that solving these problems is inevitable, because modern democratic countries, especially those adjacent to one another, are bound to seek greater integration with one another. The only question is how long it will take.

References

Aslund, A., and A. Warner (2002), 'EU Enlargement: Consequences for the CIS Countries', paper presented to the conference on 'Beyond Transition: Development Perspectives and Dilemmas', Warsaw: CASE, http://www.case.com.pl/dyn/index.php?ID=seminaria_miedzynarodowe_referaty.

Bauer, P. (1998), 'Western Subsidies and Eastern Reform', in: J.A. Dorn, S.H. Hanke, and A.A. Walters (eds.), The Revolution in Development Economics, Washington D.C.: CATO Institute.

Dynkin, A.A. and A.A. Sokolov (2001), 'Integrirovannye bizness gruppy – proryv k modernizatsii strany (Integrated Business Groups – Breakthrough to Modernization of the Country)', Moscow.

Emerson, M., M. Vahl and S. Woolcock (2002), 'Navigating by the Stars: Norway, the European Economic Area and the European Union', Brussels: CEPS.

Kuznetsova, O.V. and V.A. Mau (2002), 'Kaliningradskaya oblast': ot nepotoplyayemogo avianostsa k neotoplyaemomu sborochnomu tsekhu (Kaliningrad District: From an Unsinkable Aircraft Carrier to an Unsinkable Assembly Plant)', Moscow, RUE.

Mau, V. (2002), 'Postkommunisticheskaya Rossiya v postindustrial'nom mire: problemy dogonyayushchego rozvitiya (Post-communist Russia in Post-industrial World: Problems of Catching-up Development)', mimeo, http://www.iet.ru/personal/mau/rus-postind4art.htm or Voprosy ekonomiki, 2002, No 7.

Mau, V. and V. Novikov (2002), 'Rossiya i ES: prostranstvo vybora ili vybor prostranstva (Russia and EU: Area of Choice or Choice of the Area), Voprosy Ekonomiki, No. 6.

Round Table (2002), 'Zayavlenie Kruglogo stola promyshlennikov Rossii i Evropeiskogo soyuza (The Statement of the EU-Russian Industrialists Round Table)', Voprosy Ekonomiki, 2002, No 6.

Sachs, J.D. and Warner, A. (1995), 'Economic Reform and the Process of Global Integration', Brookings Papers on Economic Activity, Vol. 25, No. 1, pp. 1-118.

Chapter 18

Central European Experience and the CIS

Kalman Mizsei

Introduction

This volume deals mainly with second-generation economic transition issues and challenges that the countries joining the European Union in 2004 are facing. However, it is worthwhile to look into the state of transition of countries further East that do not benefit that much from the close proximity and impact of the EU. We have witnessed more than a decade of economic transition in Central Europe and the Baltic countries. Eight countries of the transforming socialist part of Europe are going to join the European Union in a few months. In the Commonwealth of Independent States (CIS), somewhat belatedly we have seen economic growth, but in many countries we also see deeply non-democratic polities and rapidly growing income gaps, much exceeding those in Central Europe.

What accounts for this difference in the transition trajectory of these two neighboring regions, whose recent histories possess many commonalties? Are there lessons that can be drawn from the successful Central European transitions for countries further east and south, or is the Central European historical experience of limited use for reasons of geography and/or sociopolitical structure? How will their absorption by the European Union change the socioeconomic dynamics in the CIS and in South Eastern Europe? While most of this book looks at the economic policy challenges of the EU accession countries, this chapter raises questions about reform challenges in the rest of the former East European socialist system, as well as the significance of the integrating Europe moving its boundaries further East, closer to the 'rest' of the transition countries.[1]

Central Europe: How Much Success?

Is it sure that Central Europe is on a better growth and modernization trajectory than the CIS-countries? At least one author, Anders Aslund, has challenged the

1 I would like to thank Olga Ioffe of UNDP New York for her assistance with data collection.

view that the long term prospects of the Central European economies are better than those of the CIS. His argument is based on the recent growth slow-down and widening fiscal (and in some cases external) imbalances seen in Central Europe (which are to a smaller extent affecting the Baltic countries that barely a decade ago left the disintegrating Soviet Union), and on the fact that these countries are joining the West European region, large parts of which are growing only slowly, if ever.[2]

When comparing the CIS with Central Europe (see Table 18.1) there are at least two factors that have to be taken into consideration: the extremely low starting levels in the CIS and the oil prices. In fact, oil prices have to be taken into account on both ends, since the Central European countries are oil (and gas) importers whereas the CIS's major economy Russia (as well as Azerbaijan, Kazakhstan, Turkmenistan, and Uzbekistan) depend critically on oil and gas exports. Russia started to grow when these two factors were extremely favorable: the country had hit the bottom after nine years of contraction, and oil prices picked up.

The most important comparative case, in many respects, is Poland since this country constitutes roughly half of the population and GDP of the ten accession countries. Polish growth was very healthy after the first reforms were introduced in the early 1990s, but in the late 1990s growth had slowed to a virtual standstill in 2001-2002. Some of the most important causes of the Polish slowdown are analyzed in earlier chapters of this volume. There was definitely a misalignment between an anti-inflationary monetary policy and an expansionary, deficit-prone fiscal policy. The markets kept upward pressures on the zloty due to Poland's anticipated adoption of the Euro and the high real yields on Polish securities, which in turn reflected the misalignment between fiscal and monetary policies. Structural factors were not sufficiently helpful: although greenfield foreign direct investment (FDI) remained relatively robust during the growth slowdown, privatization was slow and many loss-making state-owned enterprises were left unrestructured.

Still, Poland's slowdown came after nine years of dynamic economic growth. EU-accession, combined with even slow and gradual macroeconomic and structural adjustment should secure a growth rate significantly higher than the EU-average.

---

2 During his presentation to the Advisory Board of Regional Bureau for Europe and CIS (RBEC), UNDP in Moscow in May of 2003, Aslund concluded that '*Central Europe benefits from market access but suffers from the EU regulations; CIS countries are adopting a more liberal model* (that is) *likely to generate more growth*'. See also chapters 16 and 17 in this volume.

Table 18.1 Cumulative GDP growth in transition countries, 1991 = 100

Country	1992	1993	1994	1995	1996	1997	1998	1999	2000	2001
				EU accession countries						
Estonia	78.8	72.3	70.8	73.8	76.7	84.3	88.1	87.6	93.8	98.5
Hungary	96.9	96.4	99.2	100.7	102.1	106.7	111.9	116.6	122.6	127.2
Poland	102.6	106.5	112.0	119.9	127.1	135.7	142.2	148.1	154.0	155.5
Slovakia	93.3	89.8	94.5	100.6	106.5	112.5	116.9	118.5	121.1	125.1
				CIS countries						
Georgia	55.1	39.0	34.9	35.8	39.8	44.0	45.3	46.7	47.5	49.7
Kazakhstan	94.7	86.0	75.2	69.0	69.3	70.5	69.2	71.0	78.0	88.3
Kyrgyzstan	86.1	72.8	58.2	55.0	58.9	64.8	66.1	68.6	72.3	76.1
Russia	85.5	78.1	68.3	65.4	63.2	63.8	60.6	63.9	69.7	73.2
Ukraine	90.3	77.5	59.7	52.4	47.2	54.8	44.9	44.8	47.4	51.7

Source: World Bank data.

Similarly, economic growth in the other accession countries has exceeded EU averages since the recessions recorded during the first years of transition (which methodologically are themselves very questionable) (Table 18.2). They all, ironically, with the possible exception of the country with the highest per capita GDP, Slovenia, went through a critical mass of economic (and political) transition as a result of the political needs to meet the EU's accession conditions. This critical mass of reform has resulted in efficiency gains, not least because of the FDI this set of changes produced (Table 18.3).

Table 18.2 Cumulative GDP growth in the EU accession countries and EMU, 1993 = 100

Country	1994	1995	1996	1997	1998	1999	2000	2001
Czech Republic	102.7	109.3	114.6	113.1	111.9	112.5	116.1	119.9
Estonia	98.0	102.2	106.2	116.6	122.0	121.2	129.8	136.4
Hungary	103.0	104.5	105.9	110.7	116.1	120.9	127.2	132.0
Latvia	100.7	99.8	103.2	112.1	116.4	117.7	125.7	135.2
Lithuania	90.2	93.2	97.6	104.7	110.1	105.8	109.8	116.2
Poland	105.2	112.6	119.3	127.4	133.6	139.0	144.6	146.0
Slovakia	105.2	112.0	118.5	125.2	130.2	131.9	134.8	139.2
EMU	102.4	104.7	106.1	108.6	111.8	114.8	118.8	120.5

Source: World Bank.

Some of the accession countries' economic gains can be attributed to the early opening of the EU markets to these countries as a political gesture. That opening itself was an element in the accession countries' ability to attract FDI, to the extent that the investors anticipated long term access to developed markets.

Balkan Countries: European destination?

The experience of the new EU members is very relevant for the similarly small, resource-poor, open economies of the Balkans. In addition to being small, open economies, many have an institutional history within Yugoslavia that enables them to adjust to market reforms perhaps more easily than is the case in the CIS. Perhaps most importantly, these economies have their future in the European economic, and also political, area. With other words, the 'European choice' is, unlike in the CIS, unchallenged. The choice of model is thus simple.

There are some tentative signs of economic recovery and integration as well. Besides their Europe agreements, the Balkan countries, in the framework of the Stability Pact, have signed 21 bilateral free trade agreements. These agreements are not a substitute for a multinational free trade regime like the Central European Free Trade Agreement (CEFTA) that the Central European accession countries put

Table 18.3 Cumulative FDI inflows, USD million

Country	1993	1994	1995	1996	1997	1998	1999	2000	2001
EU accession countries									
Bulgaria	40	145	236	345	850	1,387	2,206	3,207	3,896
Czech Republic	654	1,522	4,084	5,513	6,813	10,531	16,855	21,841	26,757
Estonia	162	377	578	729	995	1,576	1,881	2,268	2,806
Hungary	2,339	3,485	7,938	10,213	12,386	14,422	16,366	18,009	20,423
Latvia	44	257	435	817	1,338	1,694	2,042	2,449	2,650
Lithuania	30	61	134	286	641	1,566	2,053	2,432	2,878
Poland	1,715	3,590	7,249	11,747	16,655	23,020	30,290	39,632	48,462
Romania	94	435	854	1,117	2,332	4,363	5,404	6,429	7,566
Slovakia	168	413	608	859	1 079	1,763	2,153	4,229	5,704
Slovenia	113	241	418	612	987	1,235	1,416	1,592	2 034
Other Balkan countries									
Bosnia & Herzegovina	-	-	0	-2	-1	54	202	334	498
Croatia	120	117	238	754	1,305	2,318	3,954	5,080	6,523
Serbia & Montenegro	96	159	204	204	944	1,057	1,169	1,194	1,359
CIS countries									
Georgia	-	8	13	58	300	566	648	779	939
Kazakhstan	1,271	1,931	2,915	4,589	6,696	7,929	9,397	10,675	13,435
Moldova	14	42	108	132	211	285	322	460	610
Russia	1,211	1,901	3,967	6,546	11,411	14,172	17,481	20,195	22,735
Ukraine	200	359	626	1,147	1,770	2,513	3,009	3,604	4,376

Source: UNCTAD.

in place in the early 1990s. However, in absence of a multilateral framework, these bilateral agreements are a good start and can help persuade foreign strategic investors to look at this fragmented sub-region as a whole. Indeed, FDI has increased lately but there is still a long way to go if the point of reference is Central Europe (see Table 18.4).

Table 18.4 Cumulative FDI inflows per capita, USD

Country	1993	1994	1995	1996	1997	1998	1999	2000	2001
EU accession countries									
Bulgaria	5	17	28	41	102	168	270	396	484
Czech Republic	63	147	395	534	660	1,021	1,636	2,121	2,600
Estonia	106	249	385	487	672	1,078	1,295	1,572	1,913
Hungary	228	339	775	999	1,214	1,416	1,610	1,775	2,018
Latvia	17	100	171	325	536	681	824	992	1,076
Lithuania	8	17	36	77	173	423	554	657	777
Poland	45	93	188	304	432	596	784	1,026	1,255
Romania	4	19	38	49	104	193	240	285	336
Slovakia	32	77	114	160	201	328	401	785	1,058
Slovenia	57	122	211	308	496	621	712	800	1,023
Other Balkan countries									
Bosnia & Herzegovina	-	-	0	-1	0	15	53	86	127
Croatia	26	52	78	189	307	525	876	1,119	1,428
Serbia & Montenegro	9	15	19	19	89	100	111	113	129
CIS countries									
Georgia	-	1	2	11	56	107	122	147	177
Kazakhstan	76	115	175	276	404	480	570	649	820
Moldova	3	10	25	30	49	66	74	107	142
Russia	8	13	27	44	77	96	119	137	155
Ukraine	4	7	12	22	35	49	59	71	87

Source: UNCTAD.

Overall, for the Balkans the transition as well as integration pattern is undoubtedly that of Central Europe—with admittedly some larger problems for the less developed parts of the sub-region. In institutional development, these countries are looking to the Central European countries, particularly as their desire is also to join the European Union. The Central European political model of parliamentary democracy with a weak role for the president is also attractive.

The role of the *acquis communautaire* as an institutional anchor is perhaps clearest in the case of Romania, which had a very slow start to its economic transition. When Poland, Hungary and the Czech Republic undertook their radical reforms in 1989-1991, policy makers in Romania were concerned with other matters. The revolution that overthrew Ceausescu produced democratization in Romanian political life that was deeper than in the CIS countries, but changes in the political sphere were not accompanied by commensurate economic reforms. Land was distributed to the peasants, and business formation advanced in such a way as to put Romania in between the SME explosion in Poland and the almost frozen status of Russia or Ukraine at that time. Liberalization also advanced. However, the lack of genuine conviction on the part of the first Romanian governments in market reforms and their fear of a popular backlash against privatization resulted in slow changes. Policies driven by fears of populism generated further macroeconomic problems during most of the 1990s. Inflation was high and the entrepreneurial structures developed only slowly. However, a consensus about the desirability of EU accession in the late 1990s finally resulted in a series of reforms that started to move the Romanian economy broadly in the right direction.

The above is not to deny the difficulties for Southeastern Europe in trying to follow the Central European example. One of these is relative geographic isolation. Sachs' works on the developmental disadvantages of landlocked countries highlight this issue (in perhaps an oversimplified fashion).[3] In fact, it is not so much 'landlockness' but a broader geographical isolation that means difficult access both to developed European markets as well as to the demonstration effects of these countries' market institutions and social order.

The Balkan countries have been heavily isolated in the last 'long decade' in comparison to Central Europe and also to the Baltic countries. Here such factors as which of the developed European countries are close by also play an important role. Arguably, in the case of the Baltic region, the proximity of Scandinavian countries, with their special sense of social responsibility and readiness to offer effective assistance, has played a very important role in fostering progressive change in Estonia, Latvia and Lithuania. Comparable positive influences in the Balkans have been absent. The bloody disintegration of the former Yugoslavia was also a major factor in the isolation of Southeastern Europe. This not only affected the successor states of Yugoslavia but also such neighbors as Bulgaria and Romania, which suffered further reductions in access to Western markets during the conflicts of the 1990s. On the other hand, the relative success of Albania within this region is a noteworthy phenomenon.

If conflict is receding in the Balkans, the impact of Europe in this region is likely to increase. Still, many post-conflict challenges remain. Bosnia and Herzegovina still suffers from inefficient governance originating from the shortcomings of the Dayton peace agreement of 1995. Kosovo's final constitutional status is not decided, burdening not only Kosovo's but also Serbia's development and integration perspectives. The destructive consequences of

3 In a public lecture in 1996, Sachs remarked: '(...) All else being equal, I would estimate that being landlocked subtracts between 1.5 and 2 percentage points per year of economic growth potential because if the name of the game is trade-related growth, the cost of being stuck on the inside is quite high. Possibly this cost will be reduced when neighboring countries themselves open up to world trade and let goods through at lower cost. However, the experience of the past 25 years suggests that being landlocked is a very great disadvantage.' See also Gallup, Sachs and Mellinger (1998).

organized crime were tragically underscored by the cynical assassination of Serbia's late Prime Minister Zoran Djindjic in early 2003. Europe, and European foreign policy, should play a more active role than has been the case so far in helping to consolidate democracies in the Balkans, and in promoting national and ethnic tolerance in this conflict-ridden region. A more active policy towards the Balkans should also support the development of free trade in the region. Signing mutual agreements is not enough—their enforcement will be a major challenge. The CEFTA experience should provide important lessons in this respect, and it should be promoted by the Stability Pact.

The success of Southeastern Europe in the coming years will critically depend on the strength of the European anchor: how attractive the European choice remains, and how well it is used by the European Union and its member states to foster progress in these countries. For Romania, Bulgaria, and Croatia, the Union's preparation for and interest in their accession around 2007 will be a question of particular importance.

Significant achievements in the economic arena accompany the important progress made towards political consolidation in Southeastern Europe. While socialist Yugoslavia experienced recurrent hyperinflation, the successor states have placed macroeconomic stability at their top of their policy agendas. The Latin America experience underscores the importance of macroeconomic stability if progress is to be maintained on the long haul. Still major challenges remain in the economic reform arena. For different reasons none of the Balkan countries has recorded policy successes in this respect comparable not only with what the early reforming countries achieved, but also in terms of late catching-up Slovakia.

Slovakia offers a useful comparison in this respect, since that country also wasted several years for its own reforms, and had to manage secession (fortunately peaceful) from federation and the subsequent development of national institutions. Still, since 1998 Slovakia has fully caught up with Poland, Hungary, and the Czech Republic, and may now be regarded as something of a reform frontrunner among them. This road is theoretically open to all Southeast European countries but this potential is as yet to be fully utilized. It is worth remembering that even Slovenia, with its excellent starting conditions, is a relative underperformer in reform dynamics when it comes to comparison with Slovakia.

The combined effects of lukewarm reforms, small country size, and less favorable international economic conditions, make the task of attracting FDI much more difficult in South Eastern Europe than it was for the early reforming countries. FDI is critical if the resource-poor countries of the region are to accelerate industrial restructuring and the consolidation of new, modern industrial cultures. In Central Europe, FDI was instrumental in the region's rapid economic integration into Europe. Further, FDI can also promote the spread of private enterprises (SMEs). Policies and international support need to concentrate critically on fostering FDI and eliminating the administrative and financial barriers to dynamic SME development.

Relative isolation is also a matter of transport and telecommunications infrastructure. Road and rail links to Europe in the Balkans have to improve. The experience of the Central European countries shows that connectivity was a major factor in attracting FDI and trade creation. Here active European public investments are necessary. In the telecom sector the goal should be creating a highly competitive environment. Here the EBRD should play the active role it did in Central Europe in the telecom sector and even more in bank privatization. Developed countries' investment promotion agencies should give preferential treatment to such investments, to encourage debt-ridden Western telecom companies to invest in Southeaster Europe. The privatization and subsequent business development of the Hungarian telecom MATAV should be used as a model for FDI in telecoms in the Balkans.

The CIS: The Need for an External Anchor

The emerging development pattern in the CIS is quite different—and so are the challenges. The CIS countries experienced a sharp economic decline in the first half of the 1990s due to the disintegration of the Soviet Union and of the socialist trade regime, and of the whole socialist economic experiment. But while socialism in these countries was a tremendously wasteful and inefficient economic system, its disintegration was not followed by the rapid emergence of new, market-oriented institutions that is apparent in Poland, Hungary, the Czech Republic or Estonia. Consequently, the economic decline was deeper and lasted longer in the CIS countries. One has to note, however, that statistical measurement problems severely distort the picture. Comparing output produced under conditions of shortage and forced substitute purchases of low quality products in the previous system with normal demand-driven production in the new one, or estimating different levels of distortions in different socialist economies, remain rather ambiguous territory (see Gaidar, 2001).

After initial energetic and rather unique (within the CIS) economic and institutional reform process in Russia during the early Yeltsin years, the financial collapse came in 1998. By that point basically none of the large CIS economies had reported economic growth during the 1990s (with the above-mentioned caveat). However, curiously, the financial collapse also became a turning point in the economic dynamics of the CIS. Strong economic growth for both oil producers and resource-poor countries in the CIS began around that time. The question of why the CIS economies show such a similar pattern of decline and growth during the transition is quite important. The answers of economic historians will probably reflect a mixture of different factors. Economic reforms in some of the larger CIS economies (Russia, Ukraine and Kazakhstan), oil-induced growth in Kazakhstan, Azerbaijan and Russia, the multiplier impact of the large economies' growth as well as considerable reforms in some small economies such as Armenia, Tajikistan, Moldova and Kyrgyzstan might all have contributed.

Importantly, the impact of the European Union is very limited in the CIS area—much more so than in Southeastern Europe. Russia has its own internal logic of socioeconomic dynamics. Most of the other countries are so distant geographically and geopolitically from the EU that the European influence is limited or insignificant. This lack of an anchoring role is true to all the countries, although the EU may have more influence in the Western part of the region.

Russia's future institutional dynamics and economic growth pattern are of critical importance. It is always tempting to extrapolate the future from the present and immediate past; on that basis Russia may continue its current growth path. However, a slowdown in reforms during 2003 may signal slower growth in the future, particularly if oil prices drop below current levels. The Russian tax reforms are often described as an example of institutional solutions more applicable to the CIS than the tax systems of the more developed EU accession countries, let alone the EU member states. Besides the question of whether this is true, the tax issue illustrates the kind of dilemmas the CIS countries face as they develop their socioeconomic systems: which systems and integration model to choose? The answer will be influenced by the success of Russia's economic development and its overall geopolitical influence in its 'near abroad'. International donors such as the EU, but also the IMF, the World Bank and UNDP, should play an important role in helping the countries to sort out their basic macroeconomic and institutional framework.

Here the international integration question is as important as the domestic systemic issues. These countries have fallen out of the very wasteful, top-down 'integration regime' that socialism offered them. With the exception of Russia and Ukraine, these are very small economies—and the political economy systems in Russia and Ukraine are still too young to be able to progress in isolation from their developed neighbors. From 2004, Russia, Moldova, Ukraine and Belarus will be direct neighbors of the EU. The EU's emerging trade and integration strategy towards its new neighbors will therefore be particularly important for these countries. Seen in this perspective, it is somewhat unfortunate that the EU has some of its most restrictive bilateral trading relations towards these countries (see Chapter 16). The interface of domestic reforms and external economic influences will be where the long-term development paths of the CIS countries will be decided.

In addition to the absence of a clear integration pattern, a very anachronistic political system may also hinder future reforms in CIS countries. Ultimately, the greatest challenge to this part of the world is overcoming the Soviet legacy of closeness and extreme centralization. It seems that even the countries in the Balkans with the most centralized political structures during the socialist time (Romania, Bulgaria and Albania) have distanced themselves from the Soviet legacy much more than the overwhelming majority of the CIS-countries. Centralized political structures are a problem, for a number of reasons. First, continued centralization means political continuity, preventing or obscuring the break with past inefficiencies. All the CIS countries have developed presidential frameworks in which old power relations prevail, to varying degrees. Information does not circulate freely and feedback from society comes to the higher echelons of the power structure in a very inefficient and distorted manner. Geographical isolation is in this way compounded by the isolating impact of anachronistic power structures that are supported by a social fabric inherited from the Soviet times.

Notwithstanding the great variety of concrete national situations from Kyiv to Tashkent, these systemic characteristics are common throughout the CIS.

The survival of very centralized political structures in CIS countries, combined with complete disillusionment with and cynical attitudes towards the past ideology, have gradually produced extreme forms of corrupt norms in public administration. While measurement of corruption shows some improvement in the more dynamically developing countries of the region, corruption remains an extraordinary obstacle to a long-term development there (see Table 18.5).

Table 18.5 Transparency International Corruption Perceptions Index (CPI) 2002

Rank	Country	CPI 2002
27	Slovenia	6.0
29	Estonia	5.6
33	Hungary	4.9
36	Belarus	4.8
	Lithuania	4.8
45	Bulgaria	4.0
51	Croatia	3.8
52	Czech Republic	3.7
	Latvia	3.7
	Slovakia	3.7
64	Turkey	3.2
68	Uzbekistan	2.9
71	Russia	2.7
77	Romania	2.6
85	Georgia	2.4
	Ukraine	2.4
88	Kazakhstan	2.3
89	Moldova	2.1
95	Azerbaijan	2.0

Notes: CPI scores show perceptions of the degree of corruption as seen by business people, academics and risk analysts, and ranges between 10 (highly clean) and 0 (highly corrupt); 102 countries ranked.

Source: Transparency International Corruption Perceptions Index, 2003.

Centralized political systems and cautious reforms have generated very centralized economic structures in the CIS region. This problem is further aggravated by the characteristics of the privatization process in Russia in the 1990s and by its resource-intensive nature. Ownership of large extractive companies is concentrated in very few hands, and these companies are major vehicles for FDI in other CIS countries. Bureaucracies everywhere prevent or seriously slow down badly needed small enterprise creation and expansion by trying to extort preventively large kickbacks. In addition, public administration is very heavily centralized. In Russia, this is partly justified by the centrifugal tendencies, but in many cases it also reflects the conservative nature of regional administrations. What was justified in the first years of the Putin presidency for the sake of the unity of the state and implementation of reforms is becoming an obstacle now. His centralization of public administration should give now way to transparent delegation of powers, including revenue generation, down the chain, and should be accompanied by efforts to establish the preconditions for vigorous local democracy.

Centralized political regimes, distorted economic structures, and lack of vigorous civil society organizations are the great long-term reform and modernization challenges in the CIS. It is always difficult to foresee the future. However, it may be that the post-1998 economic growth experienced in the CIS is a 'post-collapse' recovery only, i.e., the way post-war recoveries happen. In the long run, however, the lack of political reform will limit what economic reforms can achieve, as well the ability of societies to respond to such social crises as low male life expectancy, HIV/AIDS, tuberculosis, and the like. In this respect, the current growth may prove to be a seductive phenomenon: it can create a false sense of security and success for elites and thereby postpone much needed structural reforms that could unleash entrepreneurial energies.

What can improve this likely trajectory? With the partial exception of Russia, it is likely that factors of external influence will have a great role in shaping the developments in the CIS-region. The main players are here Russia itself and the EU—whereas in Central Asia the influence of other actors is also going to be important—such as China and the US. Oddly, however, because of Central Asia's distance from forces of influence, none force of gravity will necessarily have quite decisive influence on reforming institutions and the social fabric there. Russia may impact the rest of the region by its example of development and through trade as well as by its political influence.

In the immediate future, prospect for free trading regimes within the CIS, or in parts of it, are rather bleak. Free trade requires the discipline of adhering to bilateral or multilateral commitments, and this discipline is still conspicuously lacking in the region's political culture. Moreover, in some important countries in the region, such as Uzbekistan, economic reforms have not yet reached the critical mass needed for the country to run a free trade regime. While Uzbekistan is an extreme case, its reform deficiencies are to some extent shared by the rest of the CIS. Domestic economic and political factors also mitigate against the establishment of free trade regimes in these countries.

Since reform prospects within the CIS that are driven entirely by internal factors are bleak, external influence remains critical. The EU can be a significant force for change for its immediate neighbors, Ukraine, Moldova, and perhaps over time, Belarus. This will not happen, however, without active engagement. One of the most important potential forces for engagement—trade—is very underutilized, because the EU protects its markets most heavily in those sectors where these countries possess the largest comparative advantages: agriculture, steel and textiles (see Chapter 16). It is in everybody's interest to radically change this and use trade to promote positive systemic change. This engagement also has to be coupled with intelligent donor coordination so that developmental assistance acts in positive direction. The lack of anchoring and the dominant influence of any single donor underscores the importance of effective donor coordination. What definitely does not help is that many countries of the CIS are not ODA (Overseas Development Assitance) eligible. Thus development agencies' assistance to Belarus, Ukraine, Russia and a number of other countries simply does not count as ODA in the time when donor countries are very busy to show an increase of their development assistance as a sign of good international citizenship. This counts as a discriminatory practice against some of these countries and is also against the interests of the European donors as most of the developmental deficiencies of their new Eastern neighbors have direct repercussions to their own public life – suffice to remind about the high and extremely rapidly growing prevalence rate of HIV/AIDS, as well as problems with human and drugs' trafficking from these countries, and other forms of organized crime. This practice of the OECD countries actually cries for very urgent revision.

Reforms in the CIS have to result, for the foreseeable future, in smaller governments than is the case in Western Europe and the accession countries. Sweeping deregulation as well as low and simple taxes should be high on the agenda. Without deregulation and active protection of businesses from bureaucratic harassment, the necessary business creation and expansion will not happen. Similarly, as Russia's example demonstrates, only low taxes can create a favorable environment for open private enterprise to blossom. If this is the case in resource-rich Russia, then it is particularly true for the resource-poor, small and isolated countries of the region. Their potential advantage is their relatively still well trained population with comparatively low wages.

While it is true that only a very limited government can secure progress in market reforms, market failures in CIS countries—precisely because of their isolation—are more frequent and thus need corrective public actions. Also, limited budget revenues gradually erode these countries' comparative advantages deriving from their relatively well-educated populations. So, in addition to shrinking the size of government, major reforms in allocating scarce public resources are needed—which, given the undemocratic nature of politics, is an almost impossibly tall order. Hence, active engagement in economic integration with the international community needs to be accompanied by the promotion of reforms to loosen up the over-centralized nature of the state in all the CIS countries. This requires institutional changes on the national level as well as cleverly designed decentralization initiatives, in order to strengthen sub-national decision-making powers harmonized with better revenue raising abilities of regional and local governments.

Finally, the CIS countries' isolation needs to be mitigated by initiatives to link the region with the rest of the world. Here the nature and logic of the tasks are similar to those in the Balkans and the Western CIS. A very different approach is required in road and rail transport as opposed to the telecom sphere. While in the former active and large-scale European public investments are irreplaceable, in telecommunications encouraging privatization and competition with active financial support to it (in the form of EBRD assistance and public investment guarantees) should be very effective. Better connectivity can also have a major beneficial impact on the social fabric by reducing isolation—particularly in these countries with very high literacy rates.

As external factors remain critical to the long-term development of both Southeastern Europe and the CIS, it is clear that the internal dynamics (basically issues of internal cohesion) of the EU are more important than anything else for these two sub-regions: more so for the Balkans, while less so but still very important for the CIS. Russia's long run internal dynamics are the other decisive factor in the case of the CIS.

References

Aslund, A. and A. Warner (2002), 'EU Enlargement: Consequences for the CIS Countries', paper presented to the conference on 'Beyond Transition: Development Perspectives and Dilemmas', Warsaw: CASE, http://www.case.com.pl/dyn/index.php?ID=seminaria_miedzynarodowe_referaty.

Gaidar, E. (2001), 'Reforms Are Like Evolution From Dinosaurs To Mammals', An interview with Egor Gaidar, liberal economist, Author: Georgii Osipov, *Izvestiya*, November 14.

Gallup, J.L., J.D. Sachs and A.D. Mellinger (1998), 'Geography and Economic Development', *NBER Working Paper*, No. 6849, December.

Sachs, J.D. (1996), 'Globalization and Employment', Public Lecture by Jeffrey Sachs Presented at the ILO and to the International Institute for Labor Studies, Geneva, March 18, http://www.ilo.org/public/english/bureau/inst/papers/publecs/sachs/ch2.htm.

Index